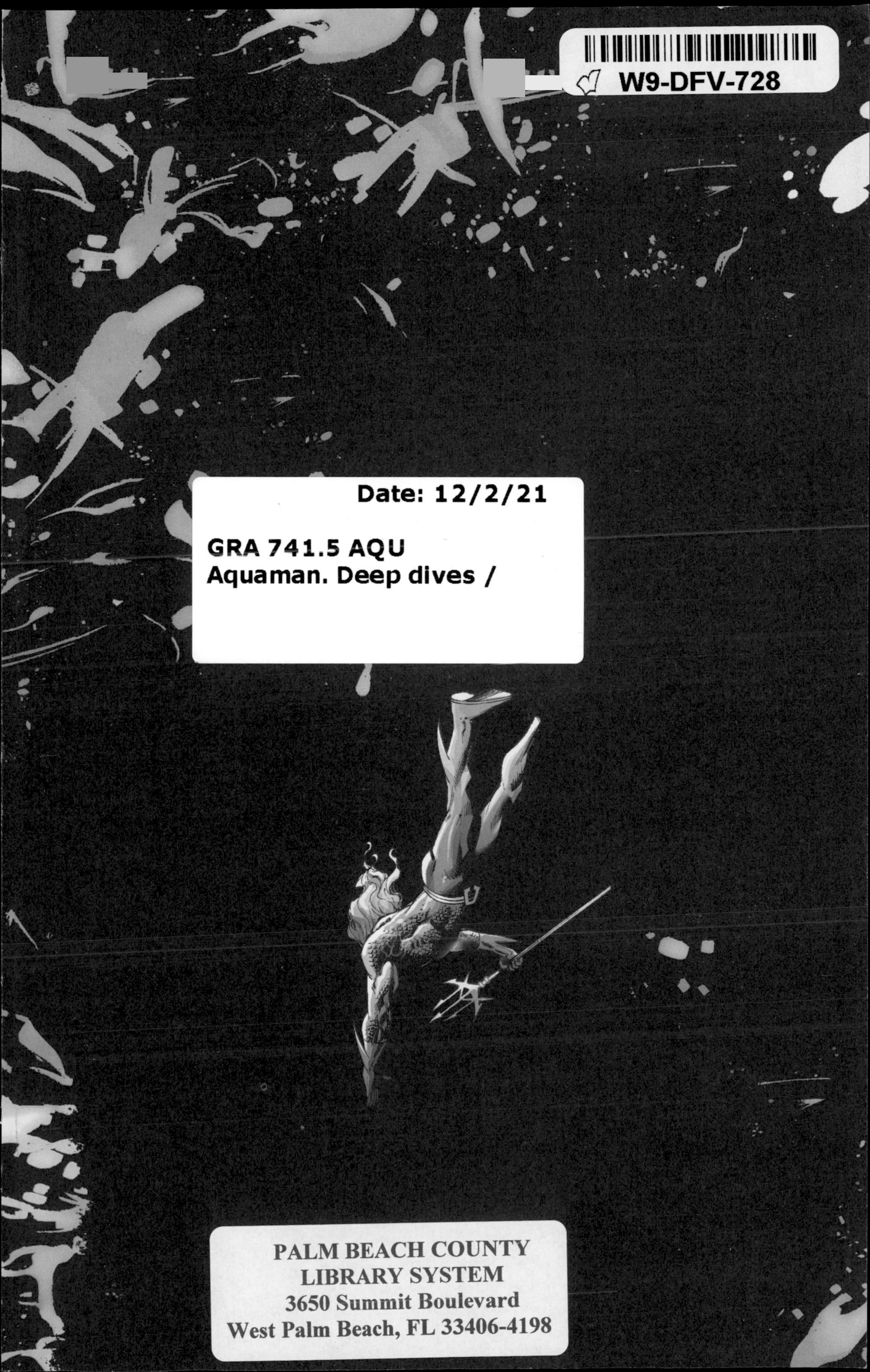

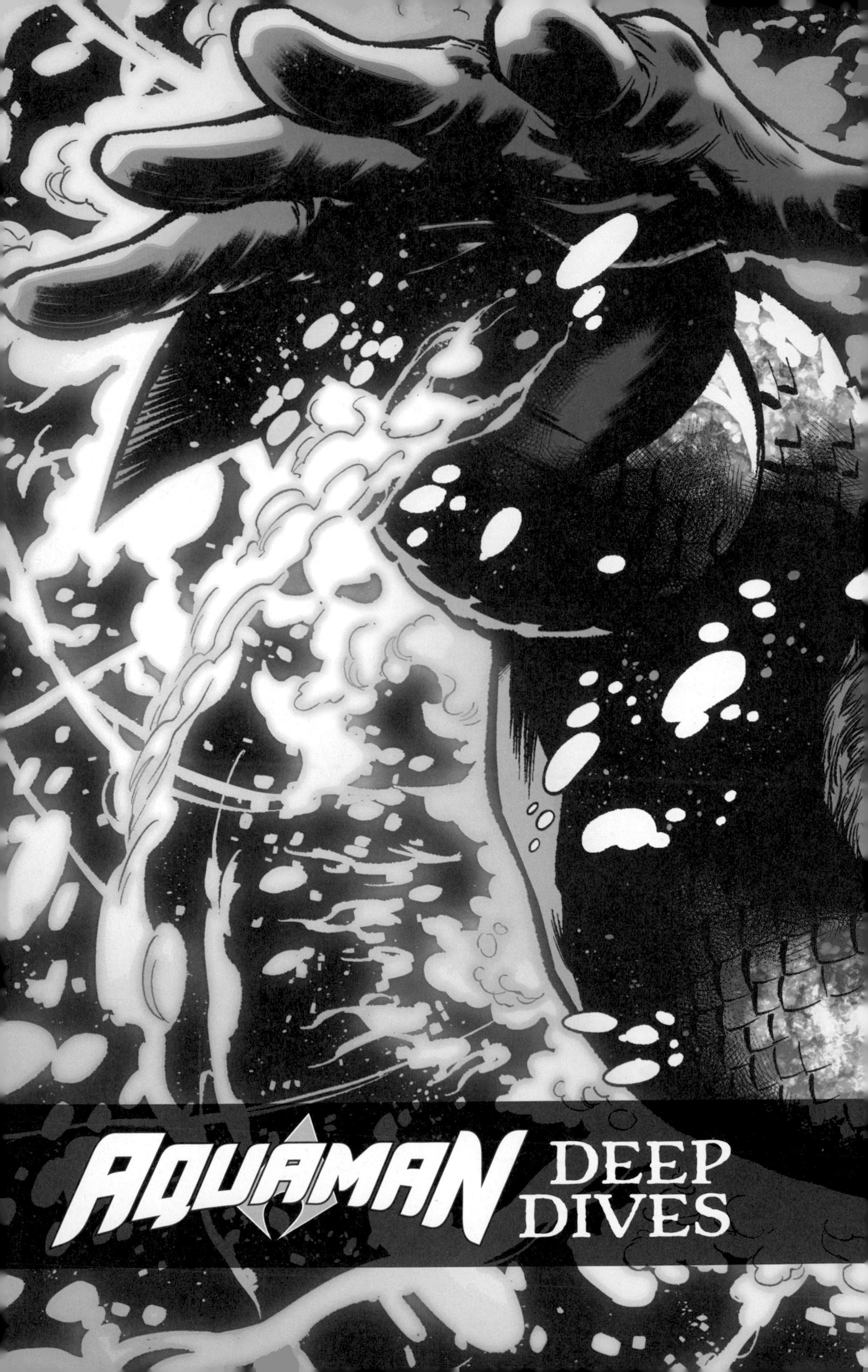

AQUAMAN DEEP DIVES

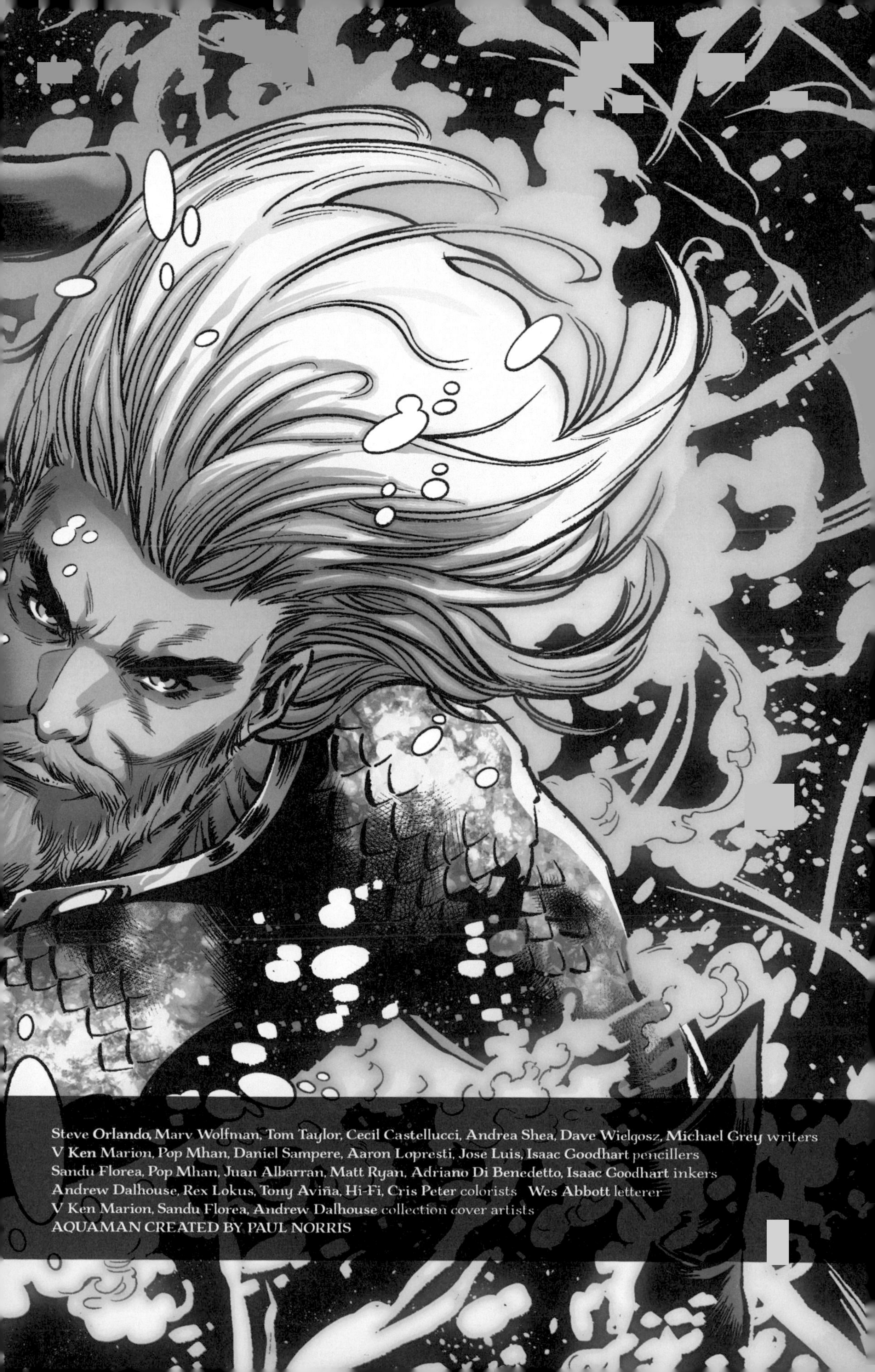

Steve Orlando, Marv Wolfman, Tom Taylor, Cecil Castellucci, Andrea Shea, Dave Wielgosz, Michael Grey writers
V Ken Marion, Pop Mhan, Daniel Sampere, Aaron Lopresti, Jose Luis, Isaac Goodhart pencillers
Sandu Florea, Pop Mhan, Juan Albarran, Matt Ryan, Adriano Di Benedetto, Isaac Goodhart inkers
Andrew Dalhouse, Rex Lokus, Tony Aviña, Hi-Fi, Cris Peter colorists Wes Abbott letterer
V Ken Marion, Sandu Florea, Andrew Dalhouse collection cover artists
AQUAMAN CREATED BY PAUL NORRIS

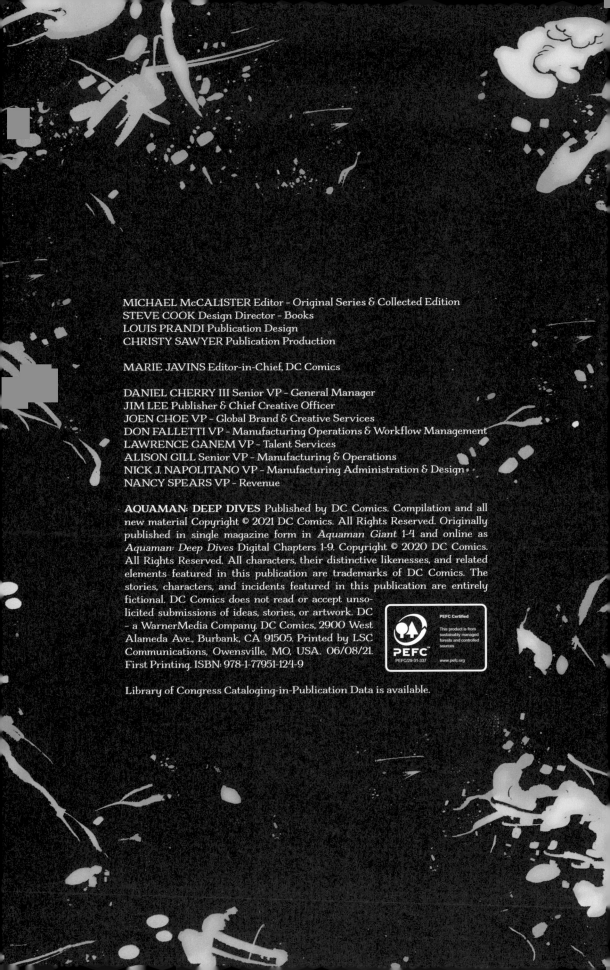

MICHAEL McCALISTER Editor - Original Series & Collected Edition
STEVE COOK Design Director - Books
LOUIS PRANDI Publication Design
CHRISTY SAWYER Publication Production

MARIE JAVINS Editor-in-Chief, DC Comics

DANIEL CHERRY III Senior VP - General Manager
JIM LEE Publisher & Chief Creative Officer
JOEN CHOE VP - Global Brand & Creative Services
DON FALLETTI VP - Manufacturing Operations & Workflow Management
LAWRENCE GANEM VP - Talent Services
ALISON GILL Senior VP - Manufacturing & Operations
NICK J. NAPOLITANO VP - Manufacturing Administration & Design
NANCY SPEARS VP - Revenue

PEFC Certified
This product is from
sustainably managed
forests and controlled
sources
PEFC/29-31-337   www.pefc.org

Library of Congress Cataloging-in-Publication Data is available.

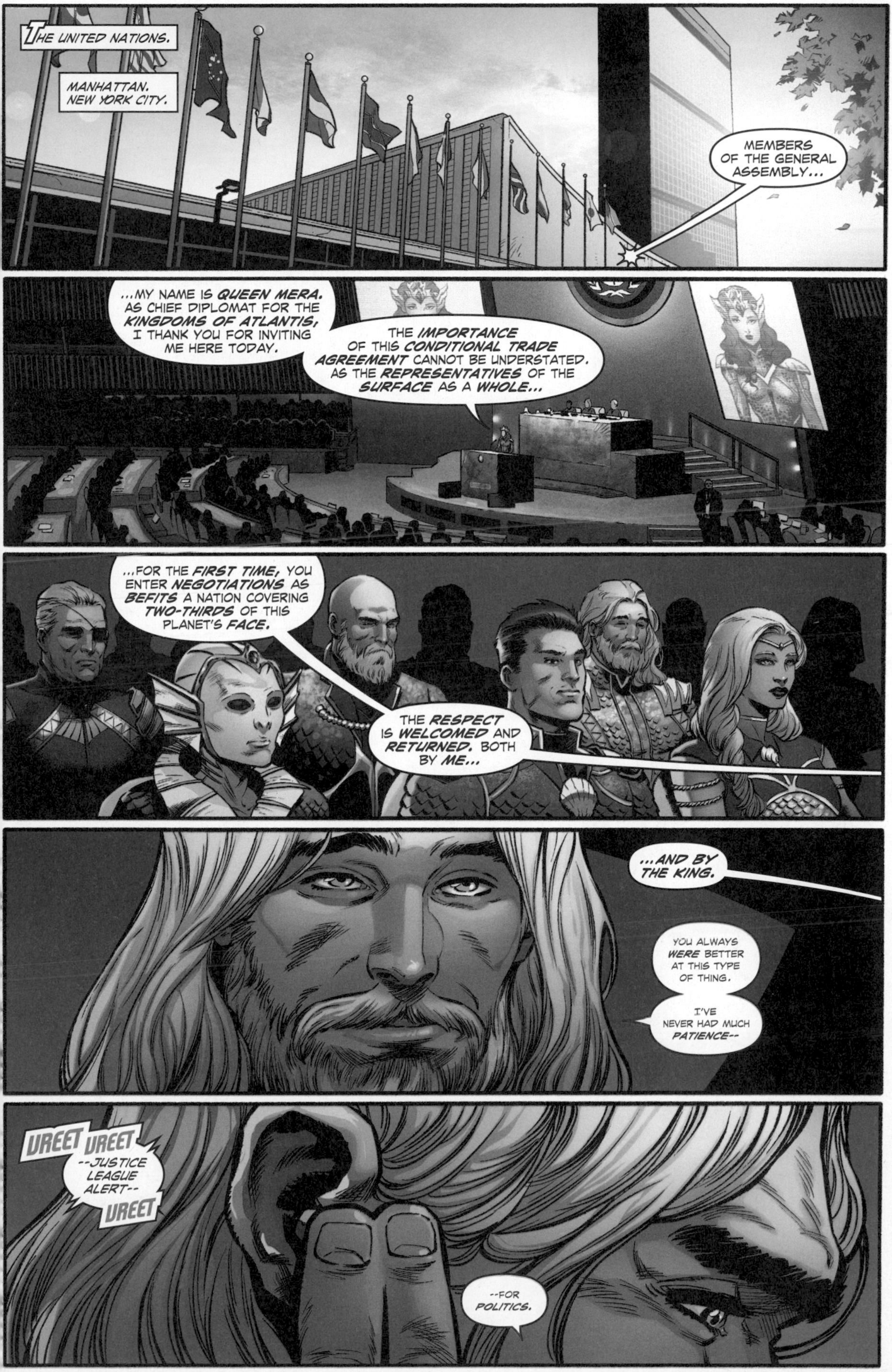
THE UNITED NATIONS.
MANHATTAN. NEW YORK CITY.
MEMBERS OF THE GENERAL ASSEMBLY...
...MY NAME IS QUEEN MERA. AS CHIEF DIPLOMAT FOR THE KINGDOMS OF ATLANTIS, I THANK YOU FOR INVITING ME HERE TODAY.
THE IMPORTANCE OF THIS CONDITIONAL TRADE AGREEMENT CANNOT BE UNDERSTATED. AS THE REPRESENTATIVES OF THE SURFACE AS A WHOLE...
...FOR THE FIRST TIME, YOU ENTER NEGOTIATIONS AS BEFITS A NATION COVERING TWO-THIRDS OF THIS PLANET'S FACE.
THE RESPECT IS WELCOMED AND RETURNED. BOTH BY ME...
...AND BY THE KING.
YOU ALWAYS WERE BETTER AT THIS TYPE OF THING.
I'VE NEVER HAD MUCH PATIENCE--
VREET VREET
--JUSTICE LEAGUE ALERT--
VREET
--FOR POLITICS.

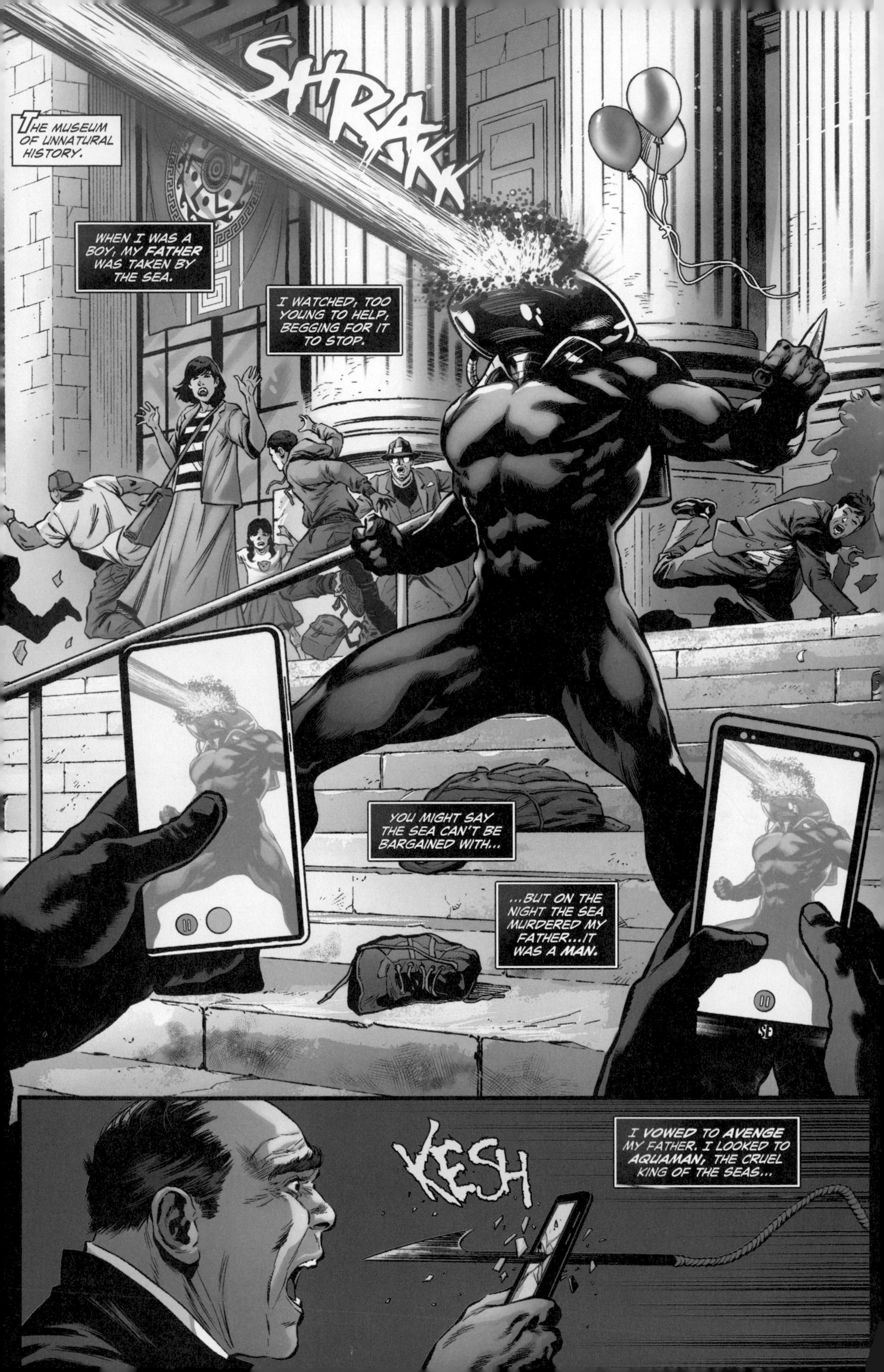
SHRAKK
THE MUSEUM OF UNNATURAL HISTORY.
WHEN I WAS A BOY, MY FATHER WAS TAKEN BY THE SEA.
I WATCHED, TOO YOUNG TO HELP, BEGGING FOR IT TO STOP.
YOU MIGHT SAY THE SEA CAN'T BE BARGAINED WITH...
...BUT ON THE NIGHT THE SEA MURDERED MY FATHER...IT WAS A MAN.
KESH
I VOWED TO AVENGE MY FATHER. I LOOKED TO AQUAMAN, THE CRUEL KING OF THE SEAS...

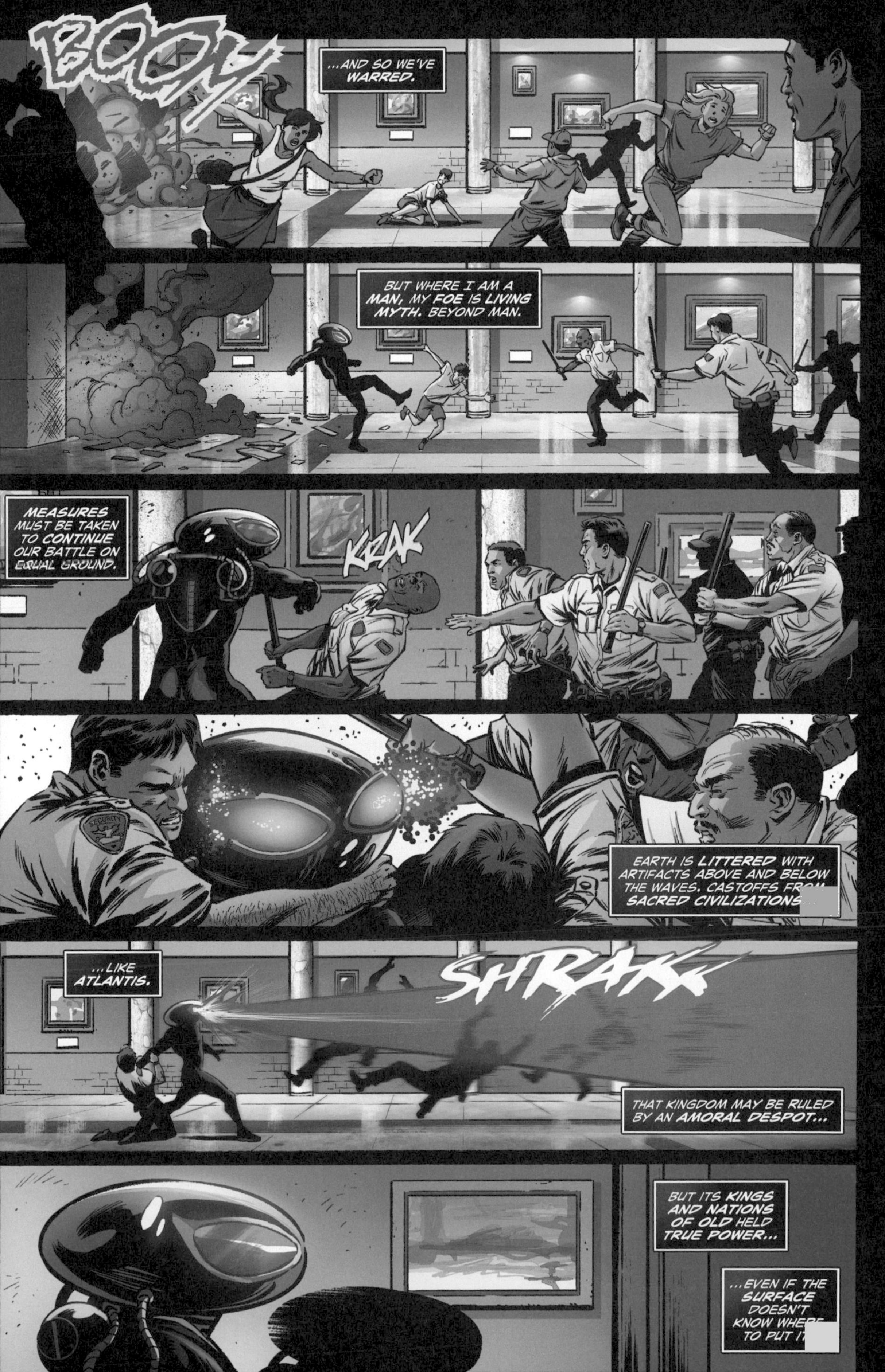
BOOM
...AND SO WE'VE WARRED.
BUT WHERE I AM A MAN, MY FOE IS LIVING MYTH. BEYOND MAN.
MEASURES MUST BE TAKEN TO CONTINUE OUR BATTLE ON EQUAL GROUND.
KRAK
EARTH IS LITTERED WITH ARTIFACTS ABOVE AND BELOW THE WAVES. CASTOFFS FROM SACRED CIVILIZATIONS...
...LIKE ATLANTIS.
SHRAKK
THAT KINGDOM MAY BE RULED BY AN AMORAL DESPOT...
BUT ITS KINGS AND NATIONS OF OLD HELD TRUE POWER...
...EVEN IF THE SURFACE DOESN'T KNOW WHERE TO PUT IT.

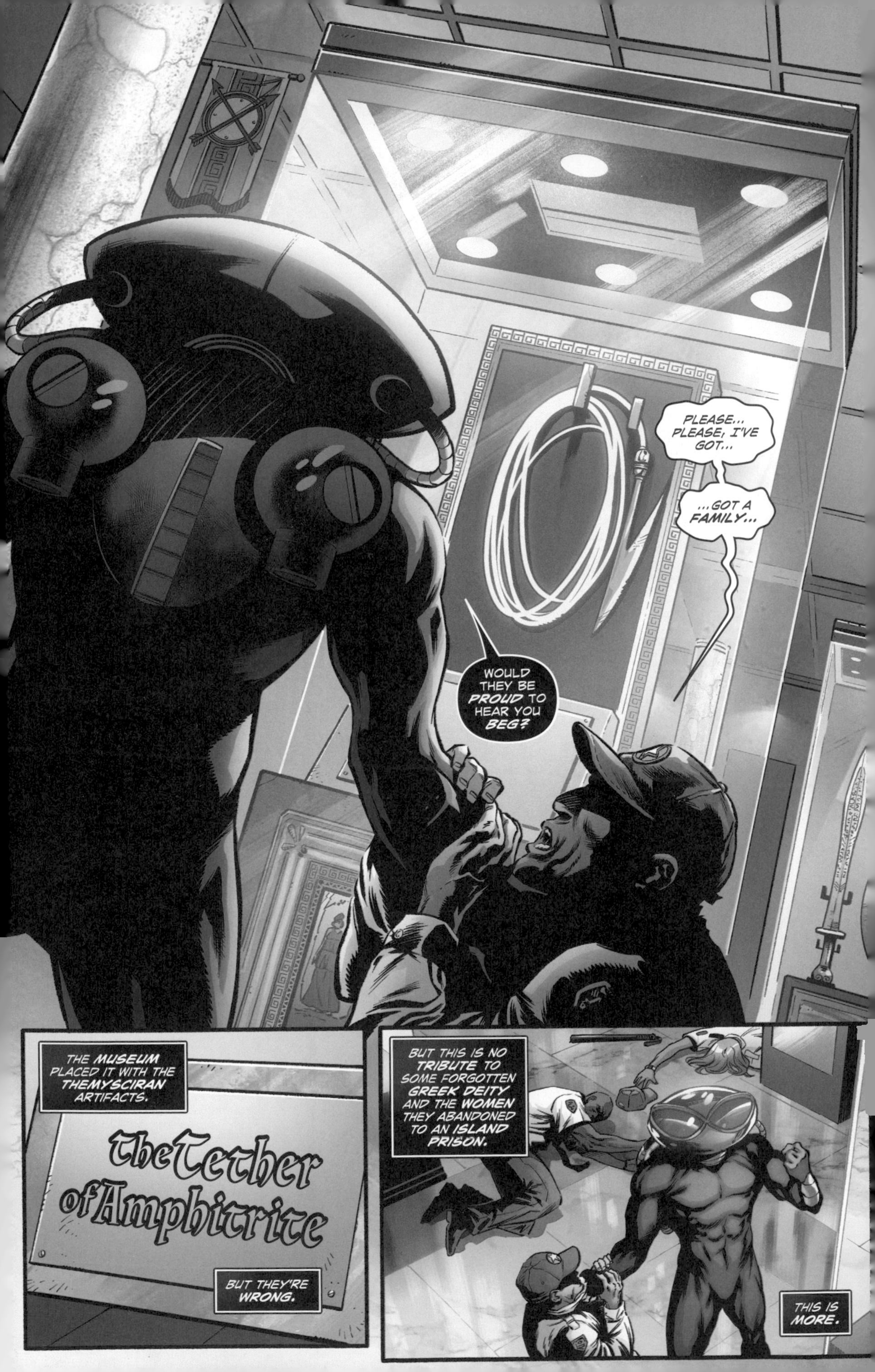
PLEASE... PLEASE, I'VE GOT...
...GOT A FAMILY...
WOULD THEY BE PROUD TO HEAR YOU BEG?
THE MUSEUM PLACED IT WITH THE THEMYSCIRAN ARTIFACTS.
The Tether of Amphitrite
BUT THEY'RE WRONG.
BUT THIS IS NO TRIBUTE TO SOME FORGOTTEN GREEK DEITY AND THE WOMEN THEY ABANDONED TO AN ISLAND PRISON.
THIS IS MORE.

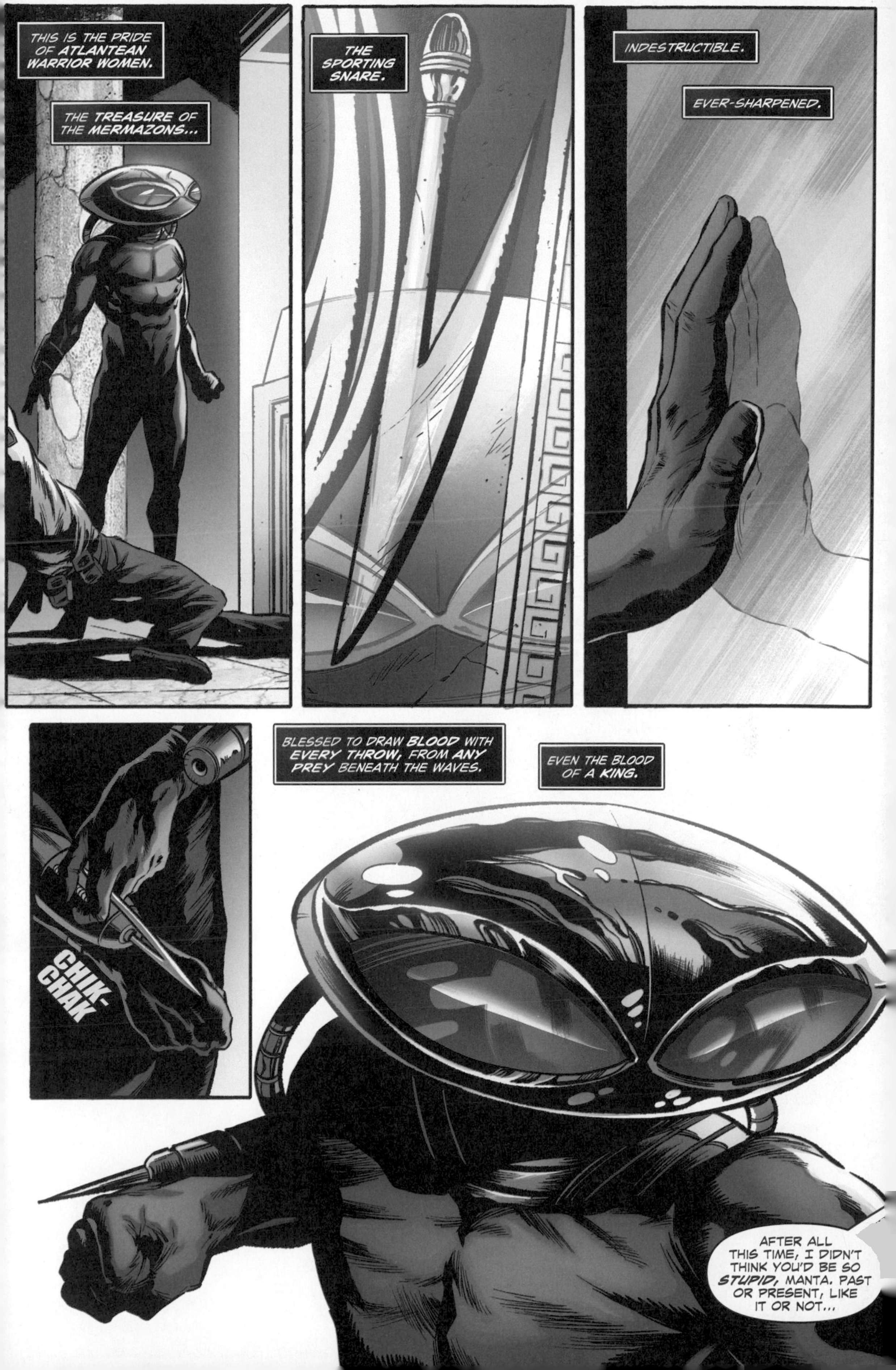
THIS IS THE PRIDE OF ATLANTEAN WARRIOR WOMEN.
THE TREASURE OF THE MERMAZONS...
THE SPORTING SNARE.
INDESTRUCTIBLE.
EVER-SHARPENED.
CHIK-CHAK
BLESSED TO DRAW BLOOD WITH EVERY THROW, FROM ANY PREY BENEATH THE WAVES.
EVEN THE BLOOD OF A KING.
AFTER ALL THIS TIME, I DIDN'T THINK YOU'D BE SO STUPID, MANTA. PAST OR PRESENT, LIKE IT OR NOT...

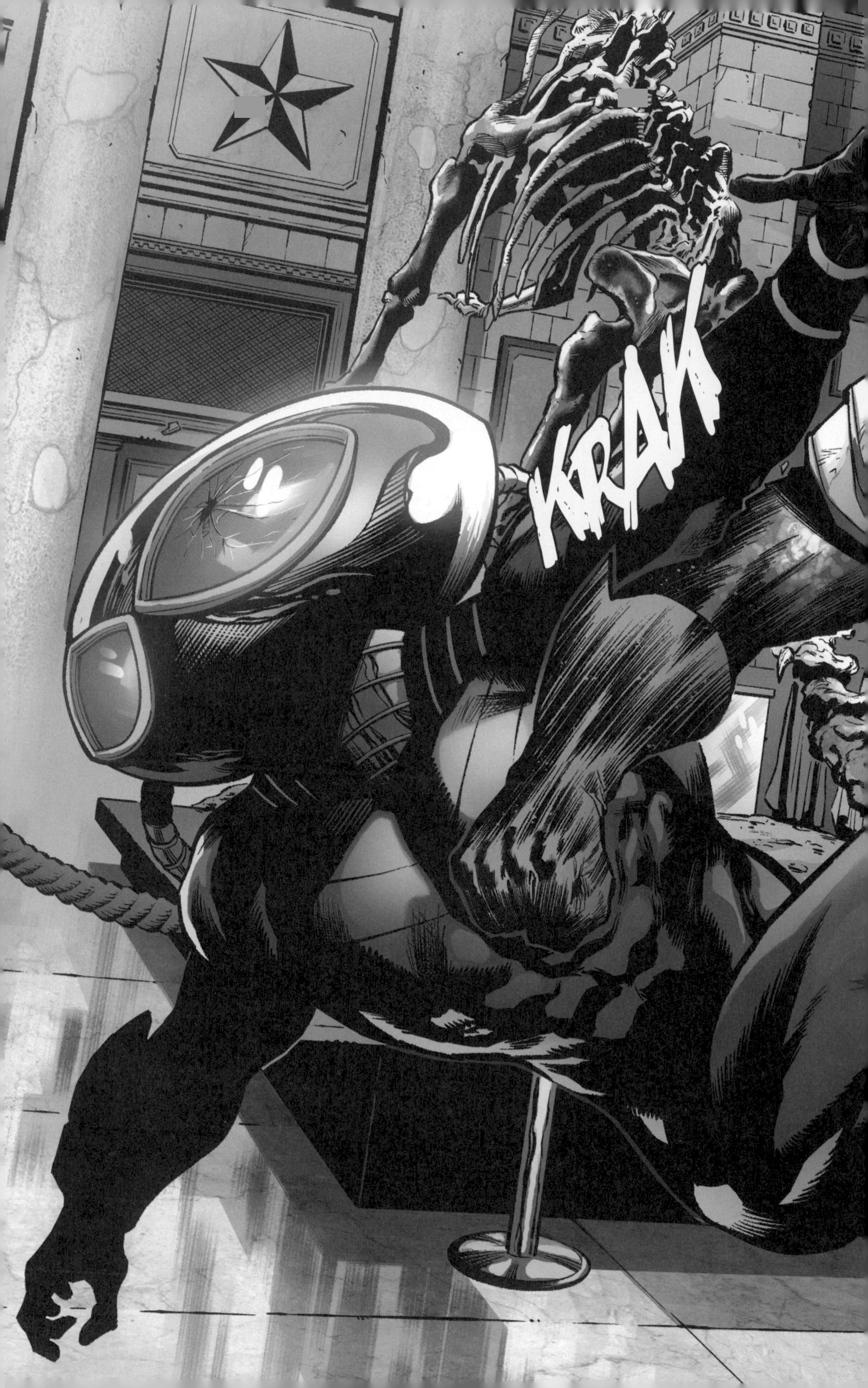
KRAK

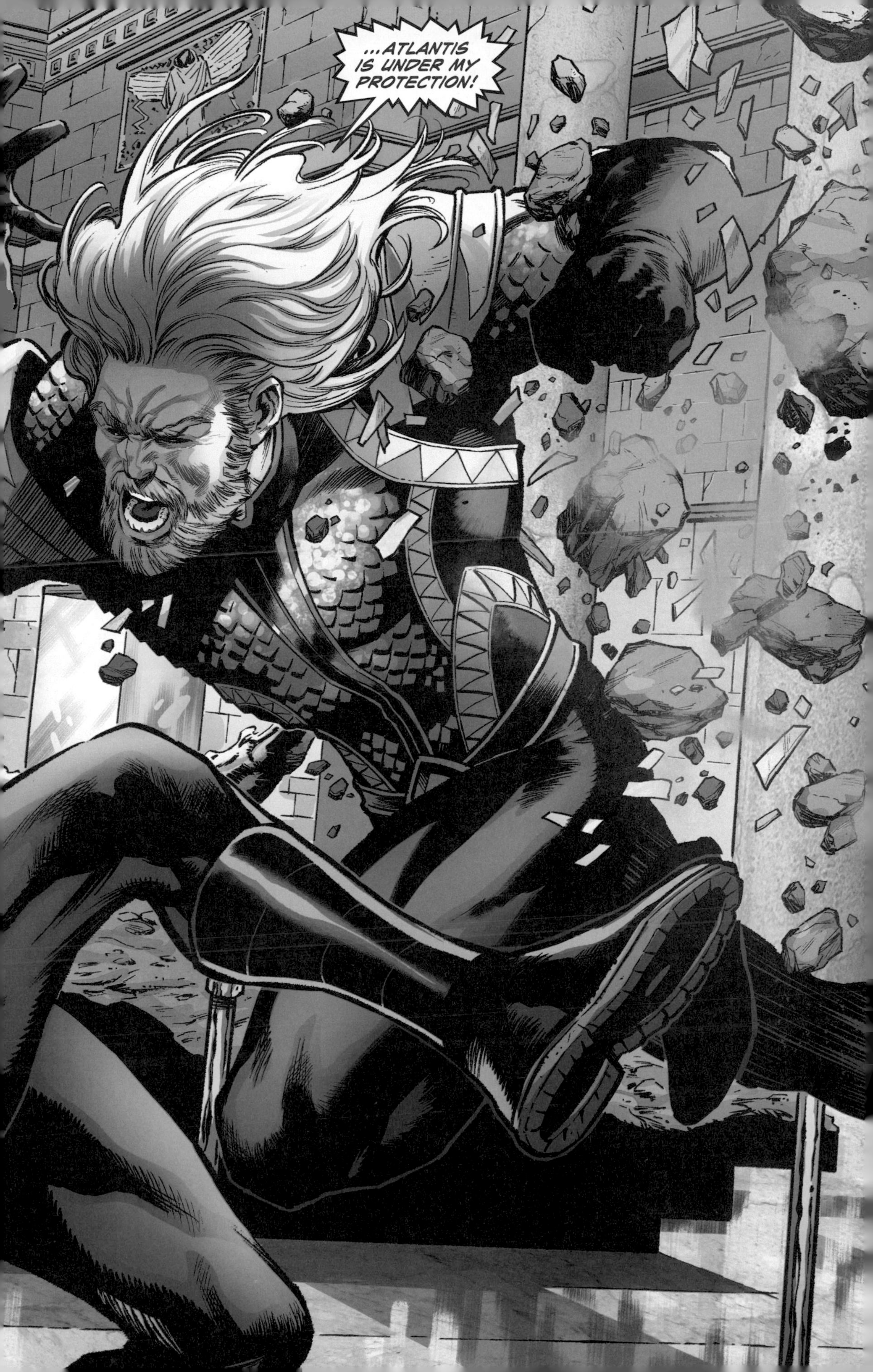
...ATLANTIS IS UNDER MY PROTECTION!

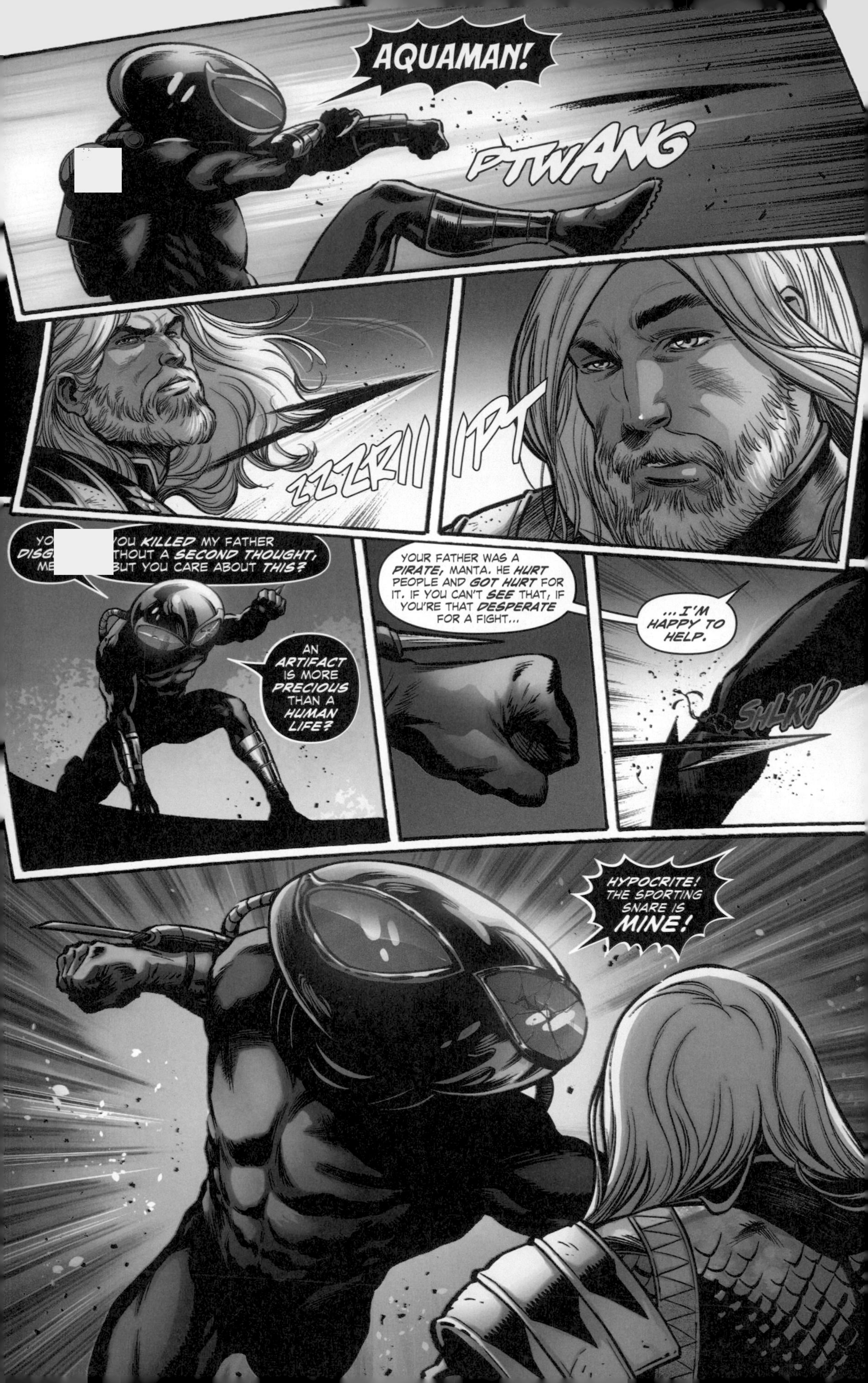
AQUAMAN!
PTWANG
ZZZRIIIIPT
YO OU KILLED MY FATHER DISG THOUT A SECOND THOUGHT, ME BUT YOU CARE ABOUT THIS?
AN ARTIFACT IS MORE PRECIOUS THAN A HUMAN LIFE?
YOUR FATHER WAS A PIRATE, MANTA. HE HURT PEOPLE AND GOT HURT FOR IT. IF YOU CAN'T SEE THAT, IF YOU'RE THAT DESPERATE FOR A FIGHT...
...I'M HAPPY TO HELP.
SHLRIP
HYPOCRITE! THE SPORTING SNARE IS MINE!

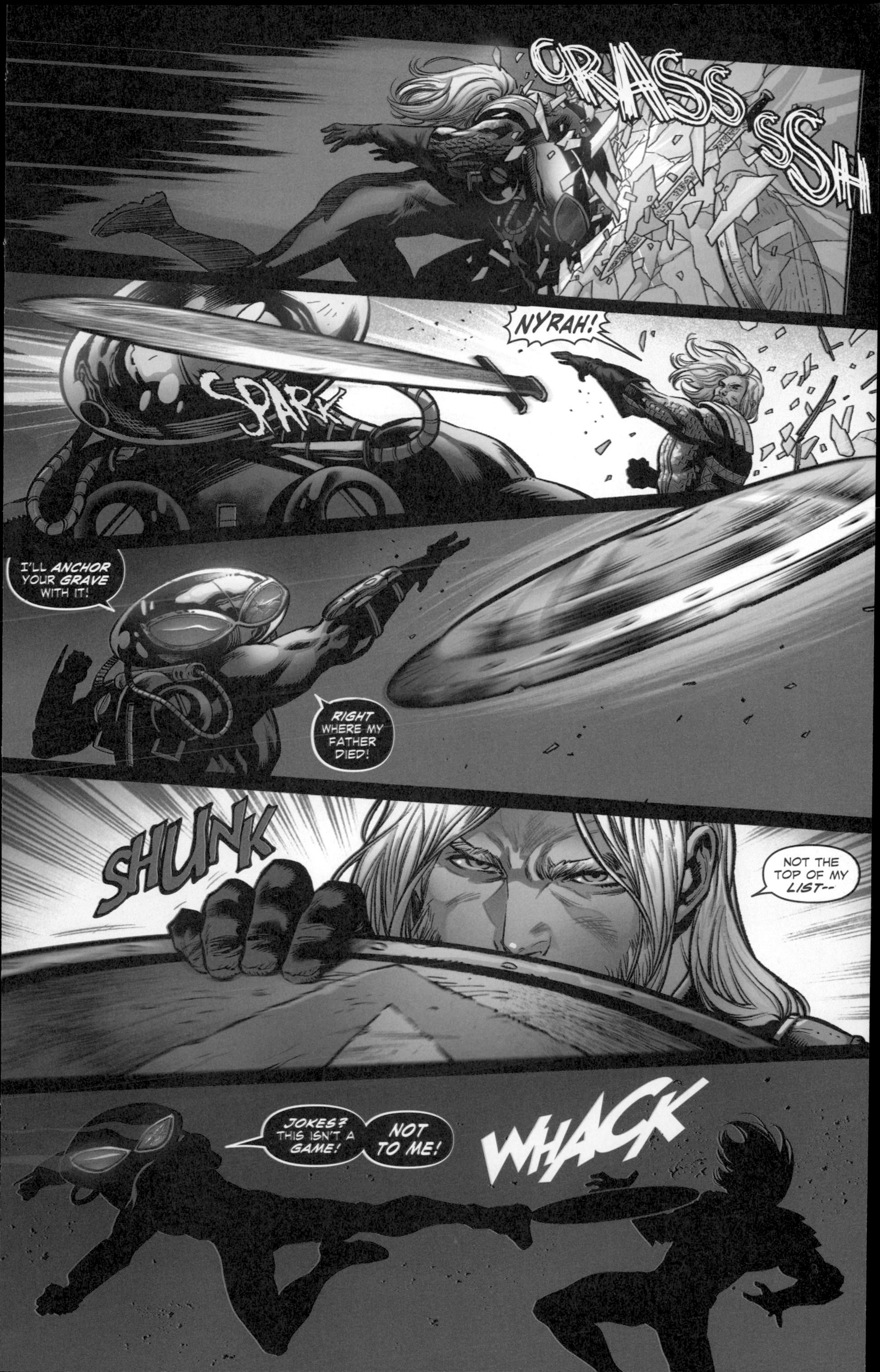
CRASSSSH
NYRAH!
SPARK
I'LL ANCHOR YOUR GRAVE WITH IT!
RIGHT WHERE MY FATHER DIED!
SHUNK
NOT THE TOP OF MY LIST--
JOKES? THIS ISN'T A GAME!
NOT TO ME!
WHACK

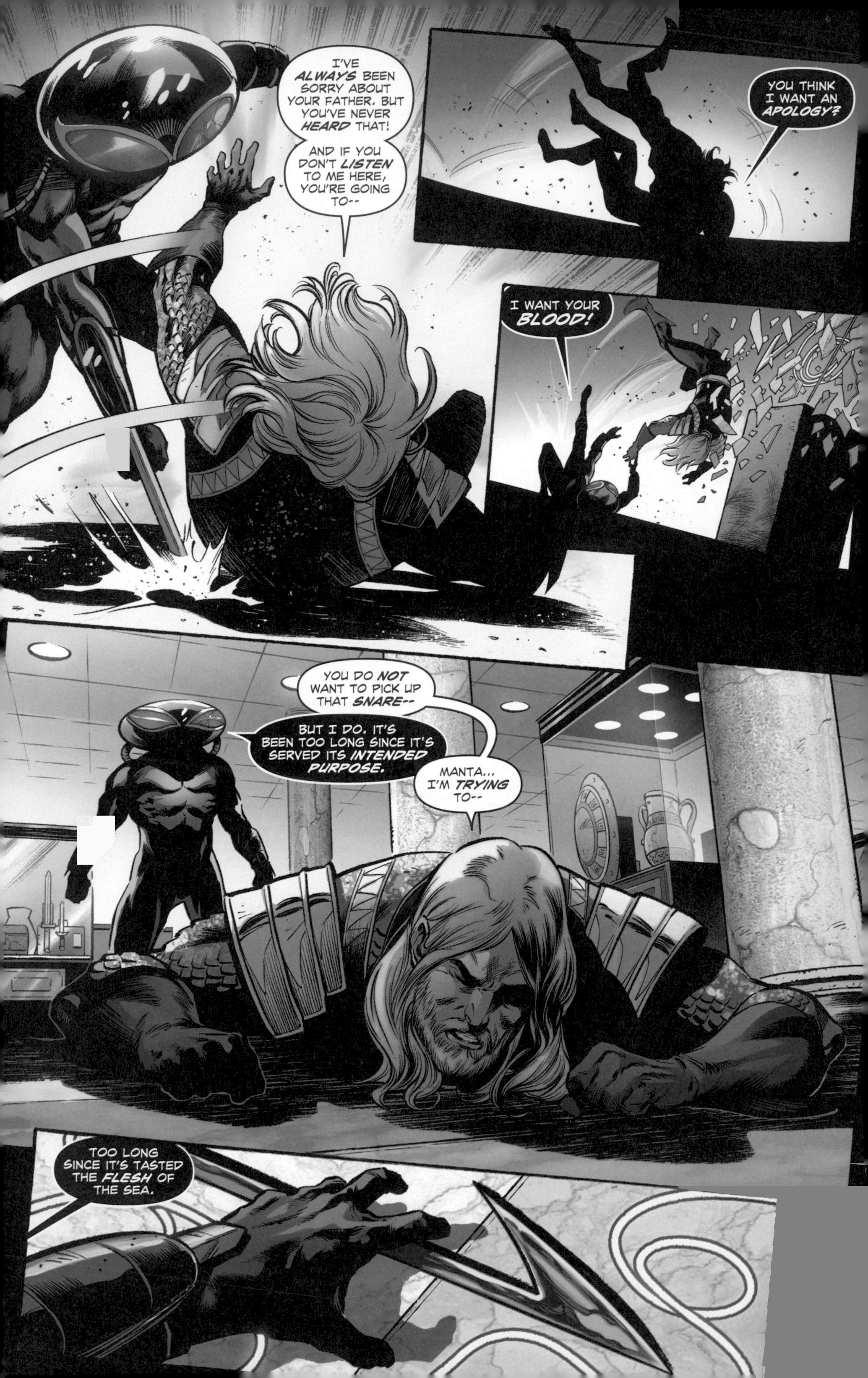
I'VE *ALWAYS* BEEN SORRY ABOUT YOUR FATHER. BUT YOU'VE NEVER *HEARD* THAT!
AND IF YOU DON'T *LISTEN* TO ME HERE, YOU'RE GOING TO--
YOU THINK I WANT AN *APOLOGY?*
I WANT YOUR *BLOOD!*
YOU DO *NOT* WANT TO PICK UP THAT *SNARE--*
BUT I DO. IT'S BEEN TOO LONG SINCE IT'S SERVED ITS *INTENDED PURPOSE.*
MANTA... I'M *TRYING* TO--
TOO LONG SINCE IT'S TASTED THE *FLESH* OF THE SEA.

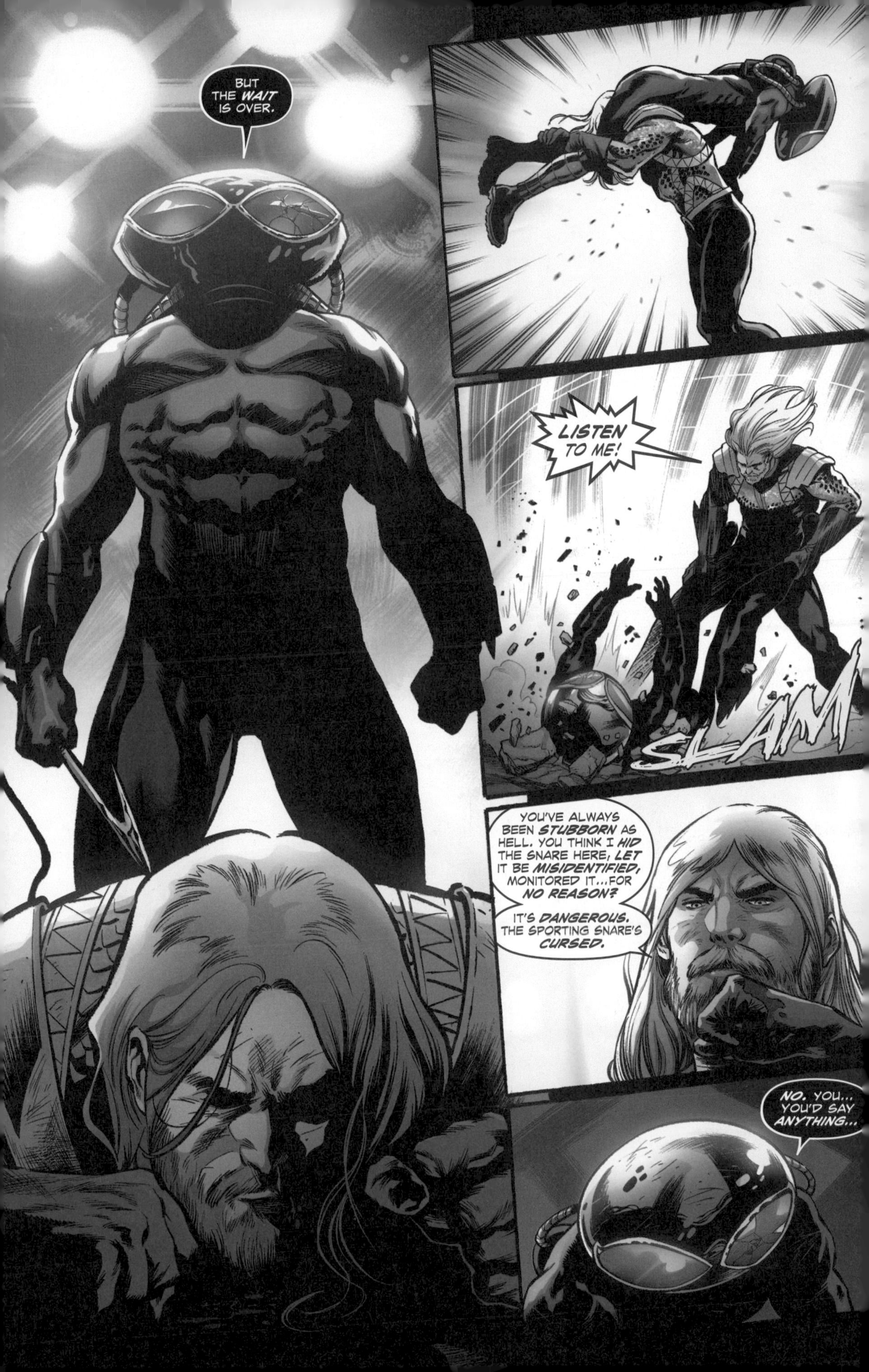
BUT THE WAIT IS OVER.
LISTEN TO ME!
SLAM
YOU'VE ALWAYS BEEN STUBBORN AS HELL. YOU THINK I HID THE SNARE HERE, LET IT BE MISIDENTIFIED, MONITORED IT...FOR NO REASON?
IT'S DANGEROUS. THE SPORTING SNARE'S CURSED.
NO. YOU... YOU'D SAY ANYTHING...

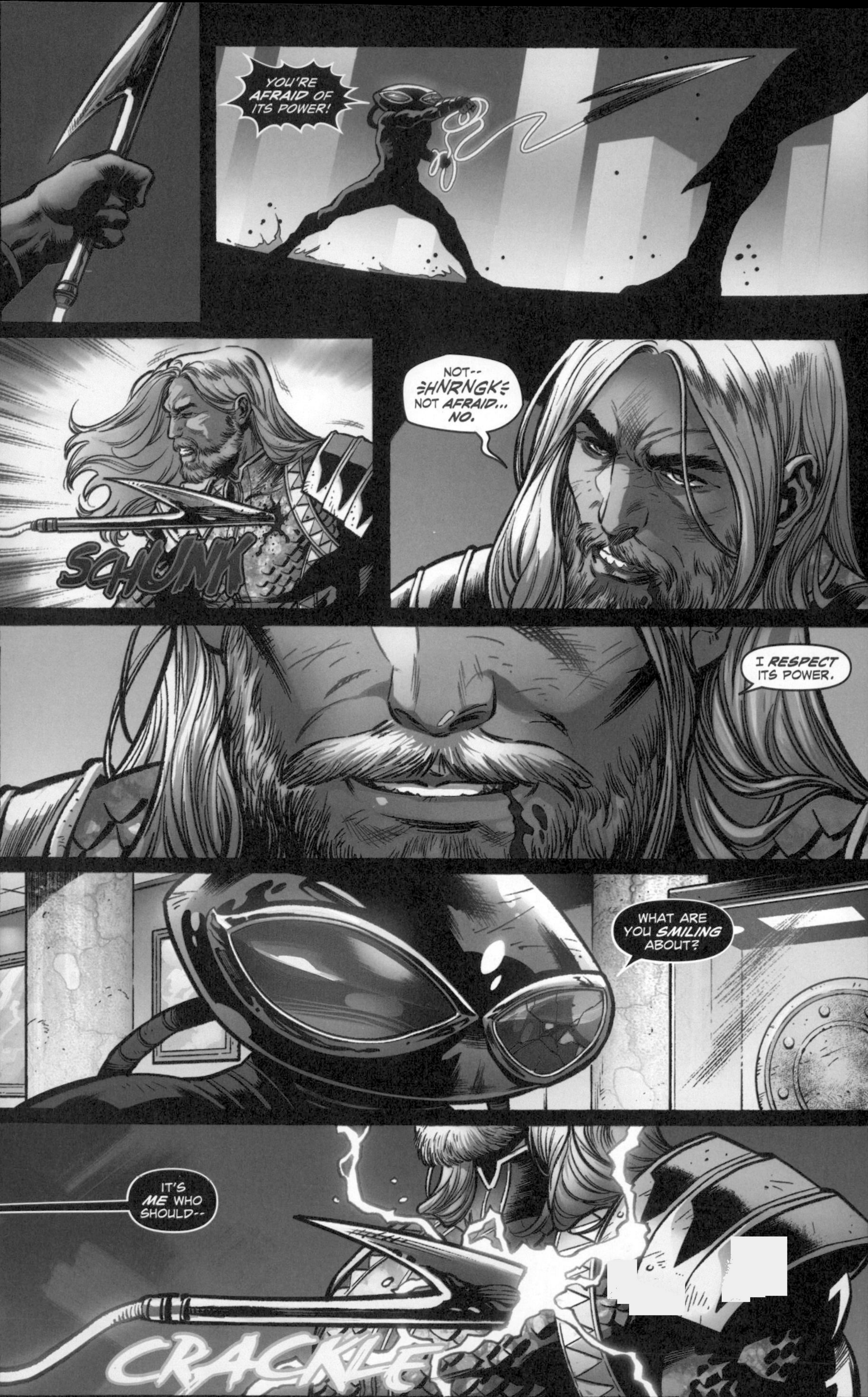
YOU'RE AFRAID OF ITS POWER!
NOT-- HNRNGK NOT AFRAID... NO.
SCHUNK
I RESPECT ITS POWER.
WHAT ARE YOU SMILING ABOUT?
IT'S ME WHO SHOULD--
CRACKLE

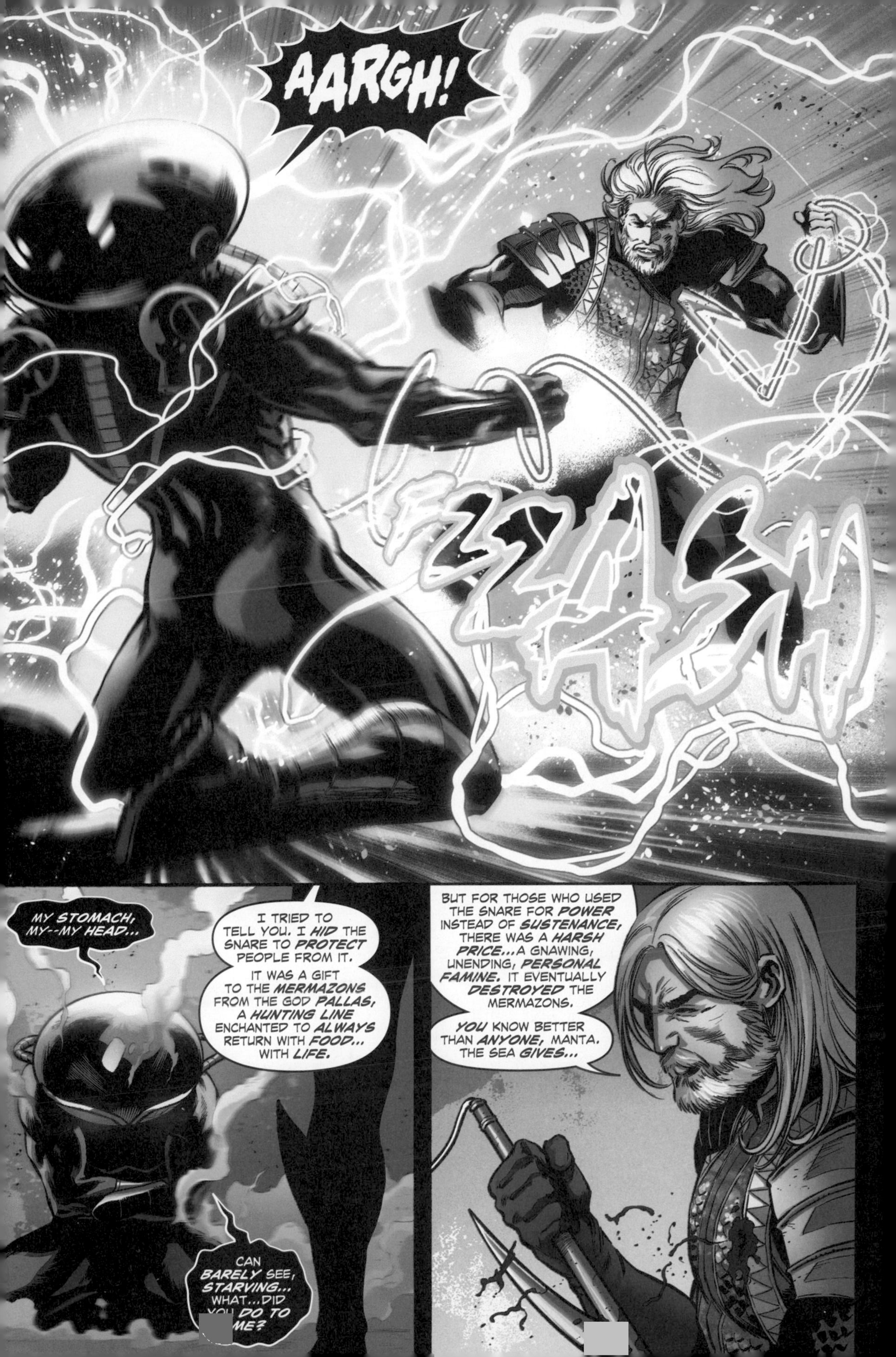
AARGH!
FZZASH
MY STOMACH, MY--MY HEAD...
I TRIED TO TELL YOU. I HID THE SNARE TO PROTECT PEOPLE FROM IT.
IT WAS A GIFT TO THE MERMAZONS FROM THE GOD PALLAS, A HUNTING LINE ENCHANTED TO ALWAYS RETURN WITH FOOD... WITH LIFE.
CAN BARELY SEE, STARVING... WHAT...DID YOU DO TO ME?
BUT FOR THOSE WHO USED THE SNARE FOR POWER INSTEAD OF SUSTENANCE, THERE WAS A HARSH PRICE...A GNAWING, UNENDING, PERSONAL FAMINE. IT EVENTUALLY DESTROYED THE MERMAZONS.
YOU KNOW BETTER THAN ANYONE, MANTA. THE SEA GIVES...

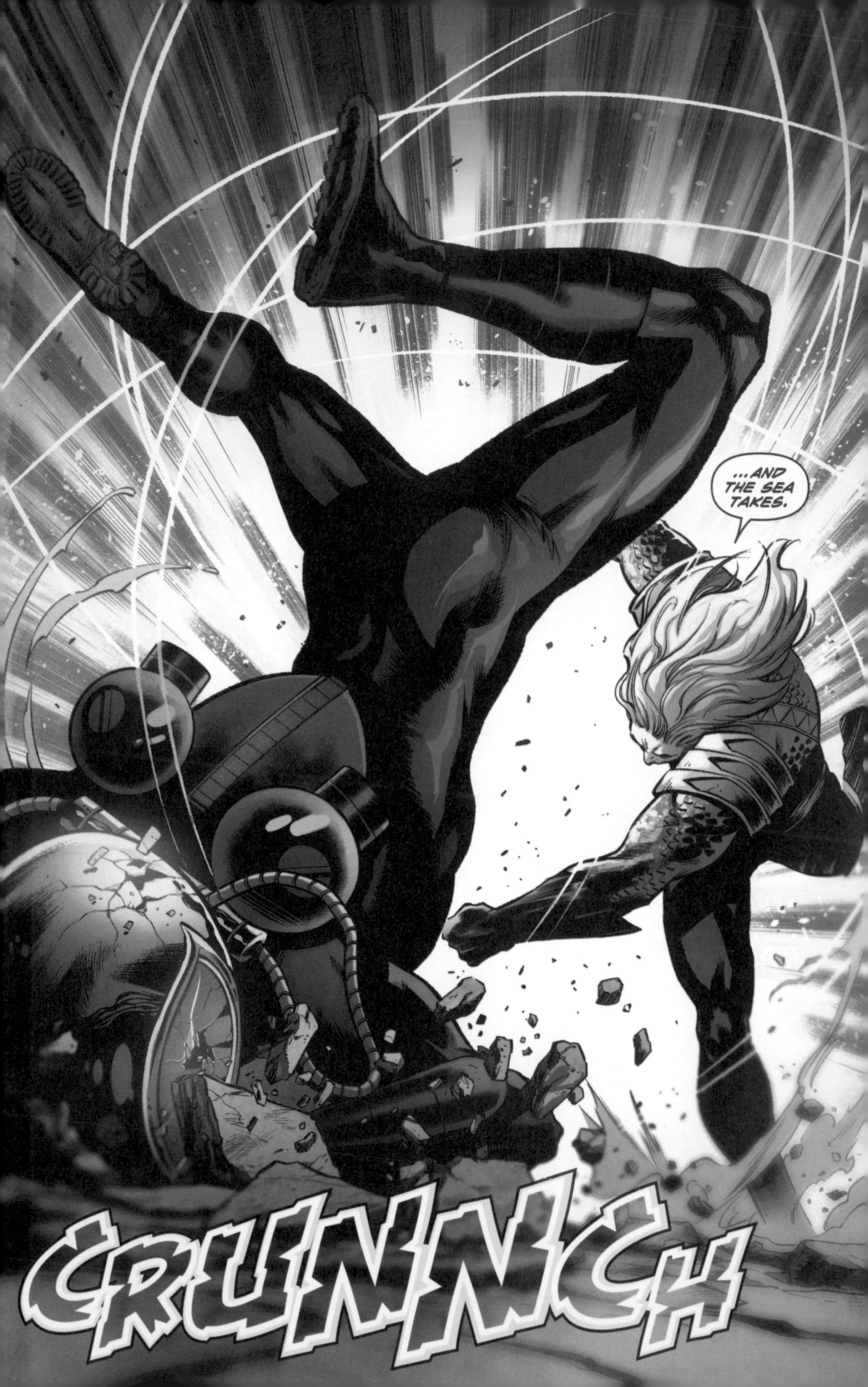
...AND THE SEA TAKES.
CRUNNCH

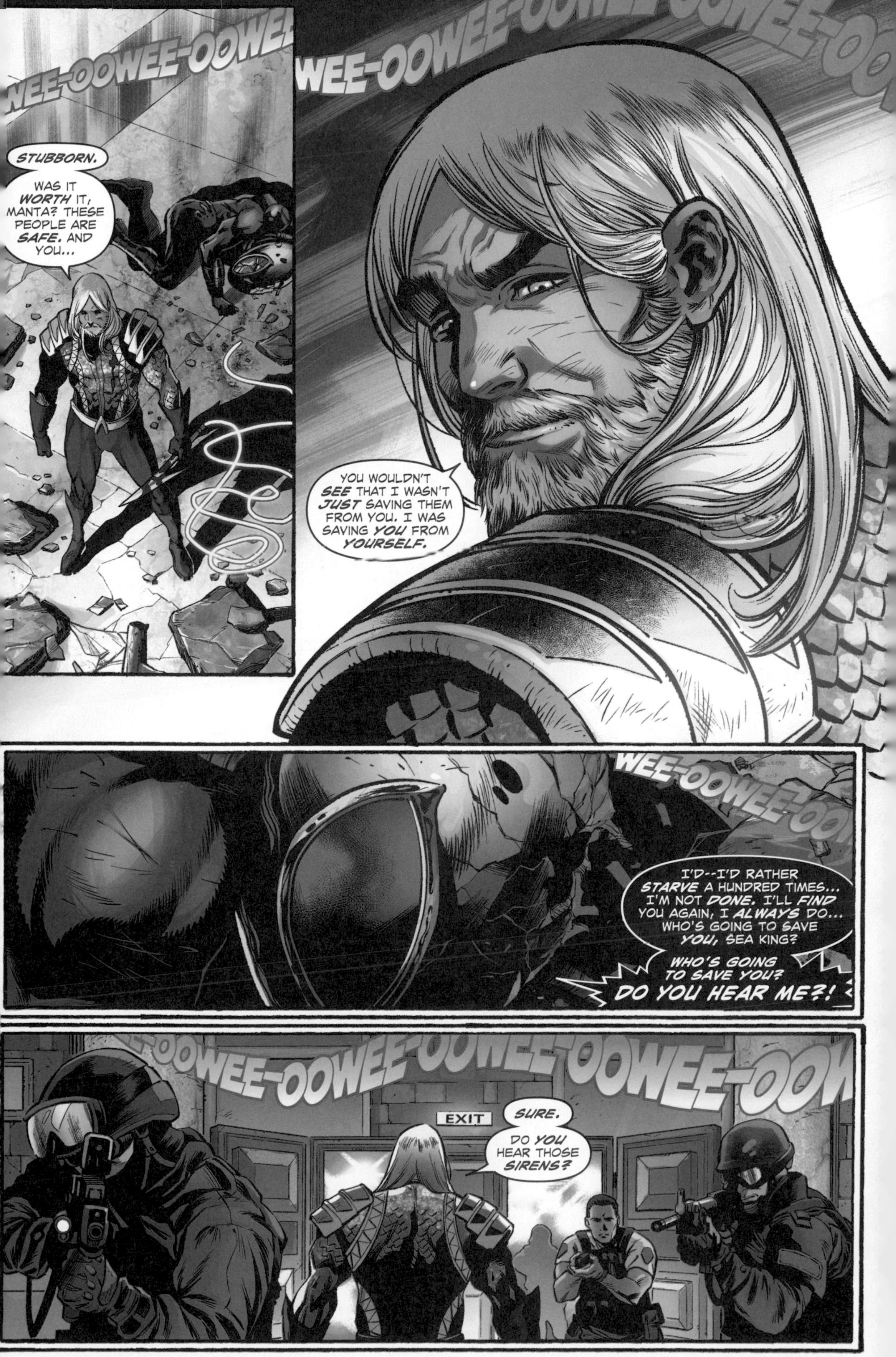
WEE-OOWEE-OOWEE
STUBBORN.
WAS IT WORTH IT, MANTA? THESE PEOPLE ARE SAFE. AND YOU...
WEE-OOWEE-OOWEE-OOWEE-OO
YOU WOULDN'T SEE THAT I WASN'T JUST SAVING THEM FROM YOU. I WAS SAVING YOU FROM YOURSELF.
WEE-OOWEE-OO
I'D--I'D RATHER STARVE A HUNDRED TIMES... I'M NOT DONE. I'LL FIND YOU AGAIN, I ALWAYS DO... WHO'S GOING TO SAVE YOU, SEA KING?
WHO'S GOING TO SAVE YOU? DO YOU HEAR ME?!
OOWEE-OOWEE-OOWEE-OOWEE-OO
EXIT
SURE.
DO YOU HEAR THOSE SIRENS?

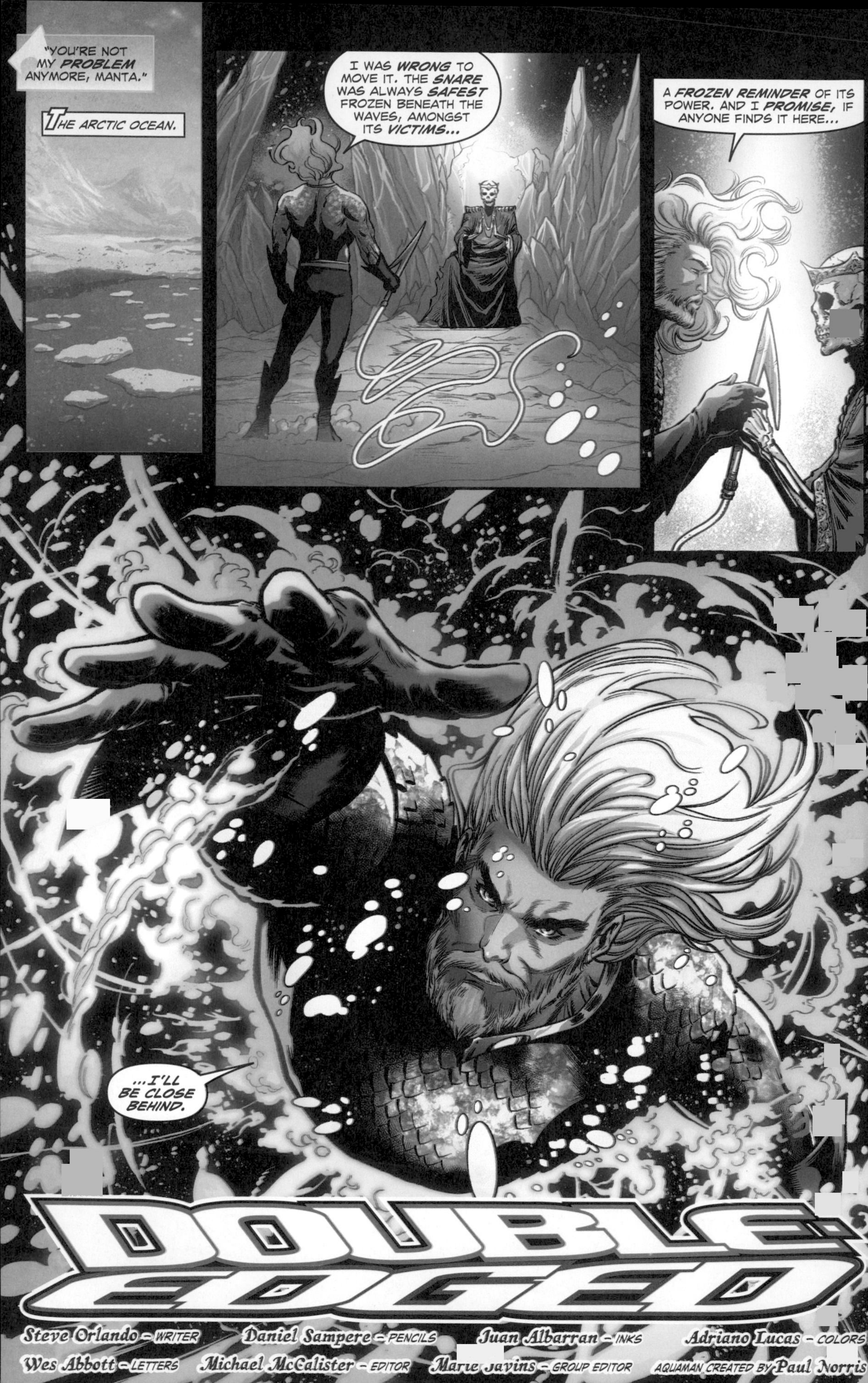
"YOU'RE NOT MY PROBLEM ANYMORE, MANTA."
THE ARCTIC OCEAN.
I WAS WRONG TO MOVE IT. THE SNARE WAS ALWAYS SAFEST FROZEN BENEATH THE WAVES, AMONGST ITS VICTIMS...
A FROZEN REMINDER OF ITS POWER. AND I PROMISE, IF ANYONE FINDS IT HERE...
...I'LL BE CLOSE BEHIND.
DOUBLE-EDGED
Steve Orlando - WRITER Daniel Sampere - PENCILS Juan Albarran - INKS Adriano Lucas - COLORS
Wes Abbott - LETTERS Michael McCalister - EDITOR Marie Javins - GROUP EDITOR AQUAMAN CREATED BY Paul Norris

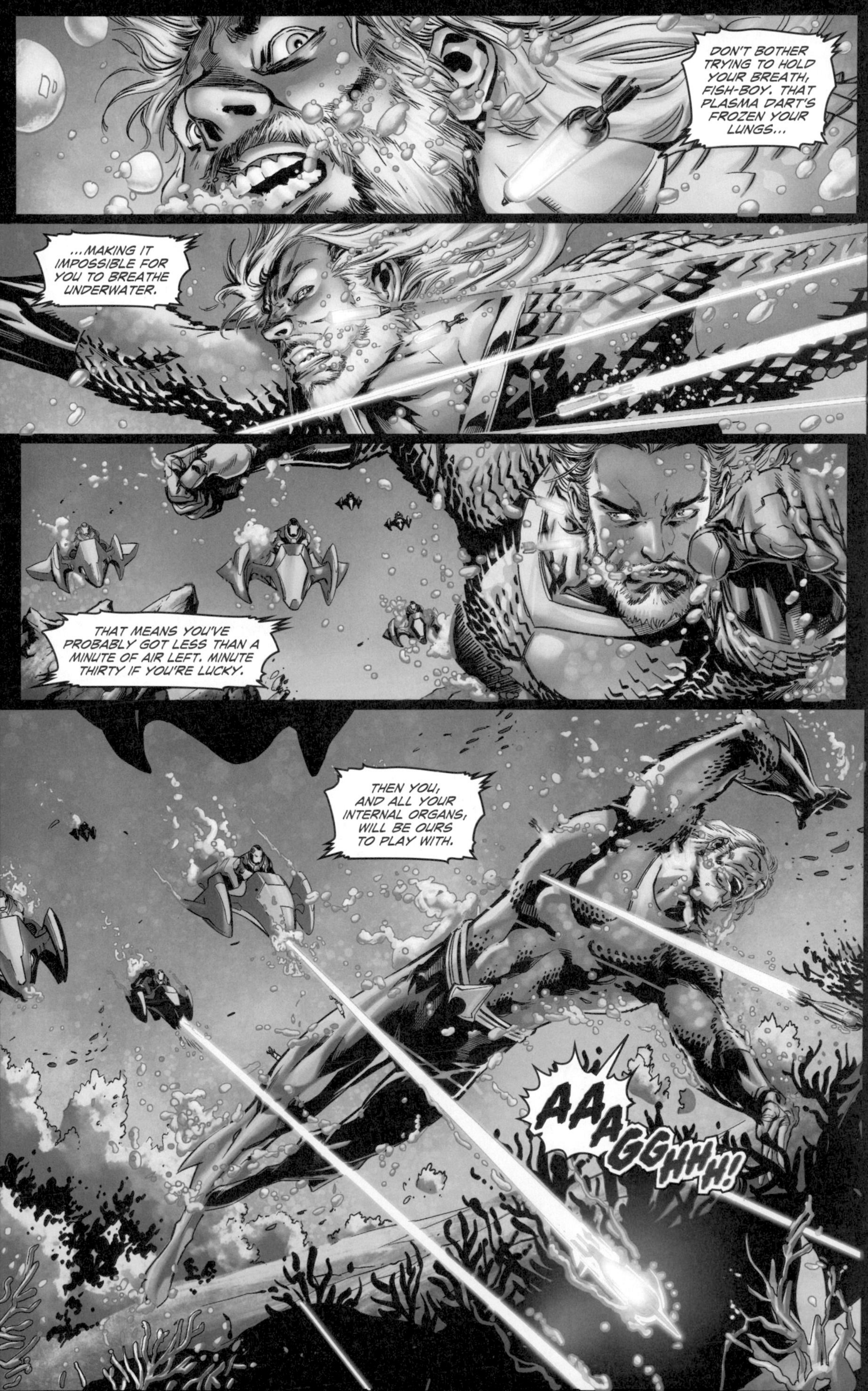
DON'T BOTHER TRYING TO HOLD YOUR BREATH, FISH-BOY. THAT PLASMA DART'S FROZEN YOUR LUNGS...
...MAKING IT IMPOSSIBLE FOR YOU TO BREATHE UNDERWATER.
THAT MEANS YOU'VE PROBABLY GOT LESS THAN A MINUTE OF AIR LEFT. MINUTE THIRTY IF YOU'RE LUCKY.
THEN YOU, AND ALL YOUR INTERNAL ORGANS, WILL BE OURS TO PLAY WITH.
AAAAGGHHH!

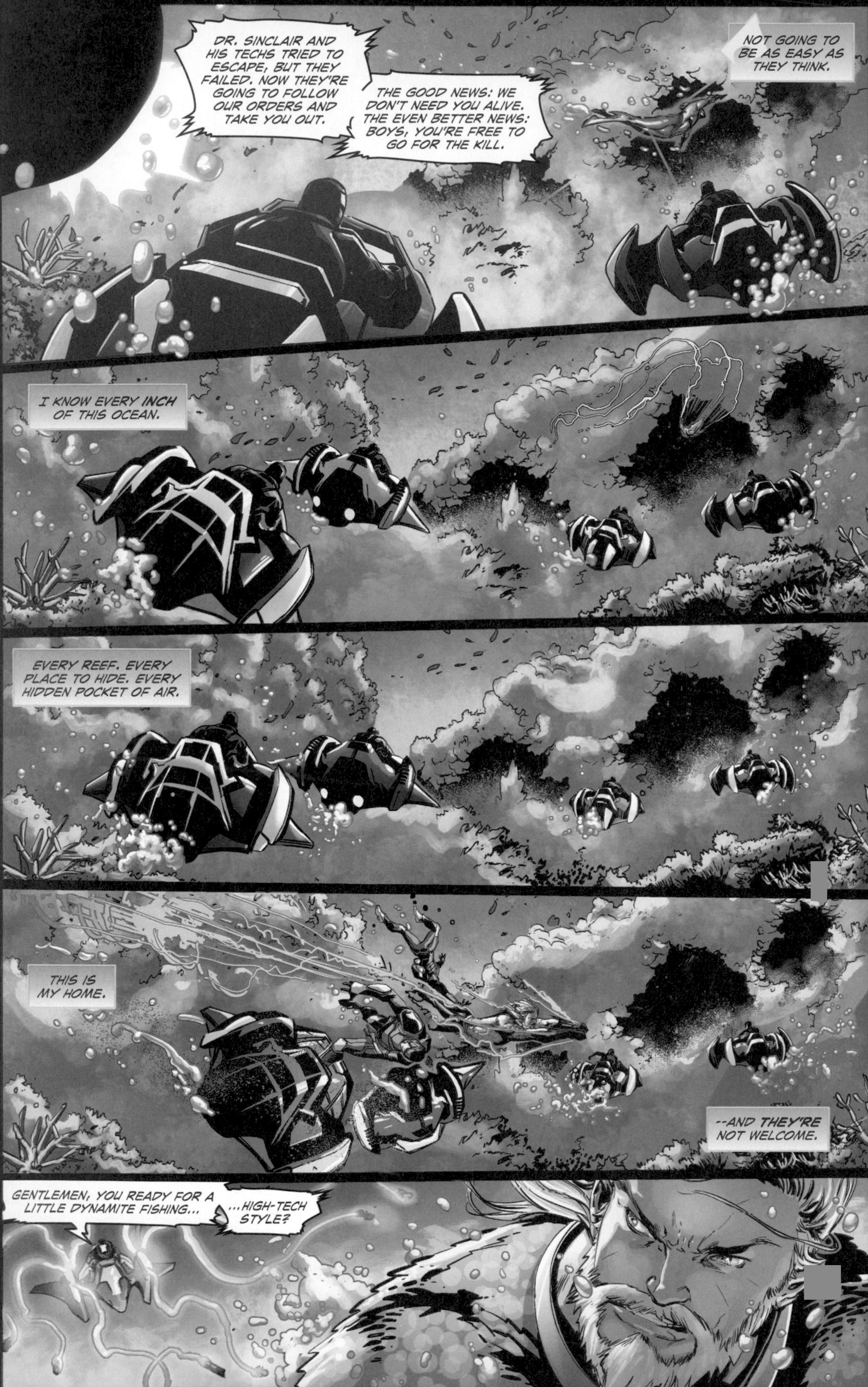
DR. SINCLAIR AND HIS TECHS TRIED TO ESCAPE, BUT THEY FAILED. NOW THEY'RE GOING TO FOLLOW OUR ORDERS AND TAKE YOU OUT.
THE GOOD NEWS: WE DON'T NEED YOU ALIVE. THE EVEN BETTER NEWS: BOYS, YOU'RE FREE TO GO FOR THE KILL.
NOT GOING TO BE AS EASY AS THEY THINK.
I KNOW EVERY INCH OF THIS OCEAN.
EVERY REEF. EVERY PLACE TO HIDE. EVERY HIDDEN POCKET OF AIR.
THIS IS MY HOME.
--AND THEY'RE NOT WELCOME.
GENTLEMEN, YOU READY FOR A LITTLE DYNAMITE FISHING...
...HIGH-TECH STYLE?

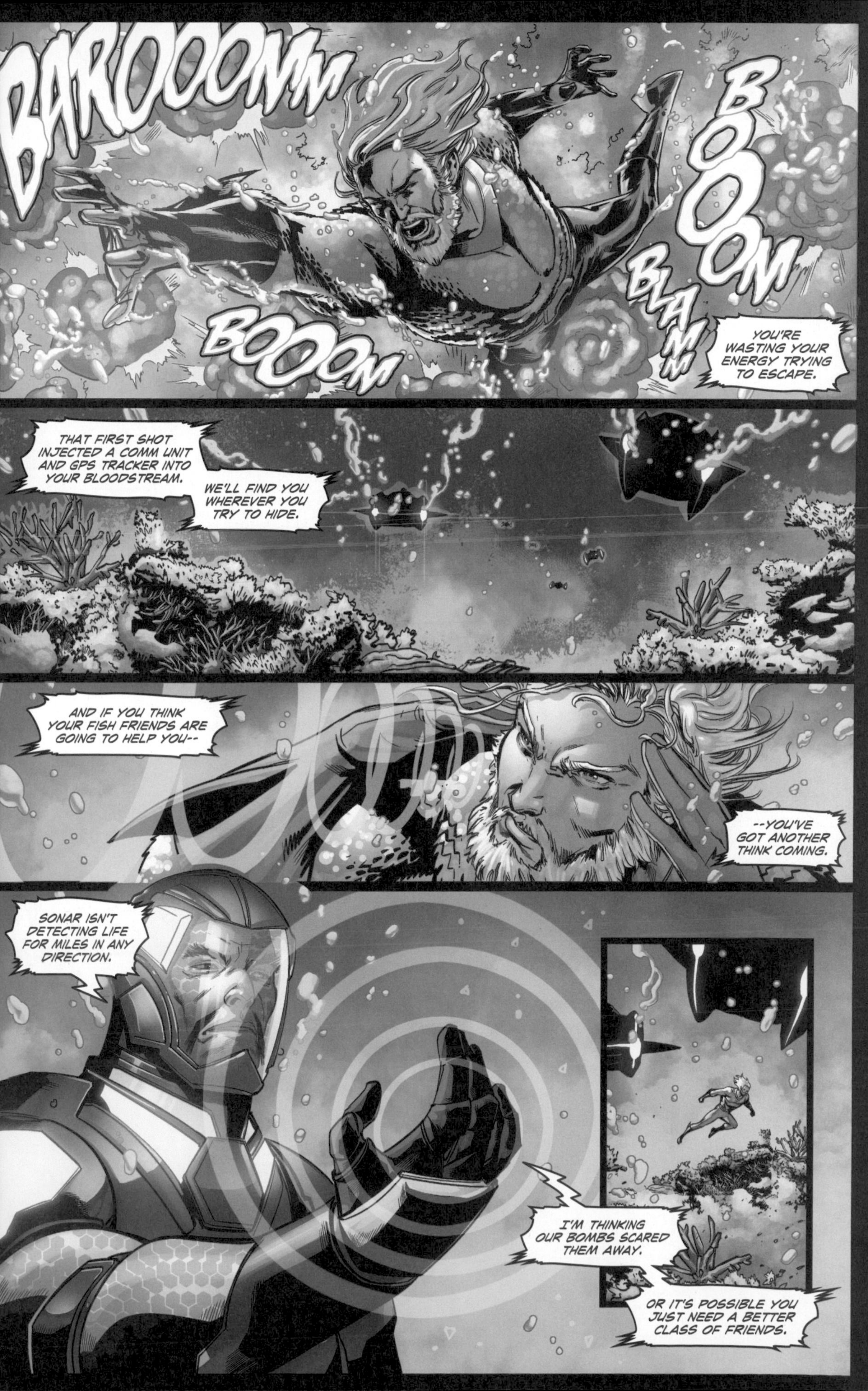
BAROOOMM
BOOOM
BLAMM
BOOOM
YOU'RE WASTING YOUR ENERGY TRYING TO ESCAPE.
THAT FIRST SHOT INJECTED A COMM UNIT AND GPS TRACKER INTO YOUR BLOODSTREAM.
WE'LL FIND YOU WHEREVER YOU TRY TO HIDE.
AND IF YOU THINK YOUR FISH FRIENDS ARE GOING TO HELP YOU--
--YOU'VE GOT ANOTHER THINK COMING.
SONAR ISN'T DETECTING LIFE FOR MILES IN ANY DIRECTION.
I'M THINKING OUR BOMBS SCARED THEM AWAY.
OR IT'S POSSIBLE YOU JUST NEED A BETTER CLASS OF FRIENDS.

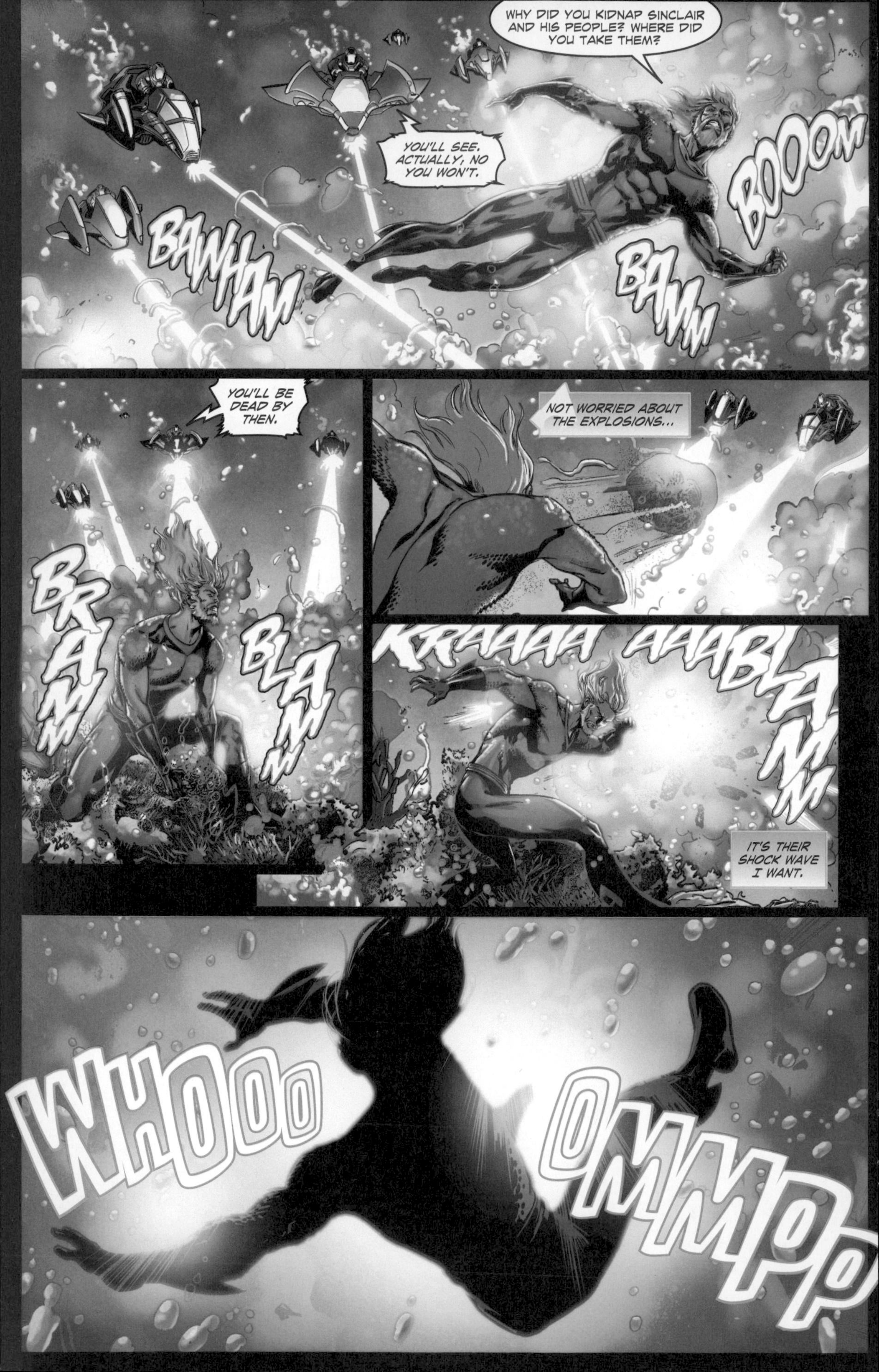
WHY DID YOU KIDNAP SINCLAIR AND HIS PEOPLE? WHERE DID YOU TAKE THEM?
YOU'LL SEE. ACTUALLY, NO YOU WON'T.
BAWHAM
BAMM
BOOOM
YOU'LL BE DEAD BY THEN.
BRAMM
BLAMM
NOT WORRIED ABOUT THE EXPLOSIONS...
KRAAAAA AAABLAMM
IT'S THEIR SHOCK WAVE I WANT.
WHOOOOOMMPP

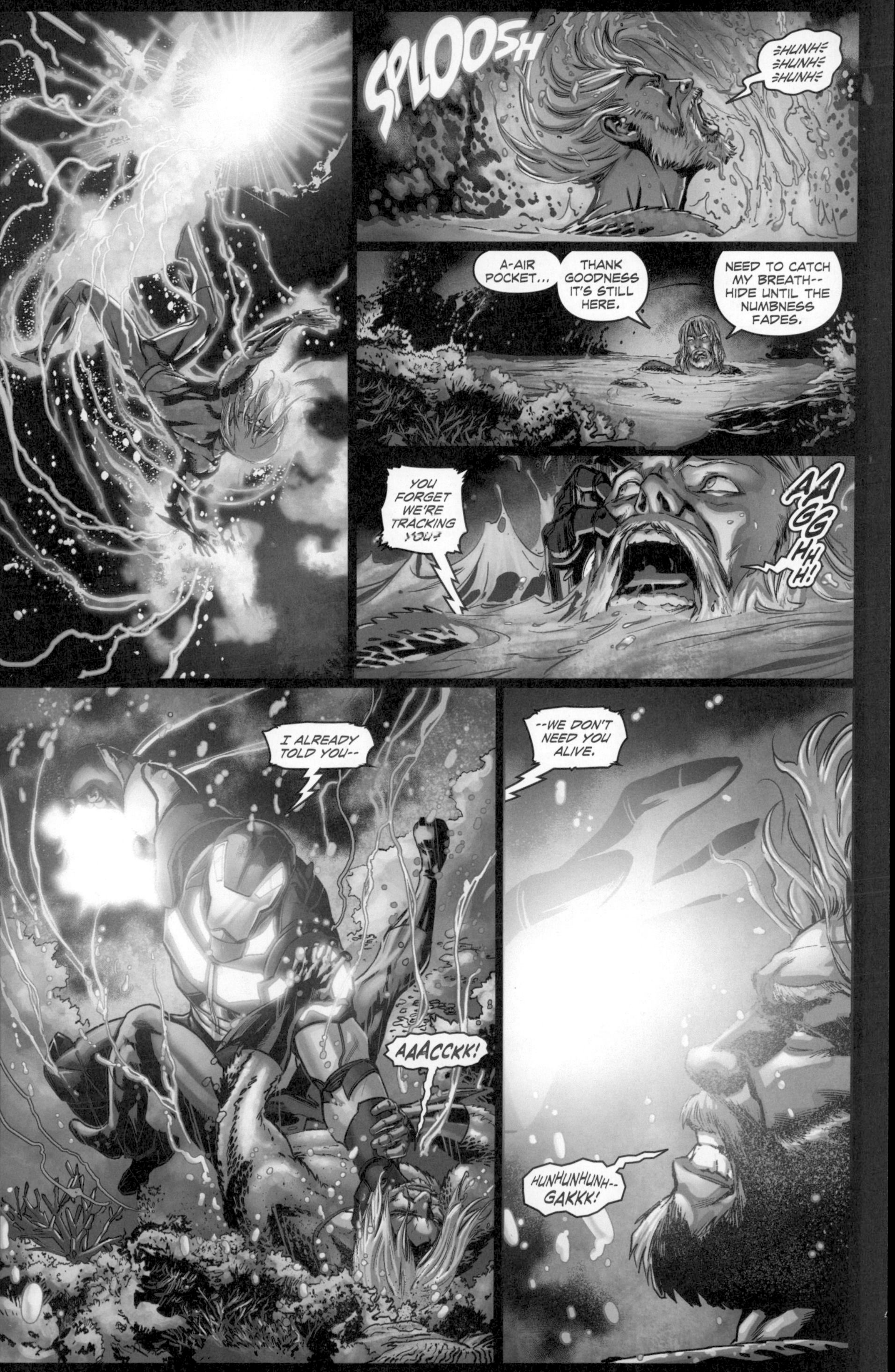

SPLOOSH
HUNH HUNH HUNH
A-AIR POCKET...
THANK GOODNESS IT'S STILL HERE.
NEED TO CATCH MY BREATH-- HIDE UNTIL THE NUMBNESS FADES.
YOU FORGET WE'RE TRACKING YOU!
AAGGHHH!
I ALREADY TOLD YOU--
AAACCKK!
--WE DON'T NEED YOU ALIVE.
HUNHUNHUNH-- GAKKK!

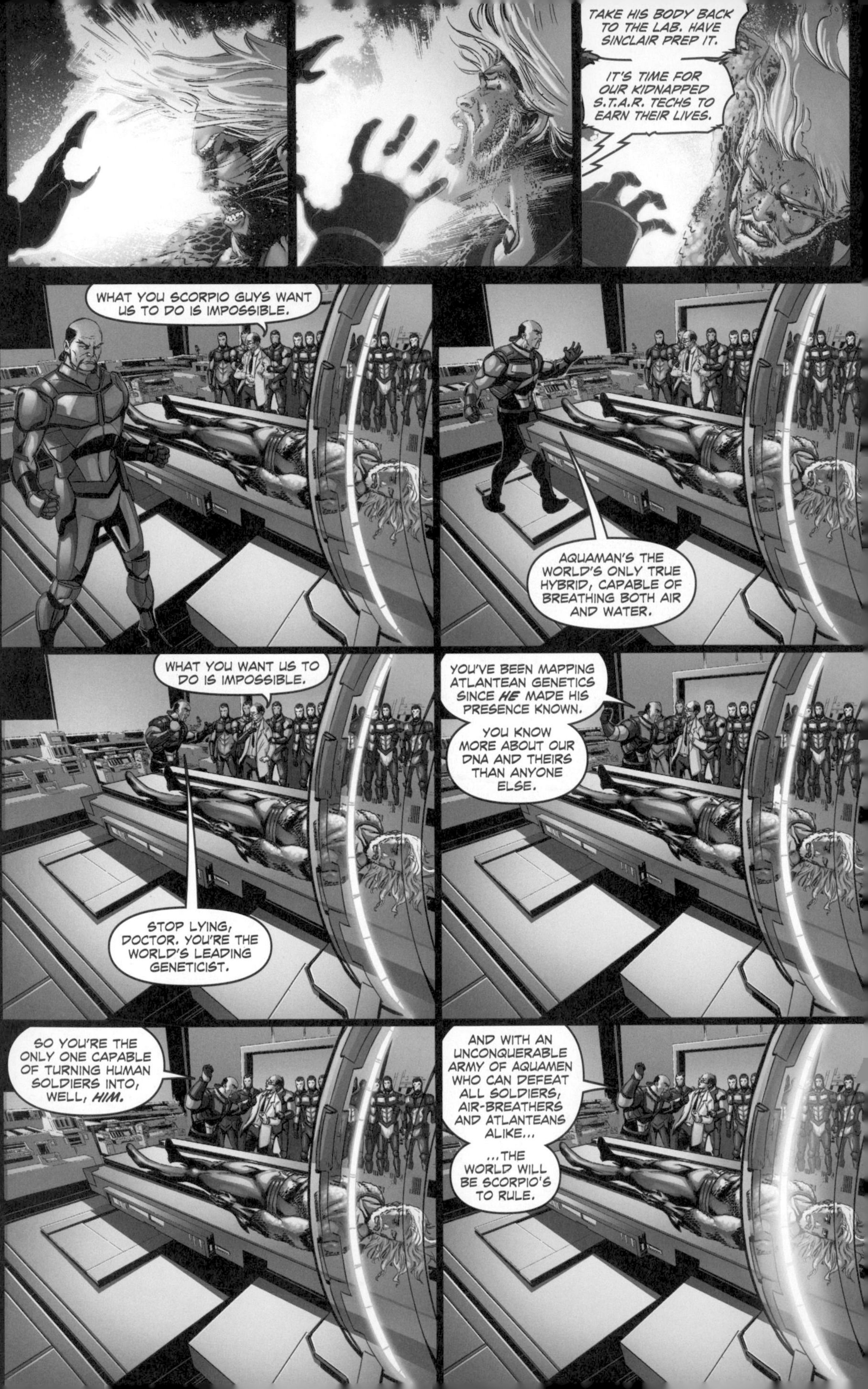
TAKE HIS BODY BACK TO THE LAB. HAVE SINCLAIR PREP IT.
IT'S TIME FOR OUR KIDNAPPED S.T.A.R. TECHS TO EARN THEIR LIVES.
WHAT YOU SCORPIO GUYS WANT US TO DO IS IMPOSSIBLE.
AQUAMAN'S THE WORLD'S ONLY TRUE HYBRID, CAPABLE OF BREATHING BOTH AIR AND WATER.
WHAT YOU WANT US TO DO IS IMPOSSIBLE.
STOP LYING, DOCTOR. YOU'RE THE WORLD'S LEADING GENETICIST.
YOU'VE BEEN MAPPING ATLANTEAN GENETICS SINCE HE MADE HIS PRESENCE KNOWN.
YOU KNOW MORE ABOUT OUR DNA AND THEIRS THAN ANYONE ELSE.
SO YOU'RE THE ONLY ONE CAPABLE OF TURNING HUMAN SOLDIERS INTO, WELL, HIM.
AND WITH AN UNCONQUERABLE ARMY OF AQUAMEN WHO CAN DEFEAT ALL SOLDIERS, AIR-BREATHERS AND ATLANTEANS ALIKE...
...THE WORLD WILL BE SCORPIO'S TO RULE.

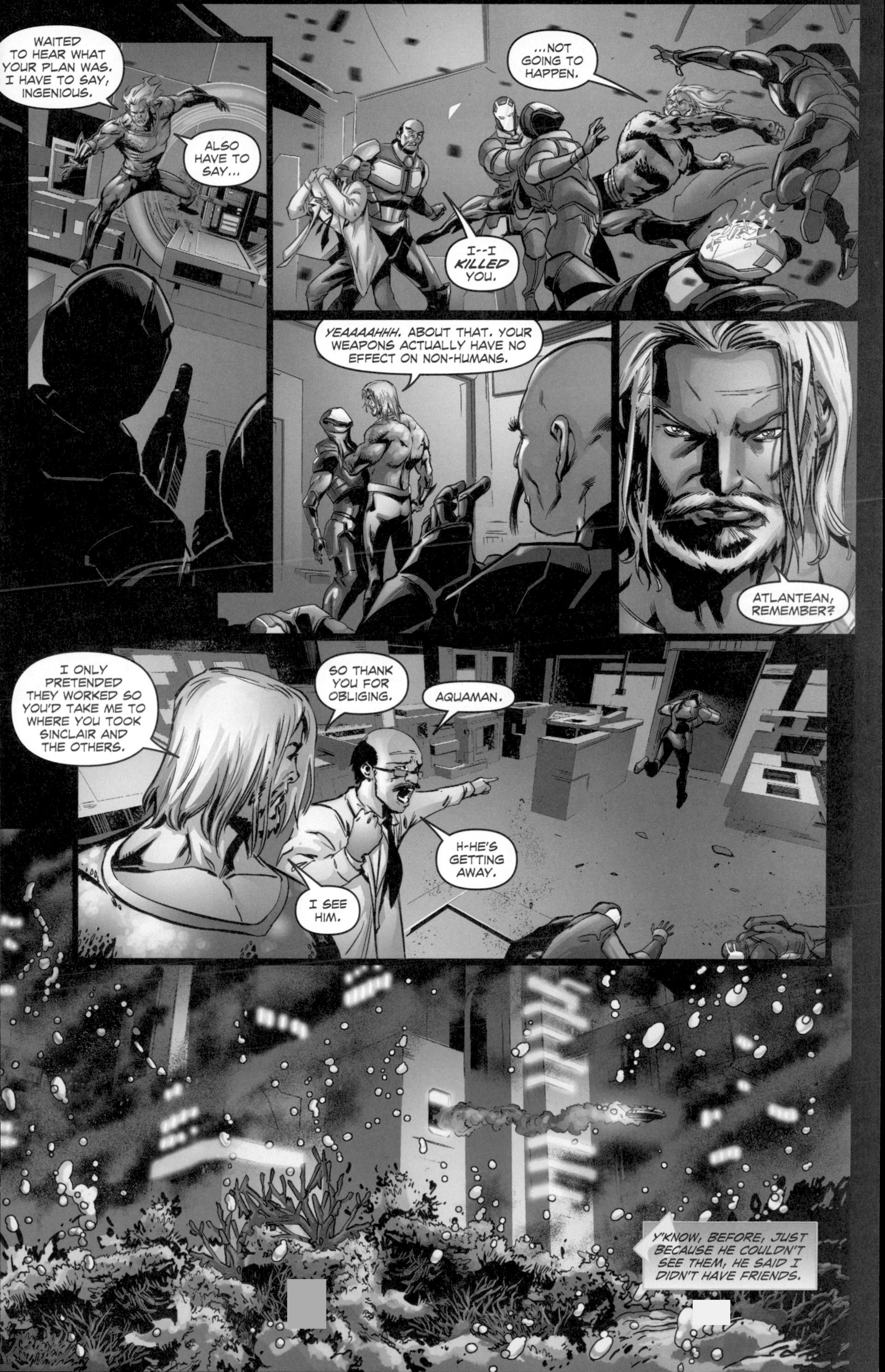
WAITED TO HEAR WHAT YOUR PLAN WAS. I HAVE TO SAY, INGENIOUS.
ALSO HAVE TO SAY...
...NOT GOING TO HAPPEN.
I--I KILLED YOU.
YEAAAAHHH. ABOUT THAT. YOUR WEAPONS ACTUALLY HAVE NO EFFECT ON NON-HUMANS.
ATLANTEAN, REMEMBER?
I ONLY PRETENDED THEY WORKED SO YOU'D TAKE ME TO WHERE YOU TOOK SINCLAIR AND THE OTHERS.
SO THANK YOU FOR OBLIGING.
AQUAMAN.
H-HE'S GETTING AWAY.
I SEE HIM.
Y'KNOW, BEFORE, JUST BECAUSE HE COULDN'T SEE THEM, HE SAID I DIDN'T HAVE FRIENDS.

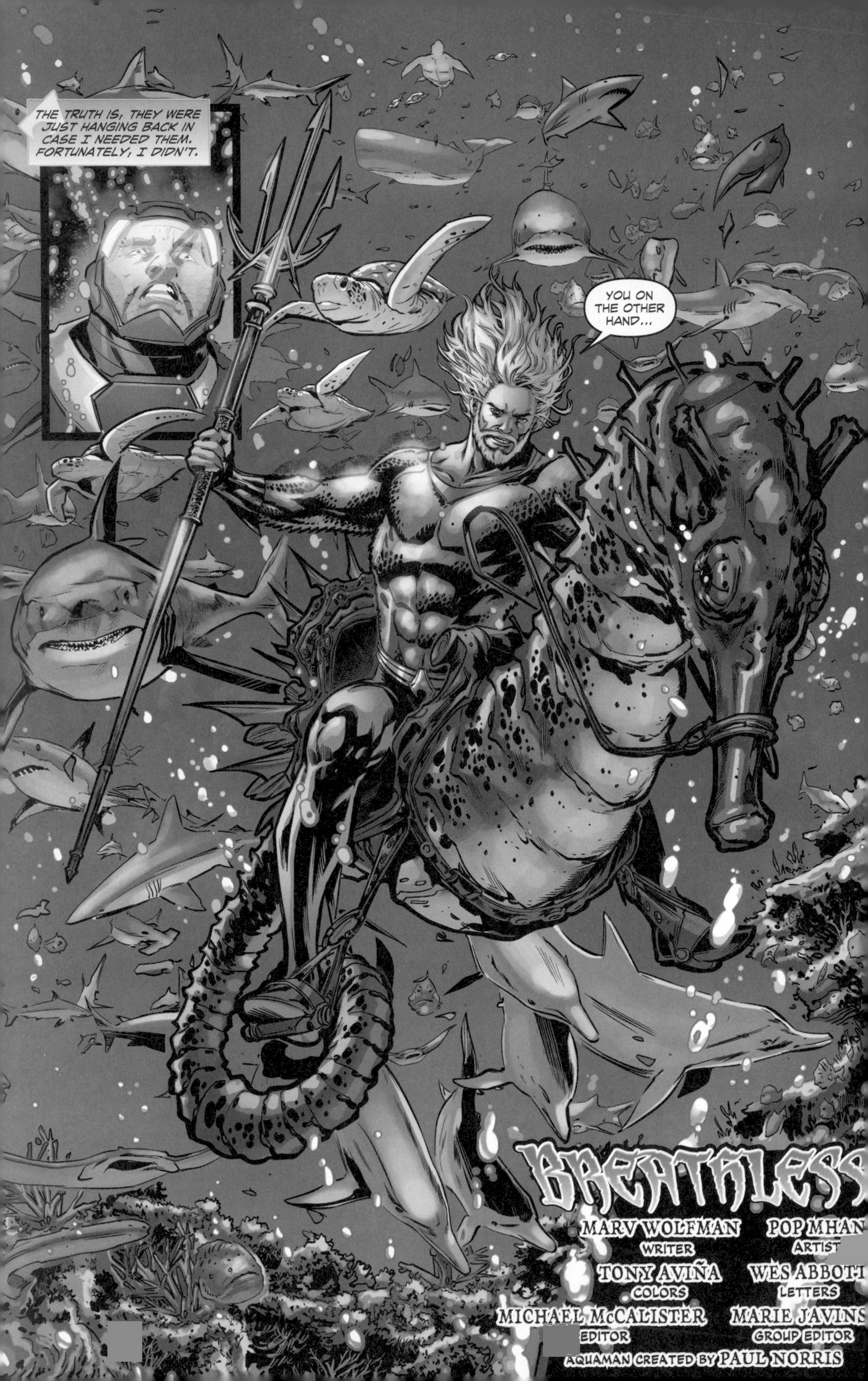
THE TRUTH IS, THEY WERE JUST HANGING BACK IN CASE I NEEDED THEM. FORTUNATELY, I DIDN'T.
YOU ON THE OTHER HAND...
BREATHLESS
MARV WOLFMAN WRITER
POP MHAN ARTIST
TONY AVIÑA COLORS
WES ABBOTT LETTERS
MICHAEL McCALISTER EDITOR
MARIE JAVINS GROUP EDITOR
AQUAMAN CREATED BY PAUL NORRIS

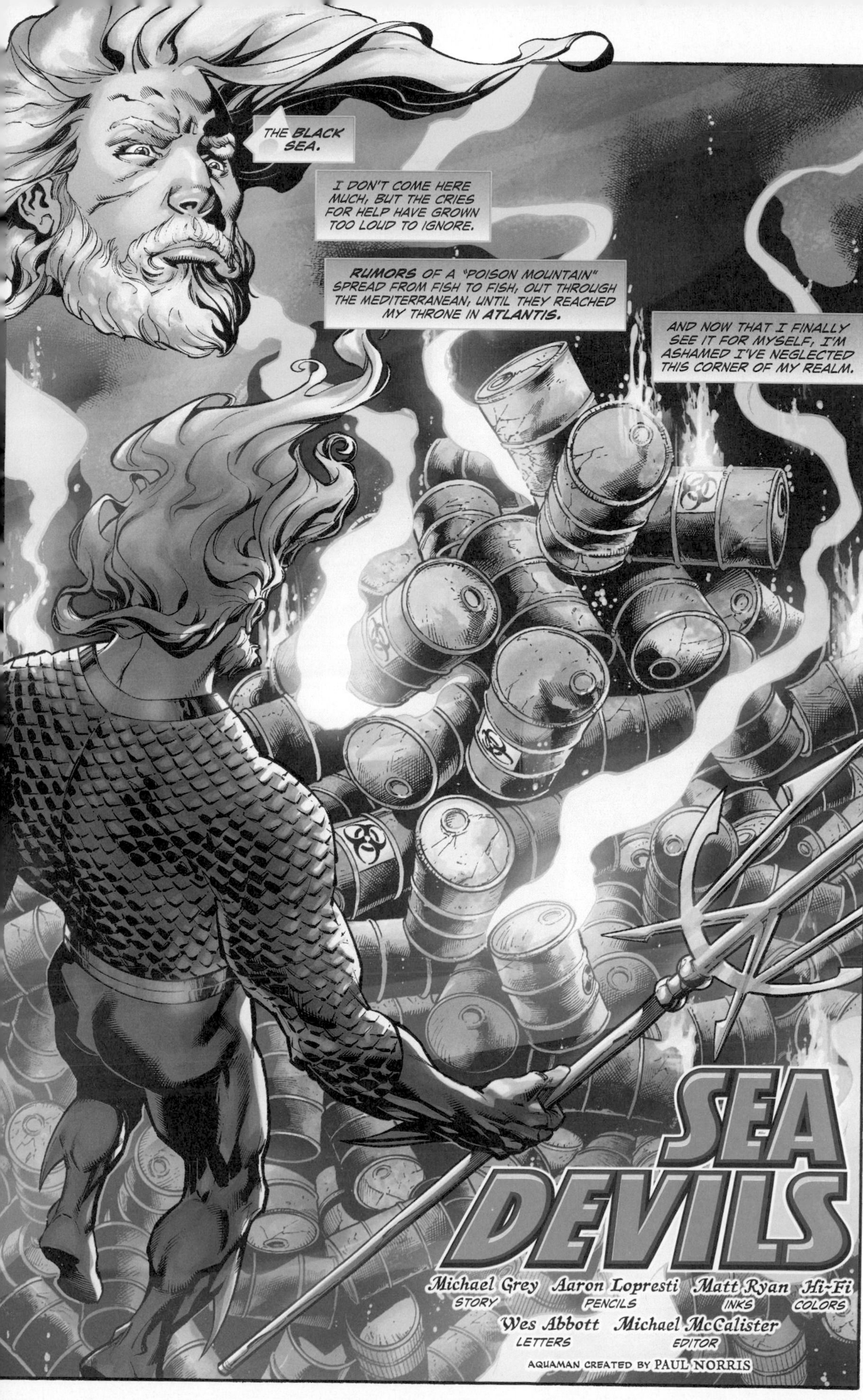
THE BLACK SEA.
I DON'T COME HERE MUCH, BUT THE CRIES FOR HELP HAVE GROWN TOO LOUD TO IGNORE.
RUMORS OF A "POISON MOUNTAIN" SPREAD FROM FISH TO FISH, OUT THROUGH THE MEDITERRANEAN, UNTIL THEY REACHED MY THRONE IN ATLANTIS.
AND NOW THAT I FINALLY SEE IT FOR MYSELF, I'M ASHAMED I'VE NEGLECTED THIS CORNER OF MY REALM.
SEA DEVILS
Michael Grey STORY
Aaron Lopresti PENCILS
Matt Ryan INKS
Hi-Fi COLORS
Wes Abbott LETTERS
Michael McCalister EDITOR
AQUAMAN CREATED BY PAUL NORRIS

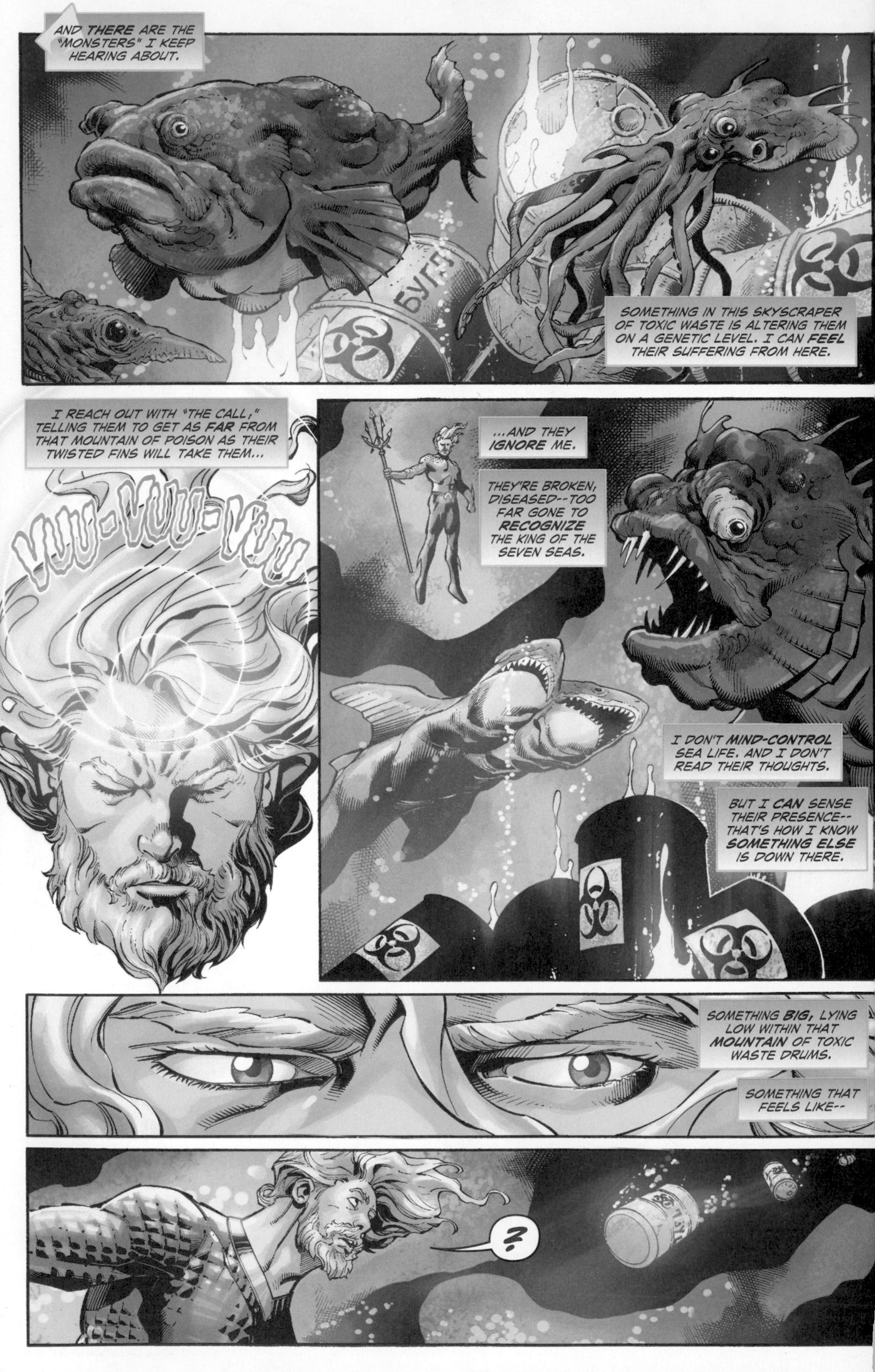

AND THERE ARE THE "MONSTERS" I KEEP HEARING ABOUT.
БУГЗ
SOMETHING IN THIS SKYSCRAPER OF TOXIC WASTE IS ALTERING THEM ON A GENETIC LEVEL. I CAN FEEL THEIR SUFFERING FROM HERE.
I REACH OUT WITH "THE CALL," TELLING THEM TO GET AS FAR FROM THAT MOUNTAIN OF POISON AS THEIR TWISTED FINS WILL TAKE THEM...
VUU-VUU-VUU
...AND THEY IGNORE ME.
THEY'RE BROKEN, DISEASED--TOO FAR GONE TO RECOGNIZE THE KING OF THE SEVEN SEAS.
I DON'T MIND-CONTROL SEA LIFE. AND I DON'T READ THEIR THOUGHTS.
BUT I CAN SENSE THEIR PRESENCE--THAT'S HOW I KNOW SOMETHING ELSE IS DOWN THERE.
SOMETHING BIG, LYING LOW WITHIN THAT MOUNTAIN OF TOXIC WASTE DRUMS.
SOMETHING THAT FEELS LIKE--
?

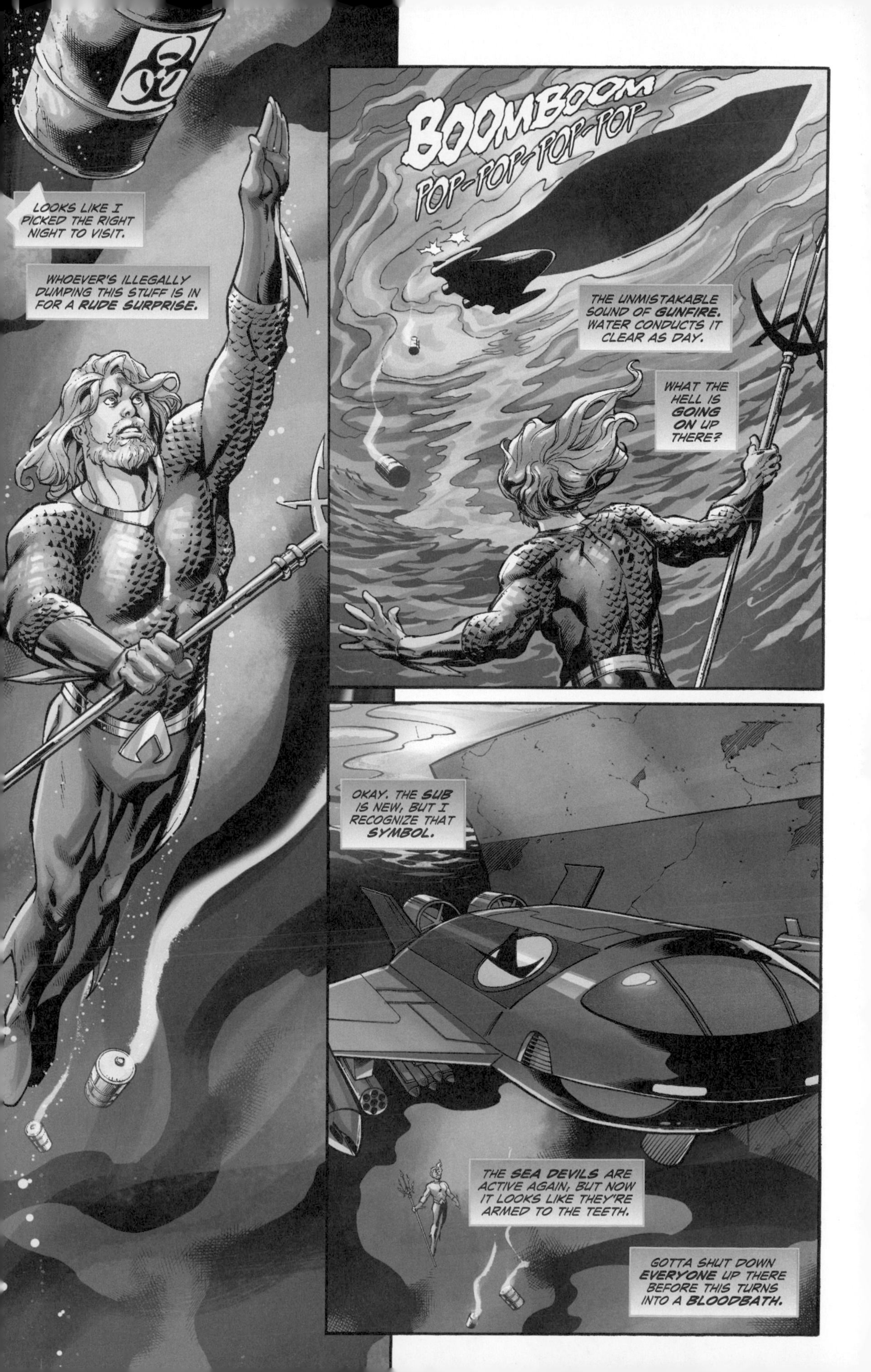
LOOKS LIKE I PICKED THE RIGHT NIGHT TO VISIT.
WHOEVER'S ILLEGALLY DUMPING THIS STUFF IS IN FOR A RUDE SURPRISE.
BOOMBOOM
POP-POP-POP-POP
THE UNMISTAKABLE SOUND OF GUNFIRE. WATER CONDUCTS IT CLEAR AS DAY.
WHAT THE HELL IS GOING ON UP THERE?
OKAY. THE SUB IS NEW, BUT I RECOGNIZE THAT SYMBOL.
THE SEA DEVILS ARE ACTIVE AGAIN, BUT NOW IT LOOKS LIKE THEY'RE ARMED TO THE TEETH.
GOTTA SHUT DOWN EVERYONE UP THERE BEFORE THIS TURNS INTO A BLOODBATH.

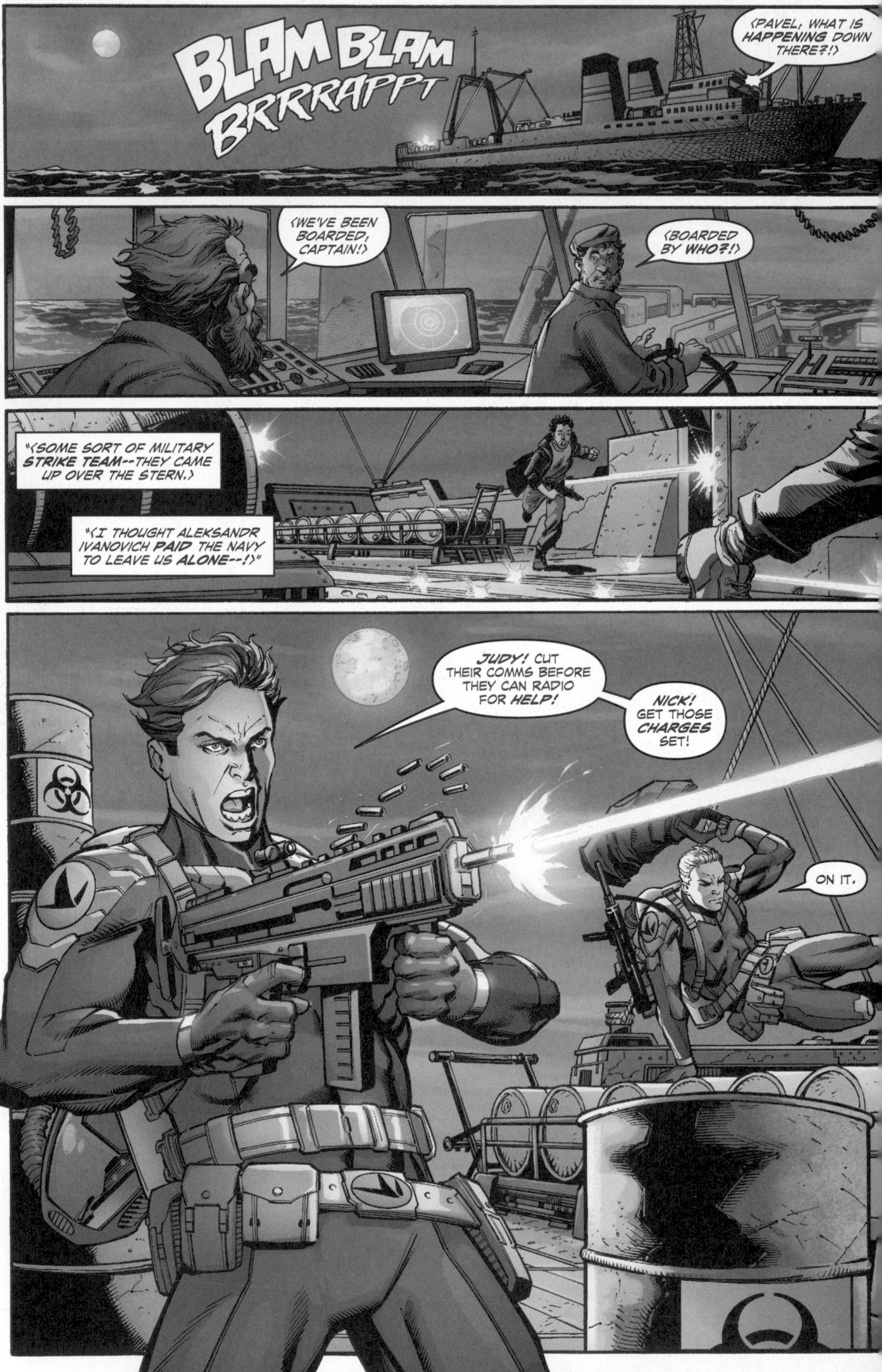
BLAM BLAM
BRRRAPPT
⟨PAVEL, WHAT IS HAPPENING DOWN THERE?!⟩
⟨WE'VE BEEN BOARDED, CAPTAIN!⟩
⟨BOARDED BY WHO?!⟩
"⟨SOME SORT OF MILITARY STRIKE TEAM--THEY CAME UP OVER THE STERN.⟩
"⟨I THOUGHT ALEKSANDR IVANOVICH PAID THE NAVY TO LEAVE US ALONE--!⟩"
JUDY! CUT THEIR COMMS BEFORE THEY CAN RADIO FOR HELP!
NICK! GET THOSE CHARGES SET!
ON IT.

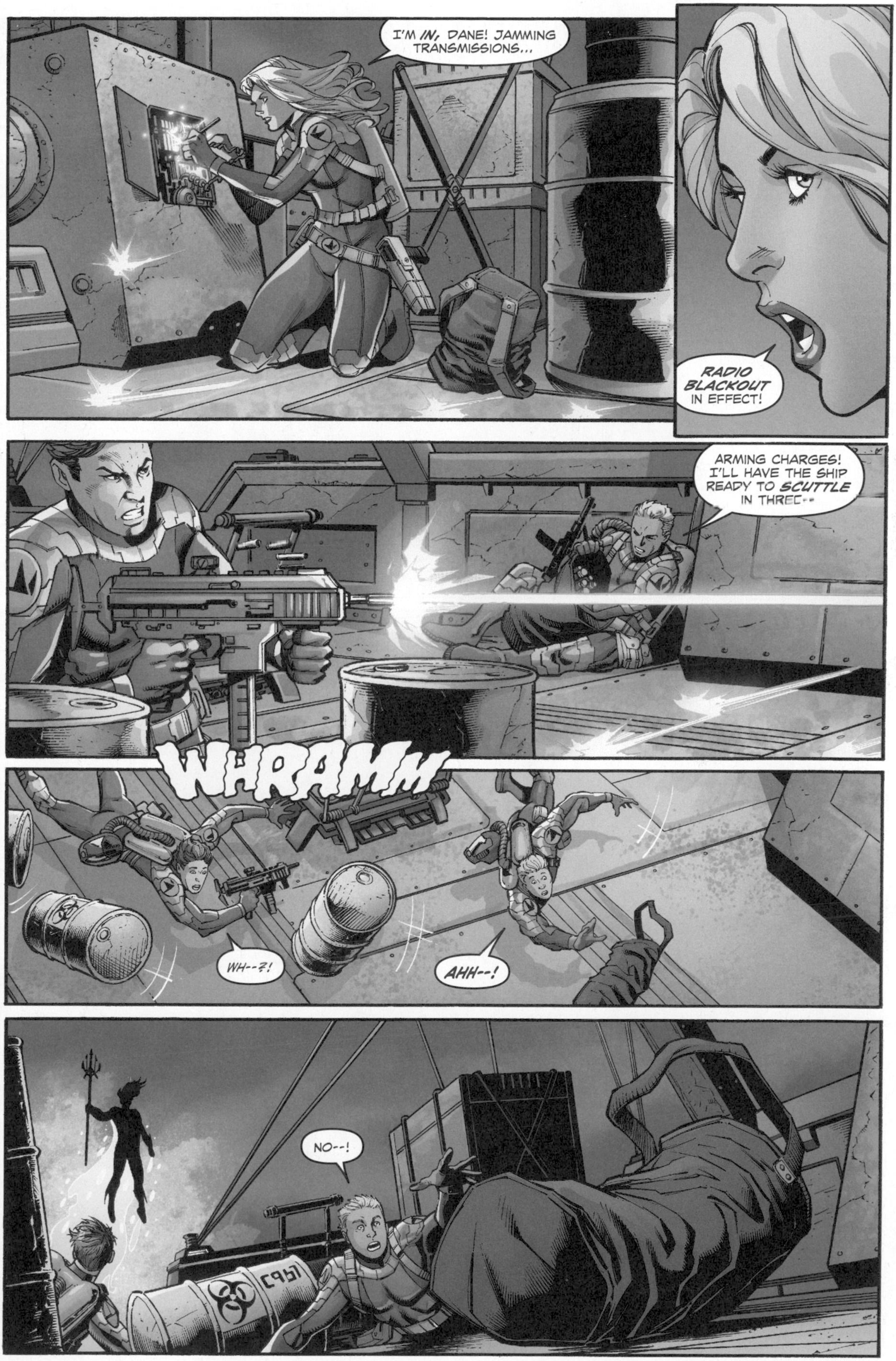
I'M IN, DANE! JAMMING TRANSMISSIONS...
RADIO BLACKOUT IN EFFECT!
ARMING CHARGES! I'LL HAVE THE SHIP READY TO SCUTTLE IN THREE--
WHRAMM
WH--?!
AHH--!
NO--!

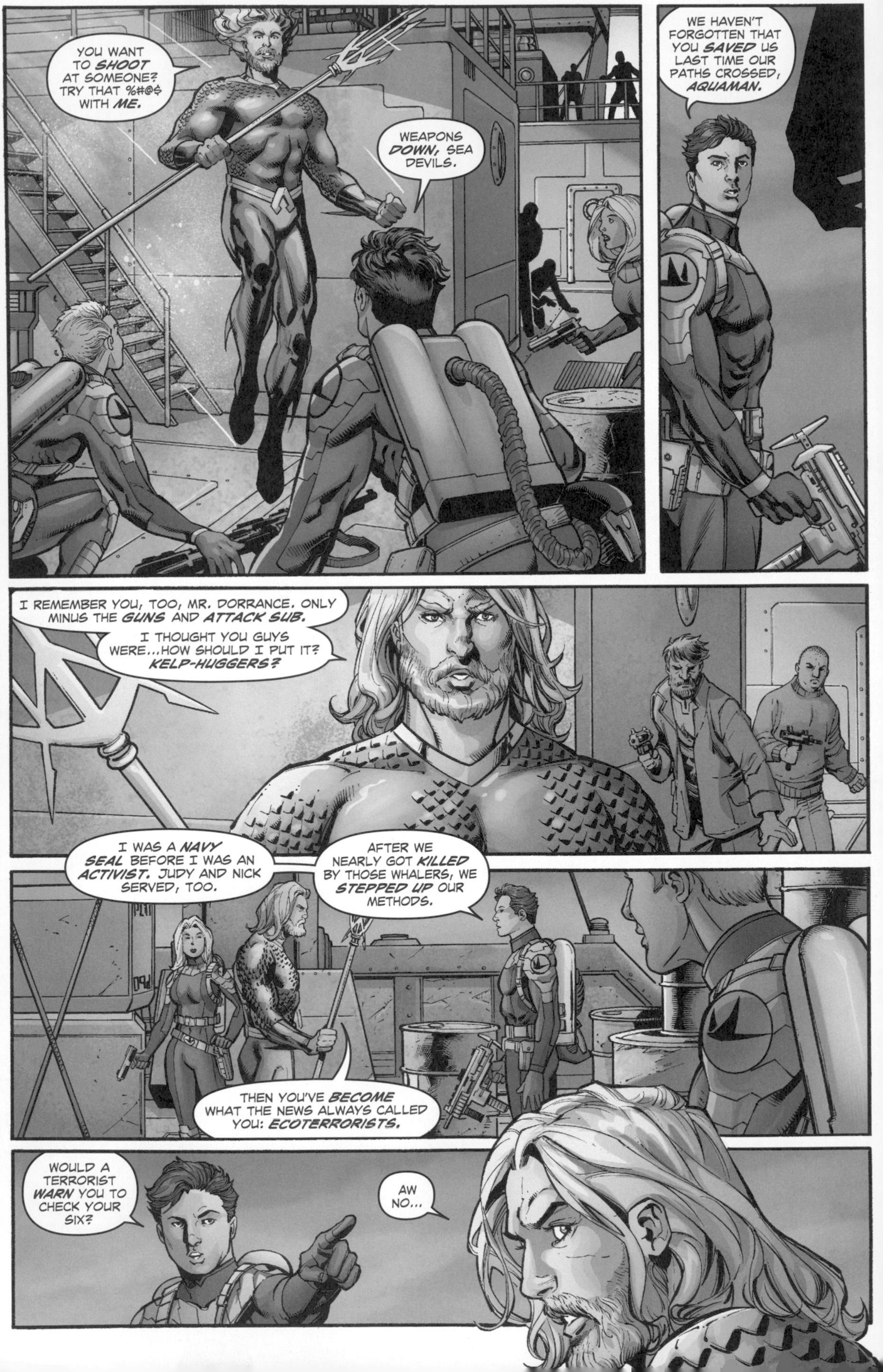
YOU WANT TO SHOOT AT SOMEONE? TRY THAT %#@$ WITH ME.
WEAPONS DOWN, SEA DEVILS.
WE HAVEN'T FORGOTTEN THAT YOU SAVED US LAST TIME OUR PATHS CROSSED, AQUAMAN.
I REMEMBER YOU, TOO, MR. DORRANCE. ONLY MINUS THE GUNS AND ATTACK SUB.
I THOUGHT YOU GUYS WERE...HOW SHOULD I PUT IT? KELP-HUGGERS?
I WAS A NAVY SEAL BEFORE I WAS AN ACTIVIST. JUDY AND NICK SERVED, TOO.
AFTER WE NEARLY GOT KILLED BY THOSE WHALERS, WE STEPPED UP OUR METHODS.
THEN YOU'VE BECOME WHAT THE NEWS ALWAYS CALLED YOU: ECOTERRORISTS.
WOULD A TERRORIST WARN YOU TO CHECK YOUR SIX?
AW NO...

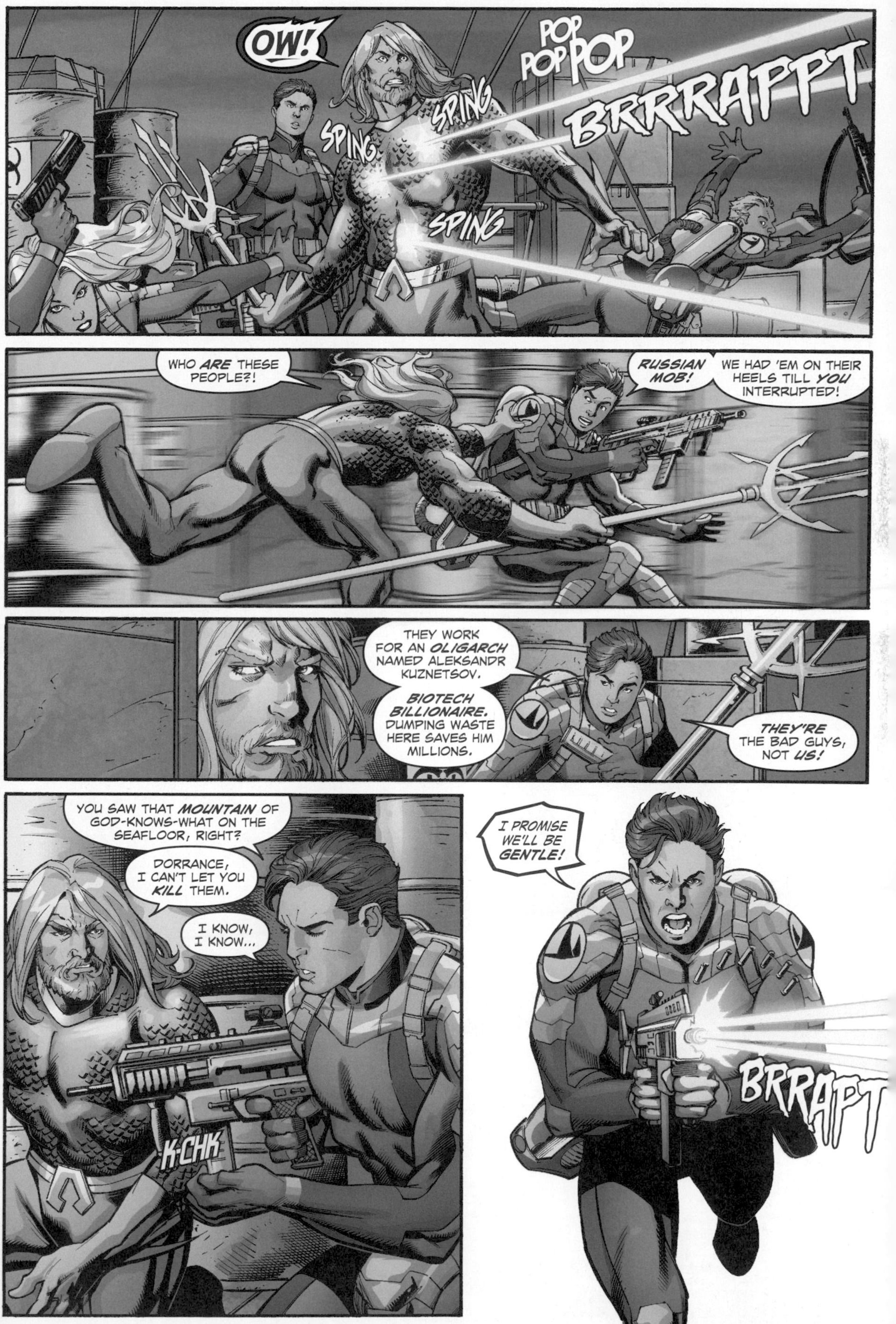
OW!
POP POP POP
BRRRAPPT
SPING
SPING
SPING
WHO ARE THESE PEOPLE?!
RUSSIAN MOB!
WE HAD 'EM ON THEIR HEELS TILL YOU INTERRUPTED!
THEY WORK FOR AN OLIGARCH NAMED ALEKSANDR KUZNETSOV.
BIOTECH BILLIONAIRE. DUMPING WASTE HERE SAVES HIM MILLIONS.
THEY'RE THE BAD GUYS, NOT US!
YOU SAW THAT MOUNTAIN OF GOD-KNOWS-WHAT ON THE SEAFLOOR, RIGHT?
DORRANCE, I CAN'T LET YOU KILL THEM.
I KNOW, I KNOW...
K-CHK
I PROMISE WE'LL BE GENTLE!
BRRAPT

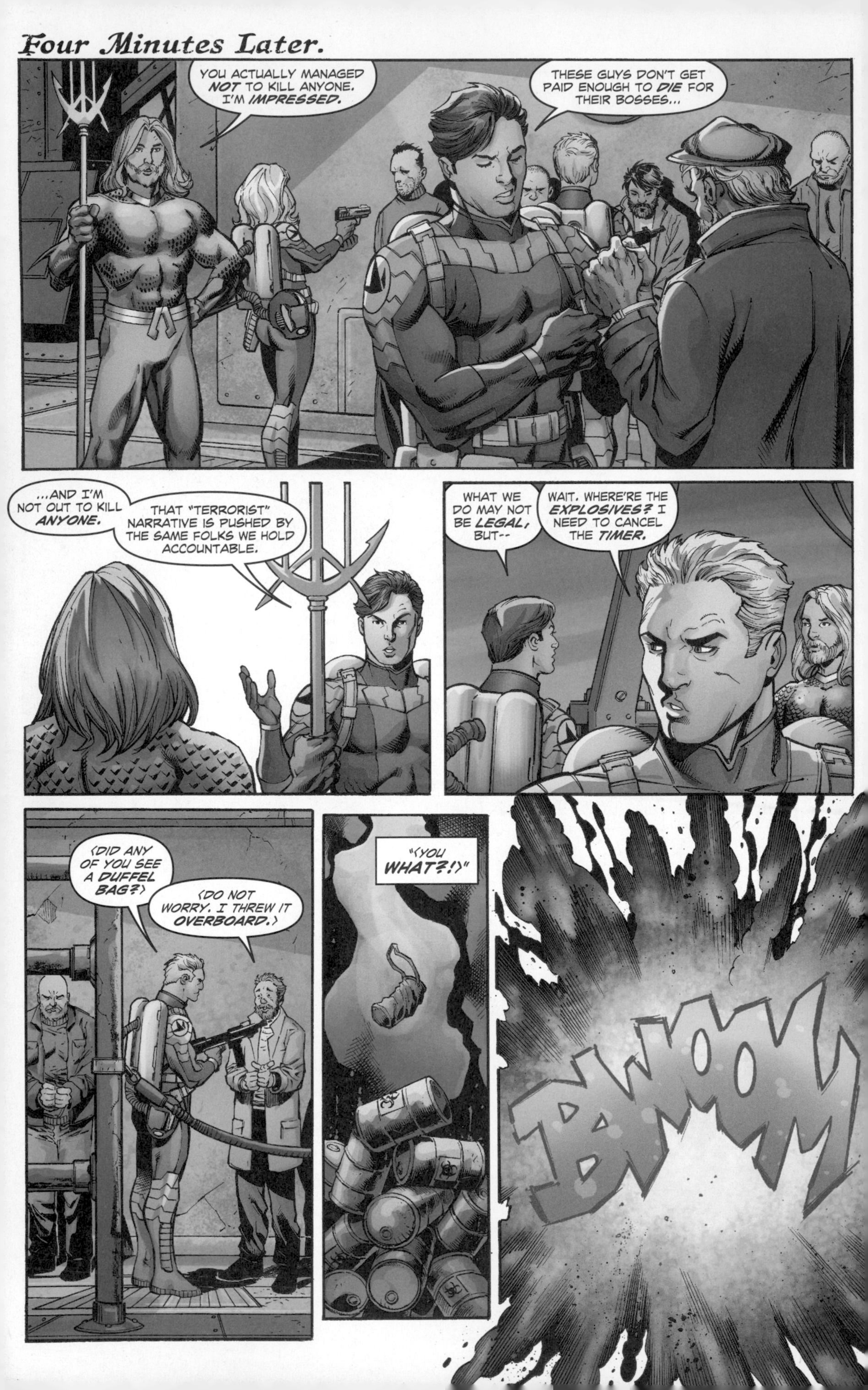
Four Minutes Later.
YOU ACTUALLY MANAGED NOT TO KILL ANYONE. I'M IMPRESSED.
THESE GUYS DON'T GET PAID ENOUGH TO DIE FOR THEIR BOSSES...
...AND I'M NOT OUT TO KILL ANYONE.
THAT "TERRORIST" NARRATIVE IS PUSHED BY THE SAME FOLKS WE HOLD ACCOUNTABLE.
WHAT WE DO MAY NOT BE LEGAL, BUT--
WAIT. WHERE'RE THE EXPLOSIVES? I NEED TO CANCEL THE TIMER.
<DID ANY OF YOU SEE A DUFFEL BAG?>
<DO NOT WORRY. I THREW IT OVERBOARD.>
"<YOU WHAT?!>"
BWOOM

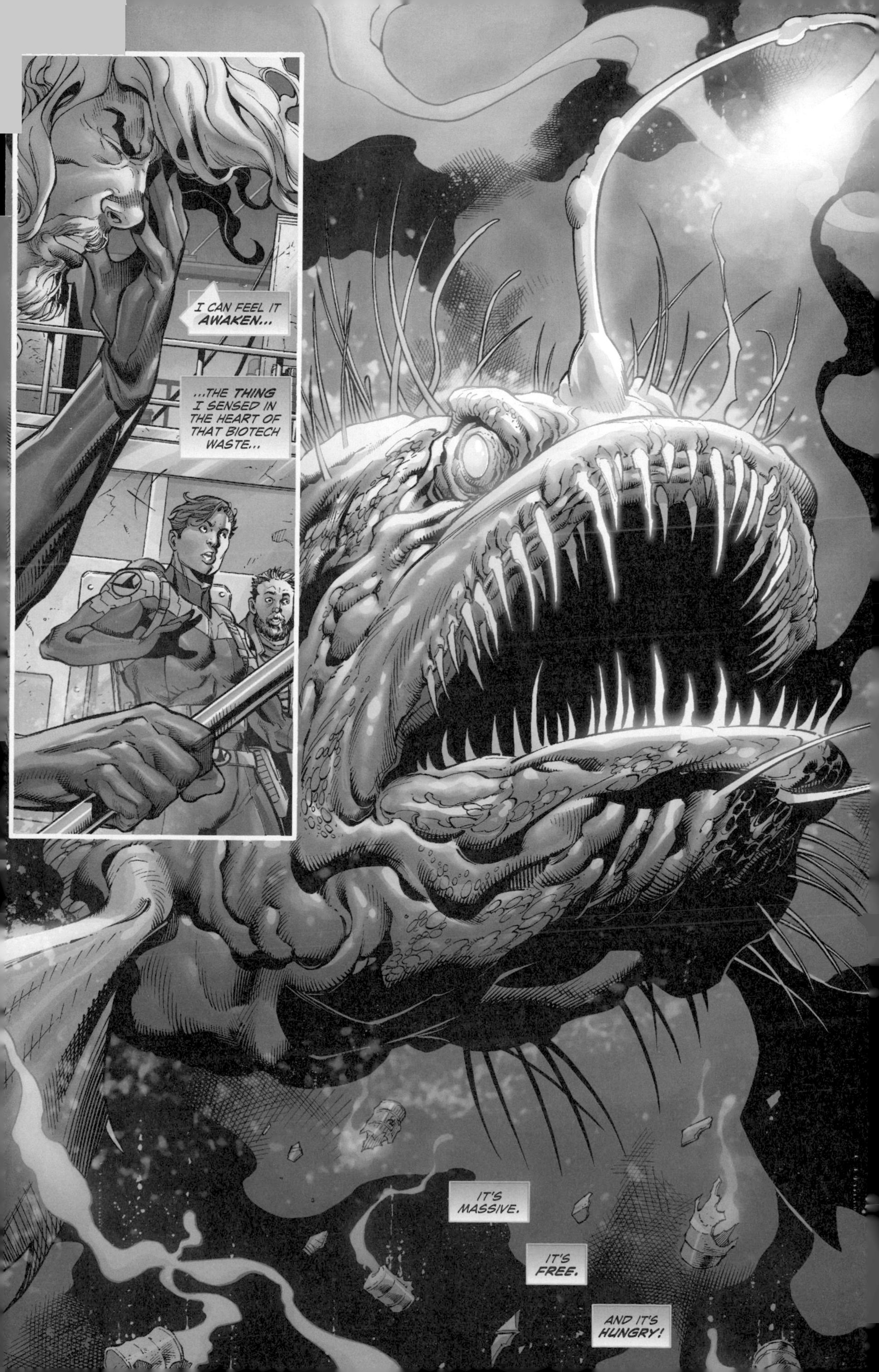
I CAN FEEL IT AWAKEN...
...THE THING I SENSED IN THE HEART OF THAT BIOTECH WASTE...
IT'S MASSIVE.
IT'S FREE.
AND IT'S HUNGRY!

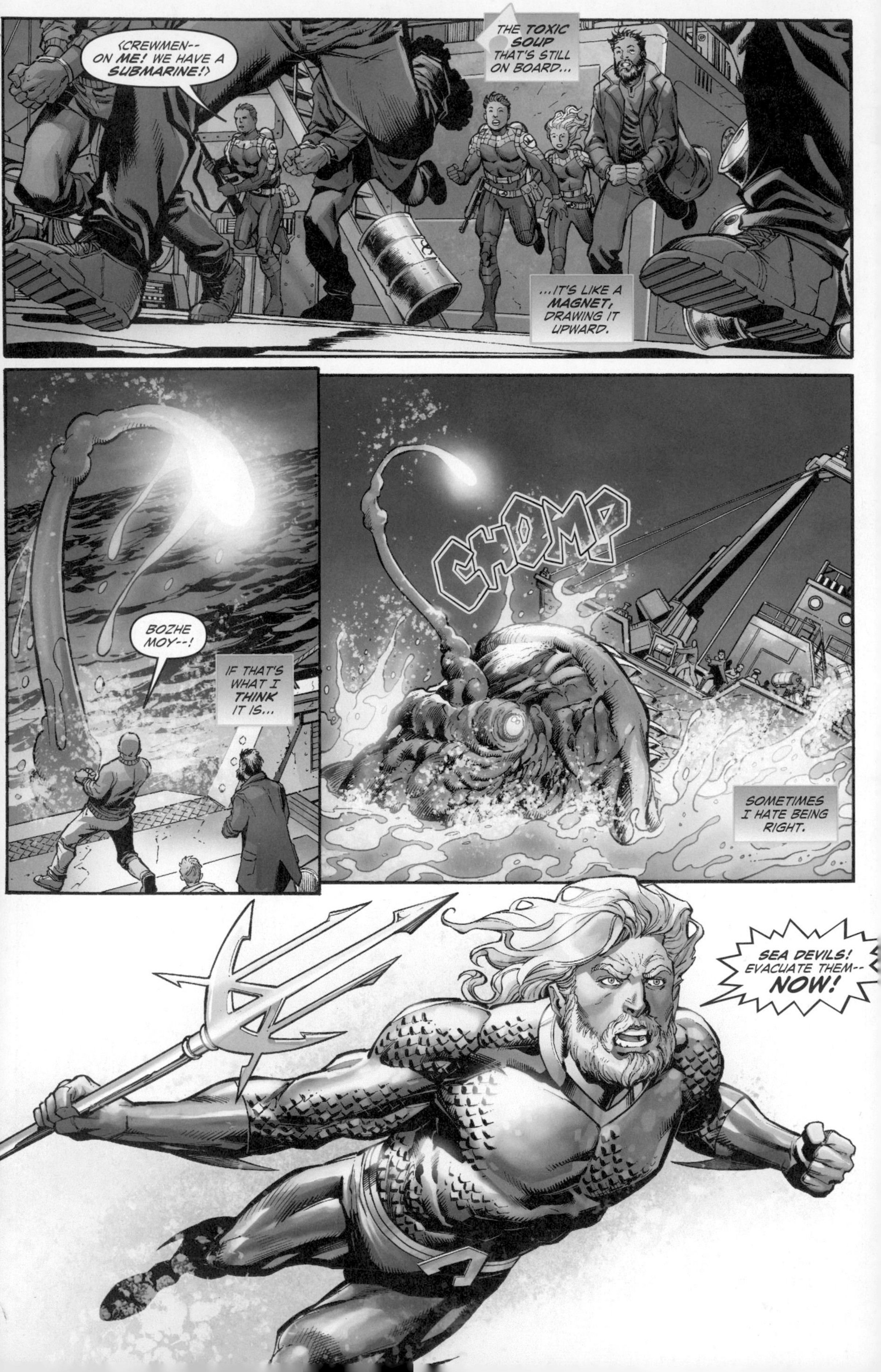
‹CREWMEN-- ON ME! WE HAVE A SUBMARINE!›
THE TOXIC SOUP THAT'S STILL ON BOARD...
...IT'S LIKE A MAGNET, DRAWING IT UPWARD.
BOZHE MOY--!
IF THAT'S WHAT I THINK IT IS...
CHOMP
SOMETIMES I HATE BEING RIGHT.
SEA DEVILS! EVACUATE THEM-- NOW!

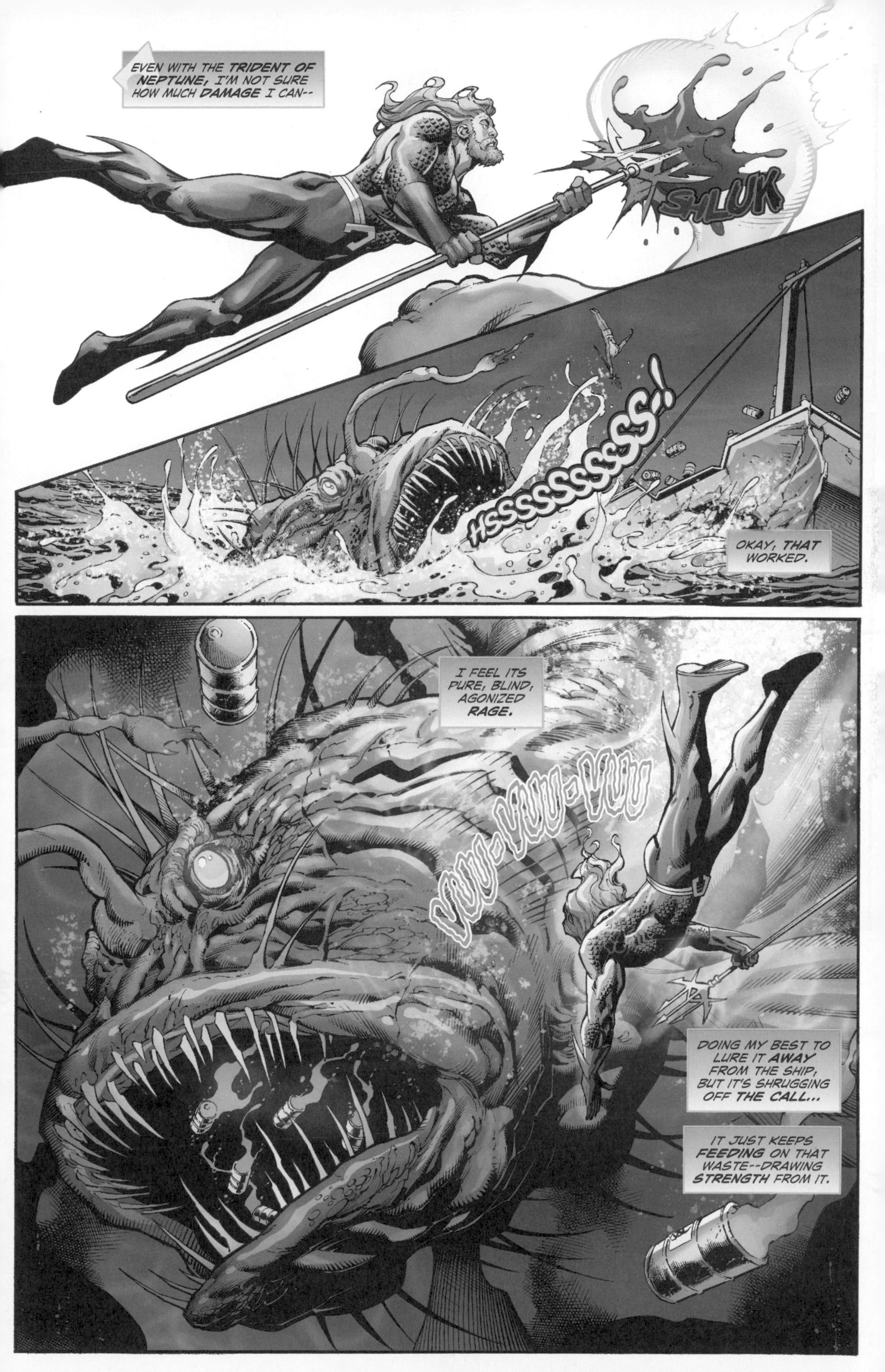
EVEN WITH THE TRIDENT OF NEPTUNE, I'M NOT SURE HOW MUCH DAMAGE I CAN--
SHLUK
HSSSSSSSSSS-!
OKAY, THAT WORKED.
I FEEL ITS PURE, BLIND, AGONIZED RAGE.
VUU-VUU-VUU
DOING MY BEST TO LURE IT AWAY FROM THE SHIP, BUT IT'S SHRUGGING OFF THE CALL...
IT JUST KEEPS FEEDING ON THAT WASTE--DRAWING STRENGTH FROM IT.

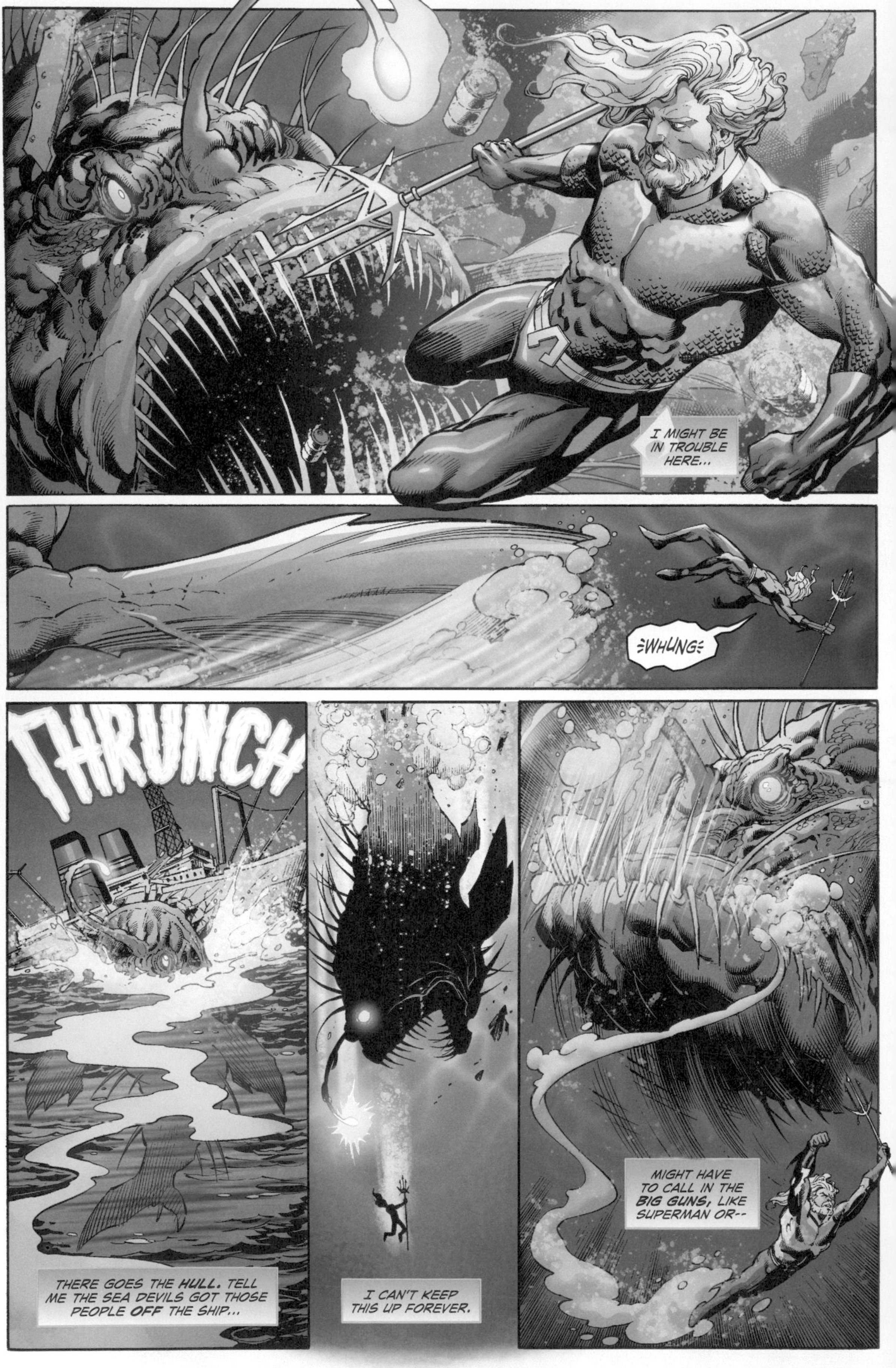
I MIGHT BE IN TROUBLE HERE...
WHUNG
THRUNCH
THERE GOES THE HULL. TELL ME THE SEA DEVILS GOT THOSE PEOPLE OFF THE SHIP...
I CAN'T KEEP THIS UP FOREVER.
MIGHT HAVE TO CALL IN THE BIG GUNS, LIKE SUPERMAN OR--

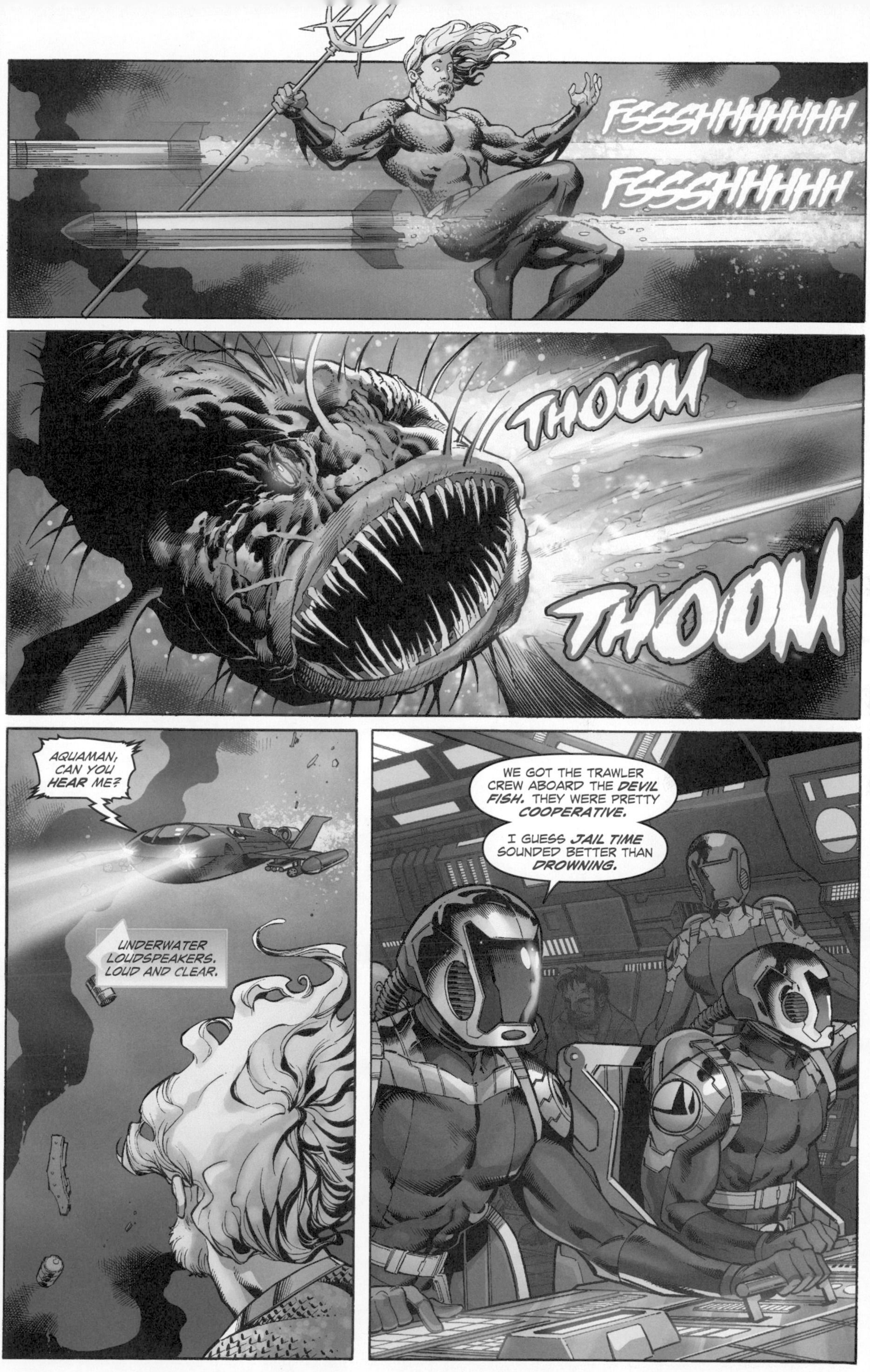
FSSSHHHHHHH
FSSSHHHHHH
THOOM
THOOM
AQUAMAN, CAN YOU HEAR ME?
UNDERWATER LOUDSPEAKERS. LOUD AND CLEAR.
WE GOT THE TRAWLER CREW ABOARD THE DEVIL FISH. THEY WERE PRETTY COOPERATIVE.
I GUESS JAIL TIME SOUNDED BETTER THAN DROWNING.

HEY, ISN'T THAT THING A LITTLE *HIGH UP* FOR A BOTTOM-FEEDER?

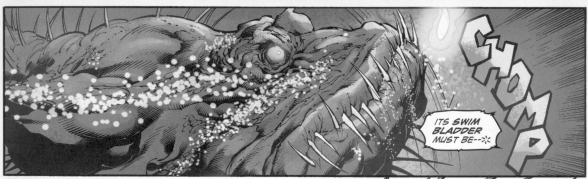

ITS SWIM BLADDER MUST BE--

CHOMP

DORRANCE--?!

DANE DORRANCE! CAN YOU HEAR ME?!

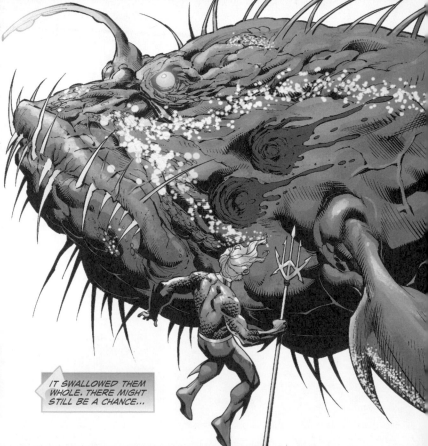

IT SWALLOWED THEM WHOLE. THERE MIGHT STILL BE A CHANCE...

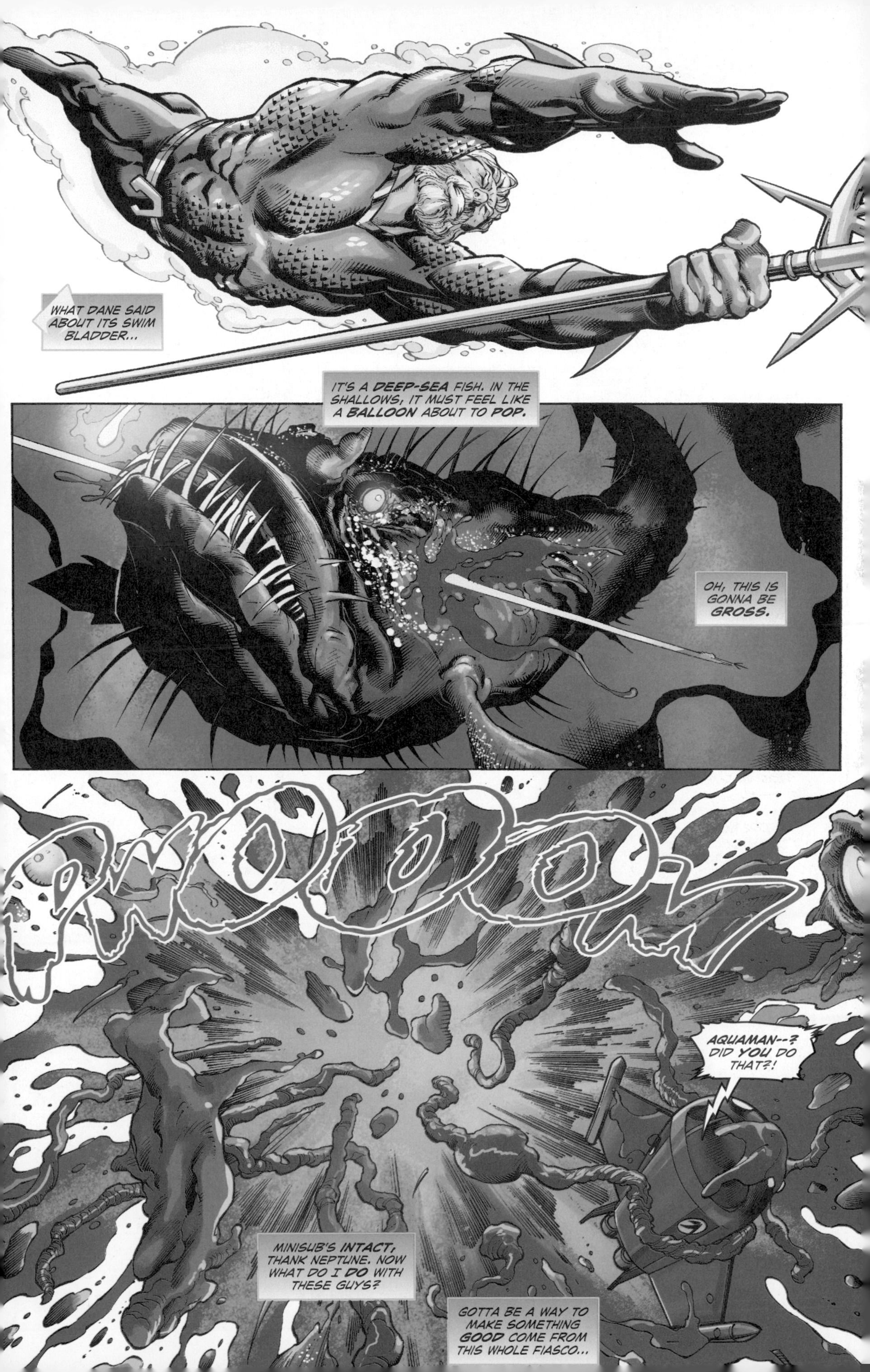
WHAT DANE SAID ABOUT ITS SWIM BLADDER...
IT'S A DEEP-SEA FISH. IN THE SHALLOWS, IT MUST FEEL LIKE A BALLOON ABOUT TO POP.
OH, THIS IS GONNA BE GROSS.
PWOOOOW
AQUAMAN--? DID YOU DO THAT?!
MINISUB'S INTACT, THANK NEPTUNE. NOW WHAT DO I DO WITH THESE GUYS?
GOTTA BE A WAY TO MAKE SOMETHING GOOD COME FROM THIS WHOLE FIASCO...

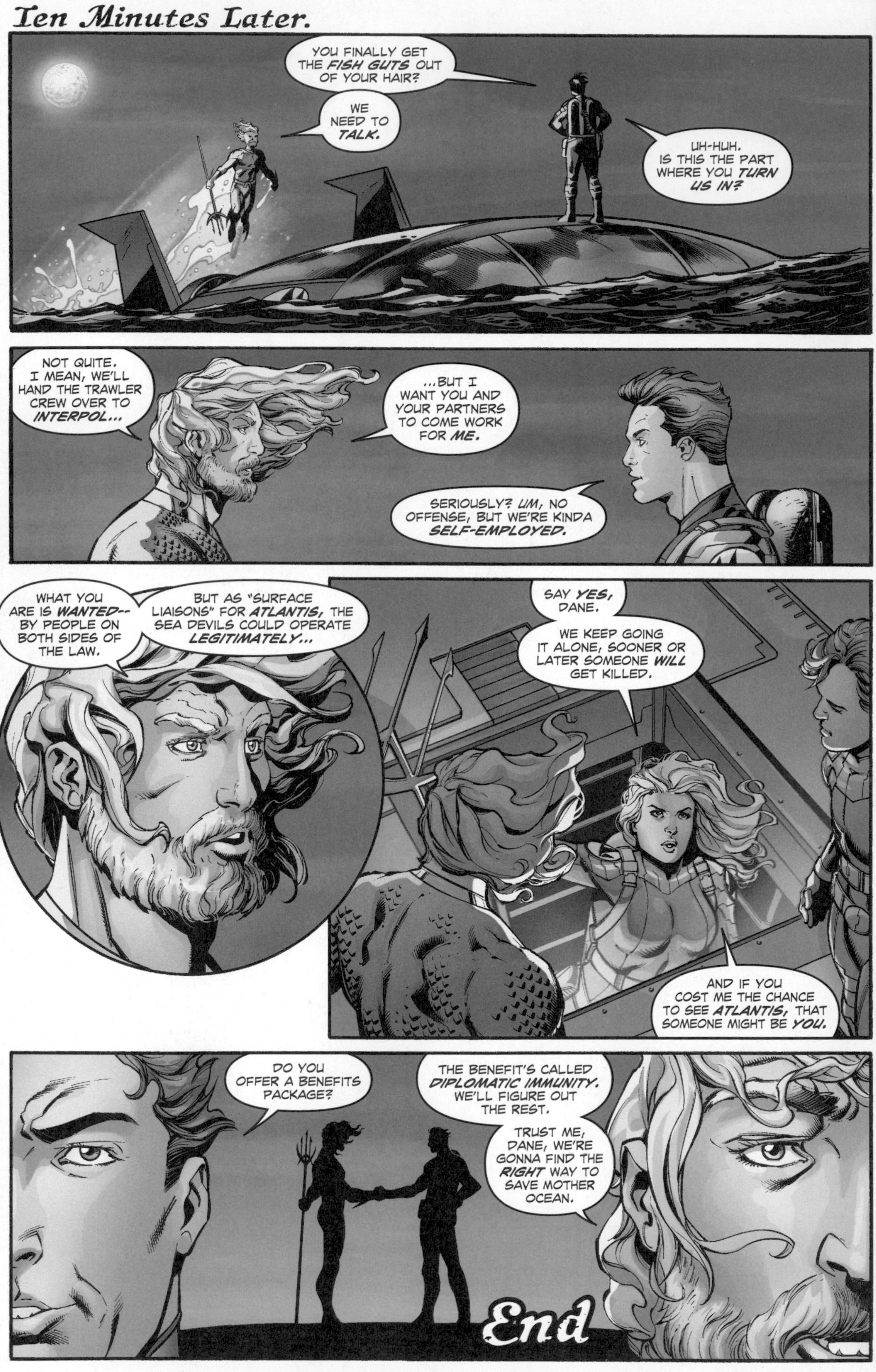
Ten Minutes Later.
YOU FINALLY GET THE FISH GUTS OUT OF YOUR HAIR?
WE NEED TO TALK.
UH-HUH. IS THIS THE PART WHERE YOU TURN US IN?
NOT QUITE. I MEAN, WE'LL HAND THE TRAWLER CREW OVER TO INTERPOL...
...BUT I WANT YOU AND YOUR PARTNERS TO COME WORK FOR ME.
SERIOUSLY? UM, NO OFFENSE, BUT WE'RE KINDA SELF-EMPLOYED.
WHAT YOU ARE IS WANTED-- BY PEOPLE ON BOTH SIDES OF THE LAW.
BUT AS "SURFACE LIAISONS" FOR ATLANTIS, THE SEA DEVILS COULD OPERATE LEGITIMATELY...
SAY YES, DANE.
WE KEEP GOING IT ALONE, SOONER OR LATER SOMEONE WILL GET KILLED.
AND IF YOU COST ME THE CHANCE TO SEE ATLANTIS, THAT SOMEONE MIGHT BE YOU.
DO YOU OFFER A BENEFITS PACKAGE?
THE BENEFIT'S CALLED DIPLOMATIC IMMUNITY. WE'LL FIGURE OUT THE REST.
TRUST ME, DANE, WE'RE GONNA FIND THE RIGHT WAY TO SAVE MOTHER OCEAN.
End

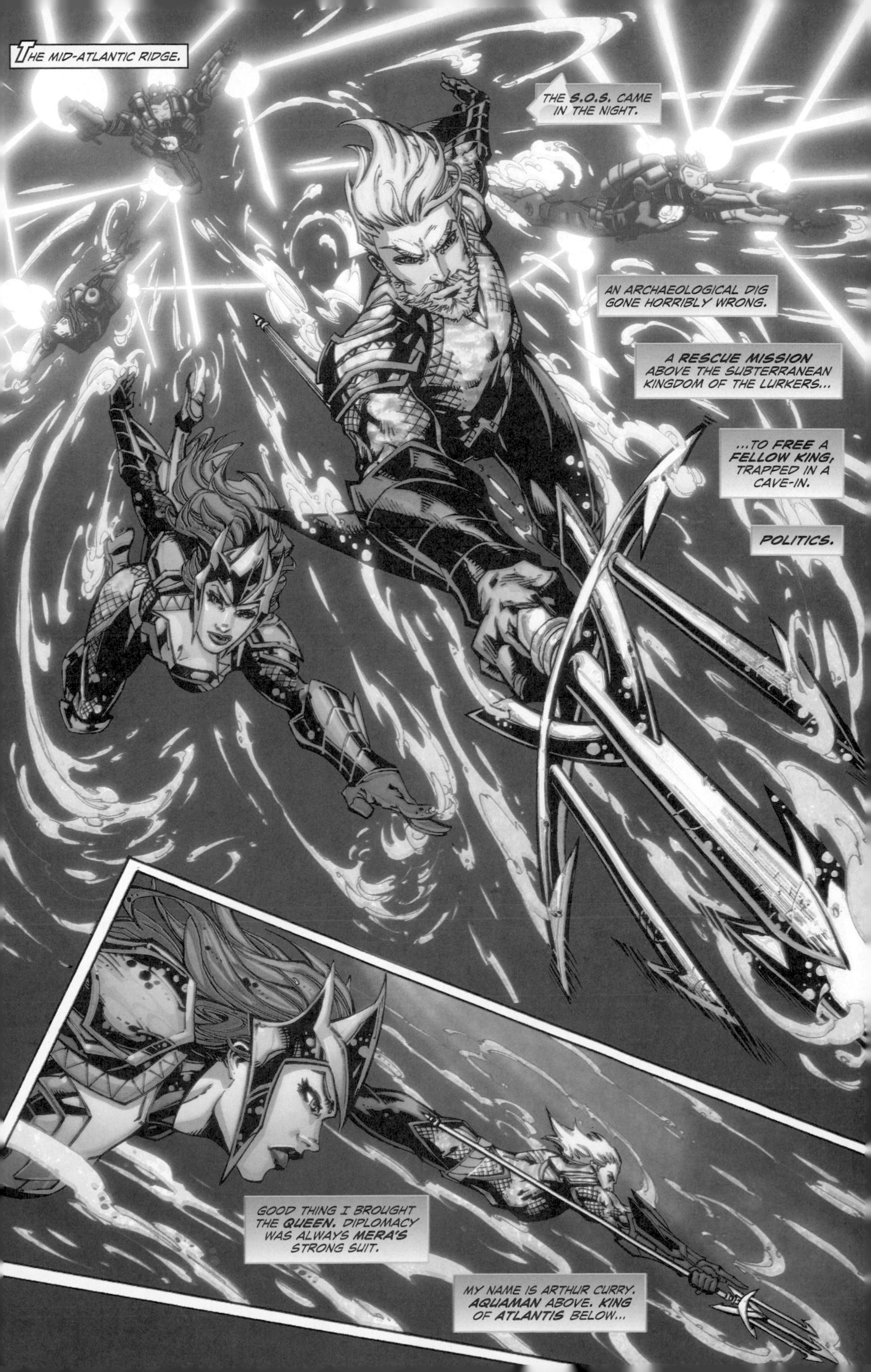
THE MID-ATLANTIC RIDGE.
THE S.O.S. CAME IN THE NIGHT.
AN ARCHAEOLOGICAL DIG GONE HORRIBLY WRONG.
A RESCUE MISSION ABOVE THE SUBTERRANEAN KINGDOM OF THE LURKERS...
...TO FREE A FELLOW KING, TRAPPED IN A CAVE-IN.
POLITICS.
GOOD THING I BROUGHT THE QUEEN. DIPLOMACY WAS ALWAYS MERA'S STRONG SUIT.
MY NAME IS ARTHUR CURRY. AQUAMAN ABOVE. KING OF ATLANTIS BELOW...

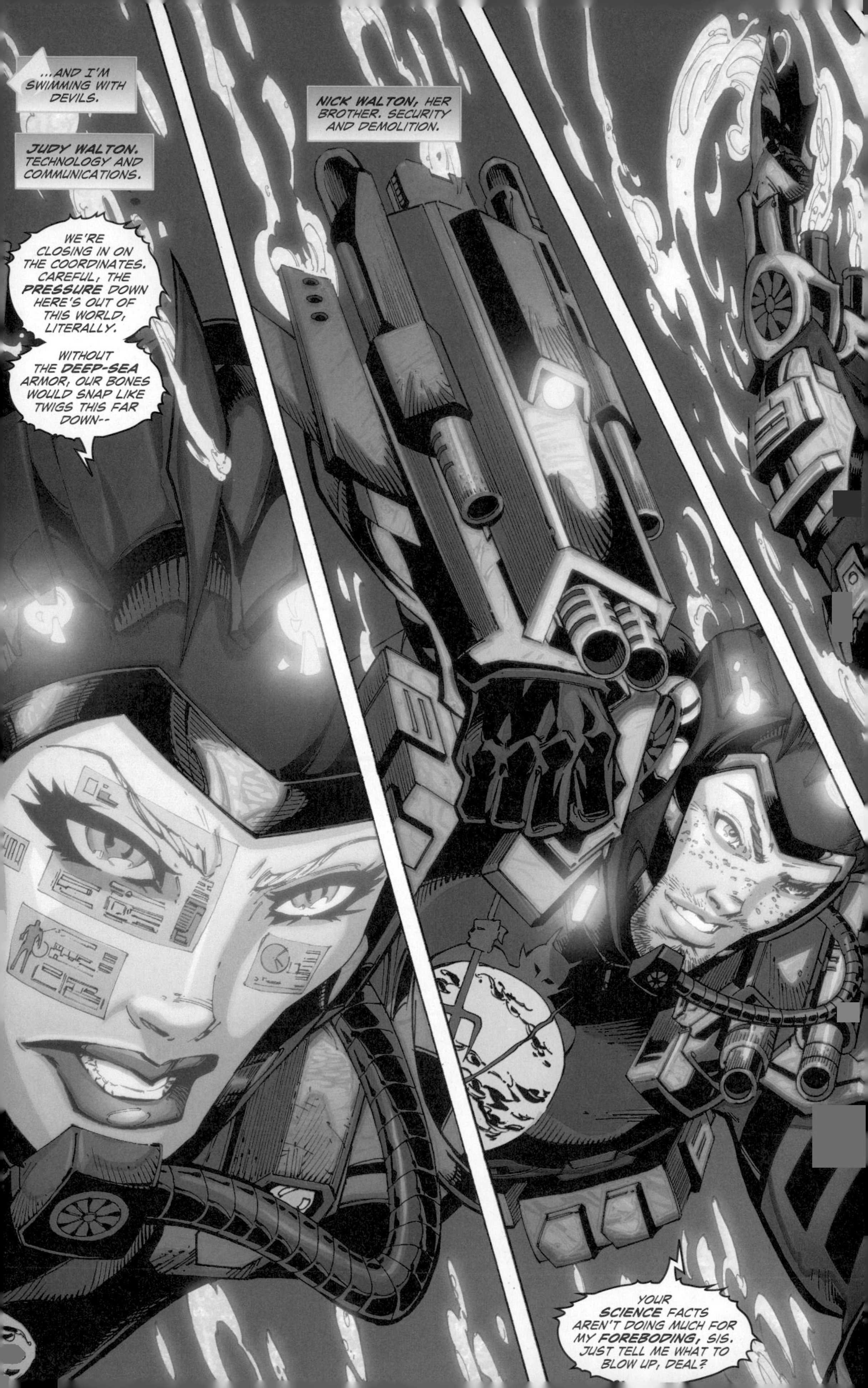
...AND I'M SWIMMING WITH DEVILS.
JUDY WALTON. TECHNOLOGY AND COMMUNICATIONS.
WE'RE CLOSING IN ON THE COORDINATES. CAREFUL, THE PRESSURE DOWN HERE'S OUT OF THIS WORLD, LITERALLY.
WITHOUT THE DEEP-SEA ARMOR, OUR BONES WOULD SNAP LIKE TWIGS THIS FAR DOWN--
NICK WALTON, HER BROTHER. SECURITY AND DEMOLITION.
YOUR SCIENCE FACTS AREN'T DOING MUCH FOR MY FOREBODING, SIS. JUST TELL ME WHAT TO BLOW UP, DEAL?

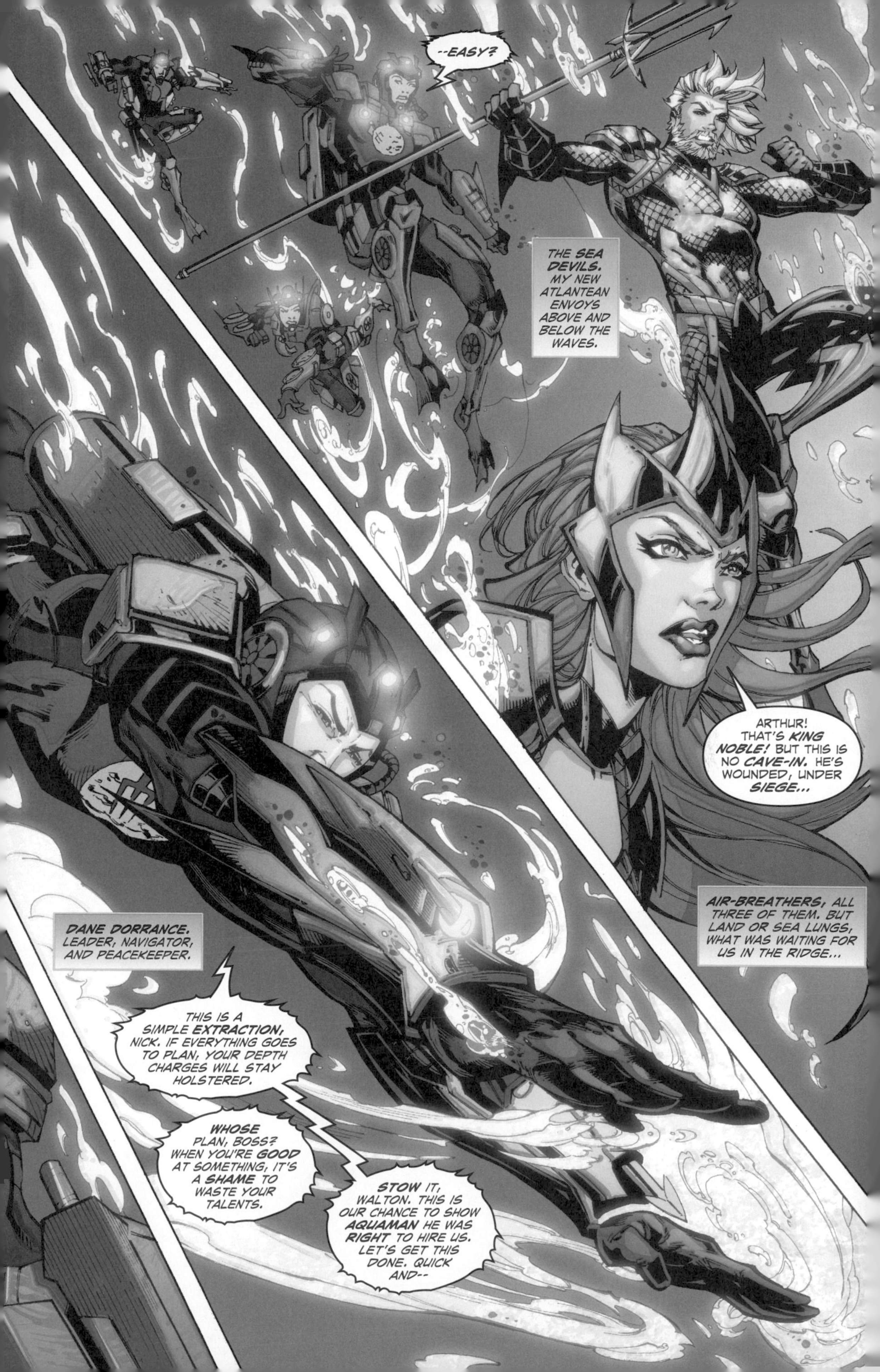
--EASY?
THE SEA DEVILS. MY NEW ATLANTEAN ENVOYS ABOVE AND BELOW THE WAVES.
ARTHUR! THAT'S KING NOBLE! BUT THIS IS NO CAVE-IN. HE'S WOUNDED, UNDER SIEGE...
AIR-BREATHERS, ALL THREE OF THEM. BUT LAND OR SEA LUNGS, WHAT WAS WAITING FOR US IN THE RIDGE...
DANE DORRANCE. LEADER, NAVIGATOR, AND PEACEKEEPER.
THIS IS A SIMPLE EXTRACTION, NICK. IF EVERYTHING GOES TO PLAN, YOUR DEPTH CHARGES WILL STAY HOLSTERED.
WHOSE PLAN, BOSS? WHEN YOU'RE GOOD AT SOMETHING, IT'S A SHAME TO WASTE YOUR TALENTS.
STOW IT, WALTON. THIS IS OUR CHANCE TO SHOW AQUAMAN HE WAS RIGHT TO HIRE US. LET'S GET THIS DONE. QUICK AND--

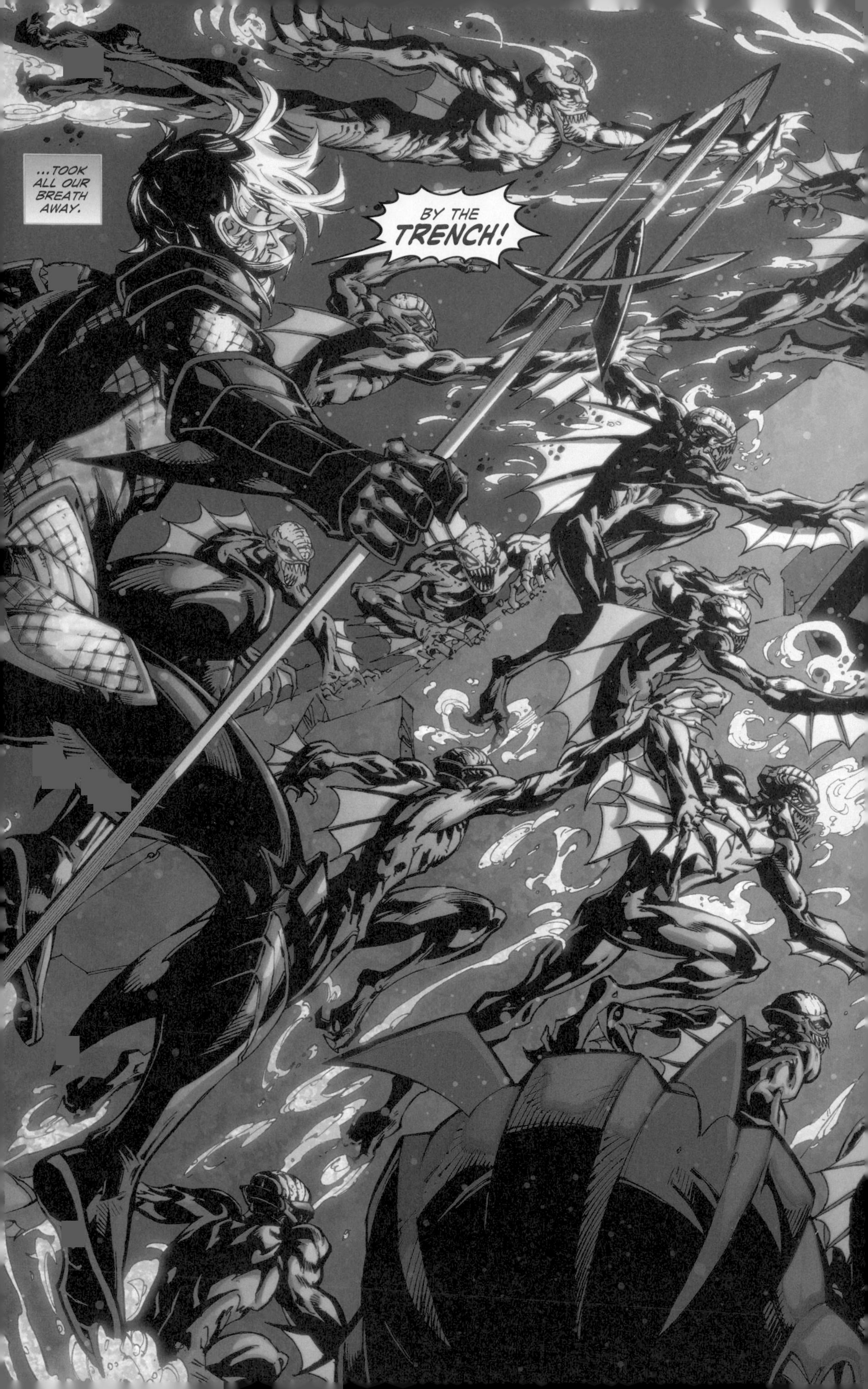
...TOOK ALL OUR BREATH AWAY.
BY THE TRENCH!

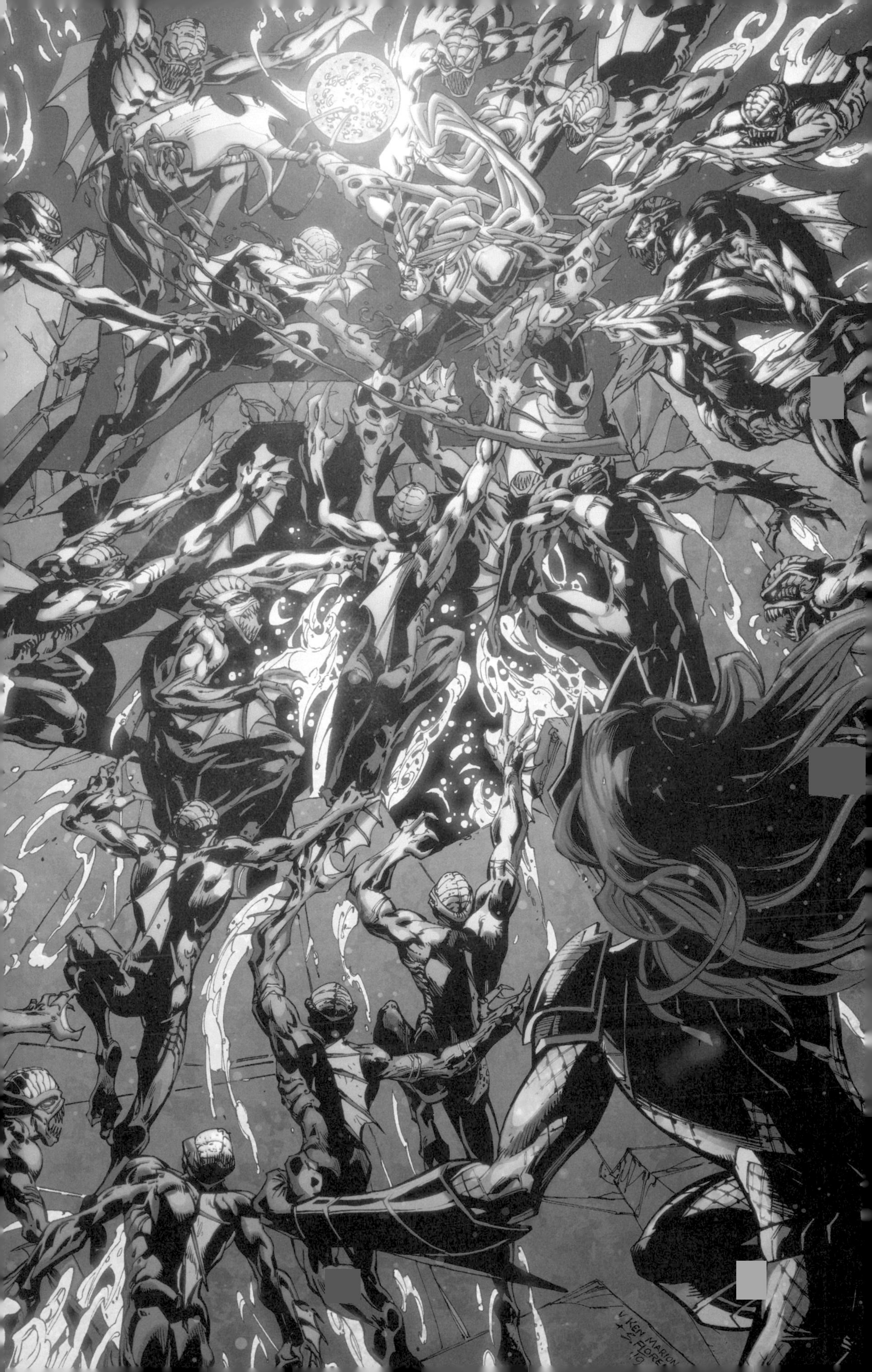

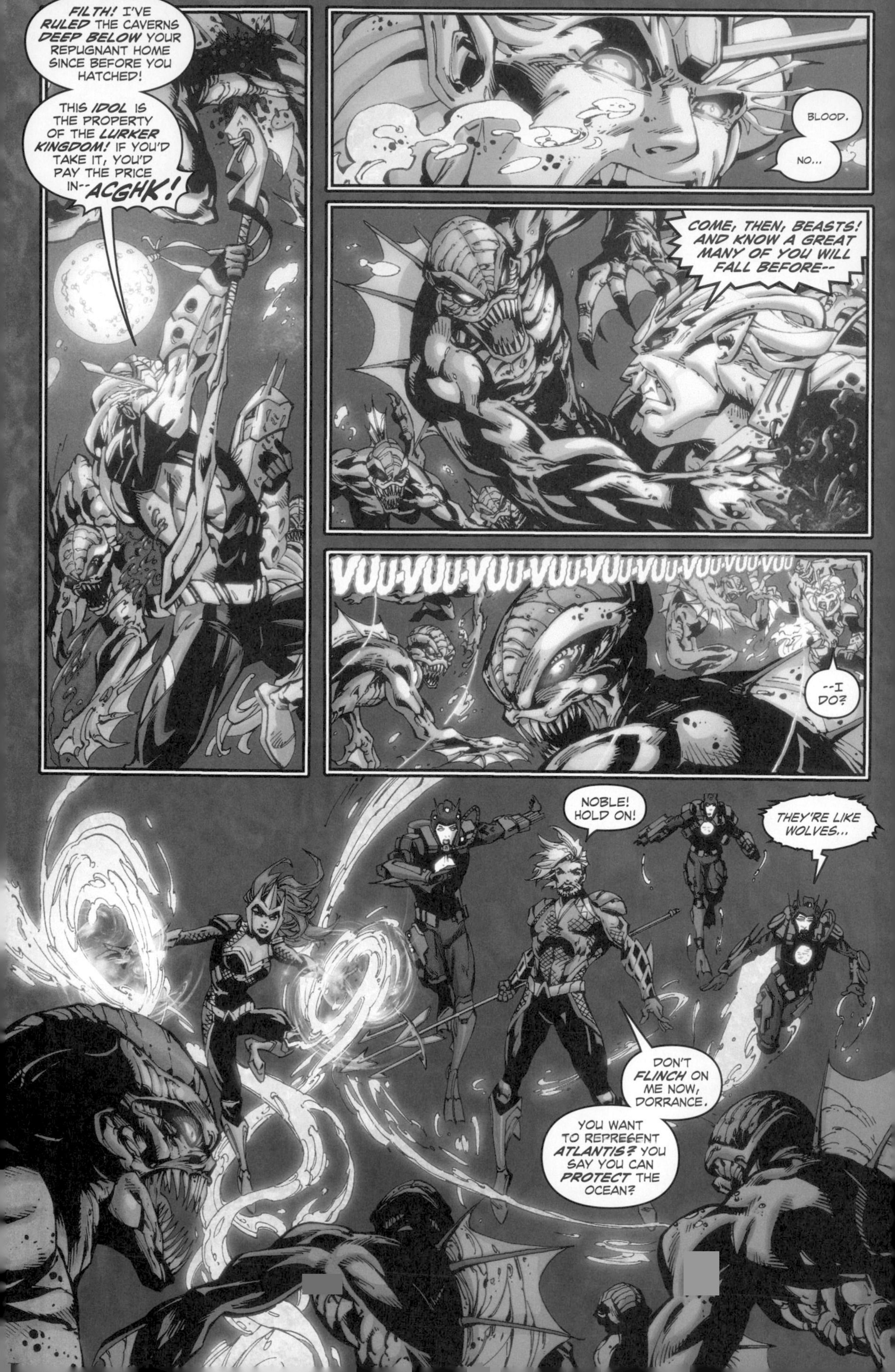
FILTH! I'VE RULED THE CAVERNS DEEP BELOW YOUR REPUGNANT HOME SINCE BEFORE YOU HATCHED!
THIS IDOL IS THE PROPERTY OF THE LURKER KINGDOM! IF YOU'D TAKE IT, YOU'D PAY THE PRICE IN--ACGHK!
BLOOD.
NO...
COME, THEN, BEASTS! AND KNOW A GREAT MANY OF YOU WILL FALL BEFORE--
VUU-VUU-VUU-VUU-VUU-VUU-VUU-VUU-VUU
--I DO?
NOBLE! HOLD ON!
THEY'RE LIKE WOLVES...
DON'T FLINCH ON ME NOW, DORRANCE.
YOU WANT TO REPRESENT ATLANTIS? YOU SAY YOU CAN PROTECT THE OCEAN?

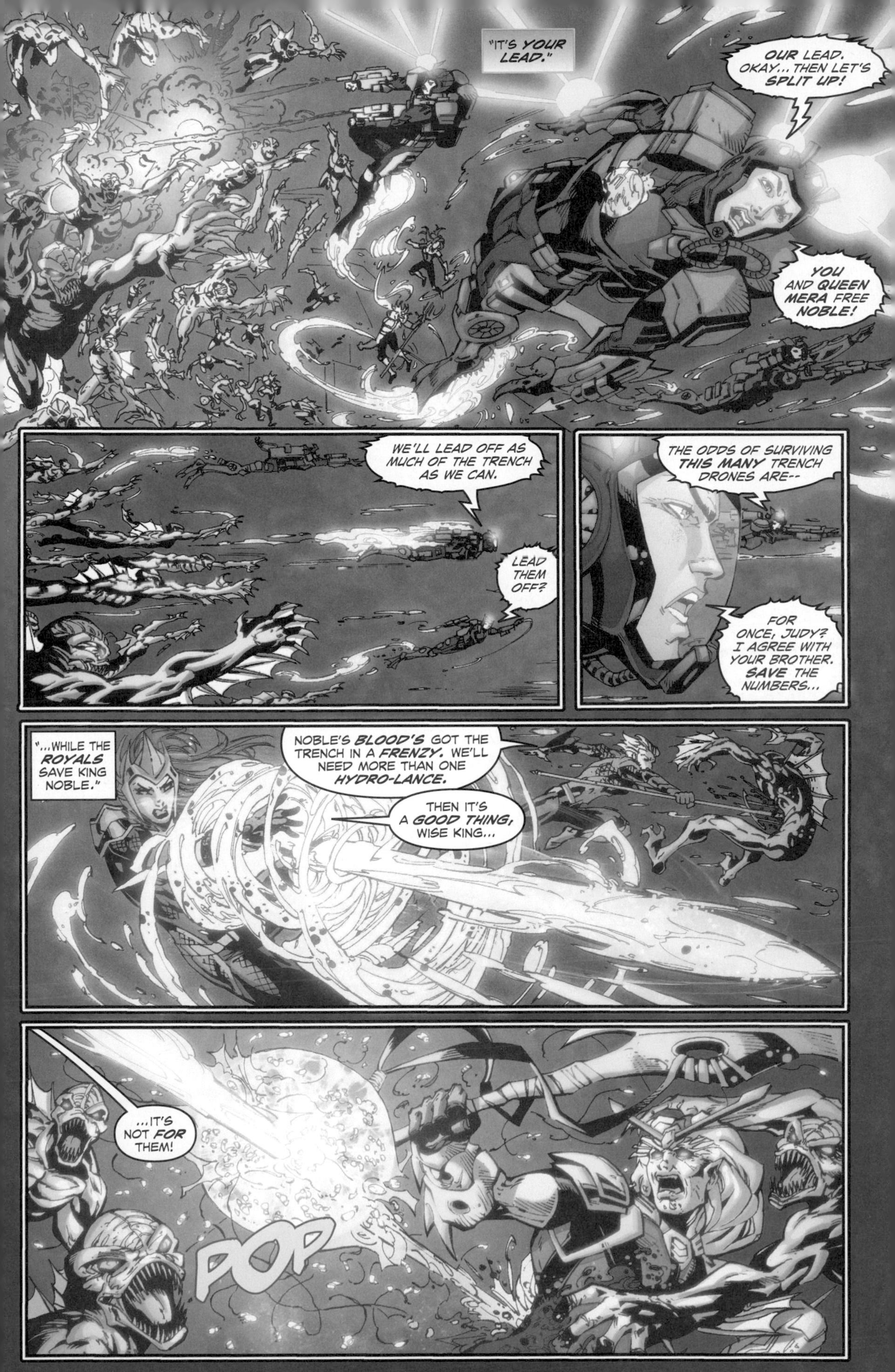

"IT'S YOUR LEAD."
OUR LEAD. OKAY... THEN LET'S SPLIT UP!
YOU AND QUEEN MERA FREE NOBLE!
WE'LL LEAD OFF AS MUCH OF THE TRENCH AS WE CAN.
LEAD THEM OFF?
THE ODDS OF SURVIVING THIS MANY TRENCH DRONES ARE--
FOR ONCE, JUDY? I AGREE WITH YOUR BROTHER. SAVE THE NUMBERS...
"...WHILE THE ROYALS SAVE KING NOBLE."
NOBLE'S BLOOD'S GOT THE TRENCH IN A FRENZY. WE'LL NEED MORE THAN ONE HYDRO-LANCE.
THEN IT'S A GOOD THING, WISE KING...
...IT'S NOT FOR THEM!
POP

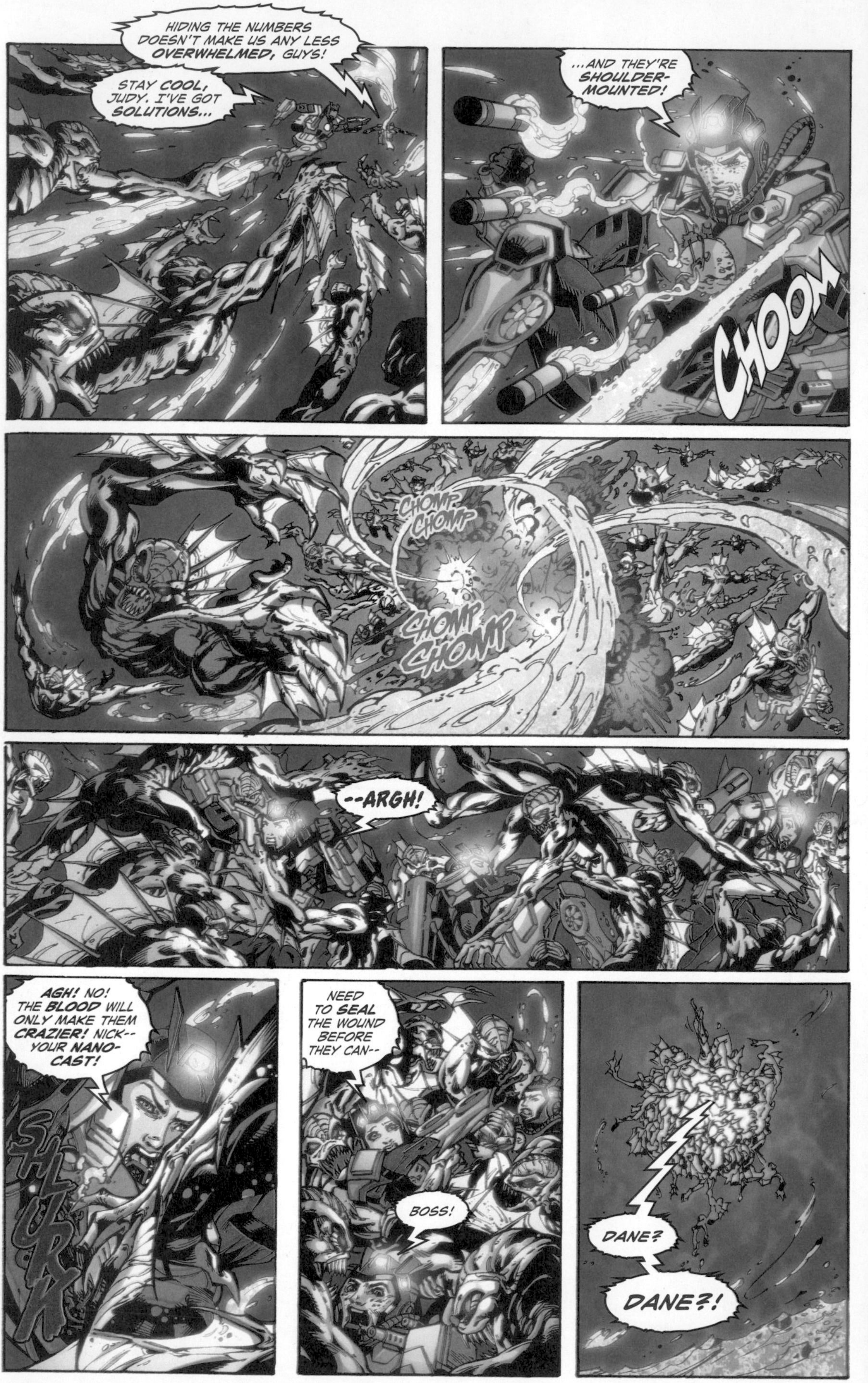
HIDING THE NUMBERS DOESN'T MAKE US ANY LESS OVERWHELMED, GUYS!
STAY COOL, JUDY. I'VE GOT SOLUTIONS...
...AND THEY'RE SHOULDER-MOUNTED!
CHOOM
CHOMP CHOMP
CHOMP CHOMP
--ARGH!
AGH! NO! THE BLOOD WILL ONLY MAKE THEM CRAZIER! NICK-- YOUR NANO-CAST!
SHLURK
NEED TO SEAL THE WOUND BEFORE THEY CAN--
BOSS!
DANE?
DANE?!

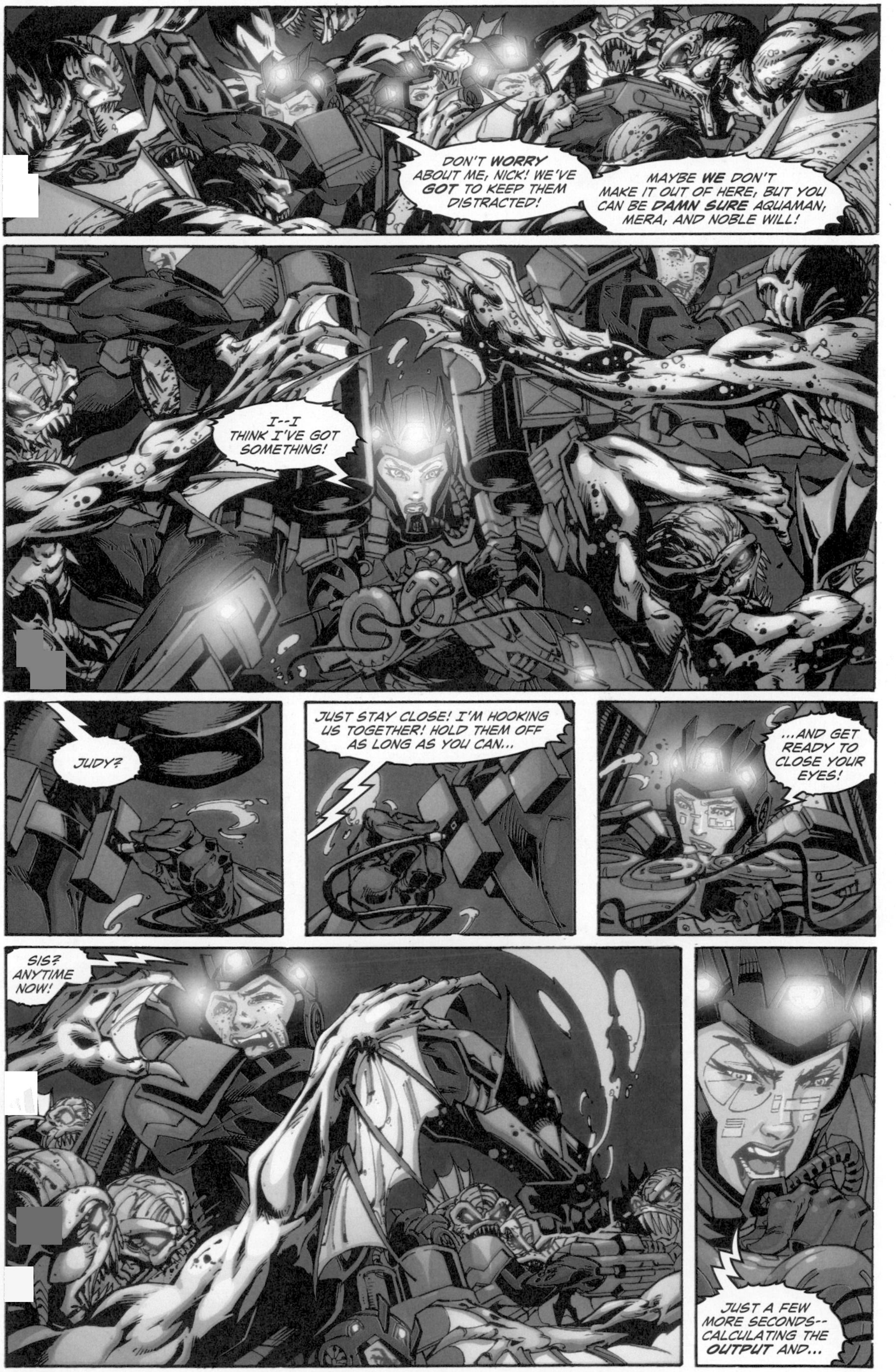
DON'T WORRY ABOUT ME, NICK! WE'VE GOT TO KEEP THEM DISTRACTED!
MAYBE WE DON'T MAKE IT OUT OF HERE; BUT YOU CAN BE DAMN SURE AQUAMAN, MERA, AND NOBLE WILL!
I--I THINK I'VE GOT SOMETHING!
JUDY?
JUST STAY CLOSE! I'M HOOKING US TOGETHER! HOLD THEM OFF AS LONG AS YOU CAN...
...AND GET READY TO CLOSE YOUR EYES!
SIS? ANYTIME NOW!
JUST A FEW MORE SECONDS-- CALCULATING THE OUTPUT AND...

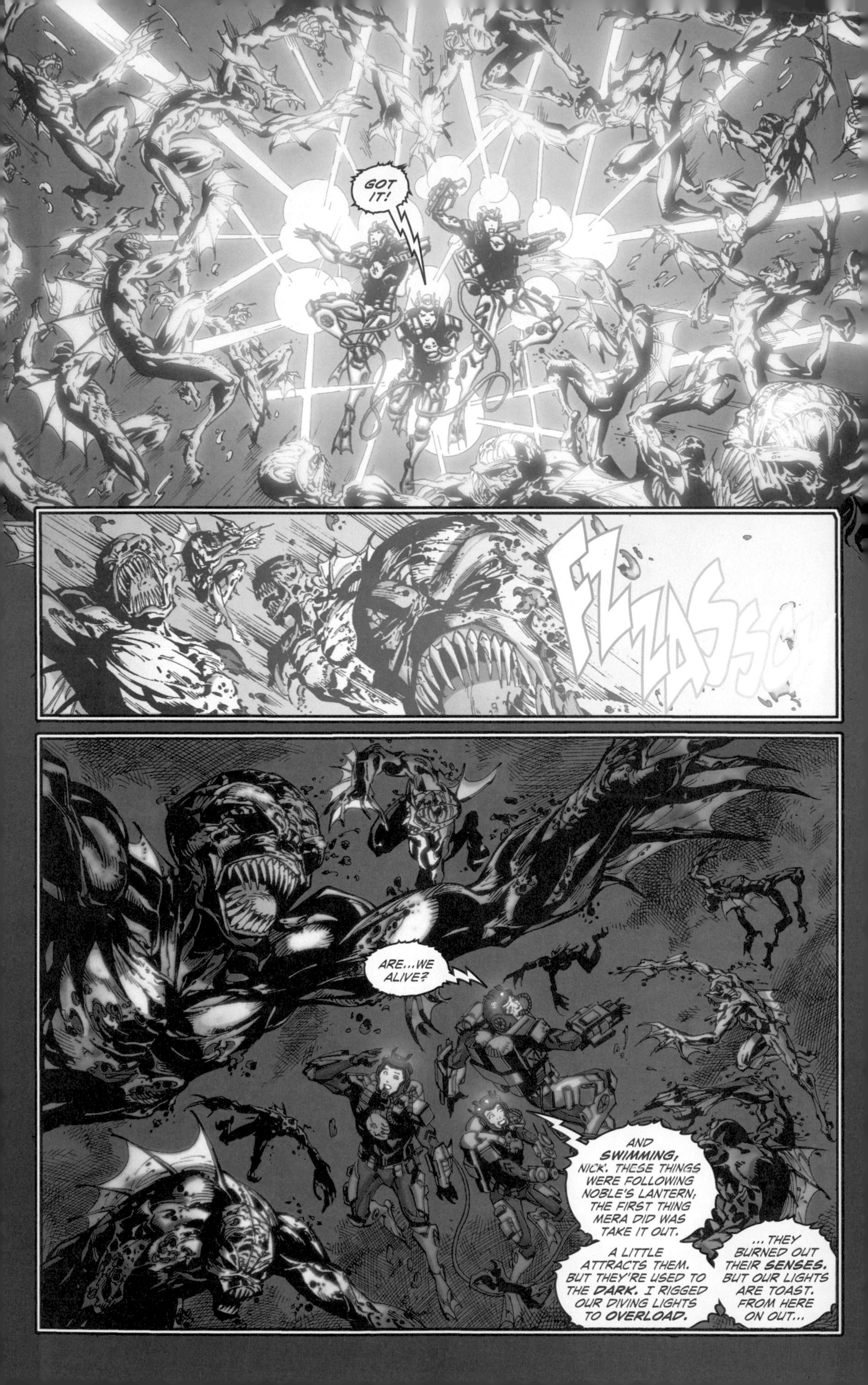
GOT IT!
FZZLASSCH
ARE...WE ALIVE?
AND SWIMMING, NICK. THESE THINGS WERE FOLLOWING NOBLE'S LANTERN, THE FIRST THING MERA DID WAS TAKE IT OUT.
A LITTLE ATTRACTS THEM. BUT THEY'RE USED TO THE DARK. I RIGGED OUR DIVING LIGHTS TO OVERLOAD.
...THEY BURNED OUT THEIR SENSES. BUT OUR LIGHTS ARE TOAST. FROM HERE ON OUT...

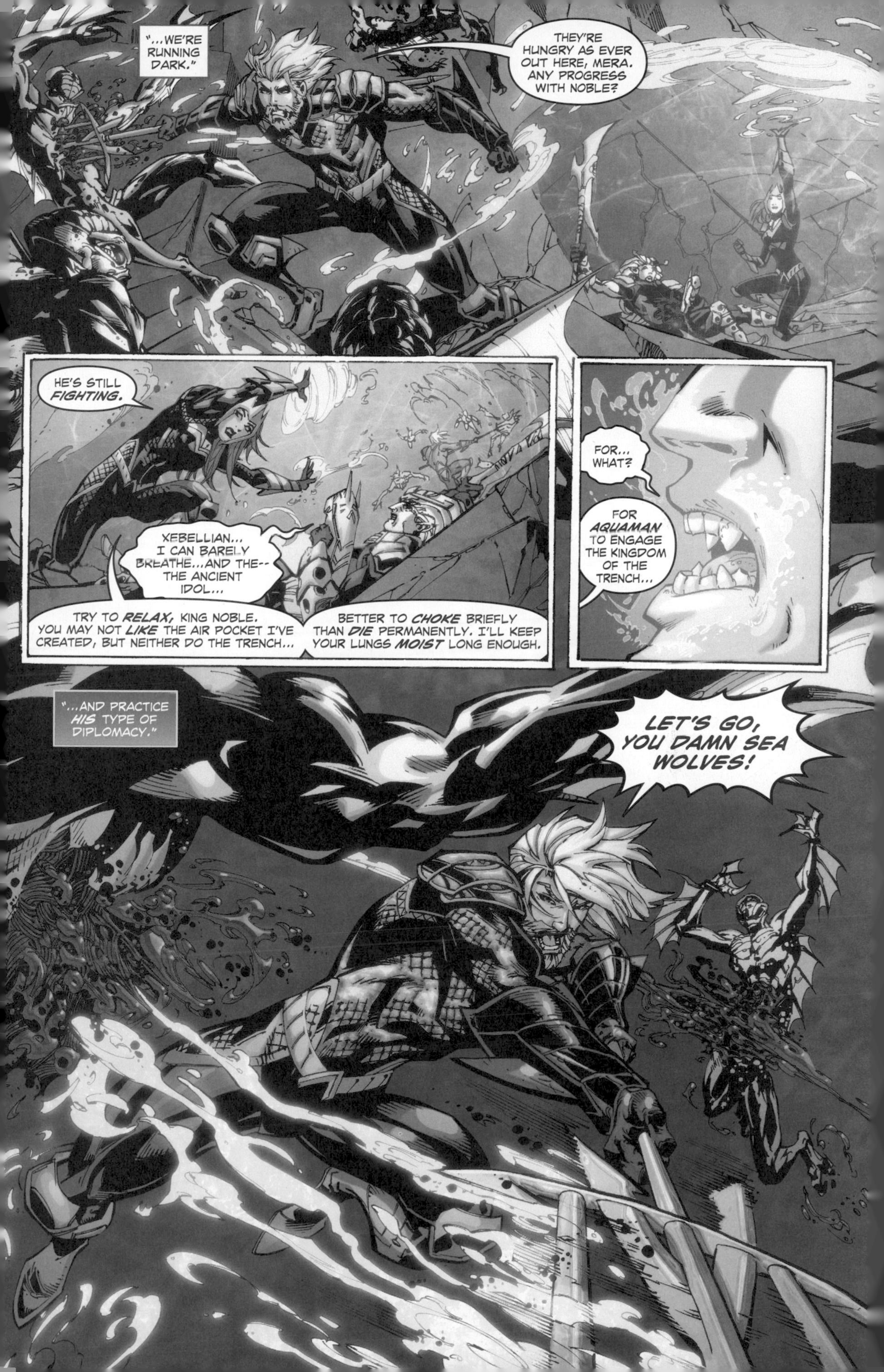
"...WE'RE RUNNING DARK."
THEY'RE HUNGRY AS EVER OUT HERE, MERA. ANY PROGRESS WITH NOBLE?
HE'S STILL *FIGHTING.*
XEBELLIAN... I CAN BARELY BREATHE...AND THE-- THE ANCIENT IDOL...
TRY TO *RELAX,* KING NOBLE. YOU MAY NOT *LIKE* THE AIR POCKET I'VE CREATED, BUT NEITHER DO THE TRENCH...
BETTER TO *CHOKE* BRIEFLY THAN *DIE* PERMANENTLY. I'LL KEEP YOUR LUNGS *MOIST* LONG ENOUGH.
FOR... WHAT?
FOR *AQUAMAN* TO ENGAGE THE KINGDOM OF THE TRENCH...
"...AND PRACTICE *HIS* TYPE OF DIPLOMACY."
LET'S GO, YOU DAMN SEA WOLVES!

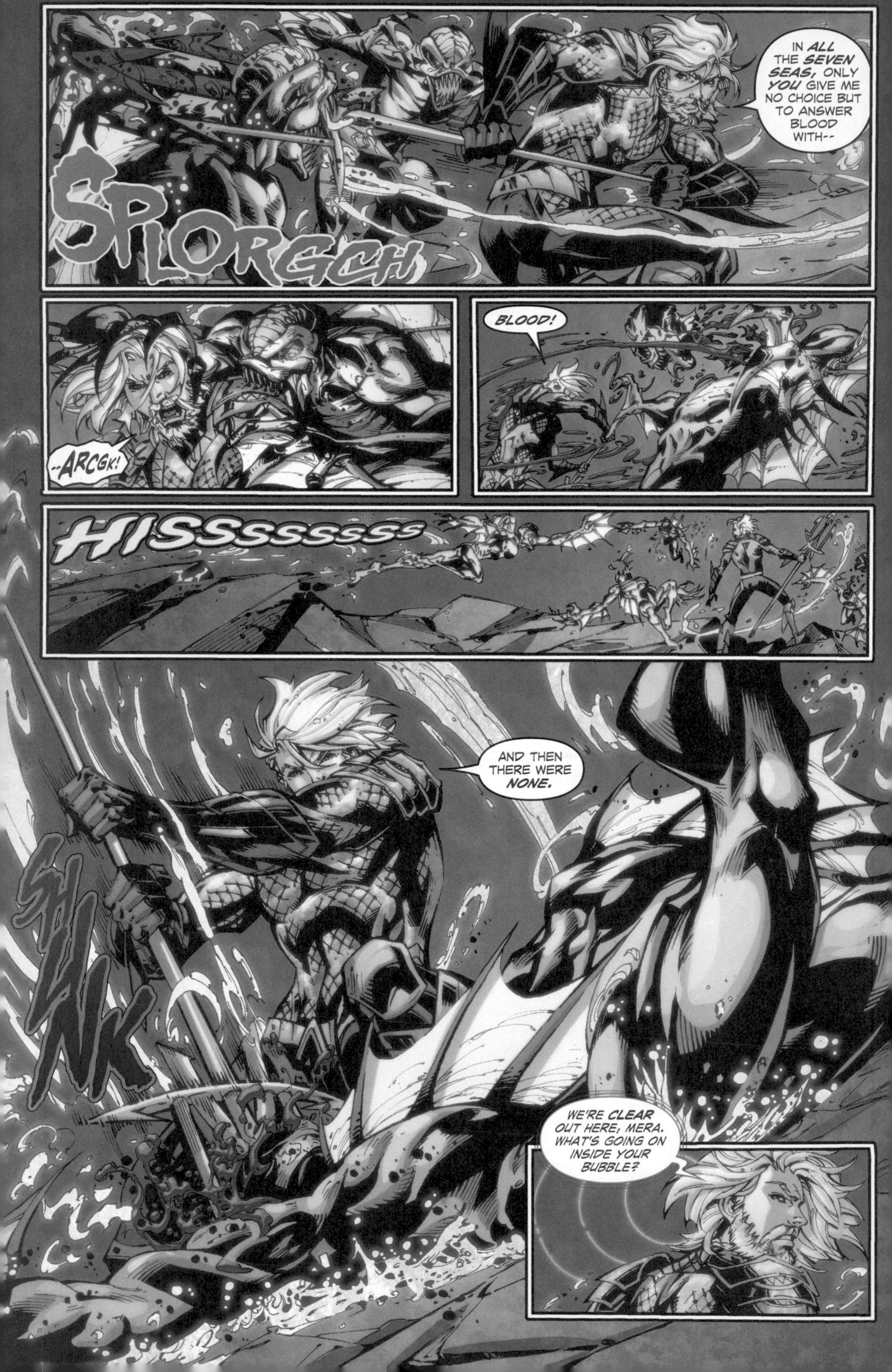

IN ALL THE SEVEN SEAS, ONLY YOU GIVE ME NO CHOICE BUT TO ANSWER BLOOD WITH--
SPLORGCH
--ARCGK!
BLOOD!
HISSSSSSSS
AND THEN THERE WERE NONE.
SHNK
WE'RE CLEAR OUT HERE, MERA. WHAT'S GOING ON INSIDE YOUR BUBBLE?

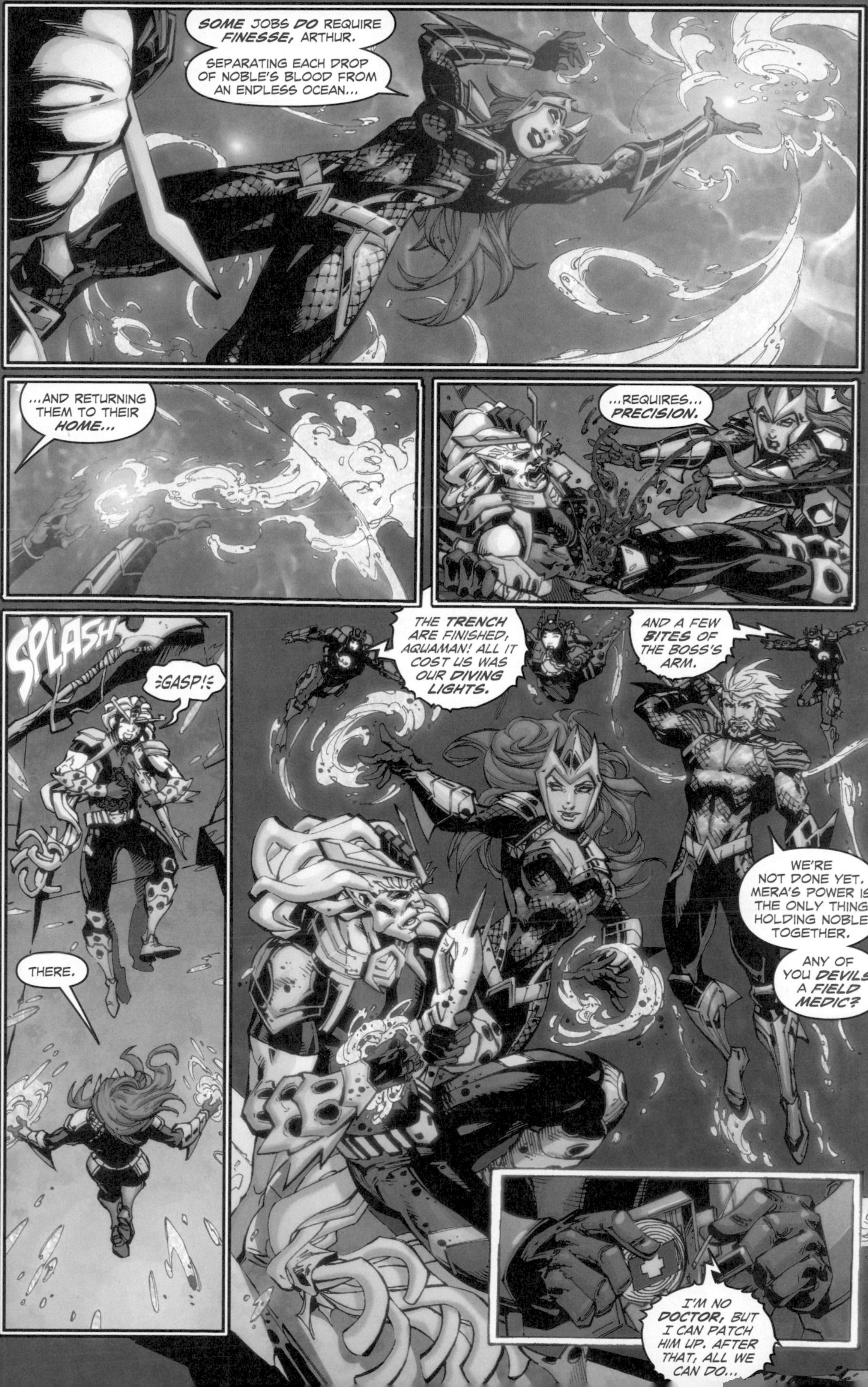
SOME JOBS DO REQUIRE FINESSE, ARTHUR.
SEPARATING EACH DROP OF NOBLE'S BLOOD FROM AN ENDLESS OCEAN...
...AND RETURNING THEM TO THEIR HOME...
...REQUIRES... PRECISION.
SPLASH
GASP!
THERE.
THE TRENCH ARE FINISHED, AQUAMAN! ALL IT COST US WAS OUR DIVING LIGHTS.
AND A FEW BITES OF THE BOSS'S ARM.
WE'RE NOT DONE YET. MERA'S POWER IS THE ONLY THING HOLDING NOBLE TOGETHER.
ANY OF YOU DEVILS A FIELD MEDIC?
I'M NO DOCTOR, BUT I CAN PATCH HIM UP. AFTER THAT, ALL WE CAN DO...

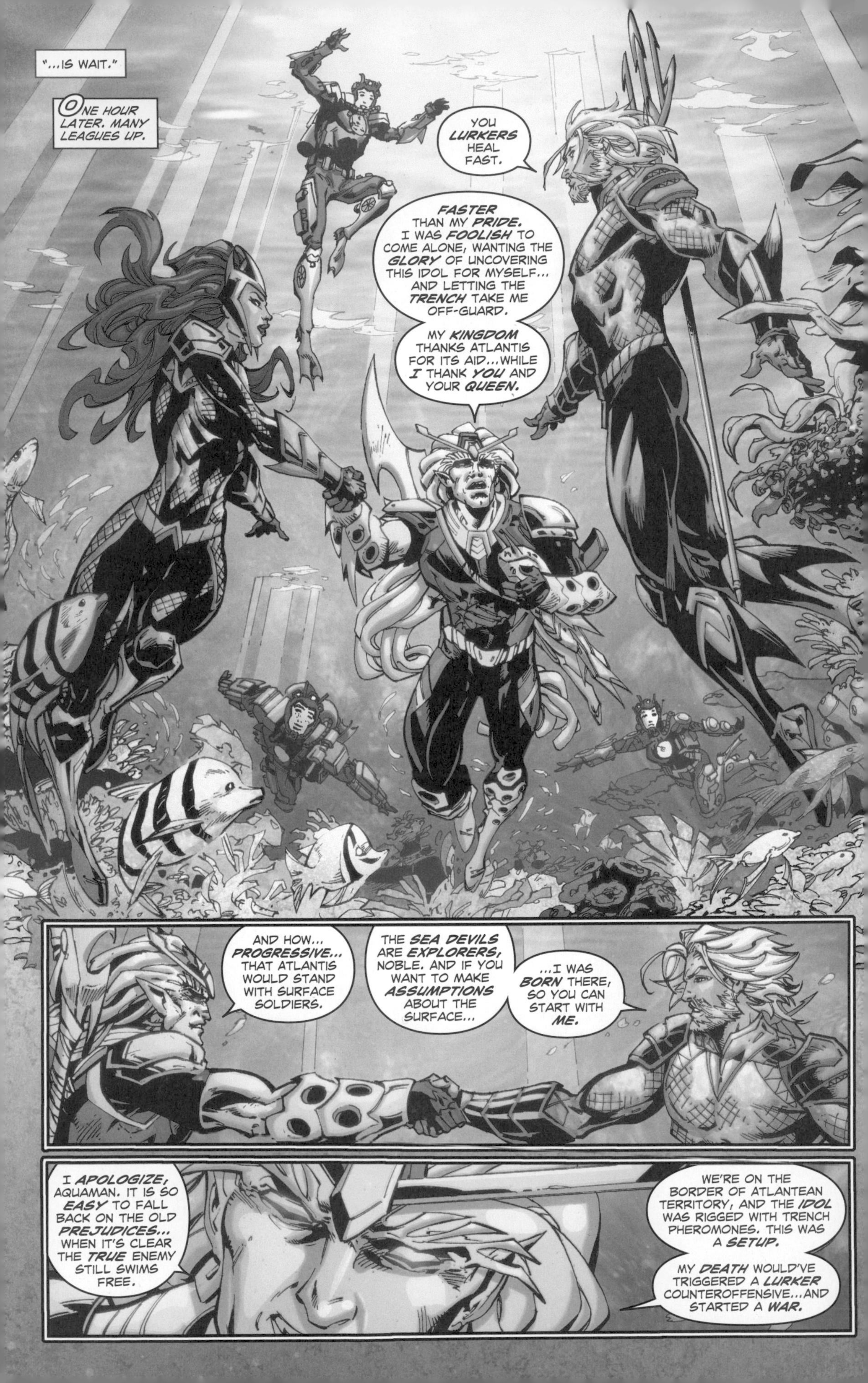
"...IS WAIT."
ONE HOUR LATER. MANY LEAGUES UP.
YOU LURKERS HEAL FAST.
FASTER THAN MY PRIDE. I WAS FOOLISH TO COME ALONE, WANTING THE GLORY OF UNCOVERING THIS IDOL FOR MYSELF... AND LETTING THE TRENCH TAKE ME OFF-GUARD.
MY KINGDOM THANKS ATLANTIS FOR ITS AID...WHILE I THANK YOU AND YOUR QUEEN.
AND HOW... PROGRESSIVE... THAT ATLANTIS WOULD STAND WITH SURFACE SOLDIERS.
THE SEA DEVILS ARE EXPLORERS, NOBLE. AND IF YOU WANT TO MAKE ASSUMPTIONS ABOUT THE SURFACE...
...I WAS BORN THERE, SO YOU CAN START WITH ME.
I APOLOGIZE, AQUAMAN. IT IS SO EASY TO FALL BACK ON THE OLD PREJUDICES... WHEN IT'S CLEAR THE TRUE ENEMY STILL SWIMS FREE.
WE'RE ON THE BORDER OF ATLANTEAN TERRITORY, AND THE IDOL WAS RIGGED WITH TRENCH PHEROMONES. THIS WAS A SETUP.
MY DEATH WOULD'VE TRIGGERED A LURKER COUNTEROFFENSIVE...AND STARTED A WAR.

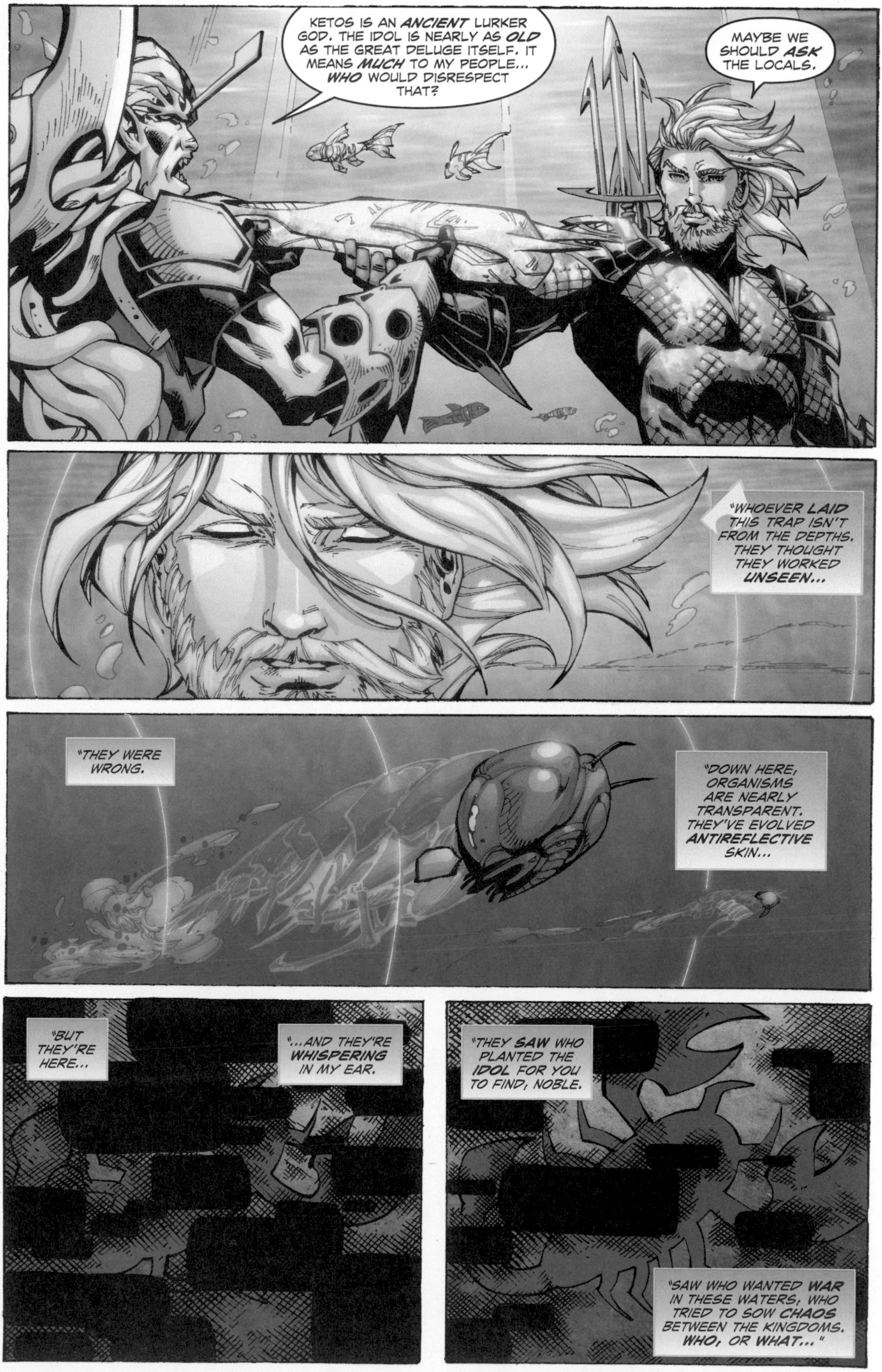
KETOS IS AN *ANCIENT* LURKER GOD. THE IDOL IS NEARLY AS *OLD* AS THE GREAT DELUGE ITSELF. IT MEANS *MUCH* TO MY PEOPLE... *WHO* WOULD DISRESPECT THAT?
MAYBE WE SHOULD *ASK* THE LOCALS.
"WHOEVER **LAID** THIS TRAP ISN'T FROM THE DEPTHS. THEY THOUGHT THEY WORKED **UNSEEN...**
"THEY WERE WRONG.
"DOWN HERE, ORGANISMS ARE NEARLY TRANSPARENT. THEY'VE EVOLVED **ANTIREFLECTIVE** SKIN...
"BUT THEY'RE HERE...
"...AND THEY'RE **WHISPERING** IN MY EAR.
"THEY **SAW** WHO PLANTED THE **IDOL** FOR YOU TO FIND, NOBLE.
"SAW WHO WANTED **WAR** IN THESE WATERS, WHO TRIED TO SOW **CHAOS** BETWEEN THE KINGDOMS. **WHO, OR WHAT...**"

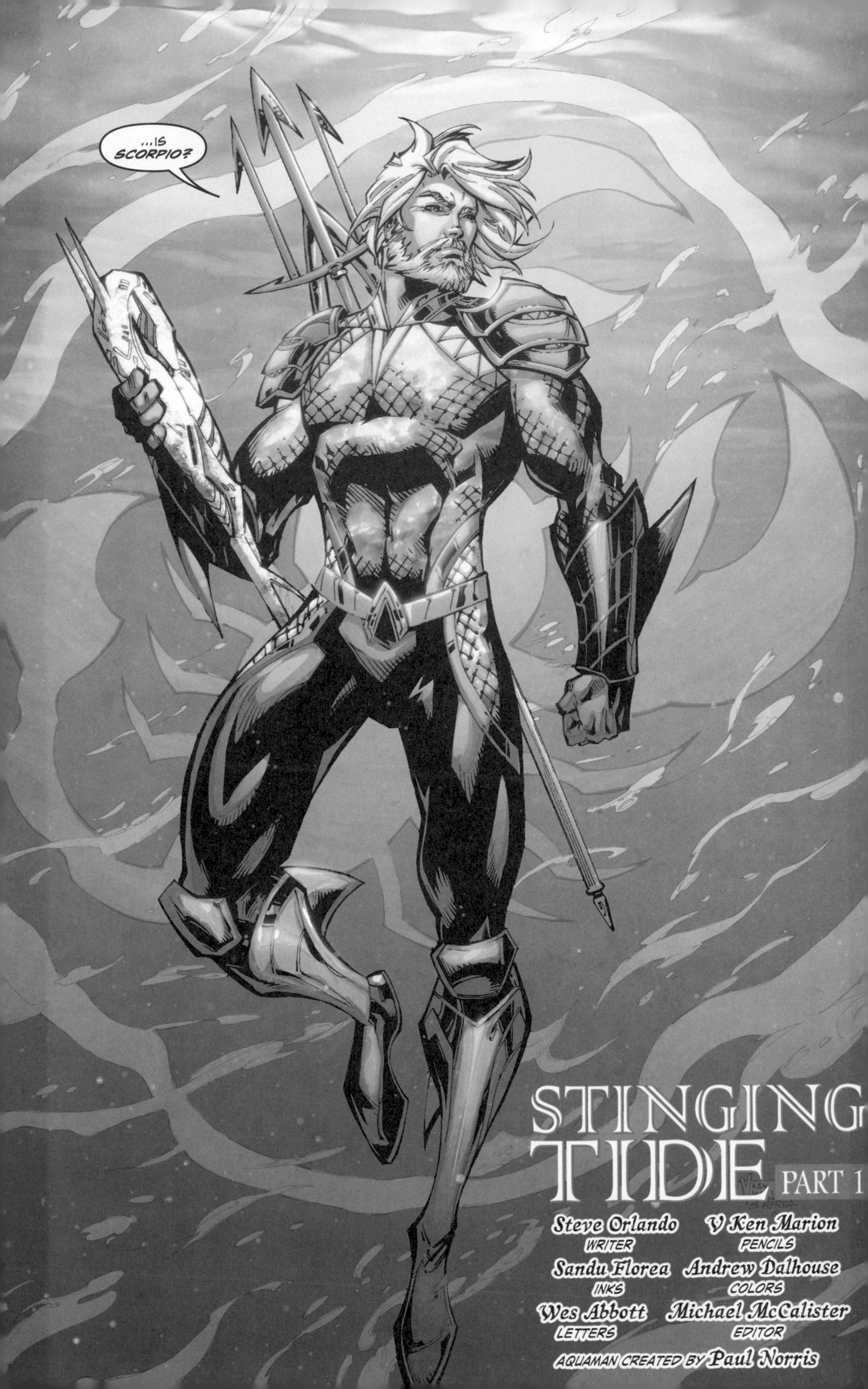
...IS SCORPIO?
STINGING TIDE PART 1
Steve Orlando WRITER
V Ken Marion PENCILS
Sandu Florea INKS
Andrew Dalhouse COLORS
Wes Abbott LETTERS
Michael McCalister EDITOR
AQUAMAN CREATED BY Paul Norris

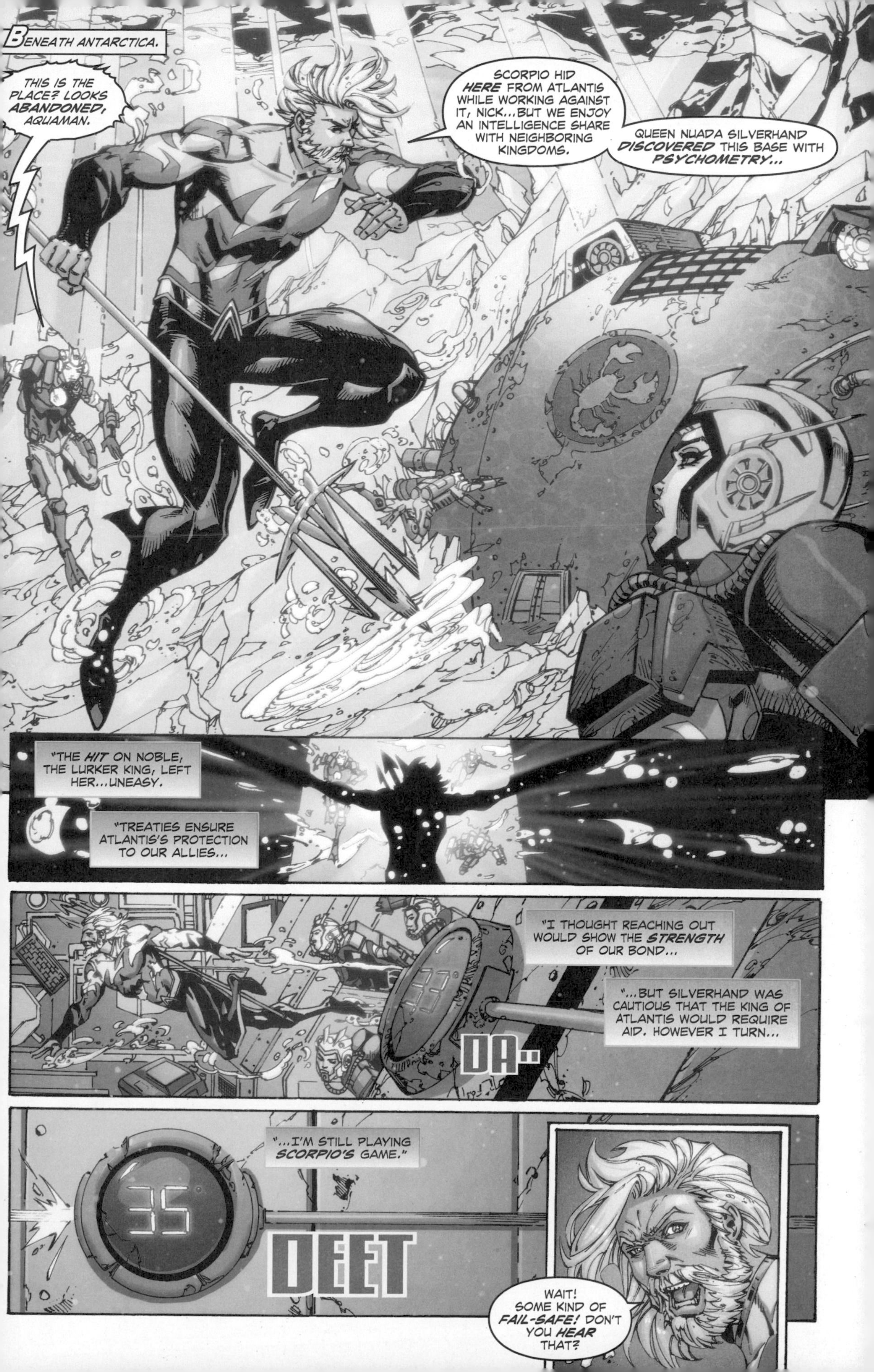
BENEATH ANTARCTICA.
THIS IS THE PLACE? LOOKS ABANDONED, AQUAMAN.
SCORPIO HID HERE FROM ATLANTIS WHILE WORKING AGAINST IT, NICK...BUT WE ENJOY AN INTELLIGENCE SHARE WITH NEIGHBORING KINGDOMS.
QUEEN NUADA SILVERHAND DISCOVERED THIS BASE WITH PSYCHOMETRY...
"THE HIT ON NOBLE, THE LURKER KING, LEFT HER...UNEASY.
"TREATIES ENSURE ATLANTIS'S PROTECTION TO OUR ALLIES...
"I THOUGHT REACHING OUT WOULD SHOW THE STRENGTH OF OUR BOND...
"...BUT SILVERHAND WAS CAUTIOUS THAT THE KING OF ATLANTIS WOULD REQUIRE AID. HOWEVER I TURN...
DA..
"...I'M STILL PLAYING SCORPIO'S GAME."
35
DEET
WAIT! SOME KIND OF FAIL-SAFE! DON'T YOU HEAR THAT?

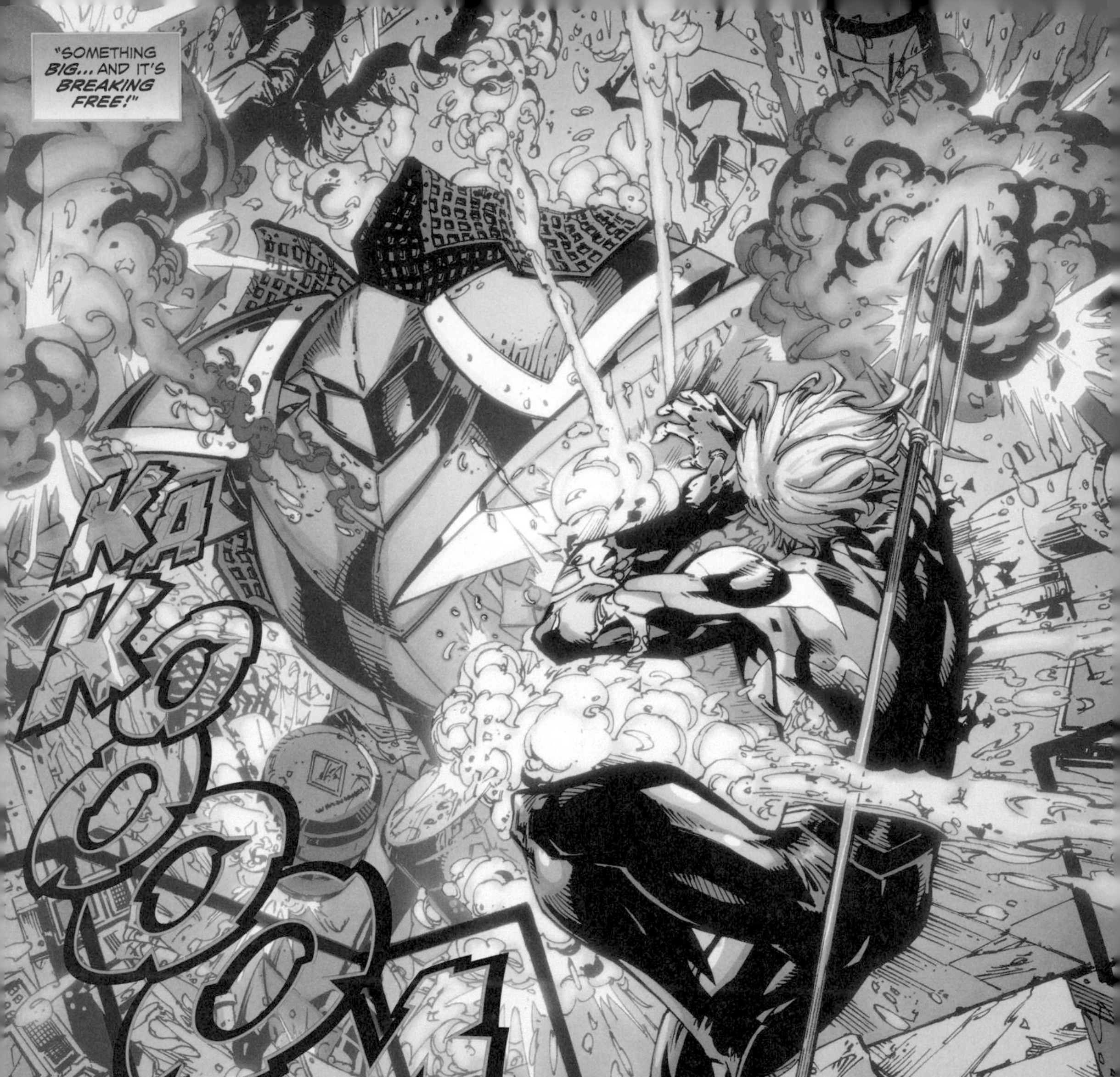
"SOMETHING BIG... AND IT'S BREAKING FREE!"
KA KOOOOM

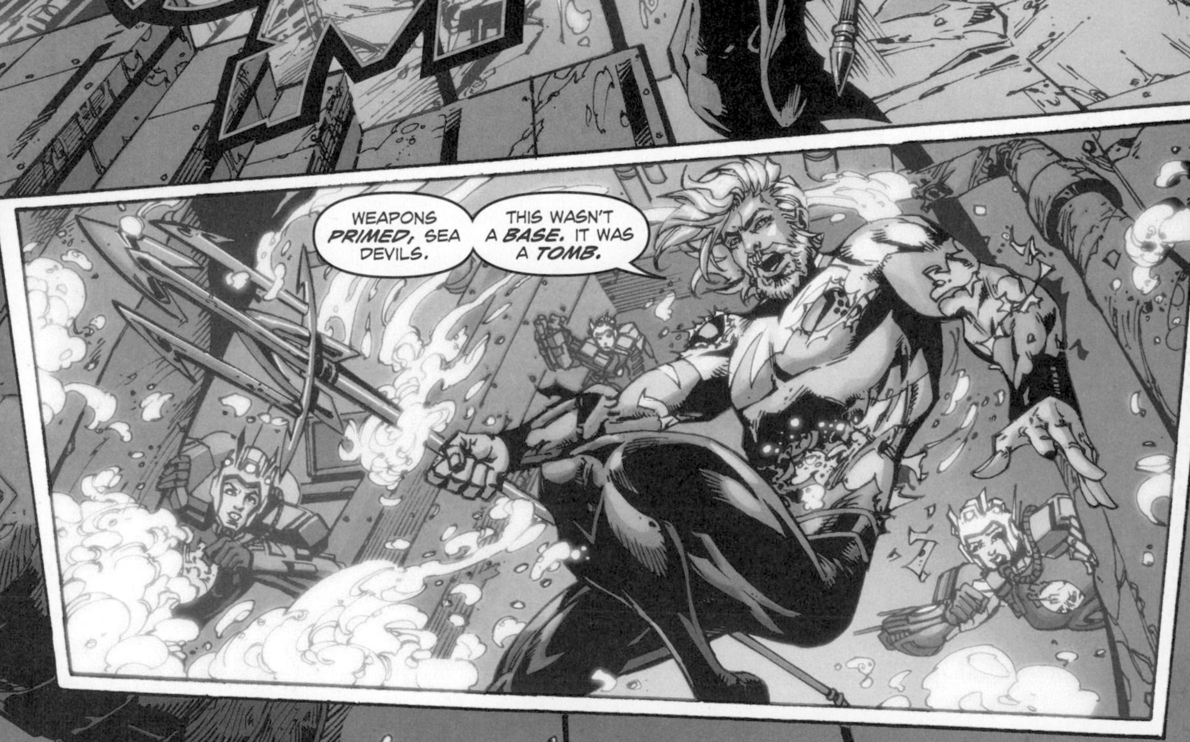
WEAPONS PRIMED, SEA DEVILS.
THIS WASN'T A BASE. IT WAS A TOMB.

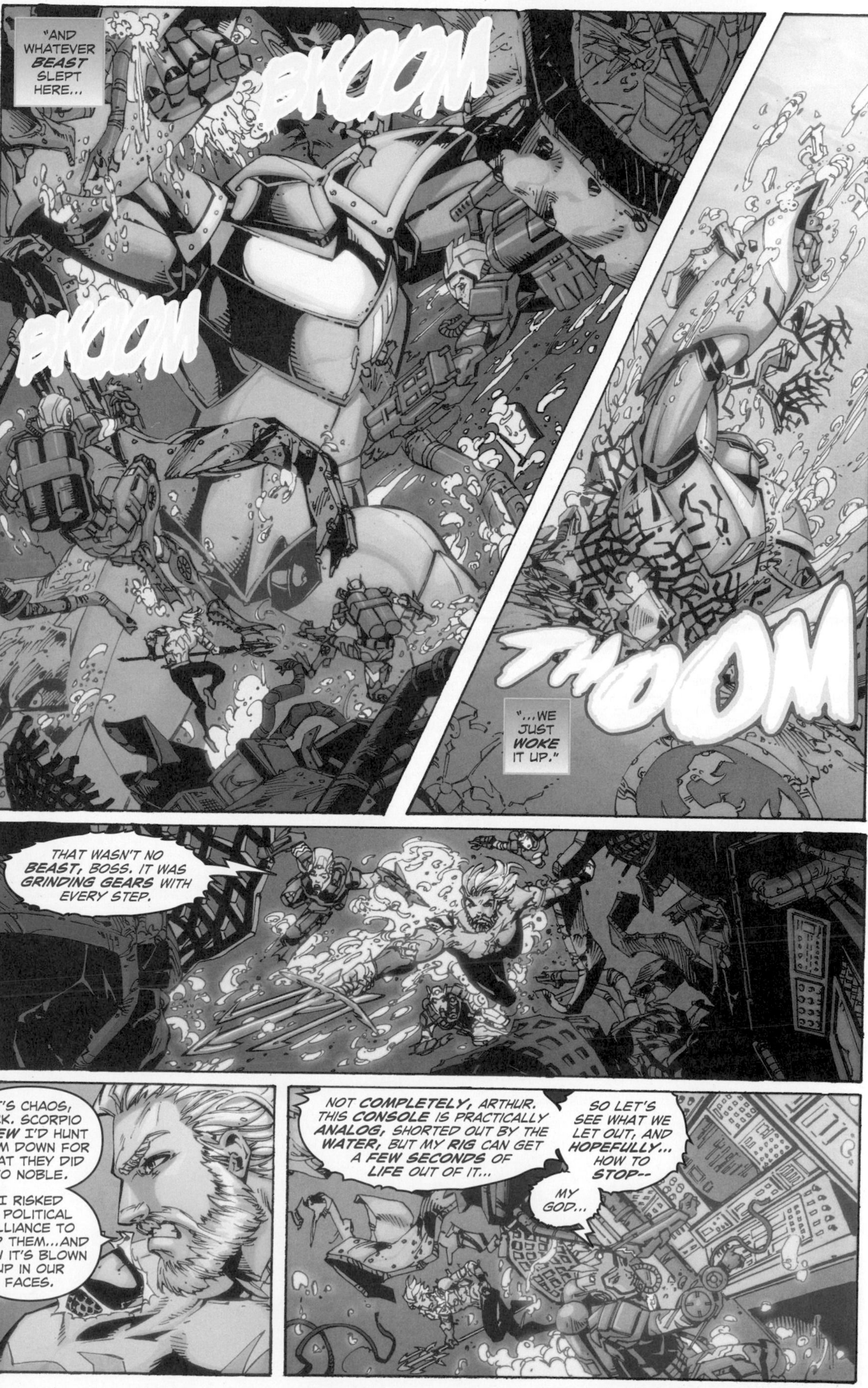
"AND WHATEVER BEAST SLEPT HERE...
BKOOM
BKOOM
THOOM
"...WE JUST WOKE IT UP."
THAT WASN'T NO BEAST, BOSS. IT WAS GRINDING GEARS WITH EVERY STEP.
IT'S CHAOS, NICK. SCORPIO NEW I'D HUNT HEM DOWN FOR HAT THEY DID TO NOBLE.
I RISKED A POLITICAL ALLIANCE TO ND THEM...AND OW IT'S BLOWN UP IN OUR FACES.
NOT COMPLETELY, ARTHUR. THIS CONSOLE IS PRACTICALLY ANALOG, SHORTED OUT BY THE WATER, BUT MY RIG CAN GET A FEW SECONDS OF LIFE OUT OF IT...
SO LET'S SEE WHAT WE LET OUT, AND HOPEFULLY... HOW TO STOP--
MY GOD...

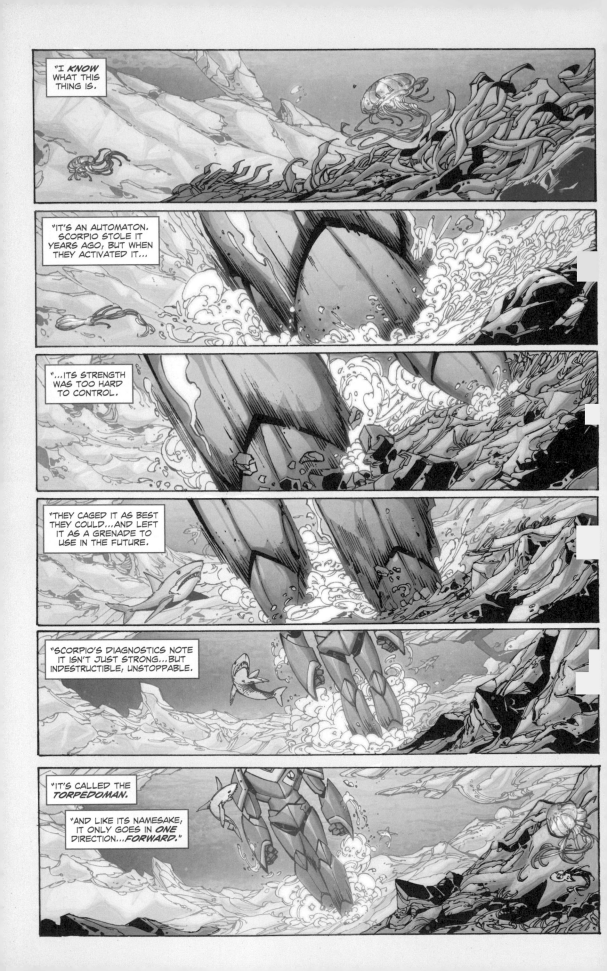

"I *KNOW* WHAT THIS THING IS.

"IT'S AN AUTOMATON. SCORPIO STOLE IT YEARS AGO, BUT WHEN THEY ACTIVATED IT...

"...ITS STRENGTH WAS TOO HARD TO CONTROL.

"THEY CAGED IT AS BEST THEY COULD...AND LEFT IT AS A GRENADE TO USE IN THE FUTURE.

"SCORPIO'S DIAGNOSTICS NOTE IT ISN'T JUST STRONG...BUT INDESTRUCTIBLE, UNSTOPPABLE.

"IT'S CALLED THE *TORPEDOMAN*.

"AND LIKE ITS NAMESAKE, IT ONLY GOES IN *ONE* DIRECTION...*FORWARD*."

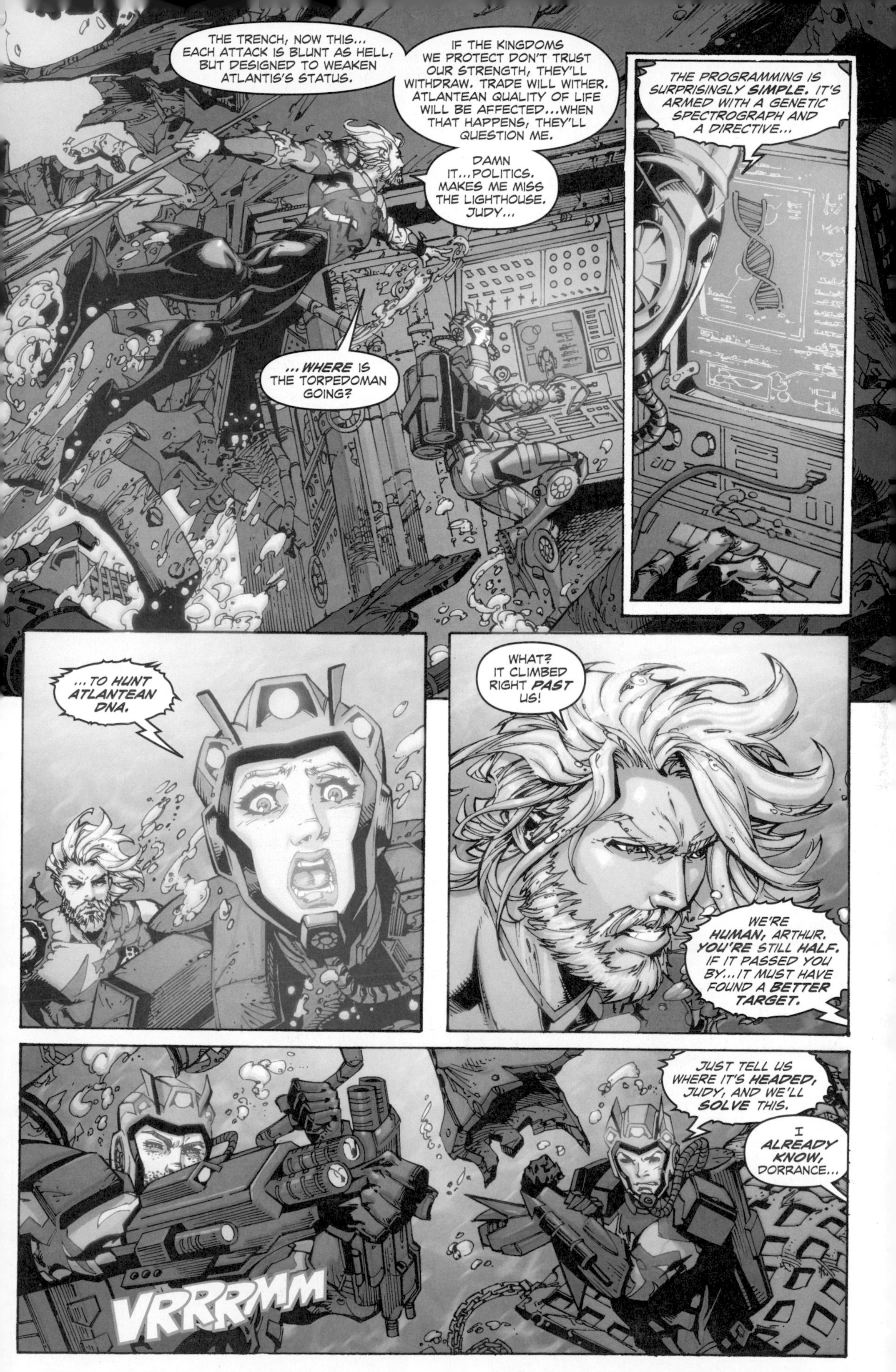
THE TRENCH, NOW THIS... EACH ATTACK IS BLUNT AS HELL, BUT DESIGNED TO WEAKEN ATLANTIS'S STATUS.
IF THE KINGDOMS WE PROTECT DON'T TRUST OUR STRENGTH, THEY'LL WITHDRAW. TRADE WILL WITHER. ATLANTEAN QUALITY OF LIFE WILL BE AFFECTED...WHEN THAT HAPPENS, THEY'LL QUESTION ME.
DAMN IT...POLITICS. MAKES ME MISS THE LIGHTHOUSE. JUDY...
...WHERE IS THE TORPEDOMAN GOING?
THE PROGRAMMING IS SURPRISINGLY SIMPLE. IT'S ARMED WITH A GENETIC SPECTROGRAPH AND A DIRECTIVE...
...TO HUNT ATLANTEAN DNA.
WHAT? IT CLIMBED RIGHT PAST US!
WE'RE HUMAN, ARTHUR. YOU'RE STILL HALF. IF IT PASSED YOU BY...IT MUST HAVE FOUND A BETTER TARGET.
JUST TELL US WHERE IT'S HEADED, JUDY, AND WE'LL SOLVE THIS.
I ALREADY KNOW, DORRANCE...
VRRRMM

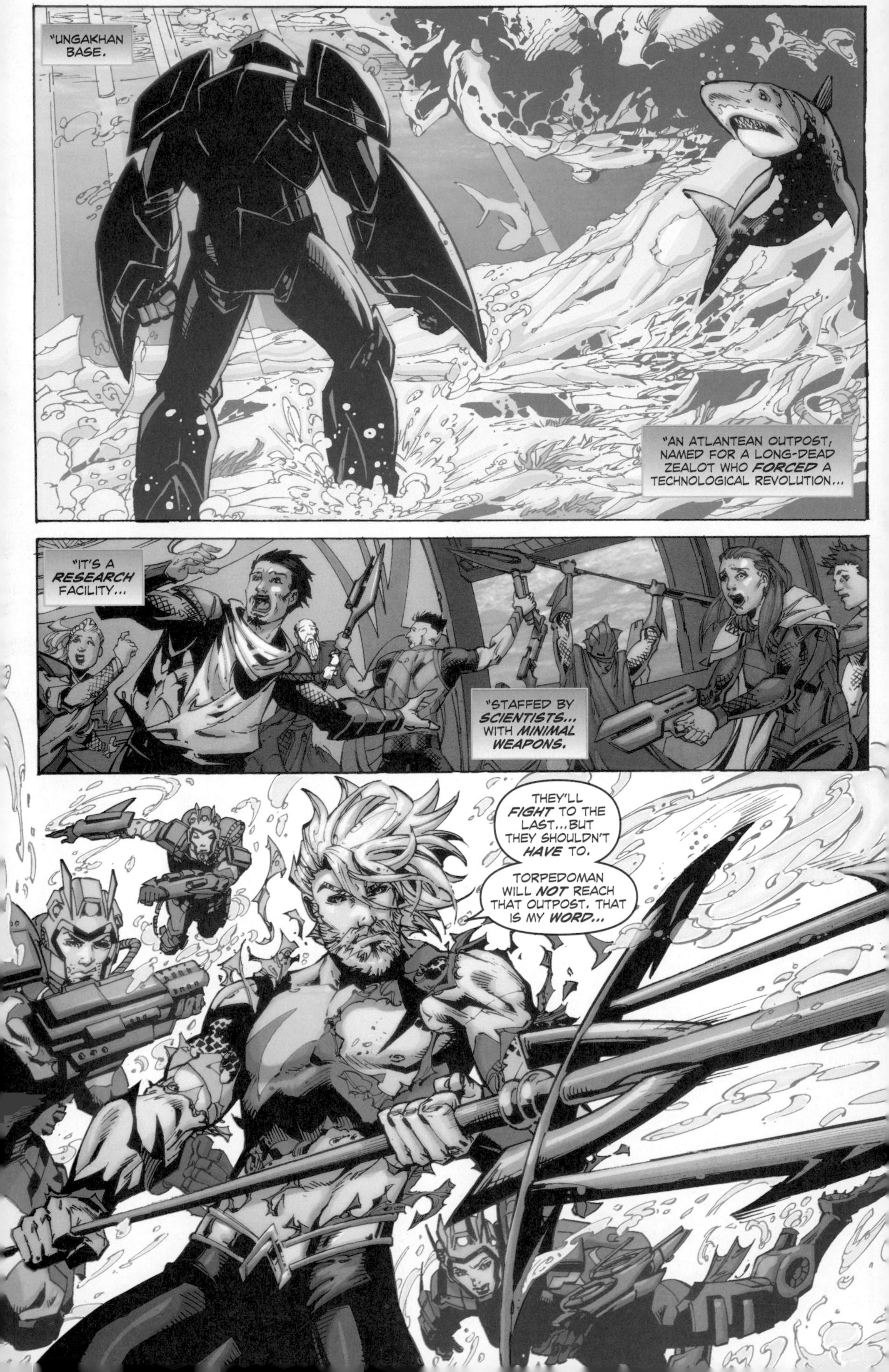
"UNGAKHAN BASE.
"AN ATLANTEAN OUTPOST, NAMED FOR A LONG-DEAD ZEALOT WHO FORCED A TECHNOLOGICAL REVOLUTION...
"IT'S A RESEARCH FACILITY...
"STAFFED BY SCIENTISTS... WITH MINIMAL WEAPONS.
THEY'LL FIGHT TO THE LAST...BUT THEY SHOULDN'T HAVE TO.
TORPEDOMAN WILL NOT REACH THAT OUTPOST. THAT IS MY WORD...

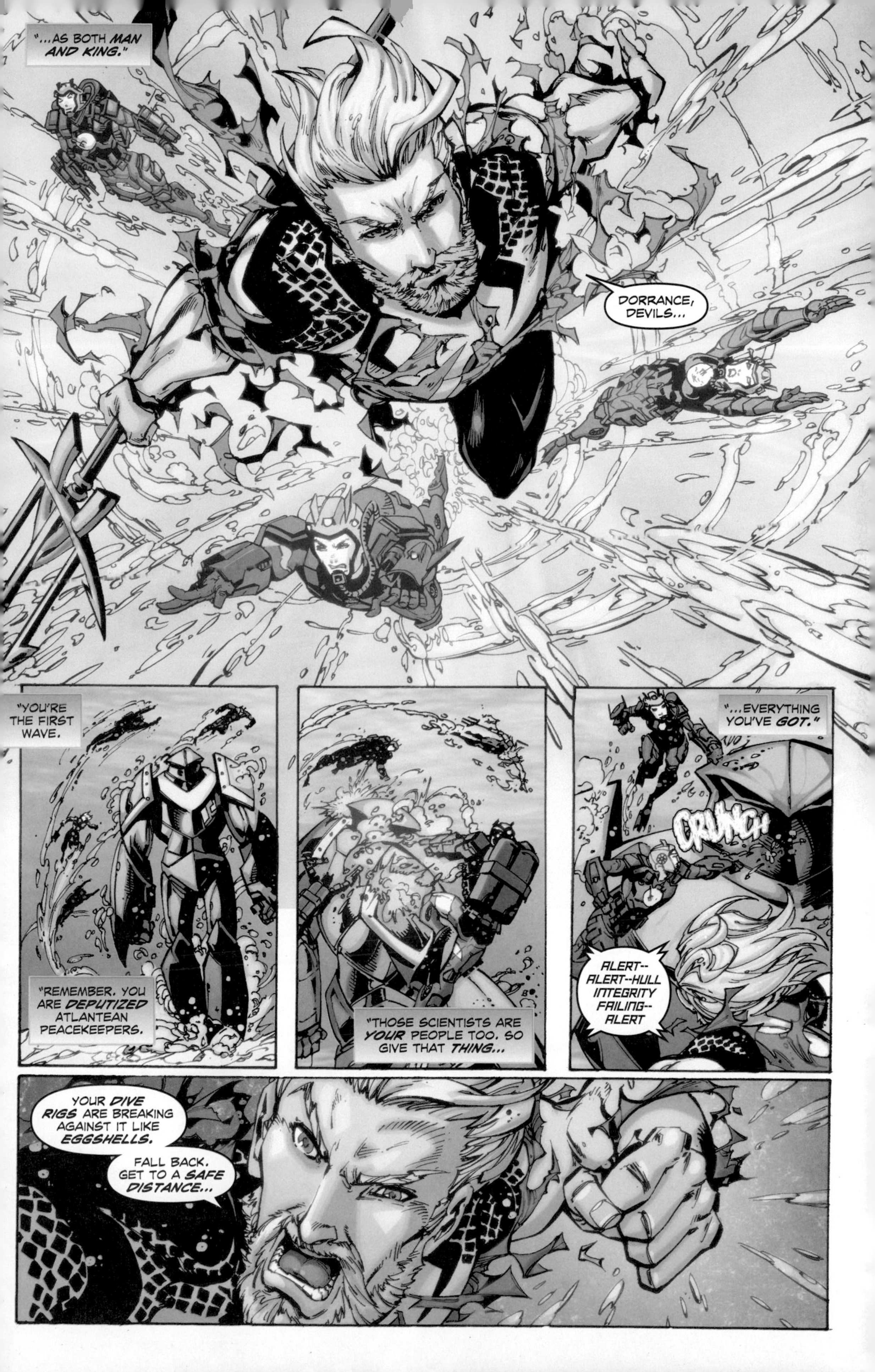
"...AS BOTH MAN AND KING."
DORRANCE, DEVILS...
"YOU'RE THE FIRST WAVE.
"REMEMBER. YOU ARE DEPUTIZED ATLANTEAN PEACEKEEPERS.
"THOSE SCIENTISTS ARE YOUR PEOPLE TOO. SO GIVE THAT THING...
"...EVERYTHING YOU'VE GOT."
CRUNCH
ALERT-- ALERT--HULL INTEGRITY FAILING-- ALERT
YOUR DIVE RIGS ARE BREAKING AGAINST IT LIKE EGGSHELLS.
FALL BACK. GET TO A SAFE DISTANCE...

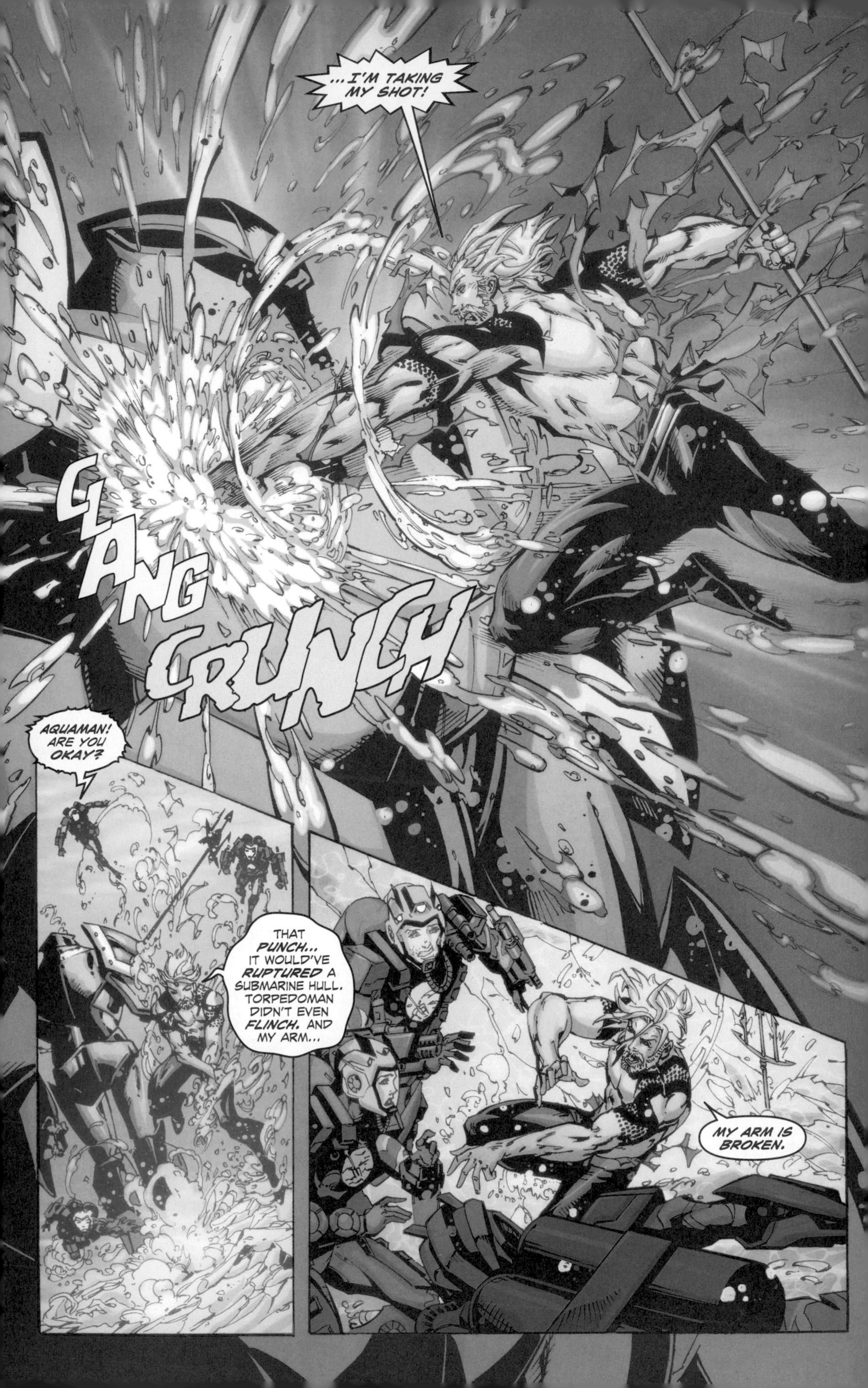
...I'M TAKING MY SHOT!
CLANG
CRUNCH
AQUAMAN! ARE YOU OKAY?
THAT PUNCH... IT WOULD'VE RUPTURED A SUBMARINE HULL. TORPEDOMAN DIDN'T EVEN FLINCH. AND MY ARM...
MY ARM IS BROKEN.

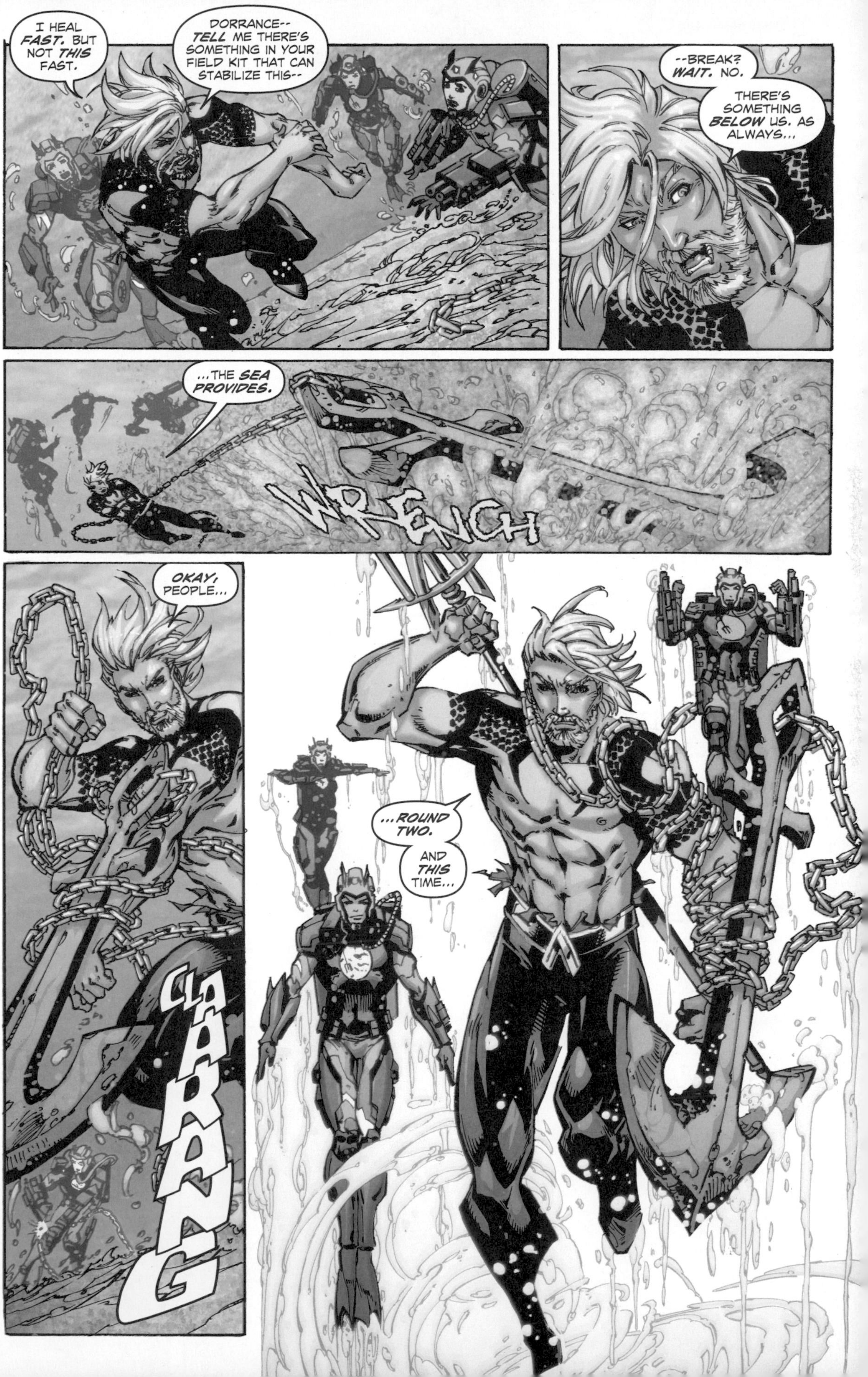

I HEAL *FAST.* BUT NOT *THIS* FAST.
DORRANCE-- *TELL* ME THERE'S SOMETHING IN YOUR FIELD KIT THAT CAN STABILIZE THIS--
--BREAK? *WAIT.* NO.
THERE'S SOMETHING *BELOW* US. AS ALWAYS...
...THE *SEA* PROVIDES.
WRENCH
OKAY, PEOPLE...
CLAAAANG
...ROUND TWO.
AND *THIS* TIME...

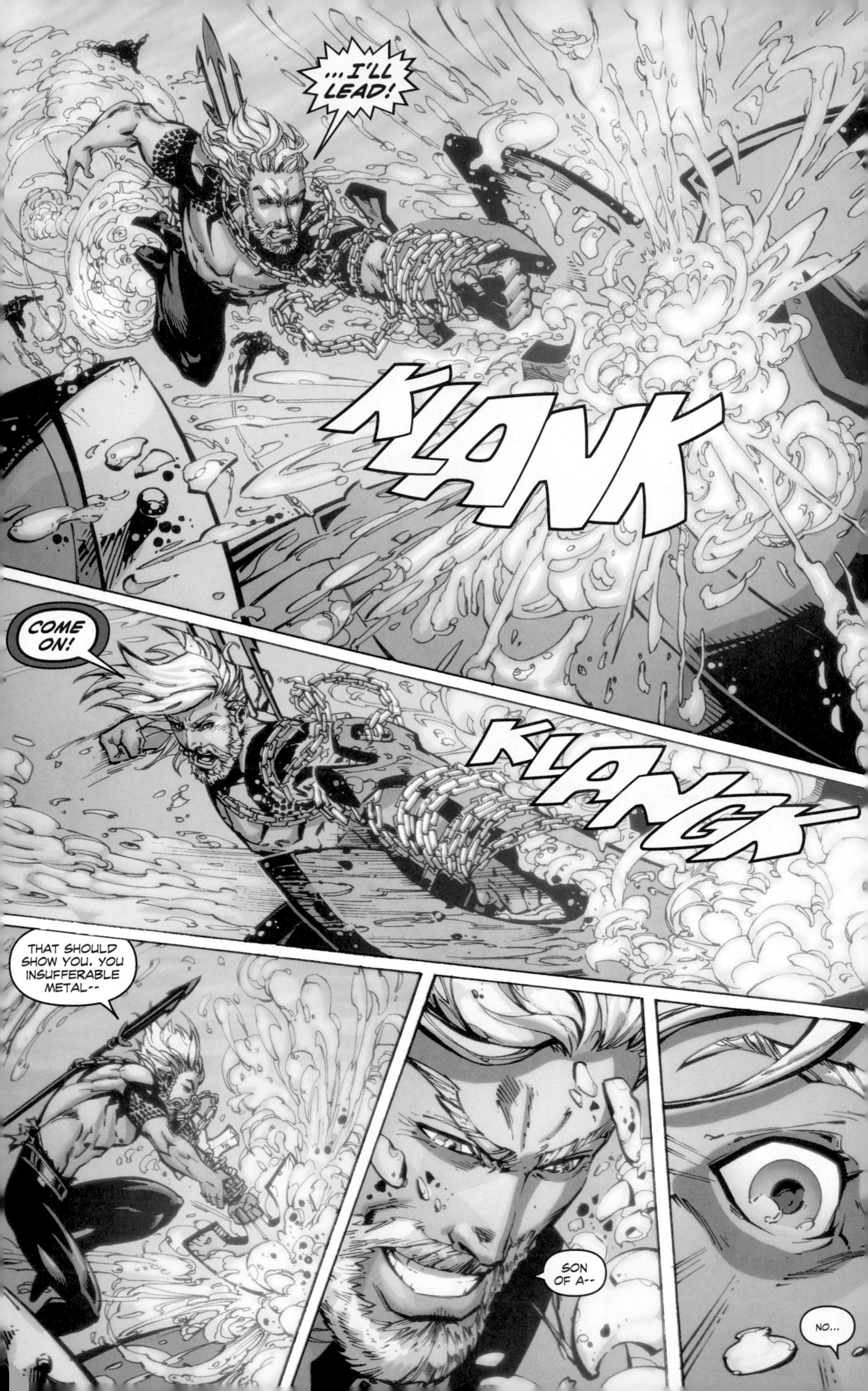
...I'LL LEAD!
KLANK
COME ON!
KLANGK
THAT SHOULD SHOW YOU. YOU INSUFFERABLE METAL--
SON OF A--
NO...

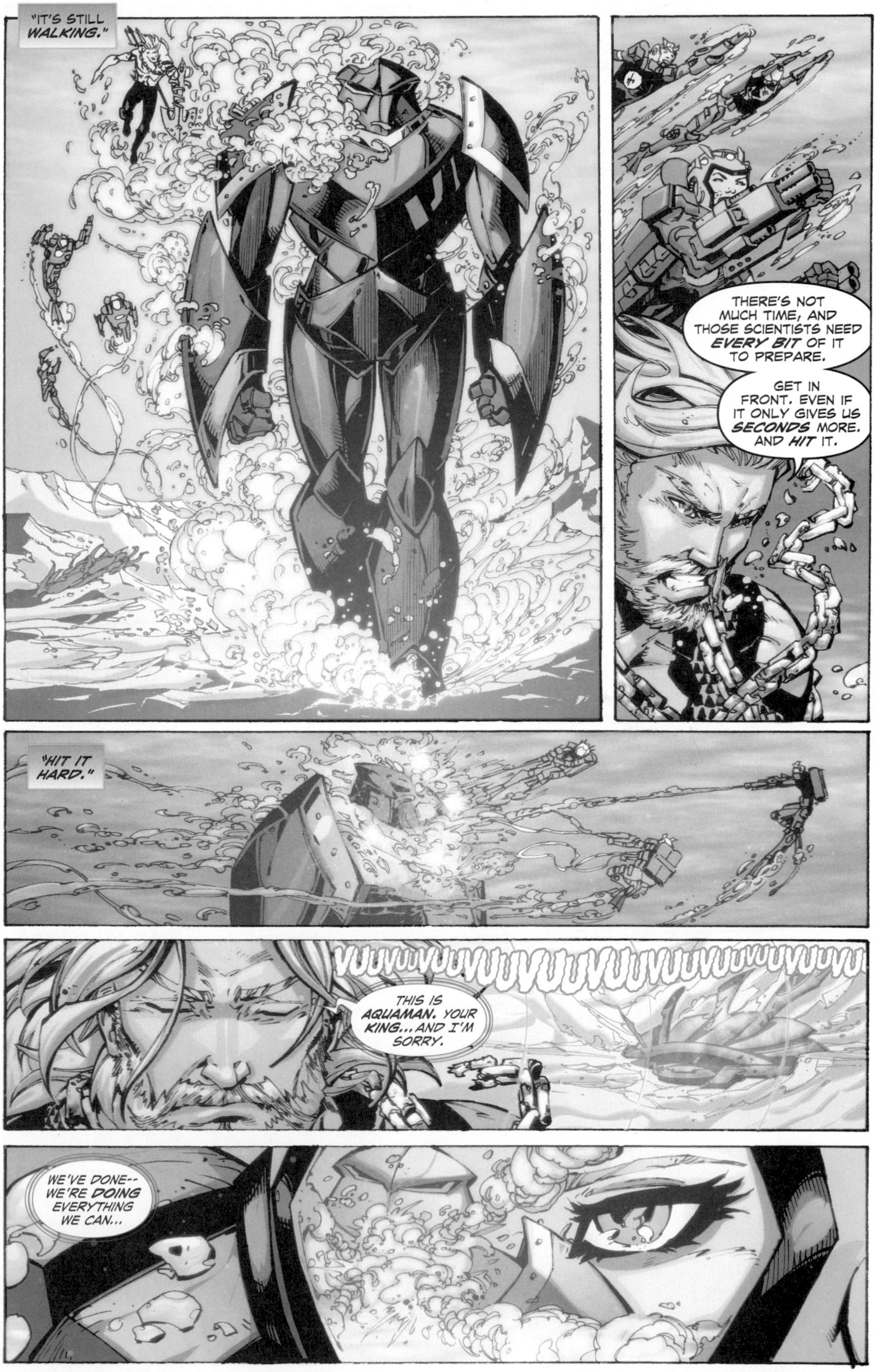
"IT'S STILL WALKING."
THERE'S NOT MUCH TIME, AND THOSE SCIENTISTS NEED EVERY BIT OF IT TO PREPARE.
GET IN FRONT. EVEN IF IT ONLY GIVES US SECONDS MORE. AND HIT IT.
"HIT IT HARD."
VUUVUUVUUVUUVUUVUUVUUVUUVUUVUUVUUV
THIS IS AQUAMAN. YOUR KING... AND I'M SORRY.
WE'VE DONE-- WE'RE DOING EVERYTHING WE CAN...

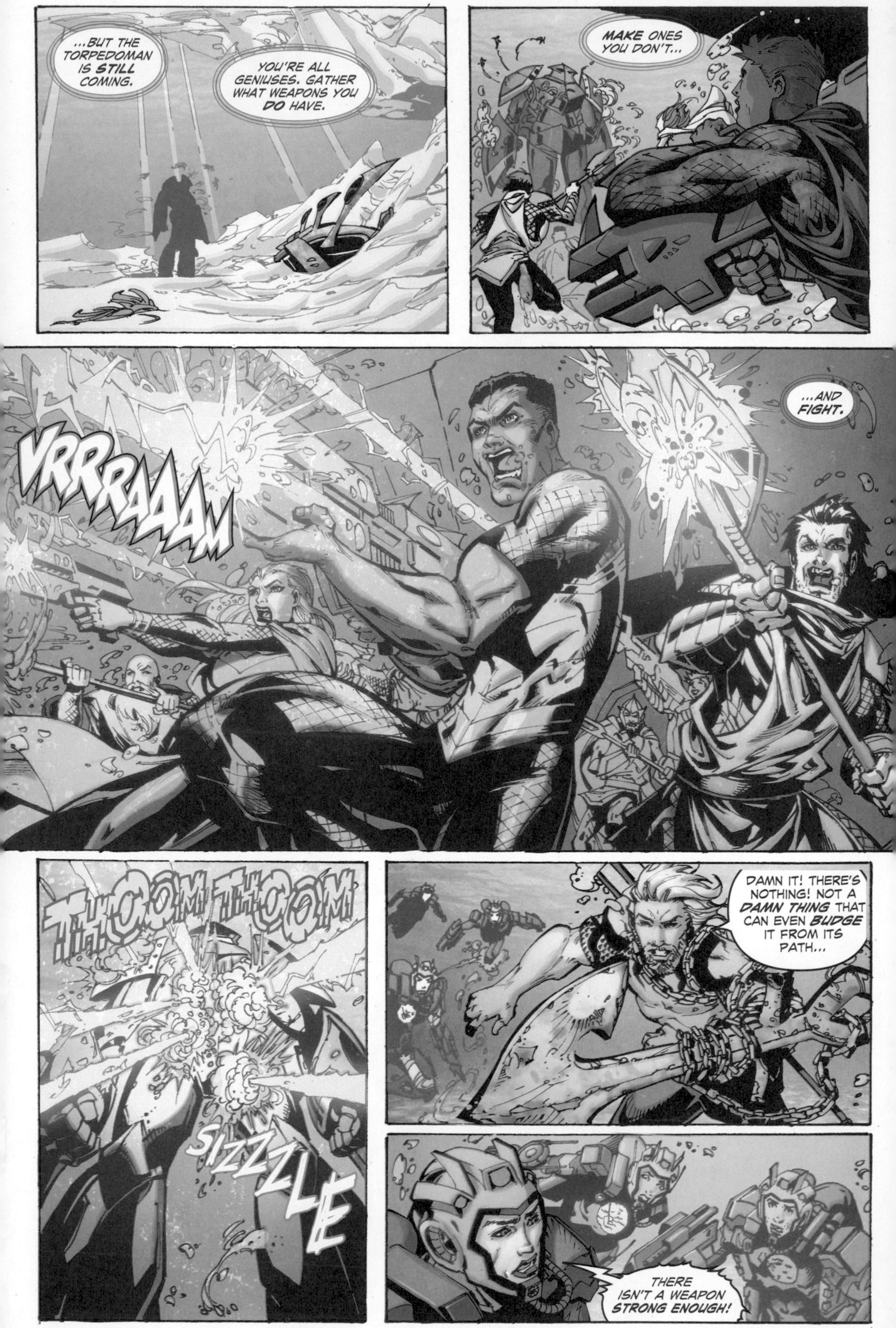
...BUT THE TORPEDOMAN IS STILL COMING.
YOU'RE ALL GENIUSES. GATHER WHAT WEAPONS YOU DO HAVE.
MAKE ONES YOU DON'T...
VRRRAAAM
...AND FIGHT.
THOOM THOOM
SIZZZLE
DAMN IT! THERE'S NOTHING! NOT A DAMN THING THAT CAN EVEN BUDGE IT FROM ITS PATH...
THERE ISN'T A WEAPON STRONG ENOUGH!

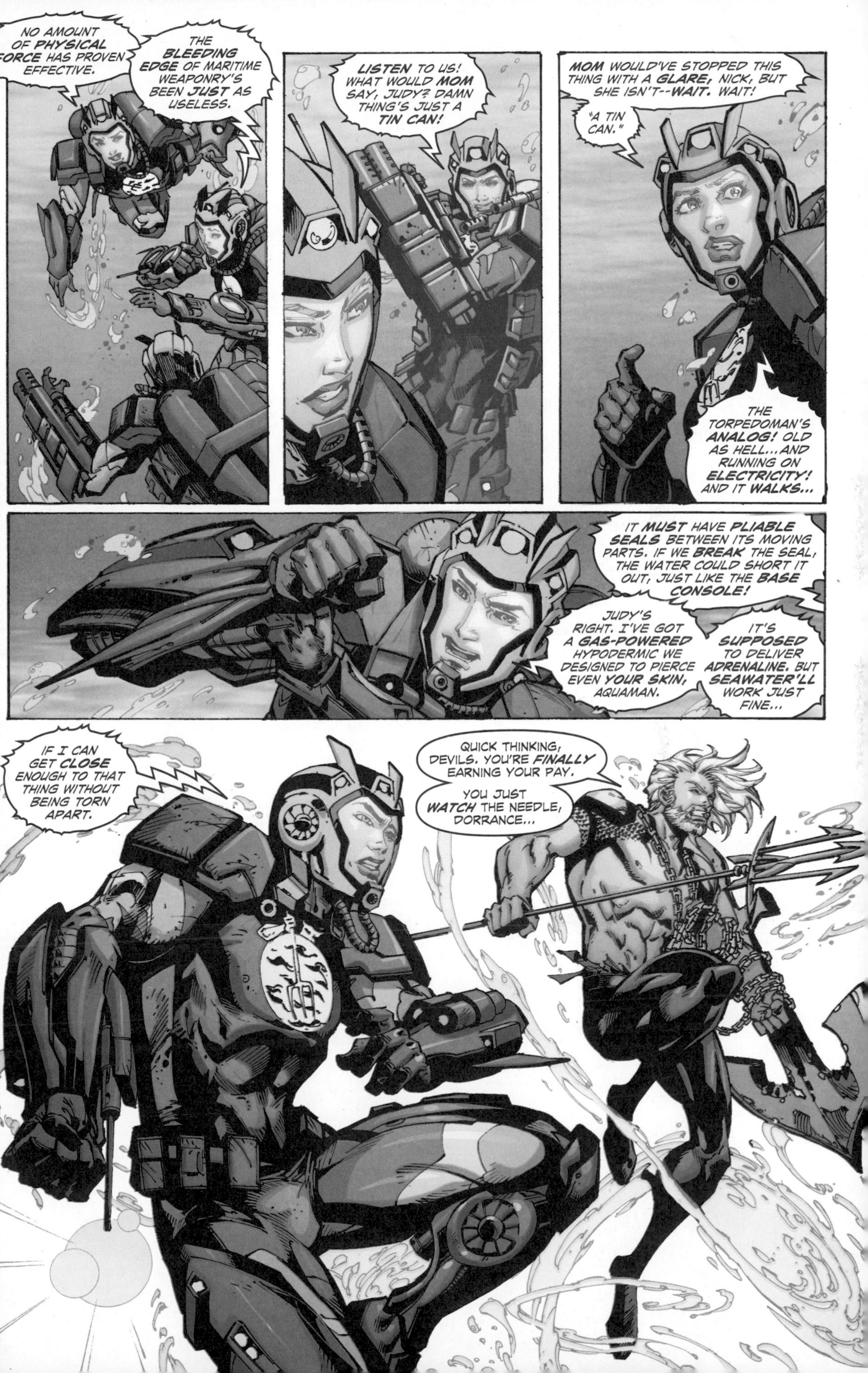
NO AMOUNT OF PHYSICAL FORCE HAS PROVEN EFFECTIVE.
THE BLEEDING EDGE OF MARITIME WEAPONRY'S BEEN JUST AS USELESS.
LISTEN TO US! WHAT WOULD MOM SAY, JUDY? DAMN THING'S JUST A TIN CAN!
MOM WOULD'VE STOPPED THIS THING WITH A GLARE, NICK, BUT SHE ISN'T--WAIT. WAIT!
"A TIN CAN."
THE TORPEDOMAN'S ANALOG! OLD AS HELL...AND RUNNING ON ELECTRICITY! AND IT WALKS...
IT MUST HAVE PLIABLE SEALS BETWEEN ITS MOVING PARTS. IF WE BREAK THE SEAL, THE WATER COULD SHORT IT OUT, JUST LIKE THE BASE CONSOLE!
JUDY'S RIGHT. I'VE GOT A GAS-POWERED HYPODERMIC WE DESIGNED TO PIERCE EVEN YOUR SKIN, AQUAMAN.
IT'S SUPPOSED TO DELIVER ADRENALINE. BUT SEAWATER'LL WORK JUST FINE...
IF I CAN GET CLOSE ENOUGH TO THAT THING WITHOUT BEING TORN APART.
QUICK THINKING, DEVILS. YOU'RE FINALLY EARNING YOUR PAY.
YOU JUST WATCH THE NEEDLE, DORRANCE...

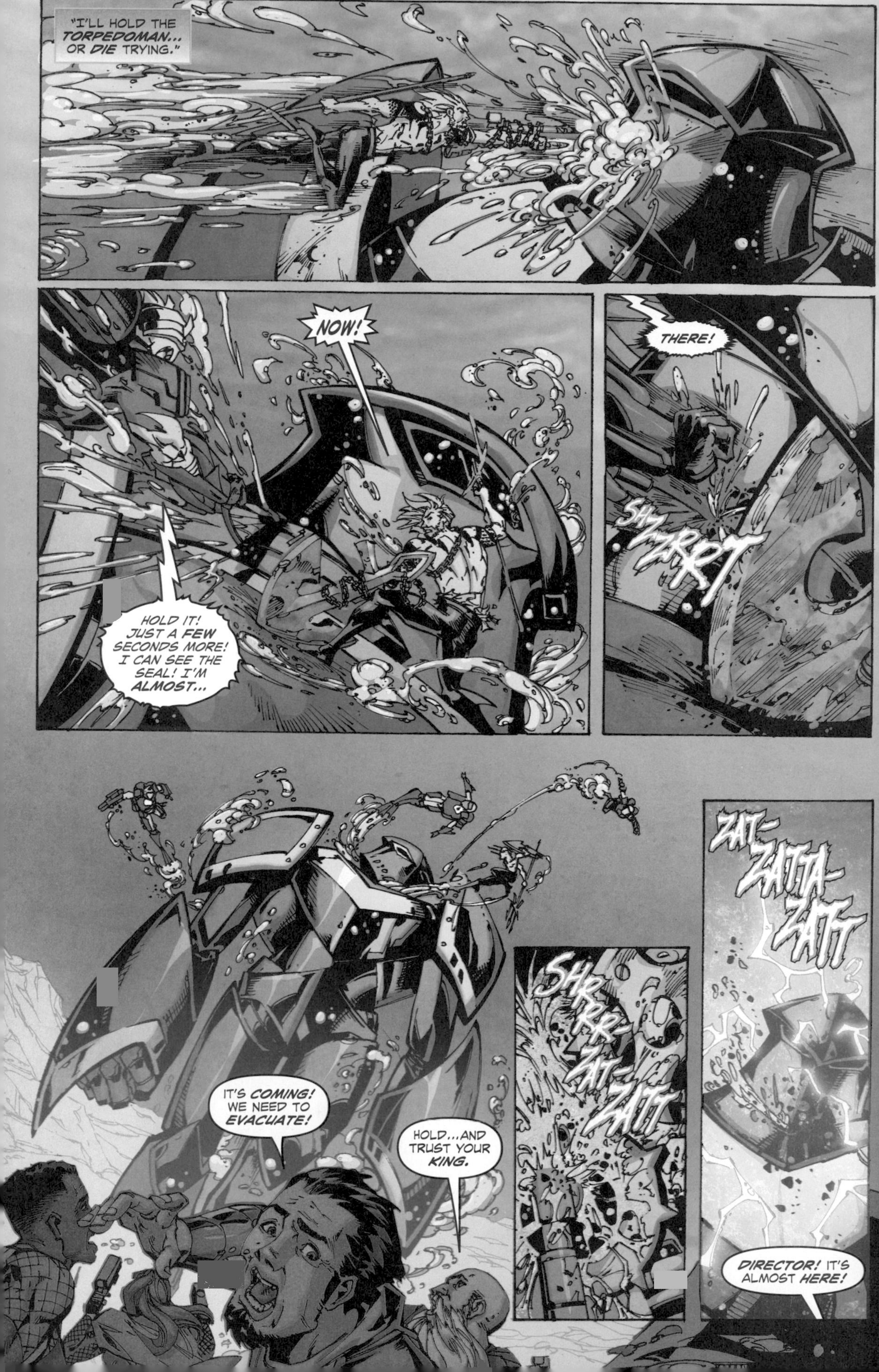
"I'LL HOLD THE TORPEDOMAN... OR DIE TRYING."
NOW!
HOLD IT! JUST A FEW SECONDS MORE! I CAN SEE THE SEAL! I'M ALMOST...
THERE!
SHZZRRRT
IT'S COMING! WE NEED TO EVACUATE!
HOLD...AND TRUST YOUR KING.
SHRRR-ZAT-ZATT
ZAT-ZATTA-ZATT
DIRECTOR! IT'S ALMOST HERE!

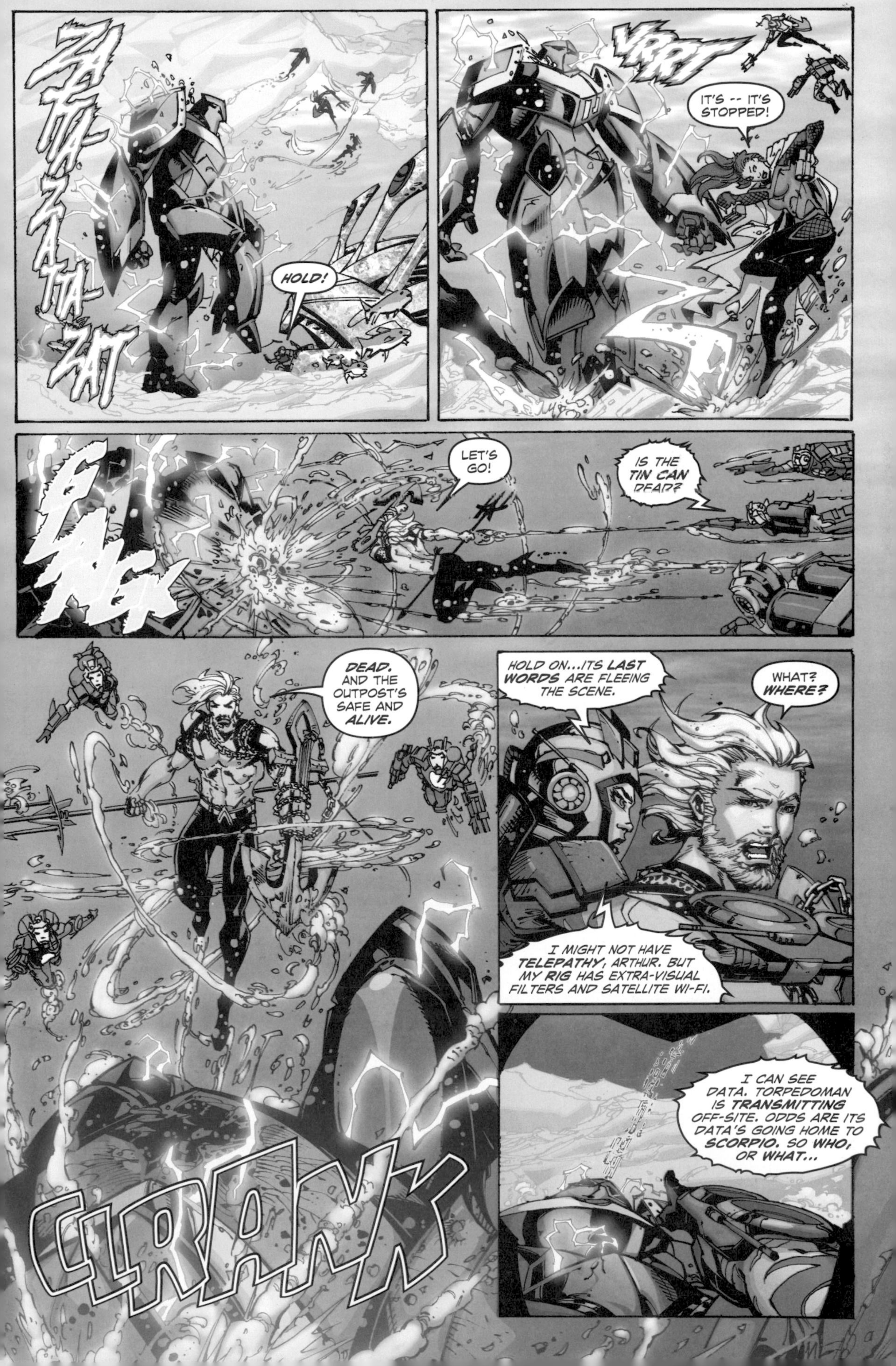

ZATTA-ZATTA-ZATTA-ZAT
HOLD!
VRRT
IT'S -- IT'S STOPPED!
KLANGK
LET'S GO!
IS THE TIN CAN DEAD?
DEAD. AND THE OUTPOST'S SAFE AND ALIVE.
HOLD ON...ITS LAST WORDS ARE FLEEING THE SCENE.
WHAT? WHERE?
I MIGHT NOT HAVE TELEPATHY, ARTHUR. BUT MY RIG HAS EXTRA-VISUAL FILTERS AND SATELLITE WI-FI.
I CAN SEE DATA. TORPEDOMAN IS TRANSMITTING OFF-SITE. ODDS ARE ITS DATA'S GOING HOME TO SCORPIO. SO WHO, OR WHAT...
CLRANK

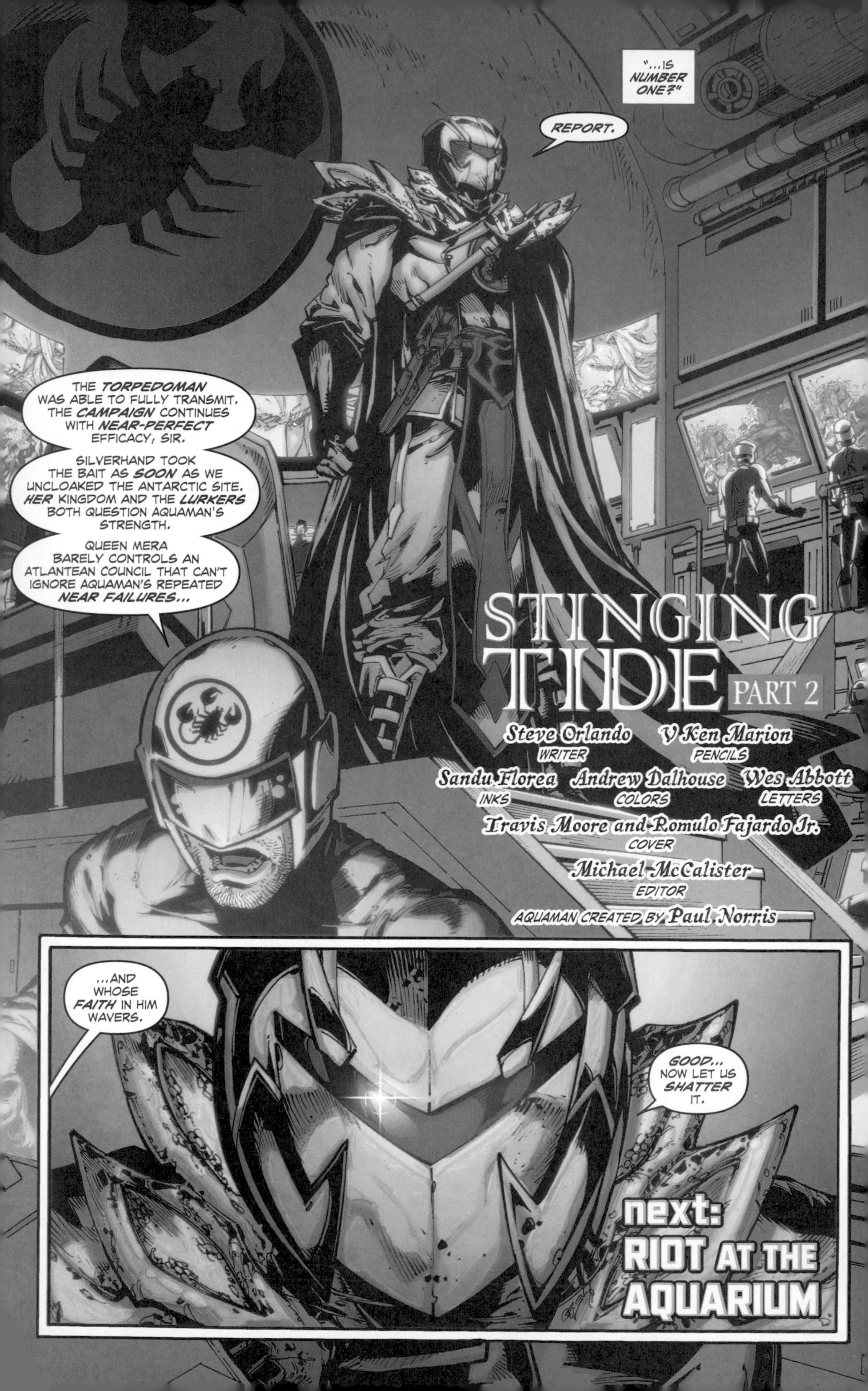
"...IS NUMBER ONE?"
REPORT.
THE TORPEDOMAN WAS ABLE TO FULLY TRANSMIT. THE CAMPAIGN CONTINUES WITH NEAR-PERFECT EFFICACY, SIR.
SILVERHAND TOOK THE BAIT AS SOON AS WE UNCLOAKED THE ANTARCTIC SITE. HER KINGDOM AND THE LURKERS BOTH QUESTION AQUAMAN'S STRENGTH.
QUEEN MERA BARELY CONTROLS AN ATLANTEAN COUNCIL THAT CAN'T IGNORE AQUAMAN'S REPEATED NEAR FAILURES...
STINGING TIDE PART 2
Steve Orlando WRITER
V Ken Marion PENCILS
Sandu Florea INKS
Andrew Dalhouse COLORS
Wes Abbott LETTERS
Travis Moore and Romulo Fajardo Jr. COVER
Michael McCalister EDITOR
AQUAMAN CREATED BY Paul Norris
...AND WHOSE FAITH IN HIM WAVERS.
GOOD... NOW LET US SHATTER IT.
next: RIOT AT THE AQUARIUM

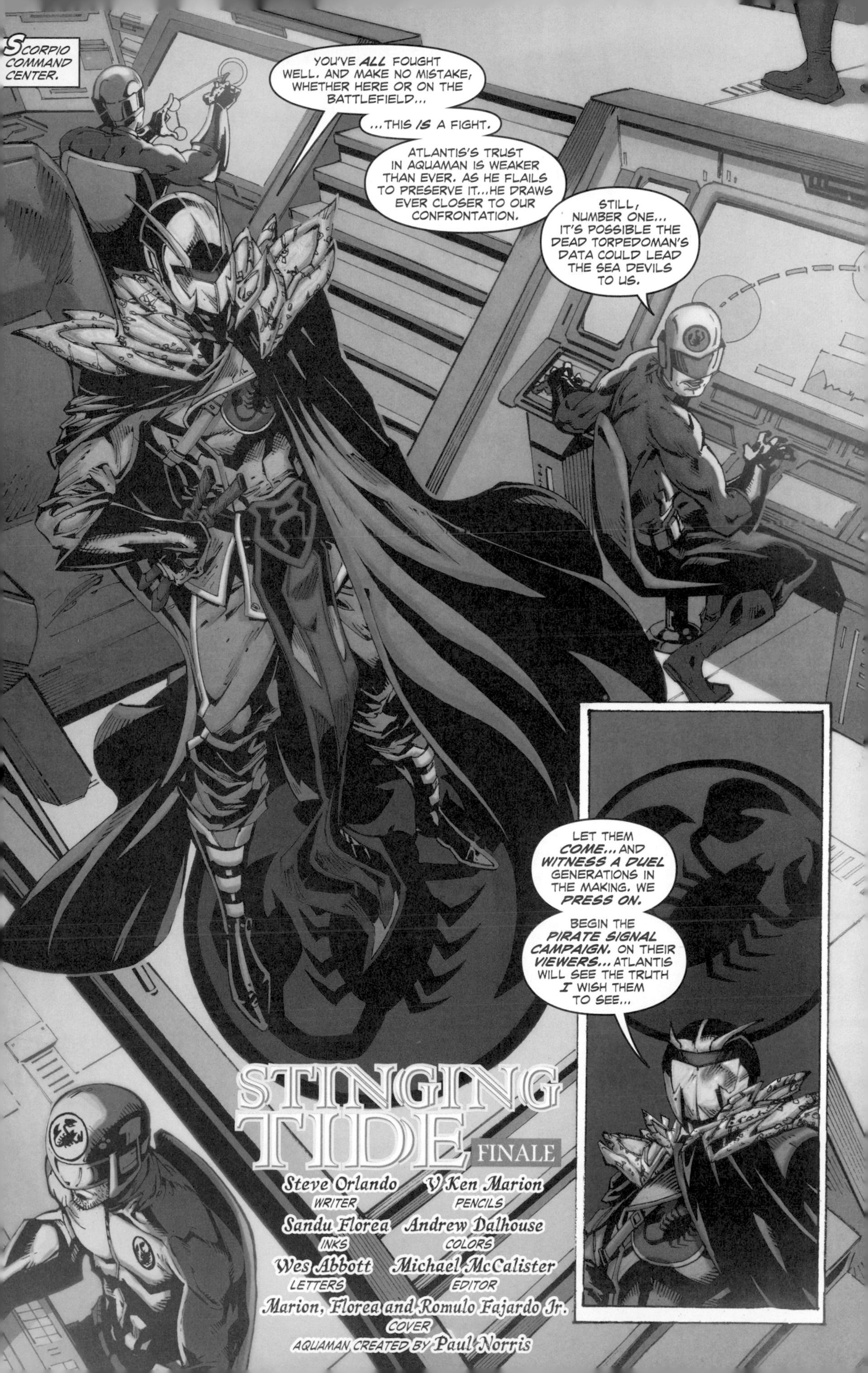
SCORPIO COMMAND CENTER.
YOU'VE ALL FOUGHT WELL. AND MAKE NO MISTAKE, WHETHER HERE OR ON THE BATTLEFIELD...
...THIS IS A FIGHT.
ATLANTIS'S TRUST IN AQUAMAN IS WEAKER THAN EVER. AS HE FLAILS TO PRESERVE IT...HE DRAWS EVER CLOSER TO OUR CONFRONTATION.
STILL, NUMBER ONE... IT'S POSSIBLE THE DEAD TORPEDOMAN'S DATA COULD LEAD THE SEA DEVILS TO US.
LET THEM COME...AND WITNESS A DUEL GENERATIONS IN THE MAKING. WE PRESS ON.
BEGIN THE PIRATE SIGNAL CAMPAIGN. ON THEIR VIEWERS...ATLANTIS WILL SEE THE TRUTH I WISH THEM TO SEE...
STINGING TIDE
FINALE
Steve Orlando WRITER
V Ken Marion PENCILS
Sandu Florea INKS
Andrew Dalhouse COLORS
Wes Abbott LETTERS
Michael McCalister EDITOR
Marion, Florea and Romulo Fajardo Jr. COVER
AQUAMAN CREATED BY Paul Norris

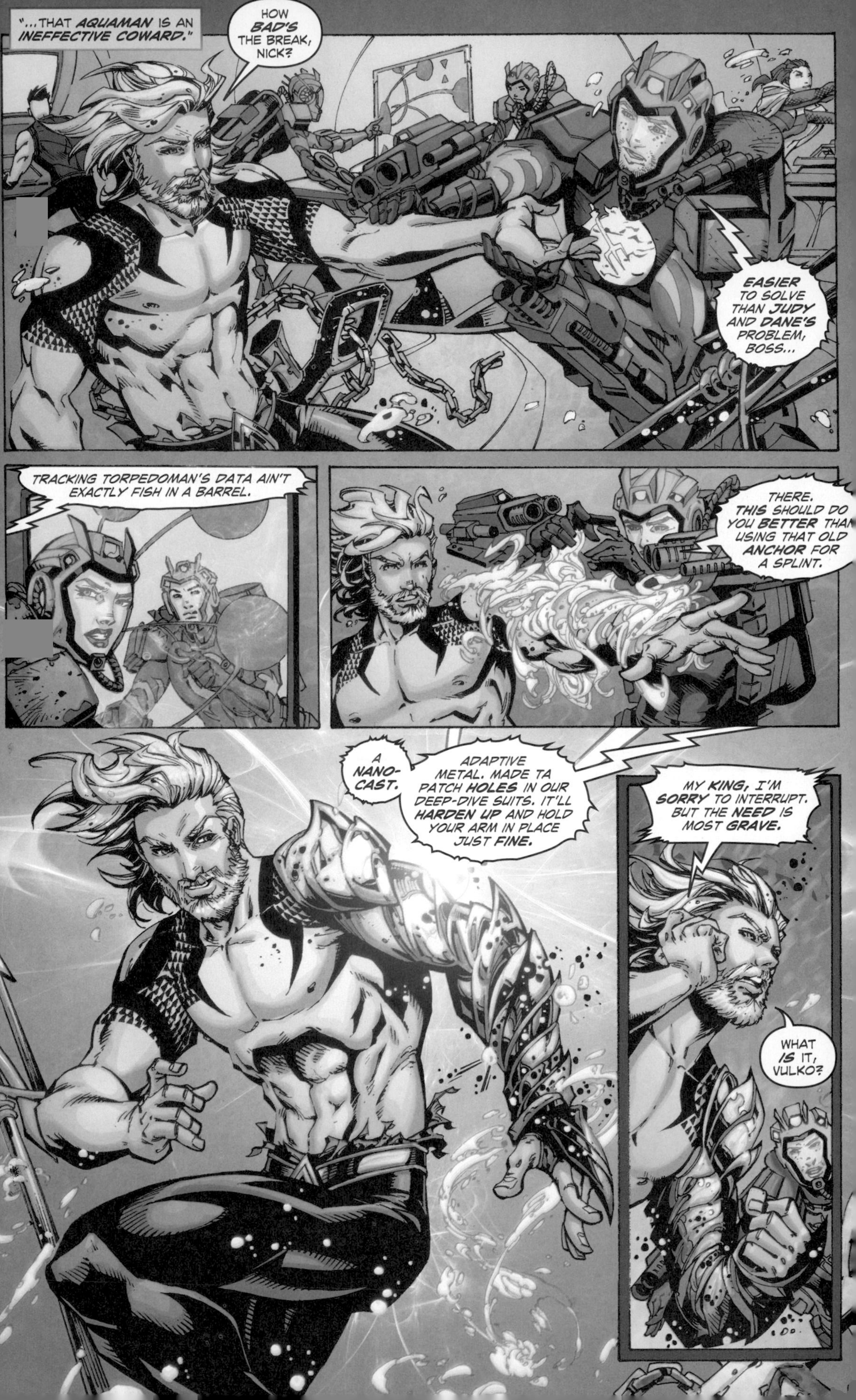
"...THAT AQUAMAN IS AN INEFFECTIVE COWARD."
HOW BAD'S THE BREAK, NICK?
EASIER TO SOLVE THAN JUDY AND DANE'S PROBLEM, BOSS...
TRACKING TORPEDOMAN'S DATA AIN'T EXACTLY FISH IN A BARREL.
THERE. THIS SHOULD DO YOU BETTER THAN USING THAT OLD ANCHOR FOR A SPLINT.
A NANO-CAST.
ADAPTIVE METAL. MADE TA PATCH HOLES IN OUR DEEP-DIVE SUITS. IT'LL HARDEN UP AND HOLD YOUR ARM IN PLACE JUST FINE.
MY KING, I'M SORRY TO INTERRUPT. BUT THE NEED IS MOST GRAVE.
WHAT IS IT, VULKO?

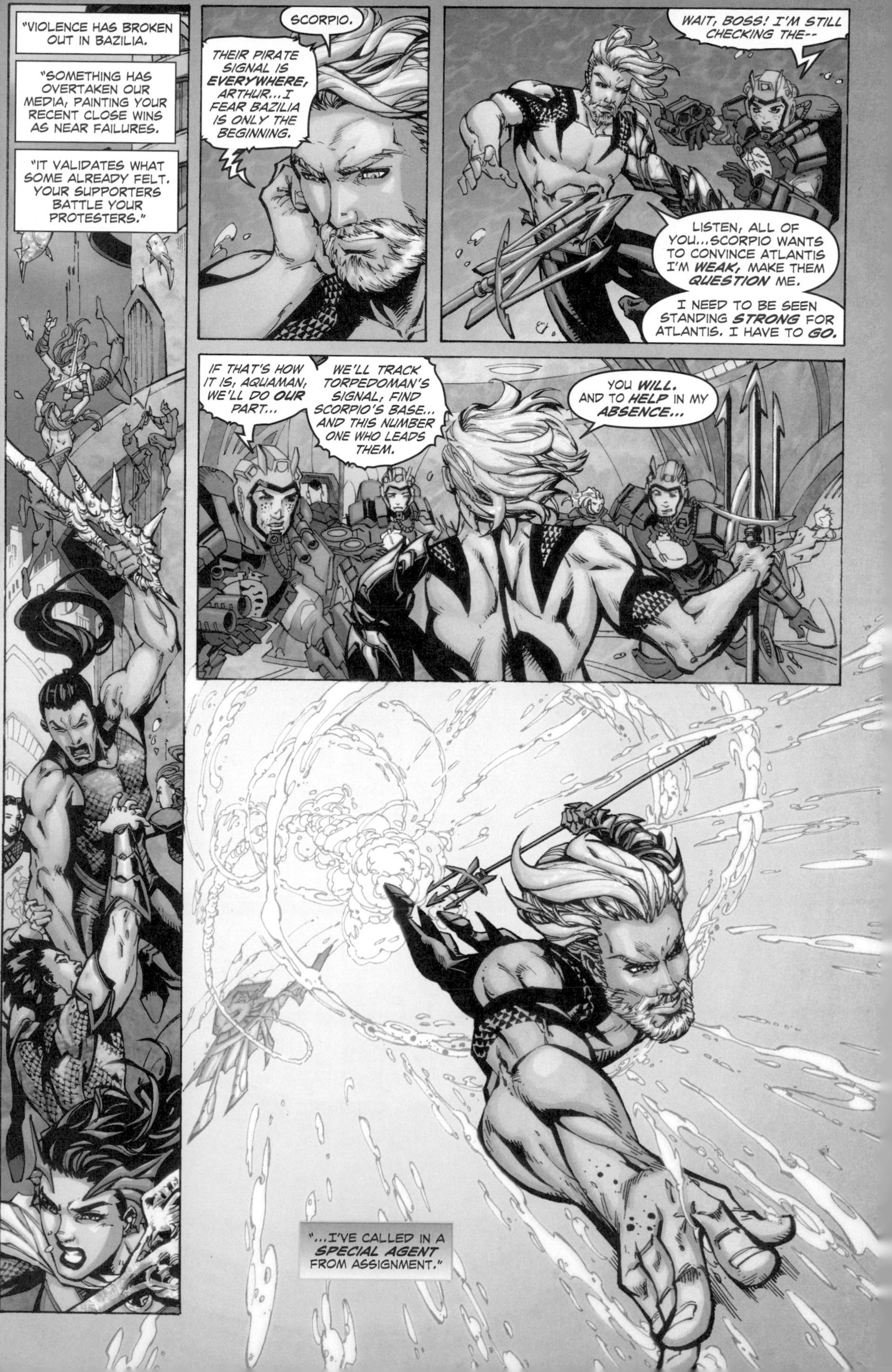
"VIOLENCE HAS BROKEN OUT IN BAZILIA.
"SOMETHING HAS OVERTAKEN OUR MEDIA, PAINTING YOUR RECENT CLOSE WINS AS NEAR FAILURES.
"IT VALIDATES WHAT SOME ALREADY FELT. YOUR SUPPORTERS BATTLE YOUR PROTESTERS."
SCORPIO.
THEIR PIRATE SIGNAL IS EVERYWHERE, ARTHUR...I FEAR BAZILIA IS ONLY THE BEGINNING.
WAIT, BOSS! I'M STILL CHECKING THE--
LISTEN, ALL OF YOU...SCORPIO WANTS TO CONVINCE ATLANTIS I'M WEAK, MAKE THEM QUESTION ME.
I NEED TO BE SEEN STANDING STRONG FOR ATLANTIS. I HAVE TO GO.
IF THAT'S HOW IT IS, AQUAMAN, WE'LL DO OUR PART...
WE'LL TRACK TORPEDOMAN'S SIGNAL, FIND SCORPIO'S BASE... AND THIS NUMBER ONE WHO LEADS THEM.
YOU WILL. AND TO HELP IN MY ABSENCE...
"...I'VE CALLED IN A SPECIAL AGENT FROM ASSIGNMENT."

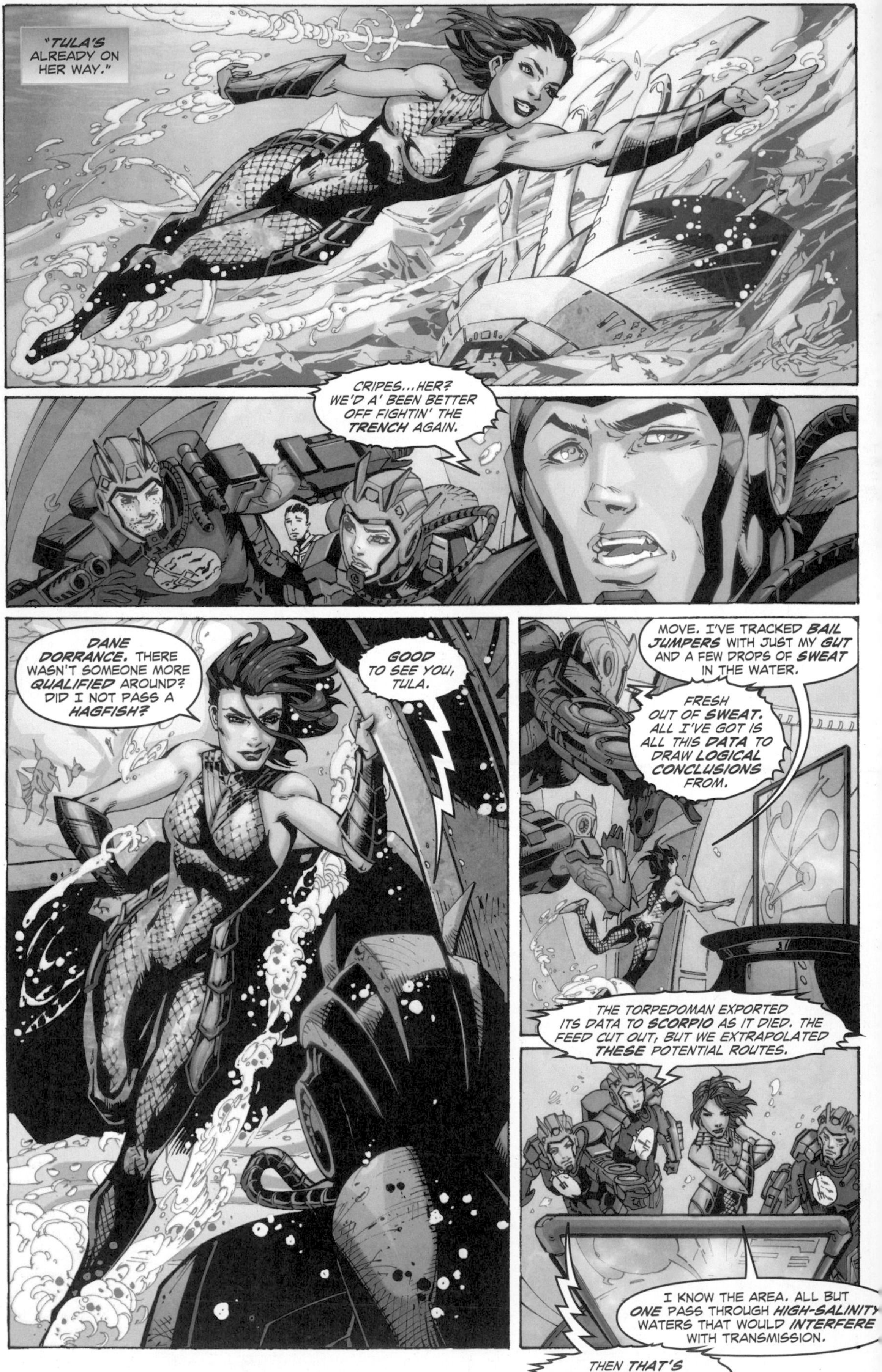
"TULA'S ALREADY ON HER WAY."
CRIPES...HER? WE'D A' BEEN BETTER OFF FIGHTIN' THE TRENCH AGAIN.
DANE DORRANCE. THERE WASN'T SOMEONE MORE QUALIFIED AROUND? DID I NOT PASS A HAGFISH?
GOOD TO SEE YOU, TULA.
MOVE. I'VE TRACKED BAIL JUMPERS WITH JUST MY GUT AND A FEW DROPS OF SWEAT IN THE WATER.
FRESH OUT OF SWEAT. ALL I'VE GOT IS ALL THIS DATA TO DRAW LOGICAL CONCLUSIONS FROM.
THE TORPEDOMAN EXPORTED ITS DATA TO SCORPIO AS IT DIED. THE FEED CUT OUT, BUT WE EXTRAPOLATED THESE POTENTIAL ROUTES.
I KNOW THE AREA. ALL BUT ONE PASS THROUGH HIGH-SALINITY WATERS THAT WOULD INTERFERE WITH TRANSMISSION.
THEN THAT'S THE ONE WE FOLLOW TO SCORPIO, TULA...

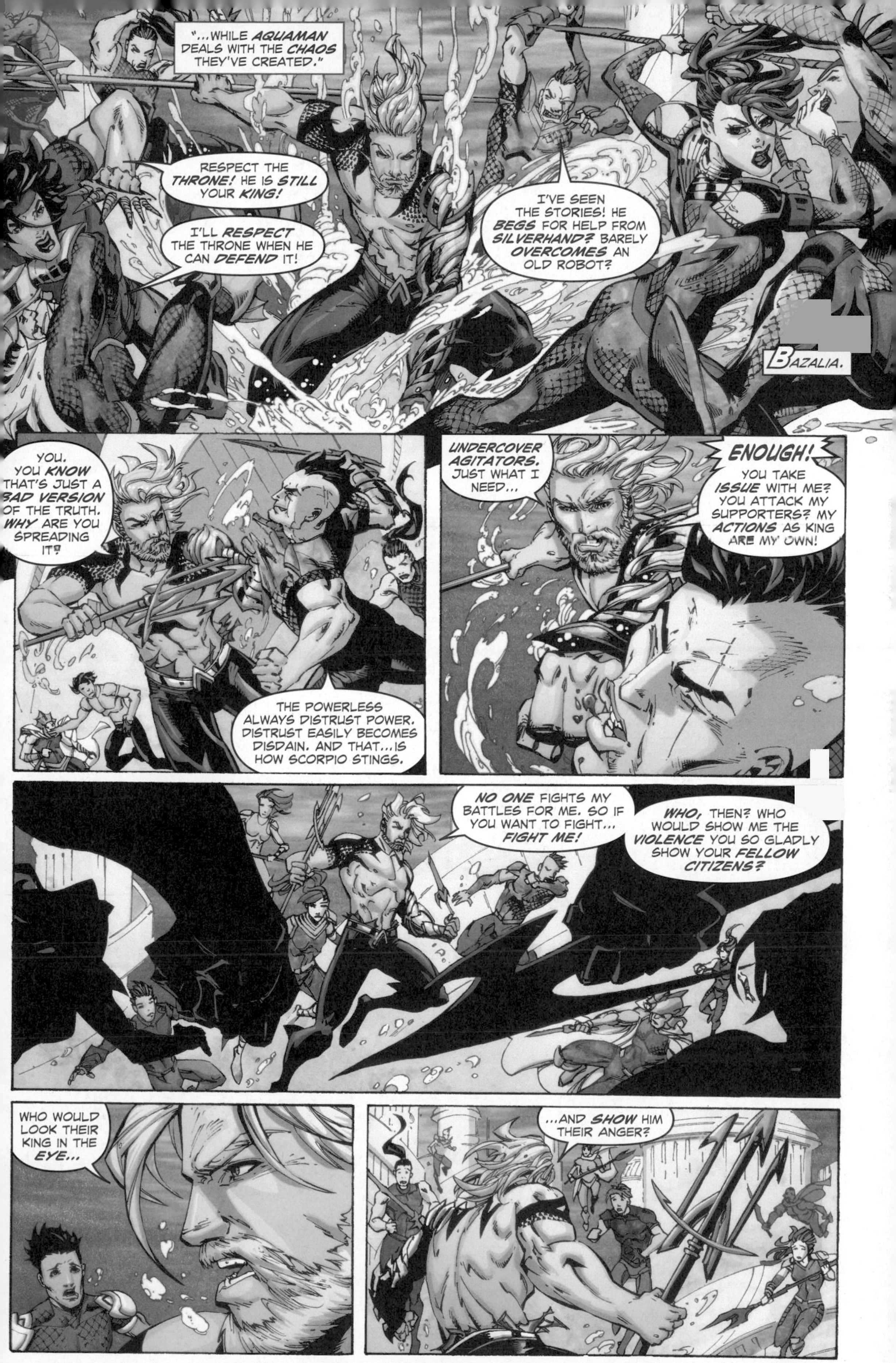

"...WHILE AQUAMAN DEALS WITH THE CHAOS THEY'VE CREATED."
RESPECT THE THRONE! HE IS STILL YOUR KING!
I'LL RESPECT THE THRONE WHEN HE CAN DEFEND IT!
I'VE SEEN THE STORIES! HE BEGS FOR HELP FROM SILVERHAND? BARELY OVERCOMES AN OLD ROBOT?
BAZALIA.
YOU. YOU KNOW THAT'S JUST A BAD VERSION OF THE TRUTH. WHY ARE YOU SPREADING IT?
THE POWERLESS ALWAYS DISTRUST POWER. DISTRUST EASILY BECOMES DISDAIN. AND THAT...IS HOW SCORPIO STINGS.
UNDERCOVER AGITATORS. JUST WHAT I NEED...
ENOUGH!
YOU TAKE ISSUE WITH ME? YOU ATTACK MY SUPPORTERS? MY ACTIONS AS KING ARE MY OWN!
NO ONE FIGHTS MY BATTLES FOR ME. SO IF YOU WANT TO FIGHT... FIGHT ME!
WHO, THEN? WHO WOULD SHOW ME THE VIOLENCE YOU SO GLADLY SHOW YOUR FELLOW CITIZENS?
WHO WOULD LOOK THEIR KING IN THE EYE...
...AND SHOW HIM THEIR ANGER?

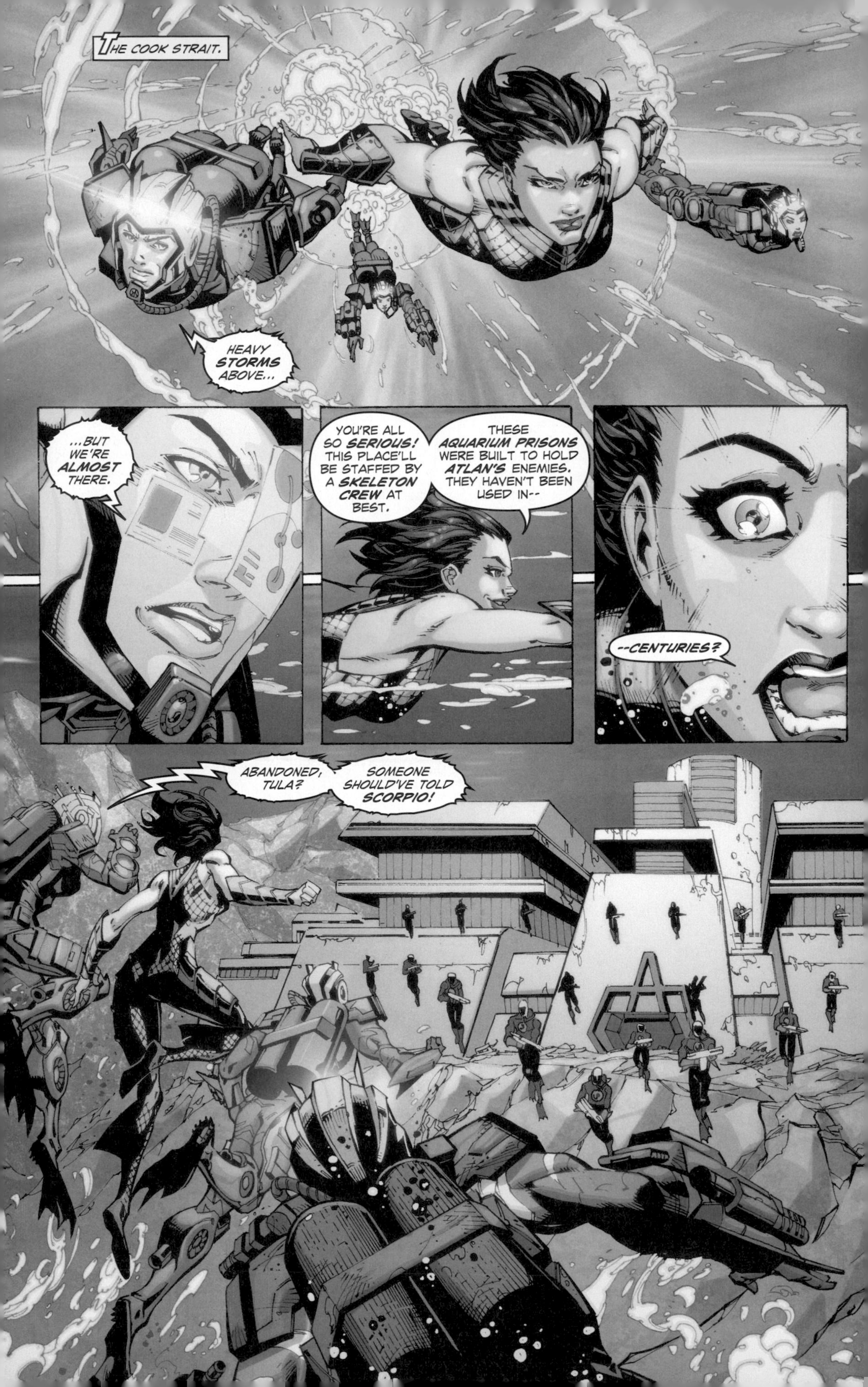
THE COOK STRAIT.
HEAVY STORMS ABOVE...
...BUT WE'RE ALMOST THERE.
YOU'RE ALL SO SERIOUS! THIS PLACE'LL BE STAFFED BY A SKELETON CREW AT BEST.
THESE AQUARIUM PRISONS WERE BUILT TO HOLD ATLAN'S ENEMIES. THEY HAVEN'T BEEN USED IN--
--CENTURIES?
ABANDONED, TULA?
SOMEONE SHOULD'VE TOLD SCORPIO!

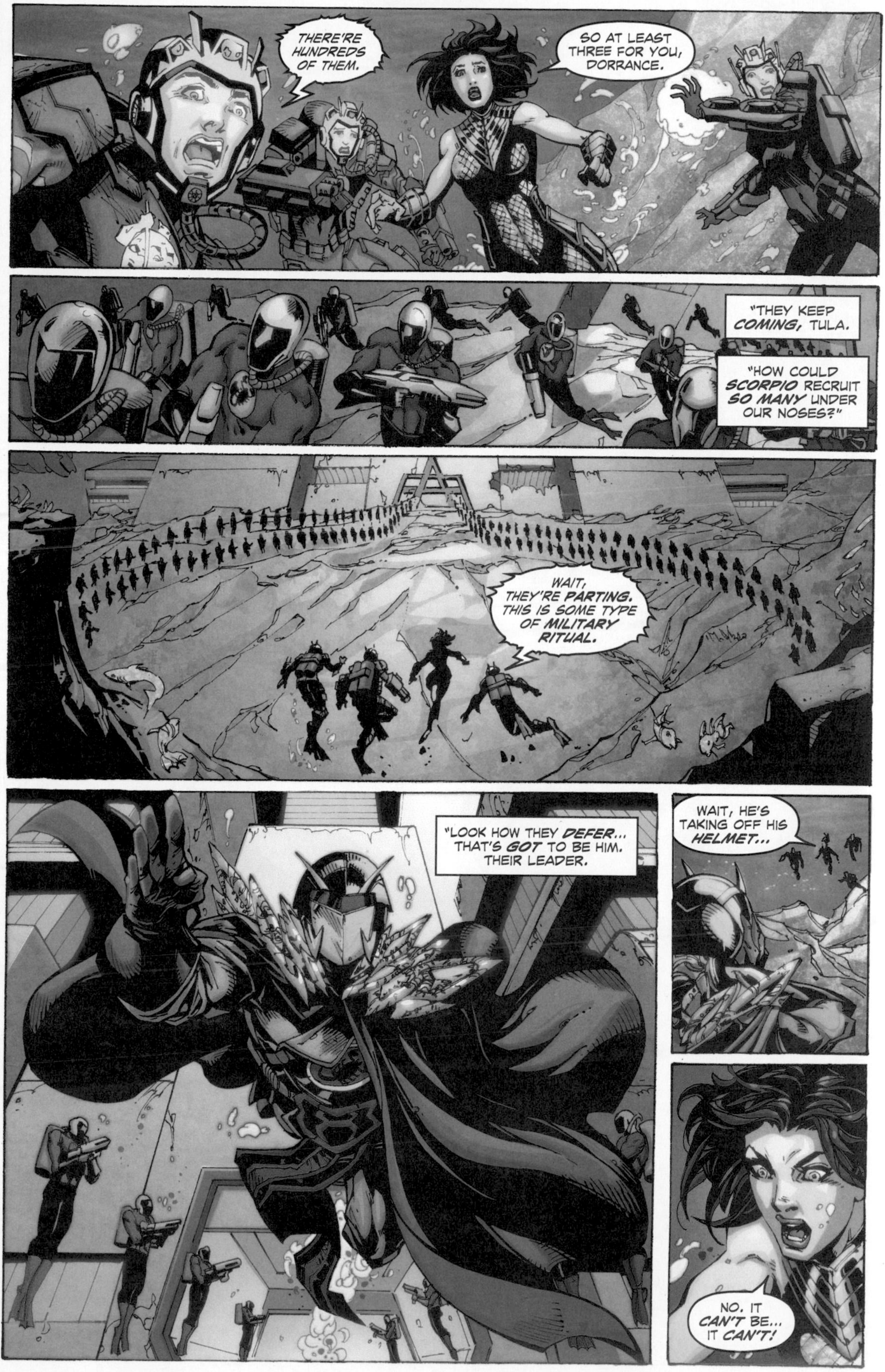
THERE'RE HUNDREDS OF THEM.
SO AT LEAST THREE FOR YOU, DORRANCE.
"THEY KEEP COMING, TULA.
"HOW COULD SCORPIO RECRUIT SO MANY UNDER OUR NOSES?"
WAIT, THEY'RE PARTING. THIS IS SOME TYPE OF MILITARY RITUAL.
"LOOK HOW THEY DEFER... THAT'S GOT TO BE HIM. THEIR LEADER.
WAIT, HE'S TAKING OFF HIS HELMET...
NO. IT CAN'T BE... IT CAN'T!

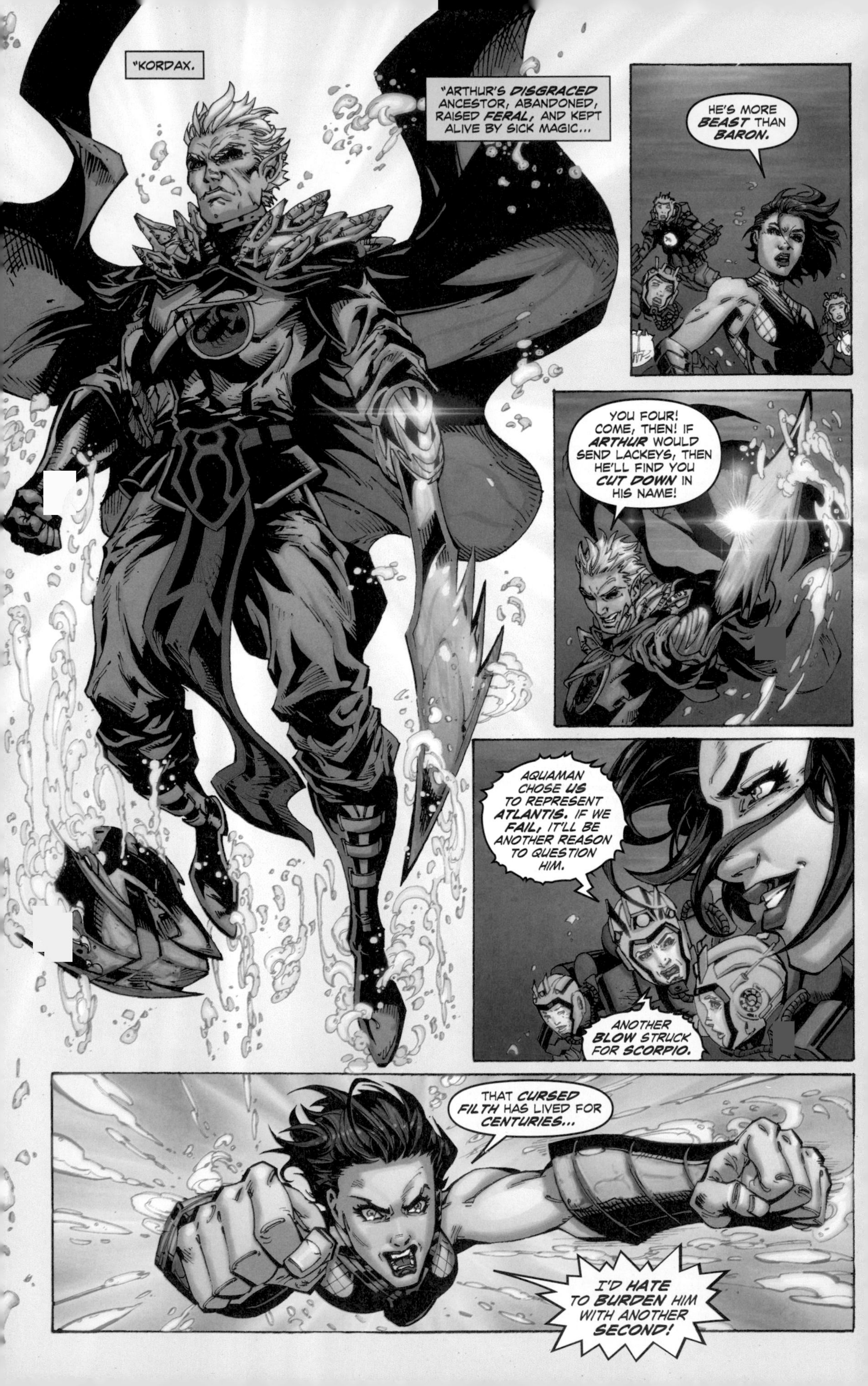
"KORDAX.
"ARTHUR'S DISGRACED ANCESTOR, ABANDONED, RAISED FERAL, AND KEPT ALIVE BY SICK MAGIC...
HE'S MORE BEAST THAN BARON.
YOU FOUR! COME, THEN! IF ARTHUR WOULD SEND LACKEYS, THEN HE'LL FIND YOU CUT DOWN IN HIS NAME!
AQUAMAN CHOSE US TO REPRESENT ATLANTIS. IF WE FAIL, IT'LL BE ANOTHER REASON TO QUESTION HIM.
ANOTHER BLOW STRUCK FOR SCORPIO.
THAT CURSED FILTH HAS LIVED FOR CENTURIES...
I'D HATE TO BURDEN HIM WITH ANOTHER SECOND!

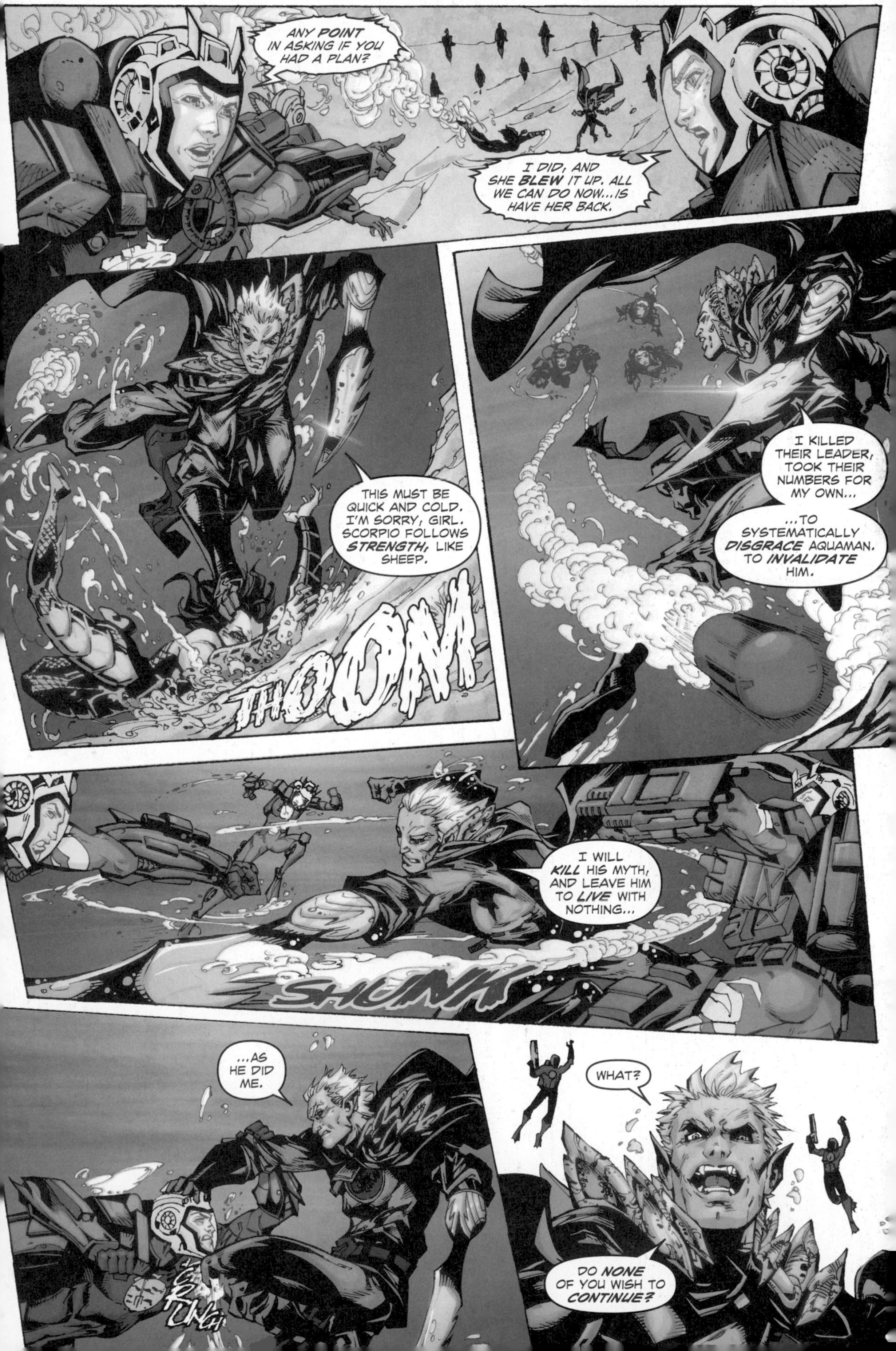
ANY POINT IN ASKING IF YOU HAD A PLAN?
I DID, AND SHE BLEW IT UP. ALL WE CAN DO NOW...IS HAVE HER BACK.
THIS MUST BE QUICK AND COLD. I'M SORRY, GIRL. SCORPIO FOLLOWS STRENGTH, LIKE SHEEP.
THOOM
I KILLED THEIR LEADER, TOOK THEIR NUMBERS FOR MY OWN...
...TO SYSTEMATICALLY DISGRACE AQUAMAN. TO INVALIDATE HIM.
I WILL KILL HIS MYTH, AND LEAVE HIM TO LIVE WITH NOTHING...
SHUNK
...AS HE DID ME.
SCRUNCH
WHAT?
DO NONE OF YOU WISH TO CONTINUE?

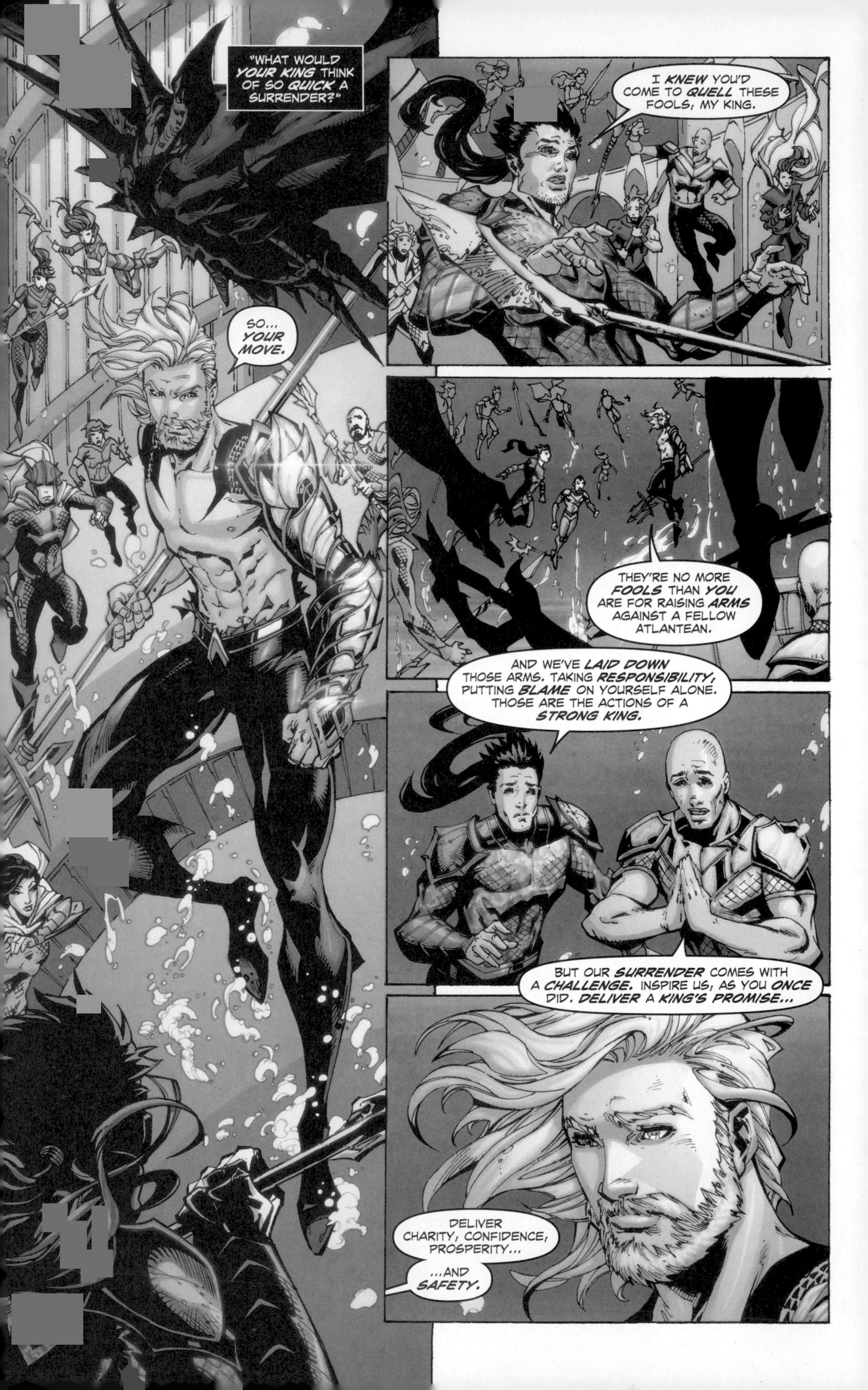
"WHAT WOULD YOUR KING THINK OF SO QUICK A SURRENDER?"
SO... YOUR MOVE.
I KNEW YOU'D COME TO QUELL THESE FOOLS, MY KING.
THEY'RE NO MORE FOOLS THAN YOU ARE FOR RAISING ARMS AGAINST A FELLOW ATLANTEAN.
AND WE'VE LAID DOWN THOSE ARMS. TAKING RESPONSIBILITY, PUTTING BLAME ON YOURSELF ALONE. THOSE ARE THE ACTIONS OF A STRONG KING.
BUT OUR SURRENDER COMES WITH A CHALLENGE. INSPIRE US, AS YOU ONCE DID. DELIVER A KING'S PROMISE...
DELIVER CHARITY, CONFIDENCE, PROSPERITY...
...AND SAFETY.

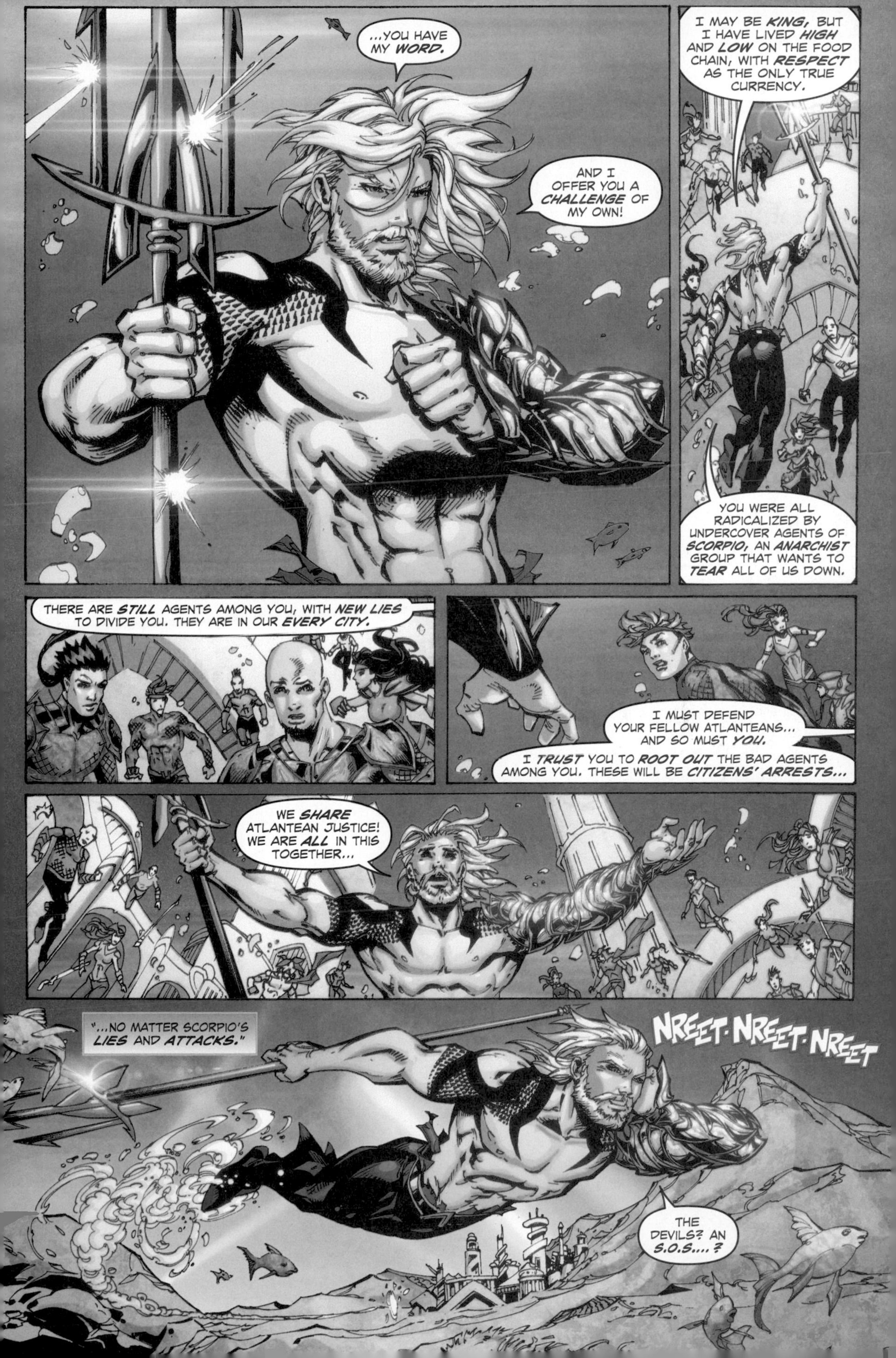
...YOU HAVE MY WORD.
AND I OFFER YOU A CHALLENGE OF MY OWN!
I MAY BE KING, BUT I HAVE LIVED HIGH AND LOW ON THE FOOD CHAIN, WITH RESPECT AS THE ONLY TRUE CURRENCY.
YOU WERE ALL RADICALIZED BY UNDERCOVER AGENTS OF SCORPIO, AN ANARCHIST GROUP THAT WANTS TO TEAR ALL OF US DOWN.
THERE ARE STILL AGENTS AMONG YOU, WITH NEW LIES TO DIVIDE YOU. THEY ARE IN OUR EVERY CITY.
I MUST DEFEND YOUR FELLOW ATLANTEANS... AND SO MUST YOU.
I TRUST YOU TO ROOT OUT THE BAD AGENTS AMONG YOU. THESE WILL BE CITIZENS' ARRESTS...
WE SHARE ATLANTEAN JUSTICE! WE ARE ALL IN THIS TOGETHER...
"...NO MATTER SCORPIO'S LIES AND ATTACKS."
NREET-NREET-NREET
THE DEVILS? AN S.O.S....?

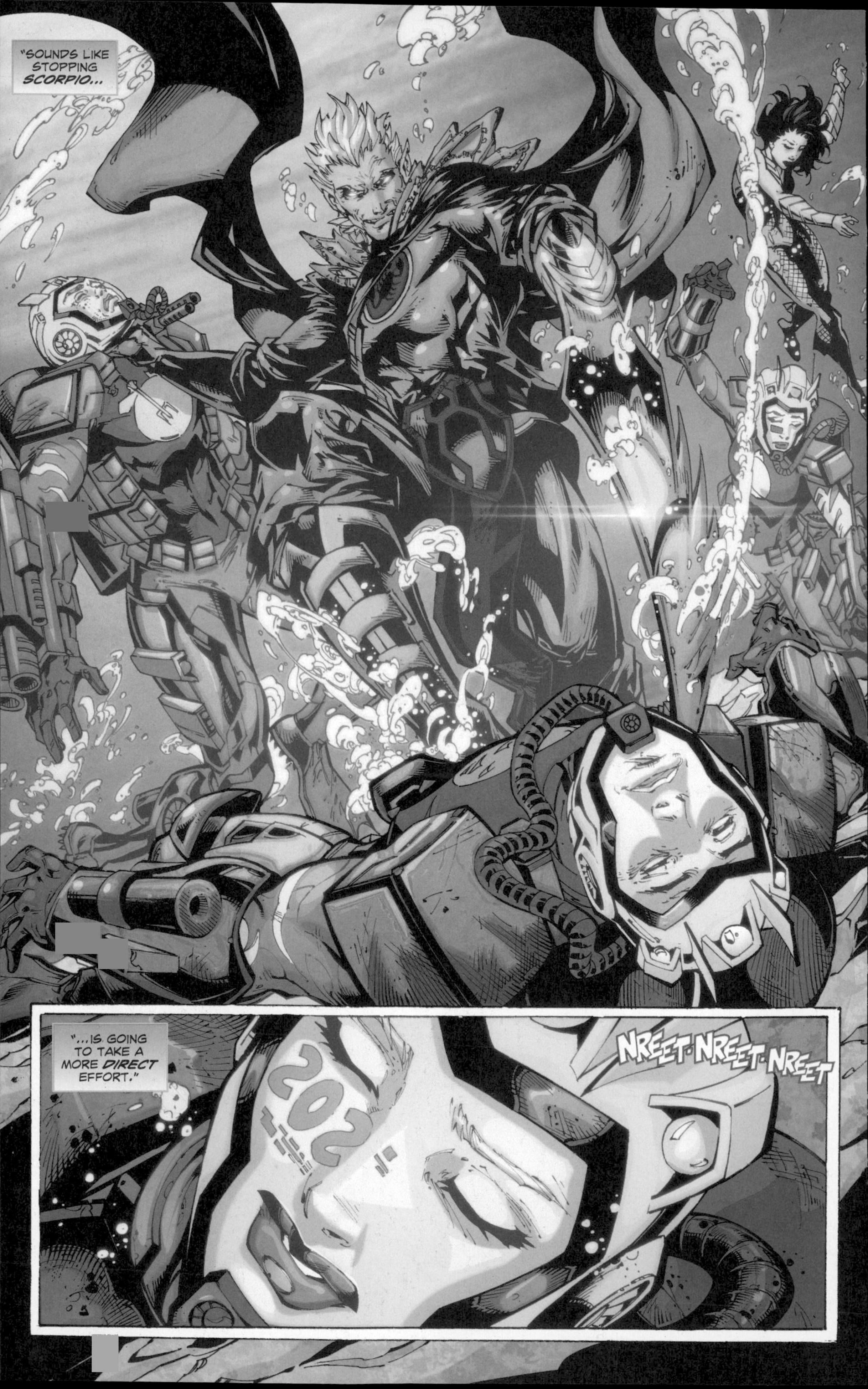
"SOUNDS LIKE STOPPING *SCORPIO*...
"...IS GOING TO TAKE A MORE *DIRECT* EFFORT."
NREET NREET NREET

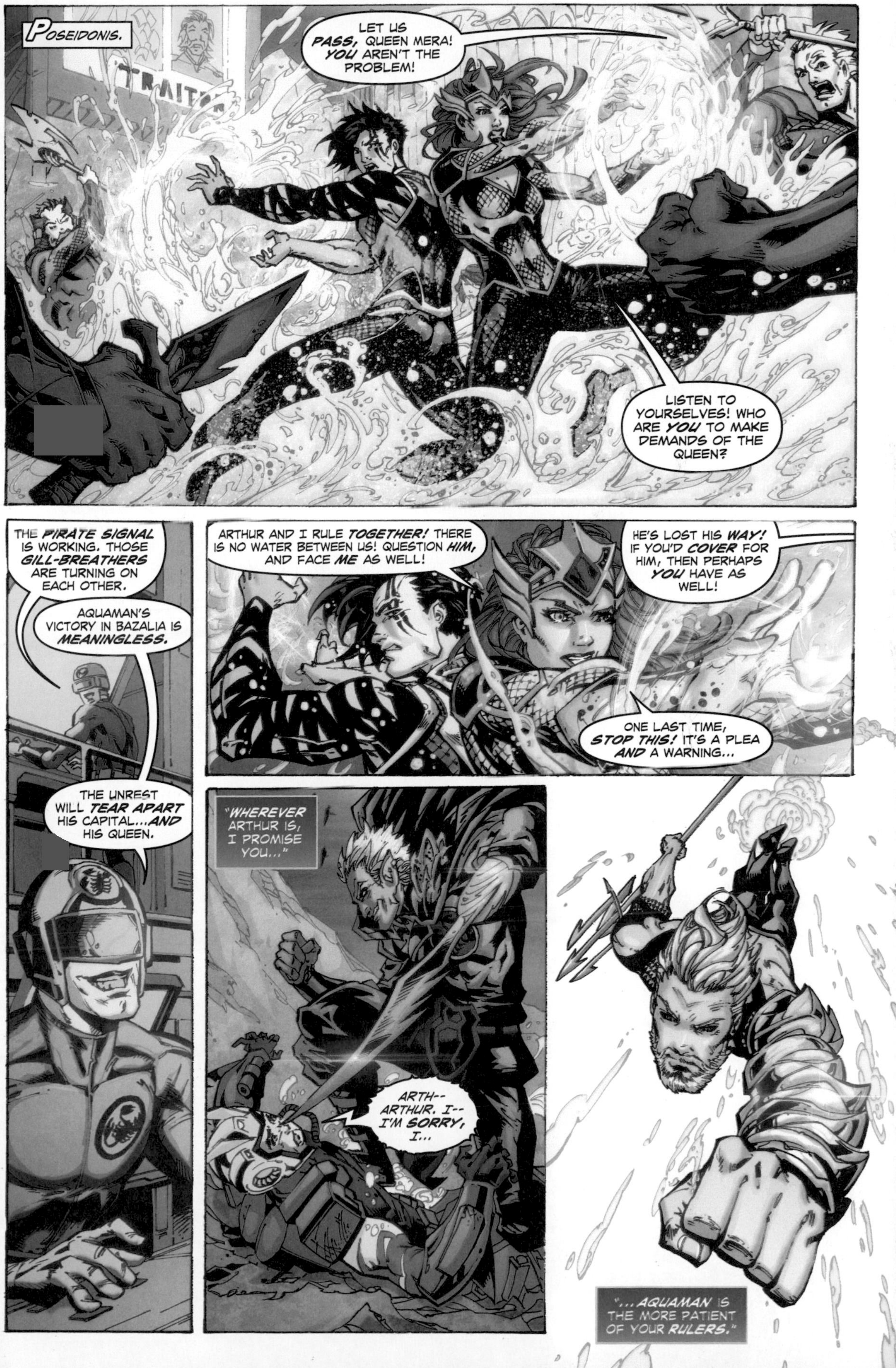
POSEIDONIS.
LET US PASS, QUEEN MERA! YOU AREN'T THE PROBLEM!
LISTEN TO YOURSELVES! WHO ARE YOU TO MAKE DEMANDS OF THE QUEEN?
THE PIRATE SIGNAL IS WORKING. THOSE GILL-BREATHERS ARE TURNING ON EACH OTHER.
AQUAMAN'S VICTORY IN BAZALIA IS MEANINGLESS.
ARTHUR AND I RULE TOGETHER! THERE IS NO WATER BETWEEN US! QUESTION HIM, AND FACE ME AS WELL!
HE'S LOST HIS WAY! IF YOU'D COVER FOR HIM, THEN PERHAPS YOU HAVE AS WELL!
ONE LAST TIME, STOP THIS! IT'S A PLEA AND A WARNING...
THE UNREST WILL TEAR APART HIS CAPITAL...AND HIS QUEEN.
"WHEREVER ARTHUR IS, I PROMISE YOU..."
ARTH-- ARTHUR. I-- I'M SORRY, I...
"...AQUAMAN IS THE MORE PATIENT OF YOUR RULERS."

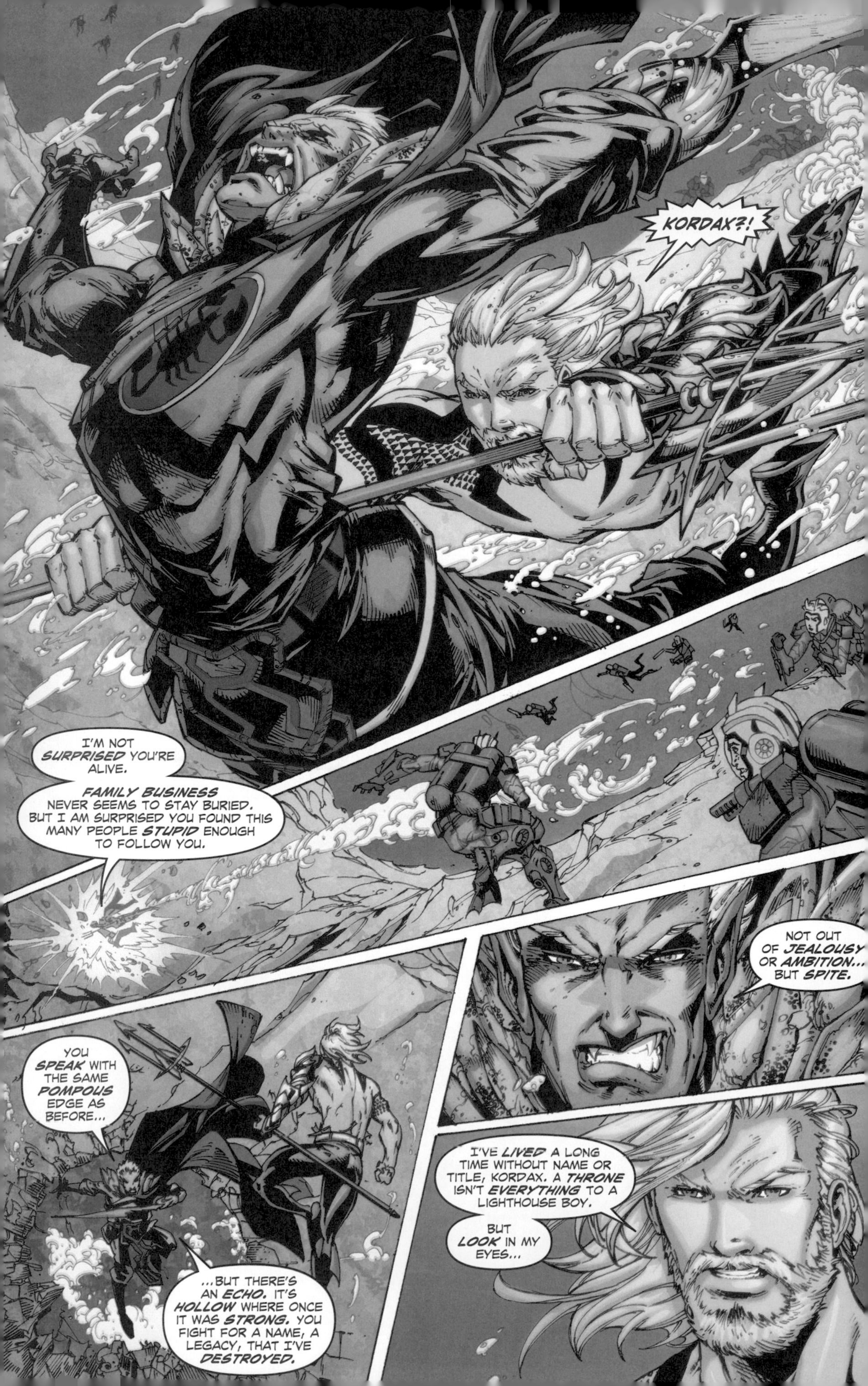
KORDAX?!
I'M NOT SURPRISED YOU'RE ALIVE.
FAMILY BUSINESS NEVER SEEMS TO STAY BURIED. BUT I AM SURPRISED YOU FOUND THIS MANY PEOPLE STUPID ENOUGH TO FOLLOW YOU.
NOT OUT OF JEALOUSY OR AMBITION... BUT SPITE.
YOU SPEAK WITH THE SAME POMPOUS EDGE AS BEFORE...
...BUT THERE'S AN ECHO. IT'S HOLLOW WHERE ONCE IT WAS STRONG. YOU FIGHT FOR A NAME, A LEGACY, THAT I'VE DESTROYED.
I'VE LIVED A LONG TIME WITHOUT NAME OR TITLE, KORDAX. A THRONE ISN'T EVERYTHING TO A LIGHTHOUSE BOY.
BUT LOOK IN MY EYES...

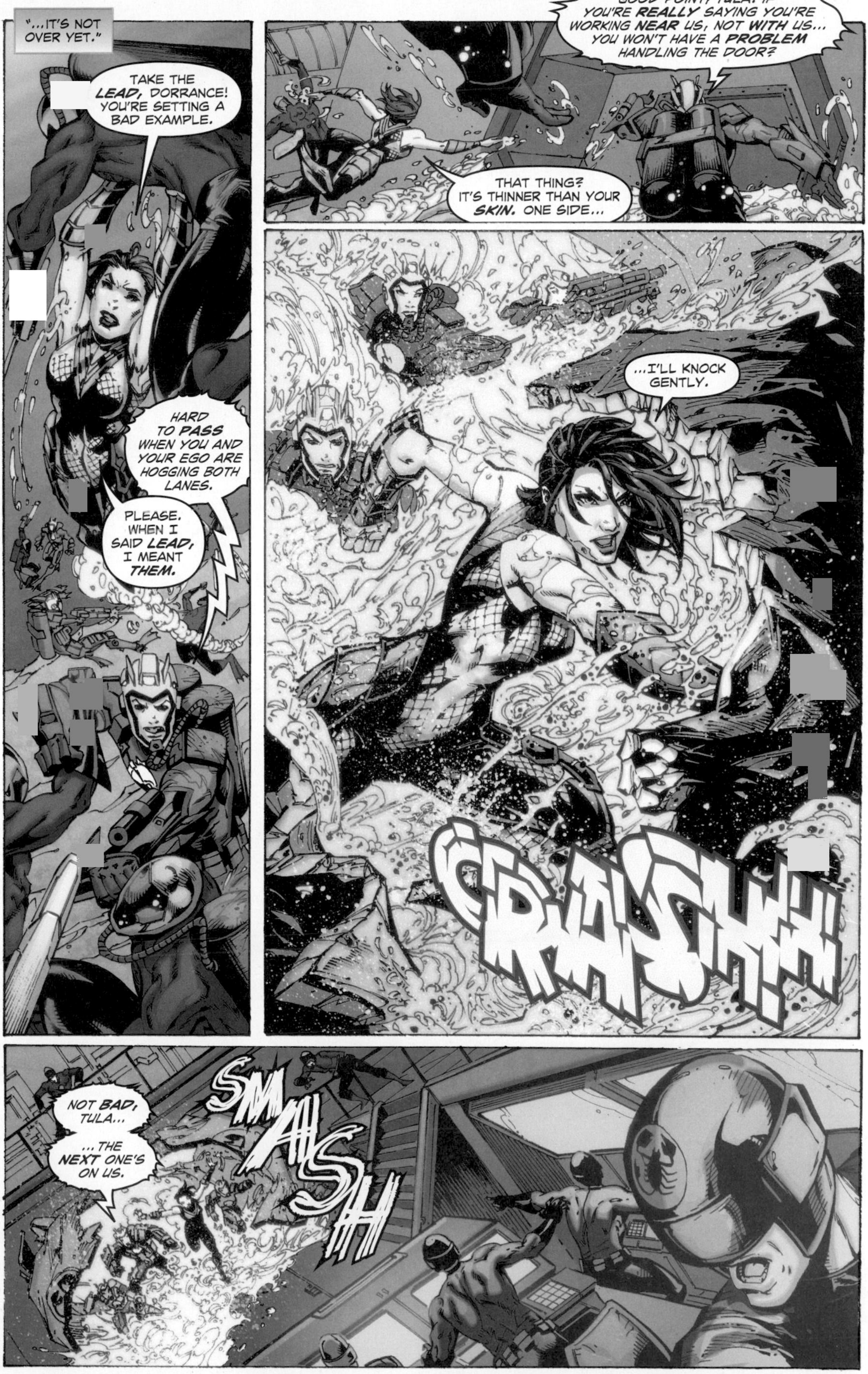
"...IT'S NOT OVER YET."
TAKE THE LEAD, DORRANCE! YOU'RE SETTING A BAD EXAMPLE.
HARD TO PASS WHEN YOU AND YOUR EGO ARE HOGGING BOTH LANES.
PLEASE. WHEN I SAID LEAD, I MEANT THEM.
GOOD POINT, TULA. IF YOU'RE REALLY SAYING YOU'RE WORKING NEAR US, NOT WITH US... YOU WON'T HAVE A PROBLEM HANDLING THE DOOR?
THAT THING? IT'S THINNER THAN YOUR SKIN. ONE SIDE...
...I'LL KNOCK GENTLY.
CRASSH!!
NOT BAD, TULA...
...THE NEXT ONE'S ON US.
SMASH

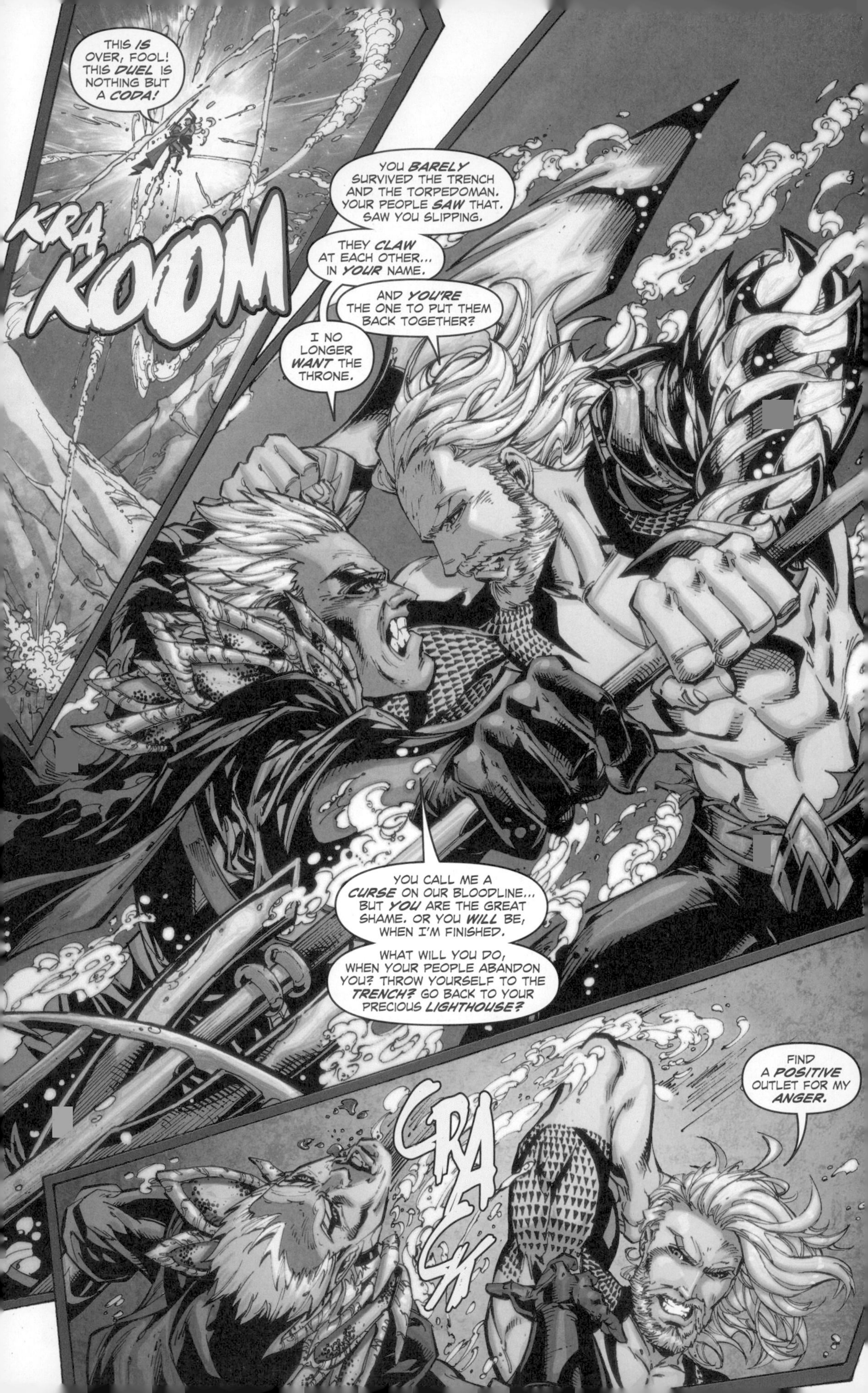
THIS IS OVER, FOOL! THIS DUEL IS NOTHING BUT A CODA!
KRA KOOM
YOU BARELY SURVIVED THE TRENCH AND THE TORPEDOMAN. YOUR PEOPLE SAW THAT. SAW YOU SLIPPING.
THEY CLAW AT EACH OTHER... IN YOUR NAME.
AND YOU'RE THE ONE TO PUT THEM BACK TOGETHER?
I NO LONGER WANT THE THRONE.
YOU CALL ME A CURSE ON OUR BLOODLINE... BUT YOU ARE THE GREAT SHAME. OR YOU WILL BE, WHEN I'M FINISHED.
WHAT WILL YOU DO, WHEN YOUR PEOPLE ABANDON YOU? THROW YOURSELF TO THE TRENCH? GO BACK TO YOUR PRECIOUS LIGHTHOUSE?
CRACK
FIND A POSITIVE OUTLET FOR MY ANGER.

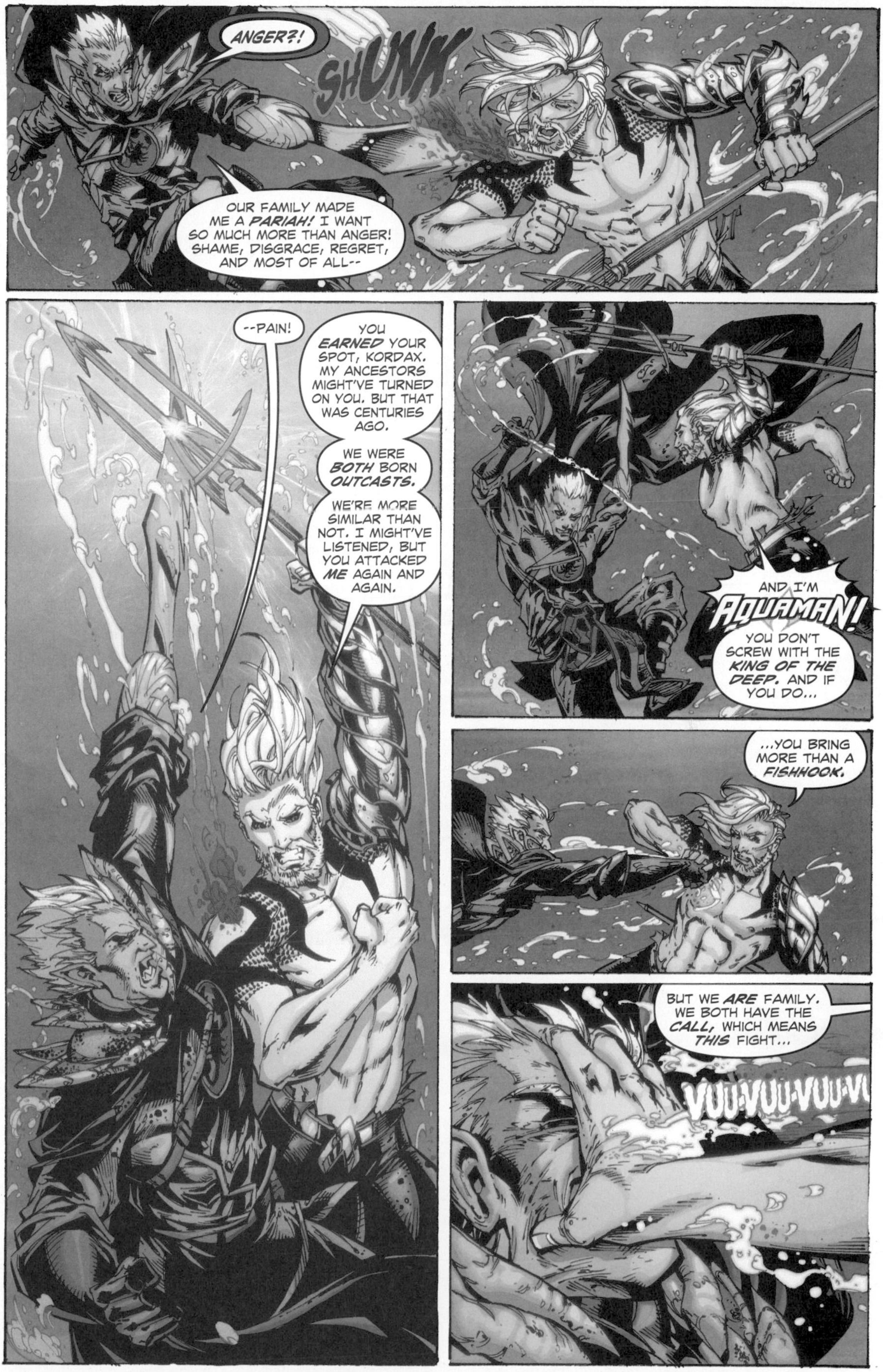
ANGER?!
SHUNK
OUR FAMILY MADE ME A PARIAH! I WANT SO MUCH MORE THAN ANGER! SHAME, DISGRACE, REGRET, AND MOST OF ALL--
--PAIN!
YOU EARNED YOUR SPOT, KORDAX. MY ANCESTORS MIGHT'VE TURNED ON YOU. BUT THAT WAS CENTURIES AGO.
WE WERE BOTH BORN OUTCASTS.
WE'RE MORE SIMILAR THAN NOT. I MIGHT'VE LISTENED, BUT YOU ATTACKED ME AGAIN AND AGAIN.
AND I'M AQUAMAN!
YOU DON'T SCREW WITH THE KING OF THE DEEP. AND IF YOU DO...
...YOU BRING MORE THAN A FISHHOOK.
BUT WE ARE FAMILY. WE BOTH HAVE THE CALL, WHICH MEANS THIS FIGHT...
VUU-VUU-VUU-VU

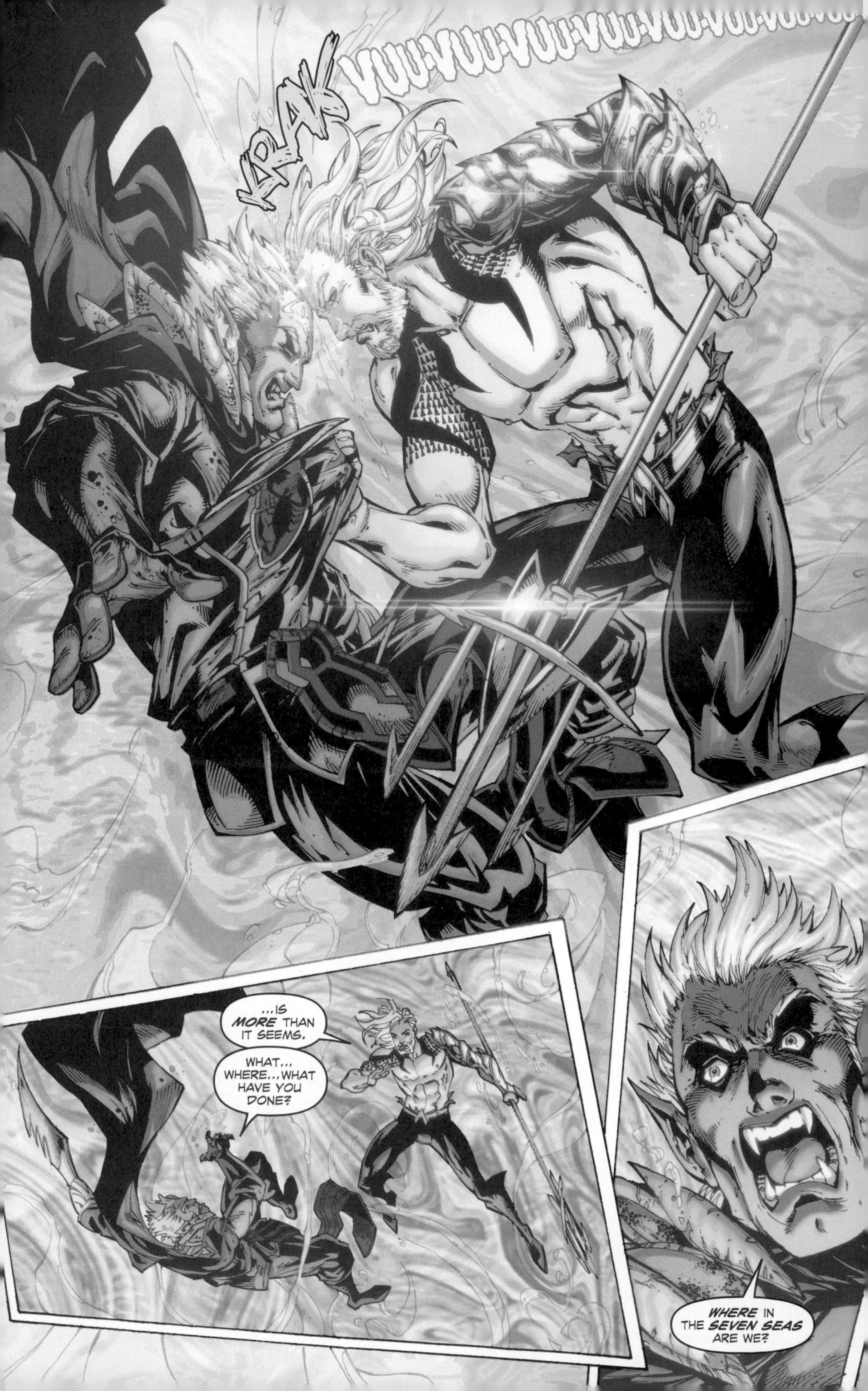
KRAK
VUU-VUU-VUU-VUU-VUU-VUU-VUU
...IS MORE THAN IT SEEMS.
WHAT... WHERE...WHAT HAVE YOU DONE?
WHERE IN THE SEVEN SEAS ARE WE?

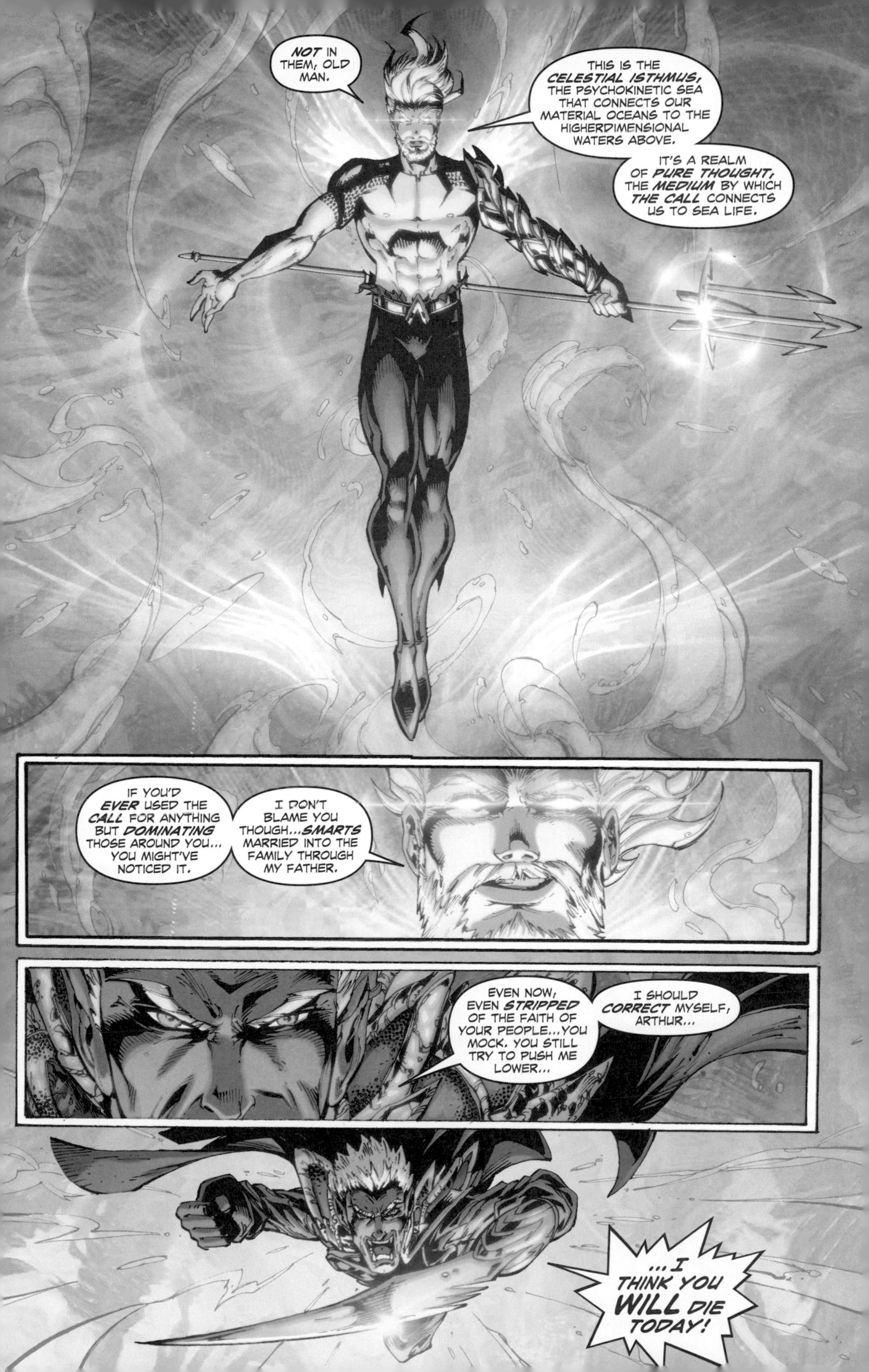
NOT IN THEM, OLD MAN.
THIS IS THE CELESTIAL ISTHMUS, THE PSYCHOKINETIC SEA THAT CONNECTS OUR MATERIAL OCEANS TO THE HIGHERDIMENSIONAL WATERS ABOVE.
IT'S A REALM OF PURE THOUGHT, THE MEDIUM BY WHICH THE CALL CONNECTS US TO SEA LIFE.
IF YOU'D EVER USED THE CALL FOR ANYTHING BUT DOMINATING THOSE AROUND YOU... YOU MIGHT'VE NOTICED IT.
I DON'T BLAME YOU THOUGH...SMARTS MARRIED INTO THE FAMILY THROUGH MY FATHER.
EVEN NOW, EVEN STRIPPED OF THE FAITH OF YOUR PEOPLE...YOU MOCK. YOU STILL TRY TO PUSH ME LOWER...
I SHOULD CORRECT MYSELF, ARTHUR...
...I THINK YOU WILL DIE TODAY!

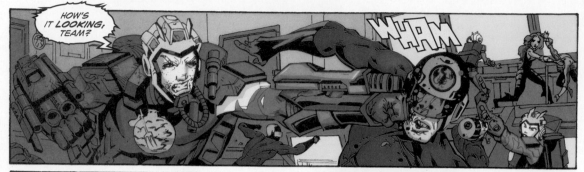

HOW'S IT *LOOKING*, TEAM?

WHAM

"*PIRATE SIGNAL'S* STILL GOING STRONG. ONLY A MATTER OF TIME UNTIL PEOPLE *REALLY* GET HURT."

THE DAMAGE HAS TO BE *COUNTERED*, NICK. I'M ALTERING THE SIGNAL SO WE CAN GET THE *TRUTH* OUT AS FAST AS SCORPIO'S LIES. ALMOST *THERE*--

NO, WE *ARE* THERE! TO THE *TRENCH* WITH CORRECTIONS...

"...WE DON'T NEED TO CHANGE THE SIGNAL. WE NEED TO *STOP* IT."

YOU HIT THE BUTTON REAL HARD. REALLY *REVELATORY*, AS STRATEGIES GO.

I *KNOW* MY PEOPLE. FOR ARTHUR TO *REGAIN* ATLANTIS'S TRUST, *HE* MUST DELIVER THE TRUTH. NOT A *COMPUTER*.

NO, REALLY. *THIS TIME...* I THINK YOU WERE RIGHT. WE COULDN'T HAVE DONE THIS *WITHOUT YOU...*

IT TAKES A *LOT* FOR YOU TO SAY THAT, DORRANCE. AND YOUR *STRATEGY* WAS *CRUCIAL* TO THIS STRIKE...

...OR A *BIG ROCK* OF SOME KIND.

...IT'S AS IF YOU HAD A *MANUAL.* PRINTED IN *VERY LARGE LETTERS.*

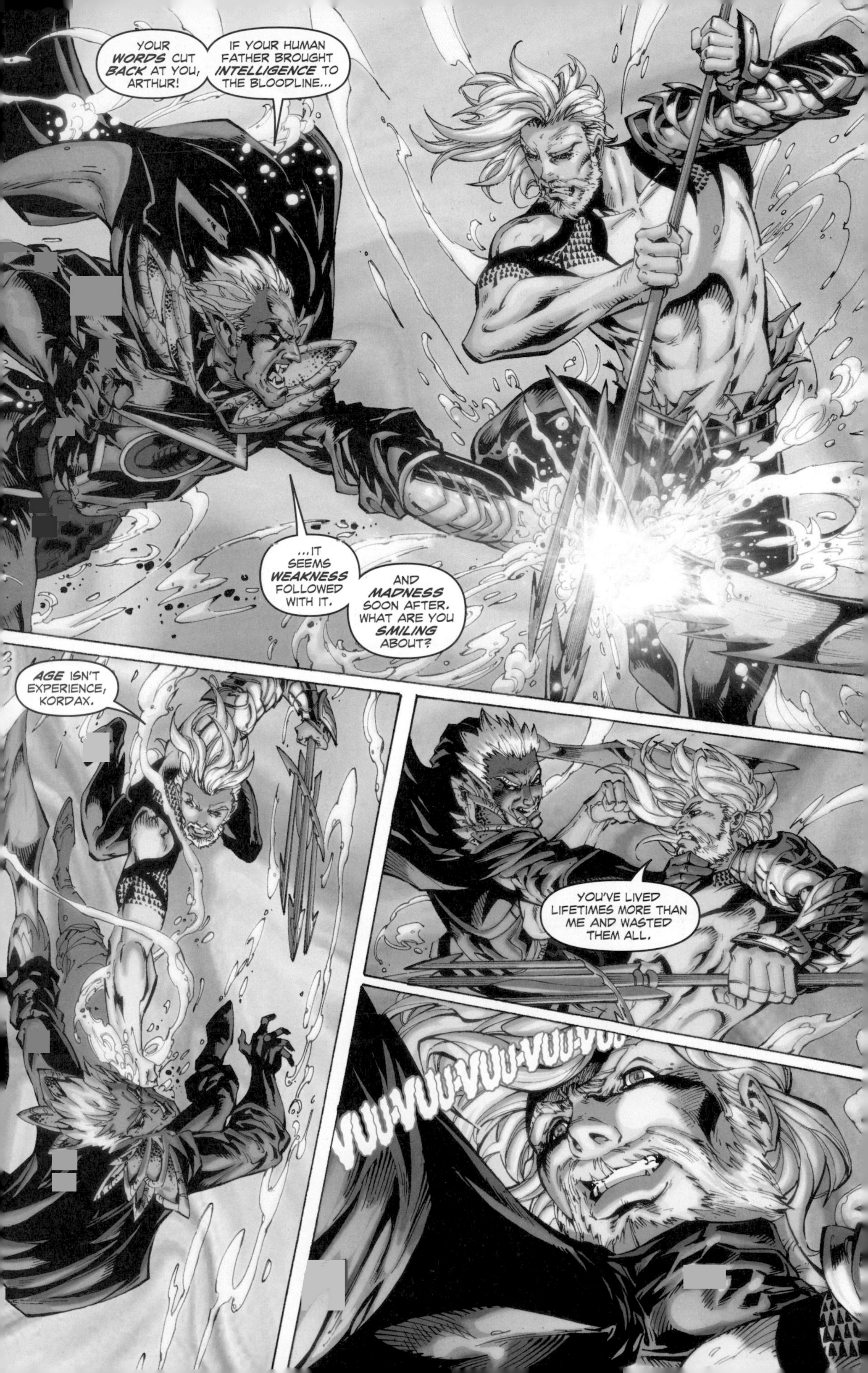
YOUR WORDS CUT BACK AT YOU, ARTHUR!
IF YOUR HUMAN FATHER BROUGHT INTELLIGENCE TO THE BLOODLINE...
...IT SEEMS WEAKNESS FOLLOWED WITH IT.
AND MADNESS SOON AFTER. WHAT ARE YOU SMILING ABOUT?
AGE ISN'T EXPERIENCE, KORDAX.
YOU'VE LIVED LIFETIMES MORE THAN ME AND WASTED THEM ALL.
VUU-VUU-VUU-VUU-VUU

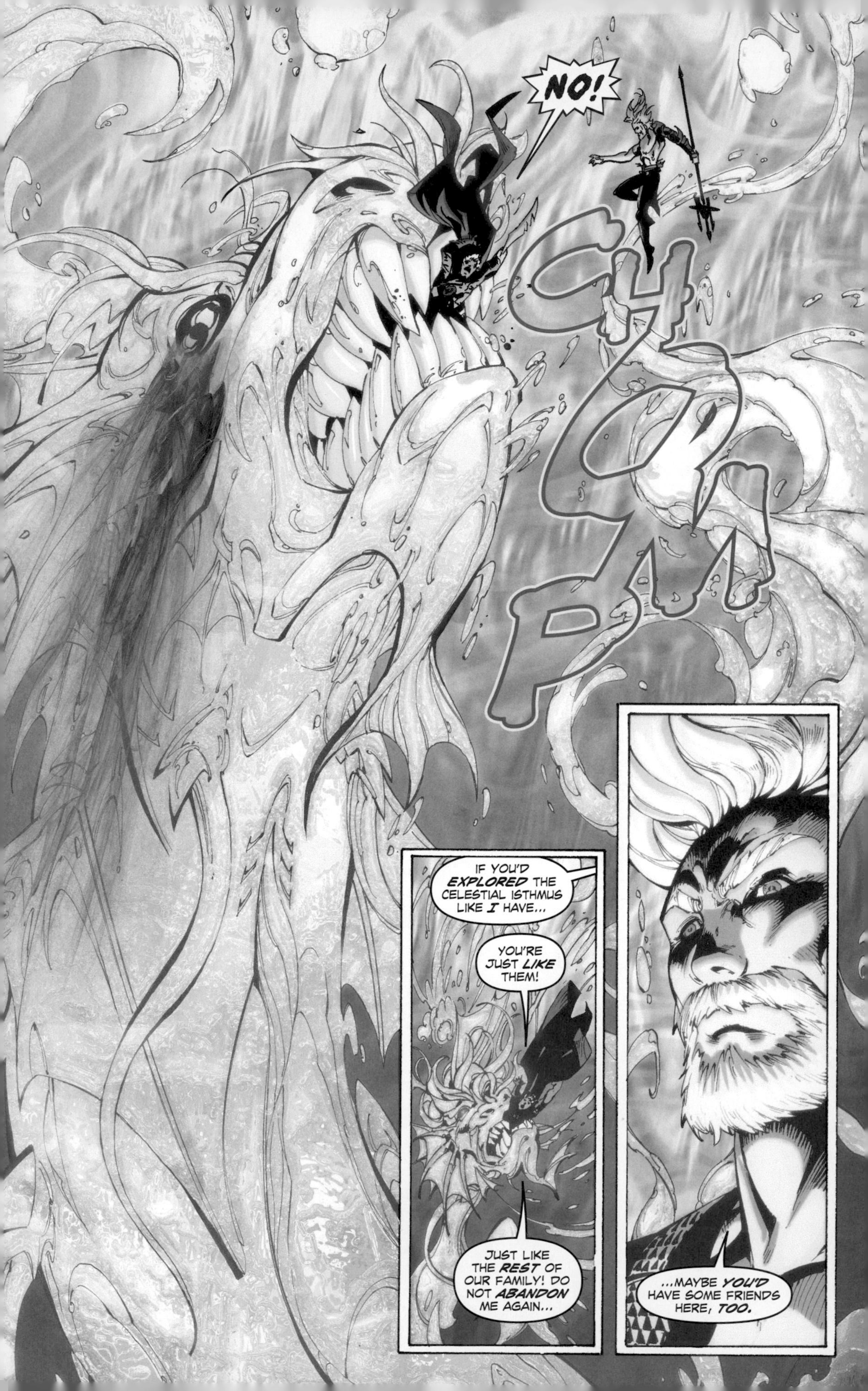

NO!
CHOMP
IF YOU'D EXPLORED THE CELESTIAL ISTHMUS LIKE I HAVE...
YOU'RE JUST LIKE THEM!
JUST LIKE THE REST OF OUR FAMILY! DO NOT ABANDON ME AGAIN...
...MAYBE YOU'D HAVE SOME FRIENDS HERE, TOO.

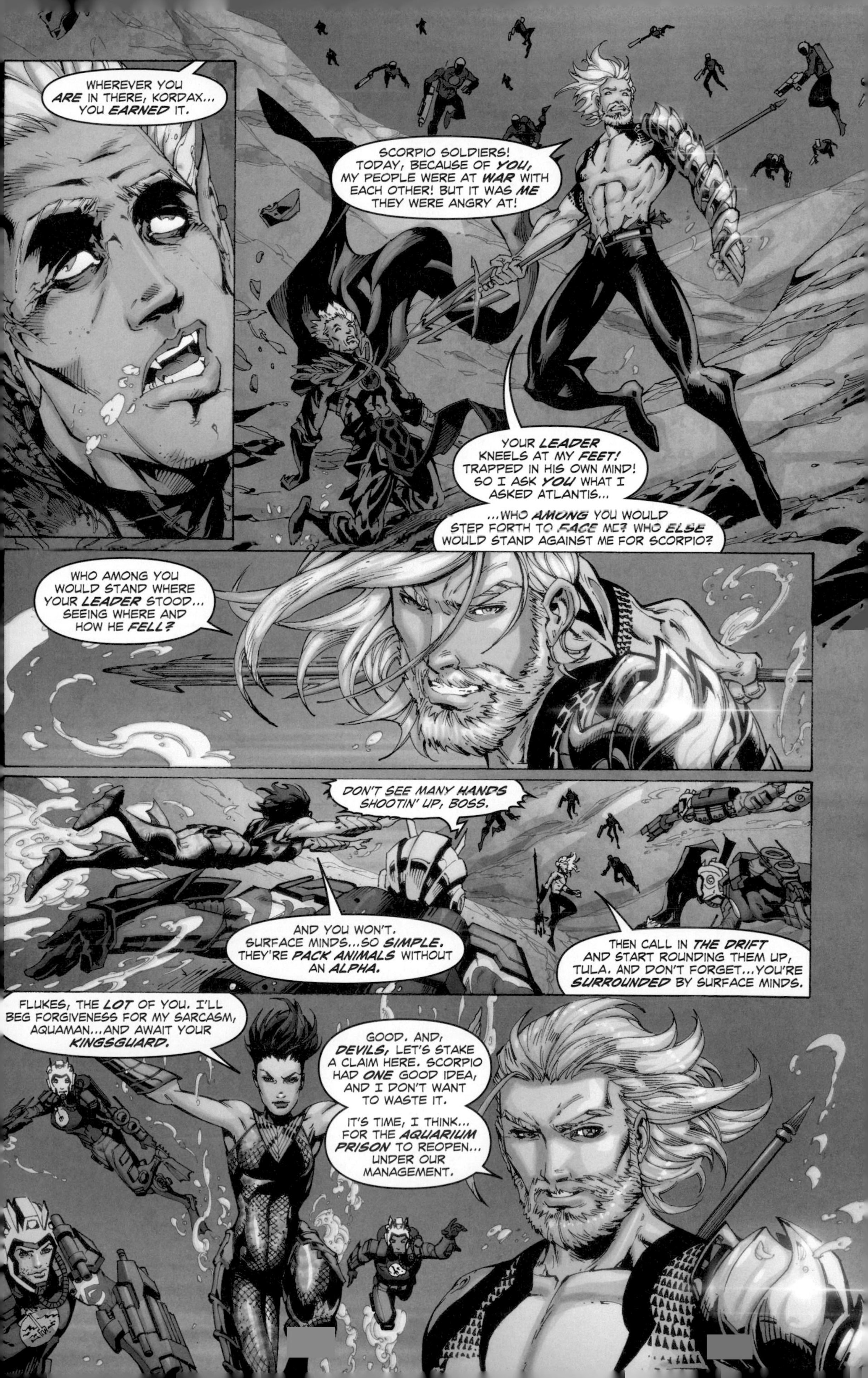
WHEREVER YOU ARE IN THERE, KORDAX... YOU EARNED IT.
SCORPIO SOLDIERS! TODAY, BECAUSE OF YOU, MY PEOPLE WERE AT WAR WITH EACH OTHER! BUT IT WAS ME THEY WERE ANGRY AT!
YOUR LEADER KNEELS AT MY FEET! TRAPPED IN HIS OWN MIND! SO I ASK YOU WHAT I ASKED ATLANTIS...
...WHO AMONG YOU WOULD STEP FORTH TO FACE ME? WHO ELSE WOULD STAND AGAINST ME FOR SCORPIO?
WHO AMONG YOU WOULD STAND WHERE YOUR LEADER STOOD... SEEING WHERE AND HOW HE FELL?
DON'T SEE MANY HANDS SHOOTIN' UP, BOSS.
AND YOU WON'T. SURFACE MINDS...SO SIMPLE. THEY'RE PACK ANIMALS WITHOUT AN ALPHA.
THEN CALL IN THE DRIFT AND START ROUNDING THEM UP, TULA. AND DON'T FORGET...YOU'RE SURROUNDED BY SURFACE MINDS.
FLUKES, THE LOT OF YOU. I'LL BEG FORGIVENESS FOR MY SARCASM, AQUAMAN...AND AWAIT YOUR KINGSGUARD.
GOOD. AND, DEVILS, LET'S STAKE A CLAIM HERE. SCORPIO HAD ONE GOOD IDEA, AND I DON'T WANT TO WASTE IT.
IT'S TIME, I THINK... FOR THE AQUARIUM PRISON TO REOPEN... UNDER OUR MANAGEMENT.

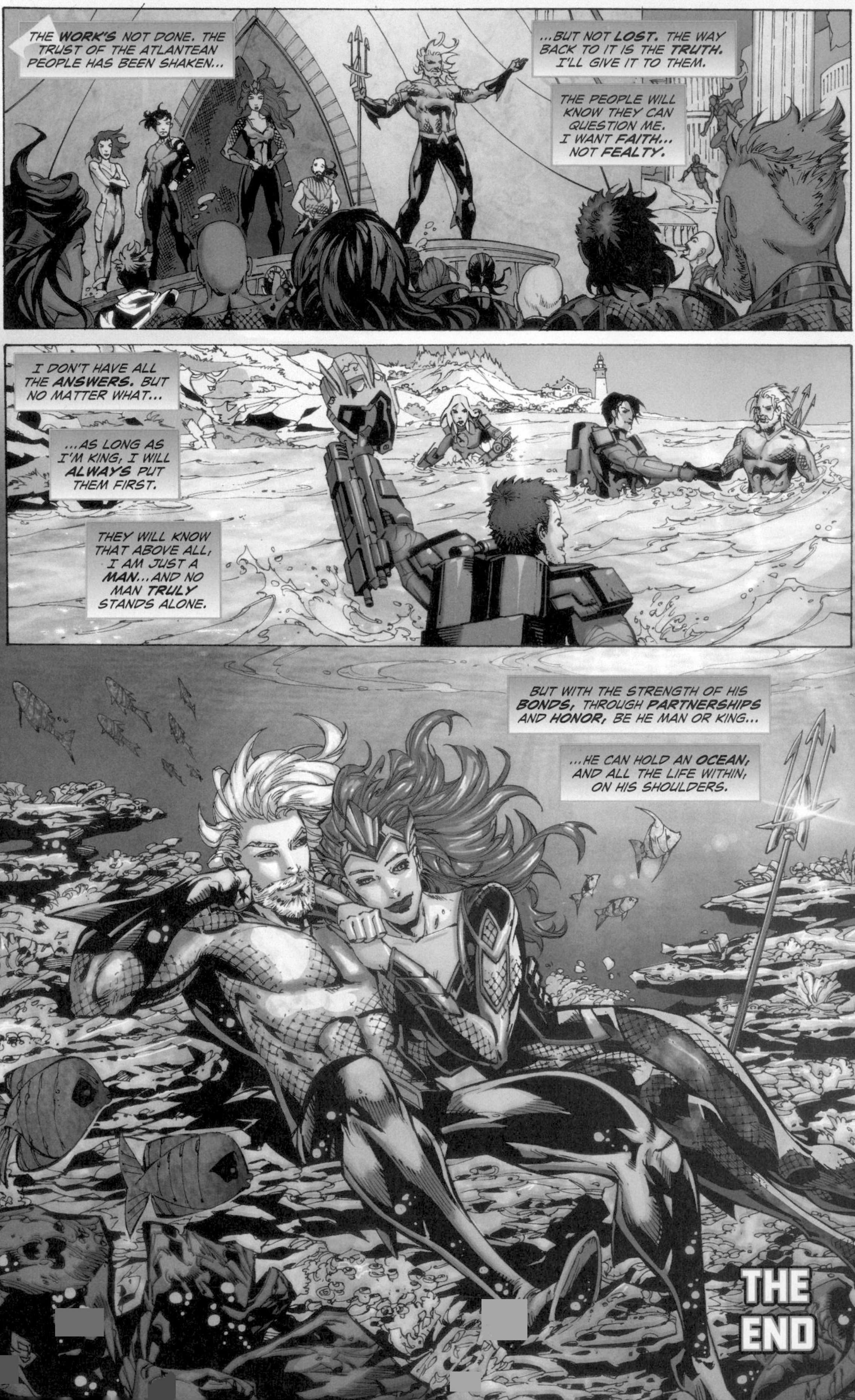
THE WORK'S NOT DONE. THE TRUST OF THE ATLANTEAN PEOPLE HAS BEEN SHAKEN...
...BUT NOT LOST. THE WAY BACK TO IT IS THE TRUTH. I'LL GIVE IT TO THEM.
THE PEOPLE WILL KNOW THEY CAN QUESTION ME. I WANT FAITH... NOT FEALTY.
I DON'T HAVE ALL THE ANSWERS. BUT NO MATTER WHAT...
...AS LONG AS I'M KING, I WILL ALWAYS PUT THEM FIRST.
THEY WILL KNOW THAT ABOVE ALL, I AM JUST A MAN...AND NO MAN TRULY STANDS ALONE.
BUT WITH THE STRENGTH OF HIS BONDS, THROUGH PARTNERSHIPS AND HONOR, BE HE MAN OR KING...
...HE CAN HOLD AN OCEAN, AND ALL THE LIFE WITHIN, ON HIS SHOULDERS.
THE END

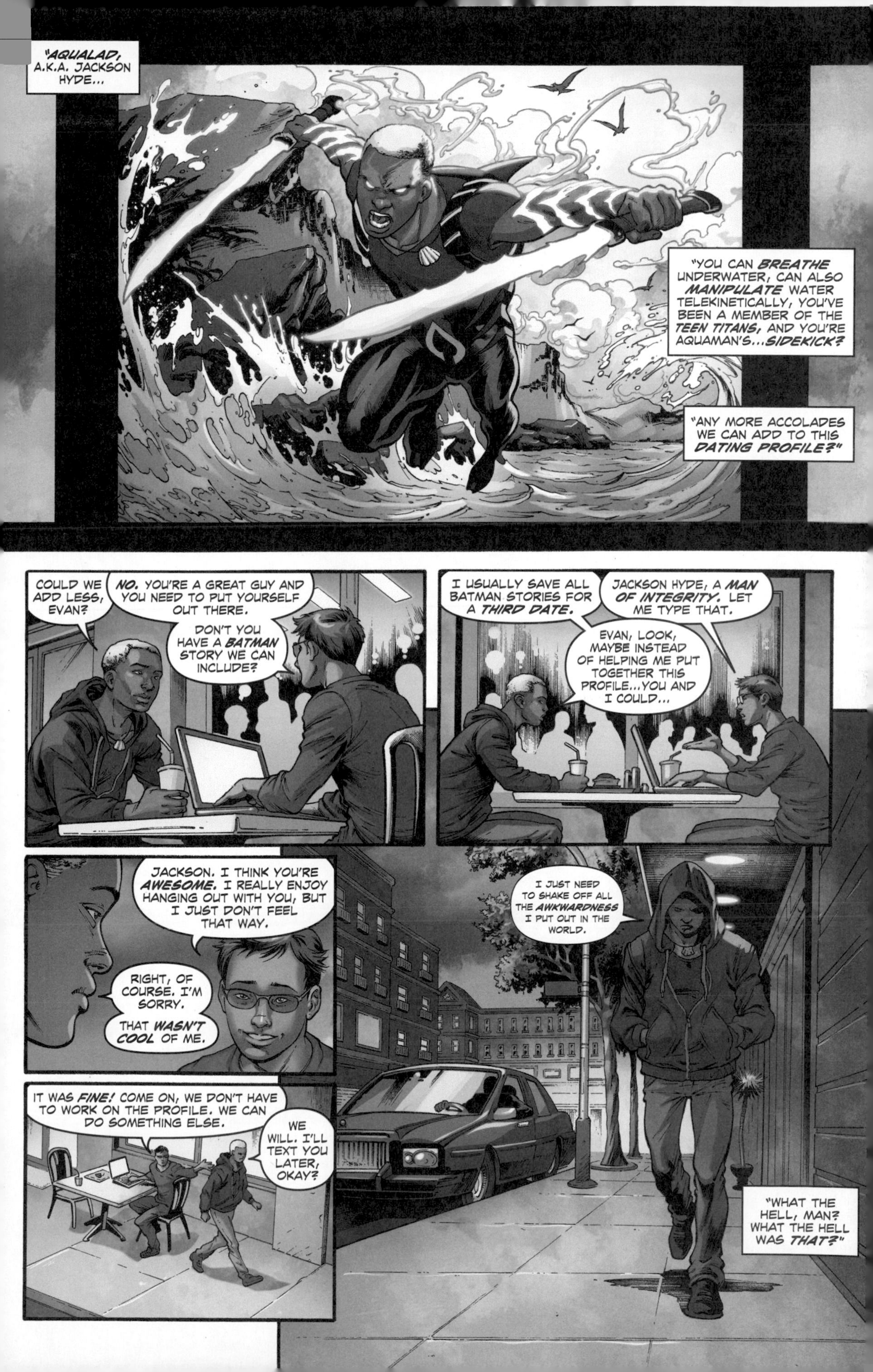

"AQUALAD, A.K.A. JACKSON HYDE...
"YOU CAN BREATHE UNDERWATER, CAN ALSO MANIPULATE WATER TELEKINETICALLY, YOU'VE BEEN A MEMBER OF THE TEEN TITANS, AND YOU'RE AQUAMAN'S...SIDEKICK?
"ANY MORE ACCOLADES WE CAN ADD TO THIS DATING PROFILE?"
COULD WE ADD LESS, EVAN?
NO. YOU'RE A GREAT GUY AND YOU NEED TO PUT YOURSELF OUT THERE.
DON'T YOU HAVE A BATMAN STORY WE CAN INCLUDE?
I USUALLY SAVE ALL BATMAN STORIES FOR A THIRD DATE.
JACKSON HYDE, A MAN OF INTEGRITY. LET ME TYPE THAT.
EVAN, LOOK, MAYBE INSTEAD OF HELPING ME PUT TOGETHER THIS PROFILE...YOU AND I COULD...
JACKSON. I THINK YOU'RE AWESOME. I REALLY ENJOY HANGING OUT WITH YOU, BUT I JUST DON'T FEEL THAT WAY.
RIGHT, OF COURSE. I'M SORRY.
THAT WASN'T COOL OF ME.
IT WAS FINE! COME ON, WE DON'T HAVE TO WORK ON THE PROFILE. WE CAN DO SOMETHING ELSE.
WE WILL. I'LL TEXT YOU LATER, OKAY?
I JUST NEED TO SHAKE OFF ALL THE AWKWARDNESS I PUT OUT IN THE WORLD.
"WHAT THE HELL, MAN? WHAT THE HELL WAS THAT?"

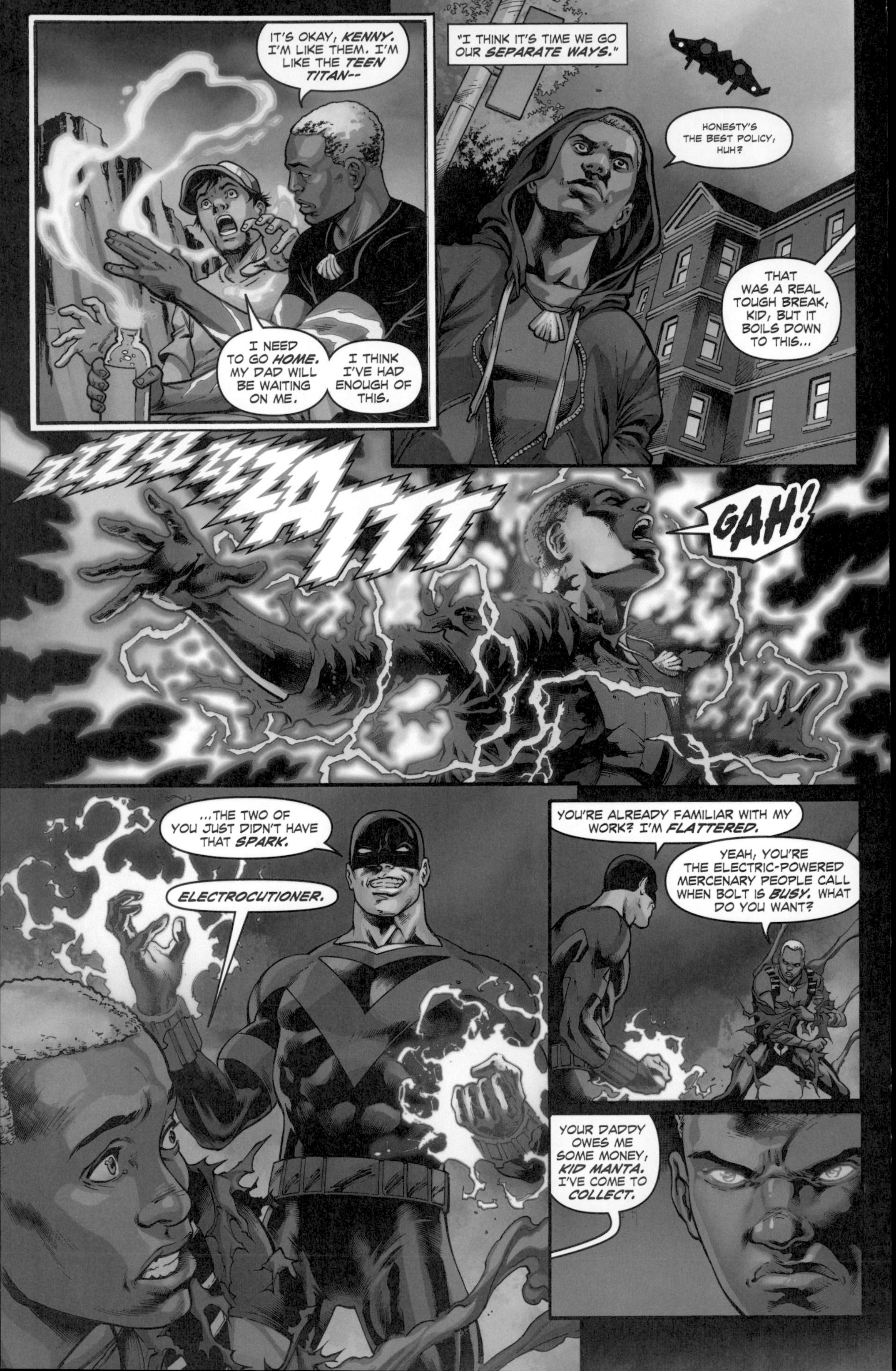
IT'S OKAY, KENNY. I'M LIKE THEM. I'M LIKE THE TEEN TITAN--
I NEED TO GO HOME. MY DAD WILL BE WAITING ON ME.
I THINK I'VE HAD ENOUGH OF THIS.
"I THINK IT'S TIME WE GO OUR SEPARATE WAYS."
HONESTY'S THE BEST POLICY, HUH?
THAT WAS A REAL TOUGH BREAK, KID, BUT IT BOILS DOWN TO THIS...
ZZZZZZZZZAPTTT
GAH!
...THE TWO OF YOU JUST DIDN'T HAVE THAT SPARK.
ELECTROCUTIONER.
YOU'RE ALREADY FAMILIAR WITH MY WORK? I'M FLATTERED.
YEAH, YOU'RE THE ELECTRIC-POWERED MERCENARY PEOPLE CALL WHEN BOLT IS BUSY. WHAT DO YOU WANT?
YOUR DADDY OWES ME SOME MONEY, KID MANTA. I'VE COME TO COLLECT.

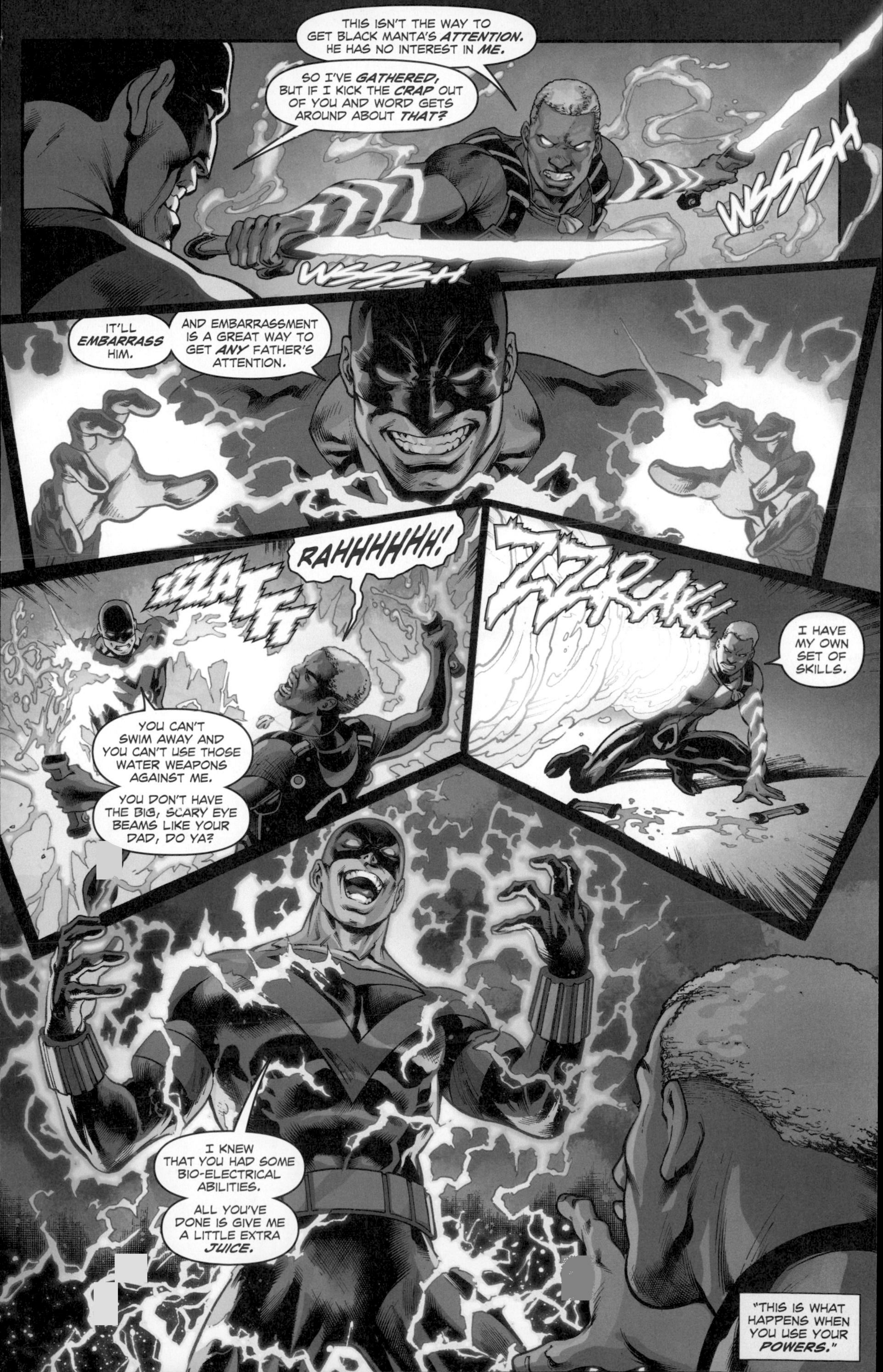

THIS ISN'T THE WAY TO GET BLACK MANTA'S ATTENTION. HE HAS NO INTEREST IN ME.
SO I'VE GATHERED, BUT IF I KICK THE CRAP OUT OF YOU AND WORD GETS AROUND ABOUT THAT?
WSSSH
WSSSH
IT'LL EMBARRASS HIM.
AND EMBARRASSMENT IS A GREAT WAY TO GET ANY FATHER'S ATTENTION.
ZZZATTT
RAHHHHHH!
YOU CAN'T SWIM AWAY AND YOU CAN'T USE THOSE WATER WEAPONS AGAINST ME.
YOU DON'T HAVE THE BIG, SCARY EYE BEAMS LIKE YOUR DAD, DO YA?
ZZZRAKK
I HAVE MY OWN SET OF SKILLS.
I KNEW THAT YOU HAD SOME BIO-ELECTRICAL ABILITIES.
ALL YOU'VE DONE IS GIVE ME A LITTLE EXTRA JUICE.
"THIS IS WHAT HAPPENS WHEN YOU USE YOUR POWERS."

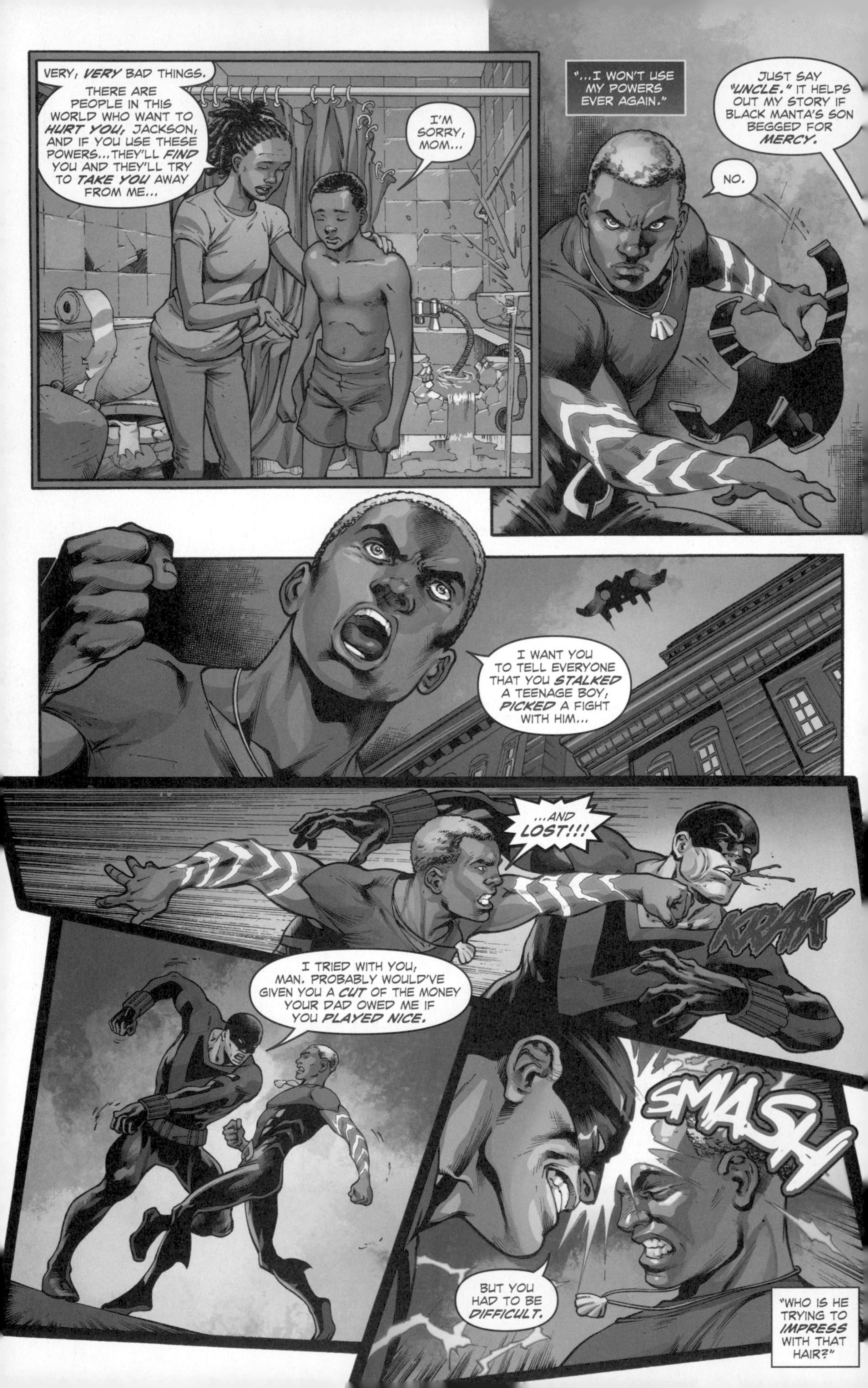

VERY, VERY BAD THINGS.
THERE ARE PEOPLE IN THIS WORLD WHO WANT TO HURT YOU, JACKSON, AND IF YOU USE THESE POWERS...THEY'LL FIND YOU AND THEY'LL TRY TO TAKE YOU AWAY FROM ME...
I'M SORRY, MOM...
"...I WON'T USE MY POWERS EVER AGAIN."
JUST SAY "UNCLE." IT HELPS OUT MY STORY IF BLACK MANTA'S SON BEGGED FOR MERCY.
NO.
I WANT YOU TO TELL EVERYONE THAT YOU STALKED A TEENAGE BOY, PICKED A FIGHT WITH HIM...
...AND LOST!!!
KRAK
I TRIED WITH YOU, MAN. PROBABLY WOULD'VE GIVEN YOU A CUT OF THE MONEY YOUR DAD OWED ME IF YOU PLAYED NICE.
SMASH
BUT YOU HAD TO BE DIFFICULT.
"WHO IS HE TRYING TO IMPRESS WITH THAT HAIR?"

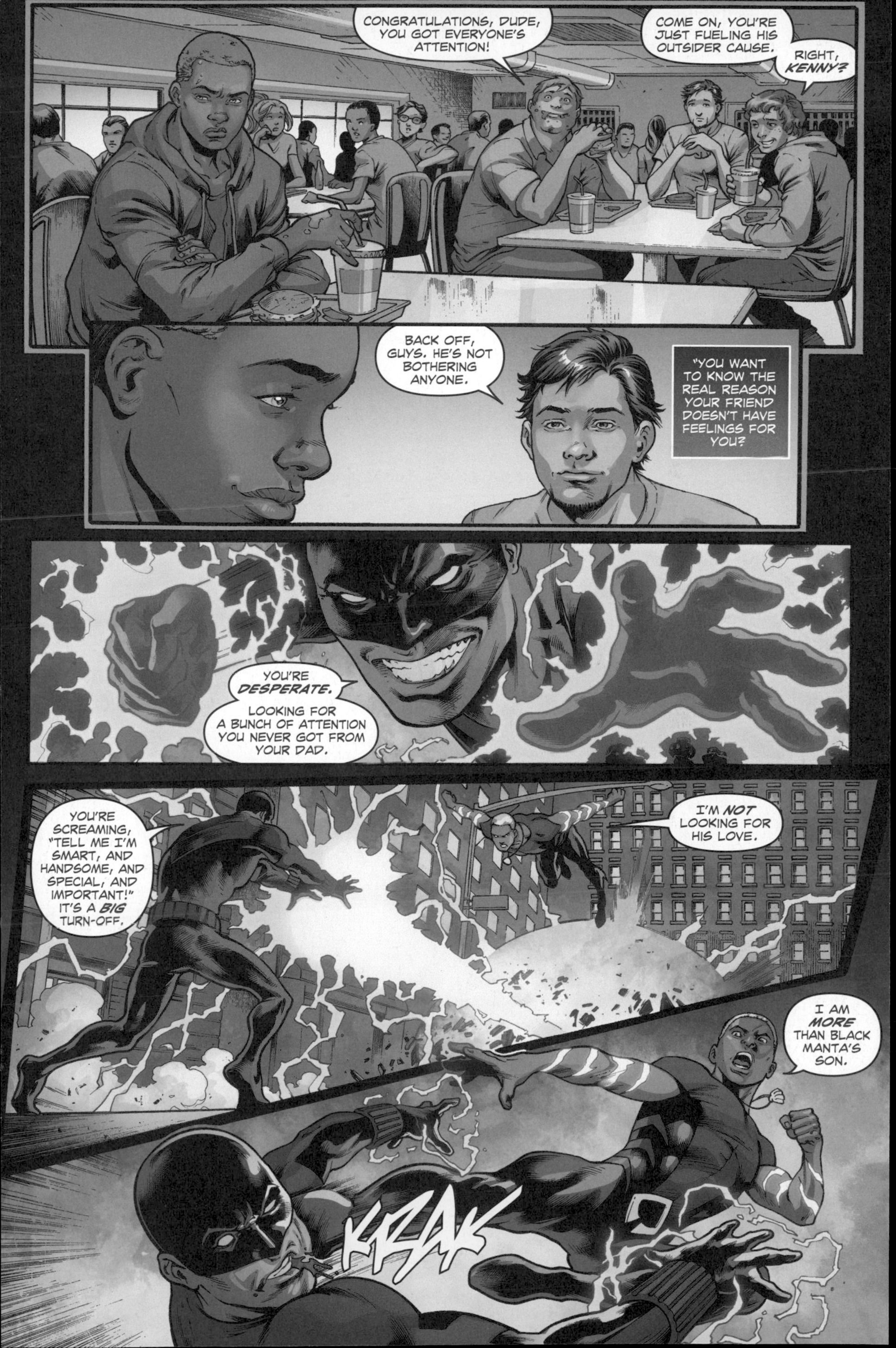

CONGRATULATIONS, DUDE, YOU GOT EVERYONE'S ATTENTION!
COME ON, YOU'RE JUST FUELING HIS OUTSIDER CAUSE.
RIGHT, KENNY?
BACK OFF, GUYS. HE'S NOT BOTHERING ANYONE.
"YOU WANT TO KNOW THE REAL REASON YOUR FRIEND DOESN'T HAVE FEELINGS FOR YOU?
YOU'RE DESPERATE.
LOOKING FOR A BUNCH OF ATTENTION YOU NEVER GOT FROM YOUR DAD.
YOU'RE SCREAMING, "TELL ME I'M SMART, AND HANDSOME, AND SPECIAL, AND IMPORTANT!" IT'S A BIG TURN-OFF.
I'M NOT LOOKING FOR HIS LOVE.
I AM MORE THAN BLACK MANTA'S SON.
KRAK

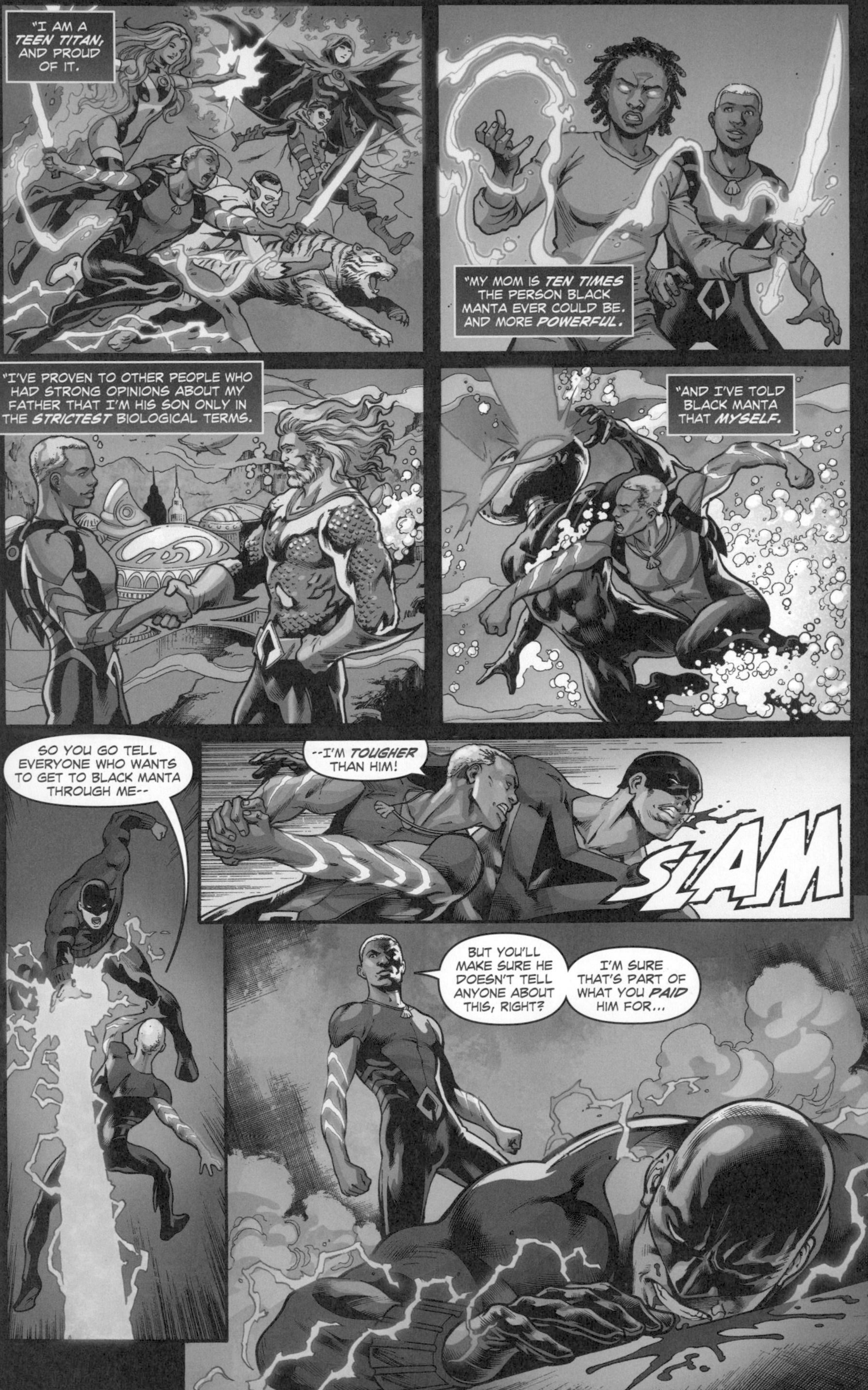
"I AM A TEEN TITAN, AND PROUD OF IT.
"MY MOM IS TEN TIMES THE PERSON BLACK MANTA EVER COULD BE. AND MORE POWERFUL.
"I'VE PROVEN TO OTHER PEOPLE WHO HAD STRONG OPINIONS ABOUT MY FATHER THAT I'M HIS SON ONLY IN THE STRICTEST BIOLOGICAL TERMS.
"AND I'VE TOLD BLACK MANTA THAT MYSELF.
SO YOU GO TELL EVERYONE WHO WANTS TO GET TO BLACK MANTA THROUGH ME--
--I'M TOUGHER THAN HIM!
SLAM
BUT YOU'LL MAKE SURE HE DOESN'T TELL ANYONE ABOUT THIS, RIGHT?
I'M SURE THAT'S PART OF WHAT YOU PAID HIM FOR...

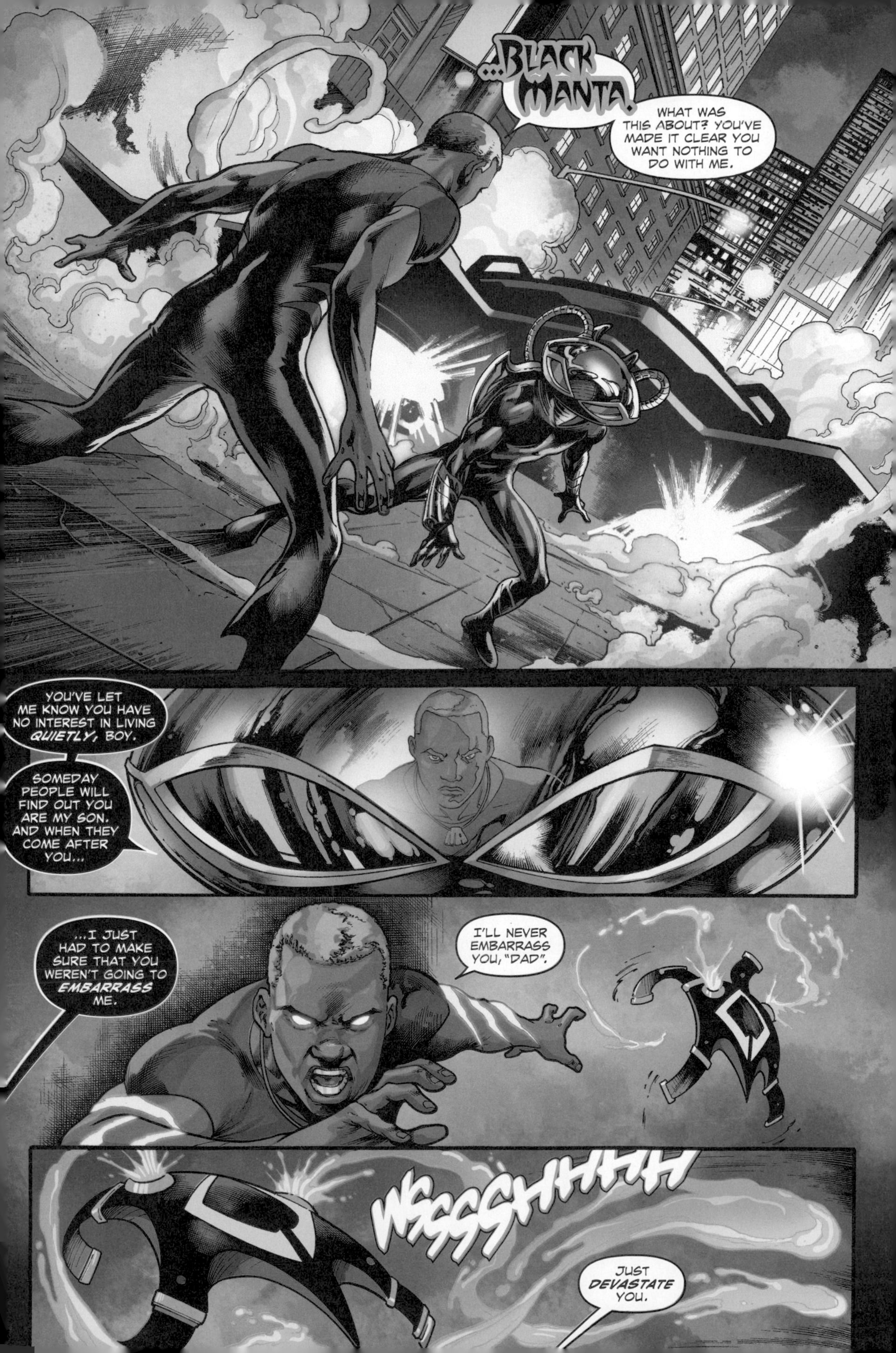
...BLACK MANTA.
WHAT WAS THIS ABOUT? YOU'VE MADE IT CLEAR YOU WANT NOTHING TO DO WITH ME.
YOU'VE LET ME KNOW YOU HAVE NO INTEREST IN LIVING *QUIETLY*, BOY.
SOMEDAY PEOPLE WILL FIND OUT YOU ARE MY SON. AND WHEN THEY COME AFTER YOU...
...I JUST HAD TO MAKE SURE THAT YOU WEREN'T GOING TO *EMBARRASS* ME.
I'LL NEVER EMBARRASS YOU, "DAD".
WSSSHHHHH
JUST *DEVASTATE* YOU.

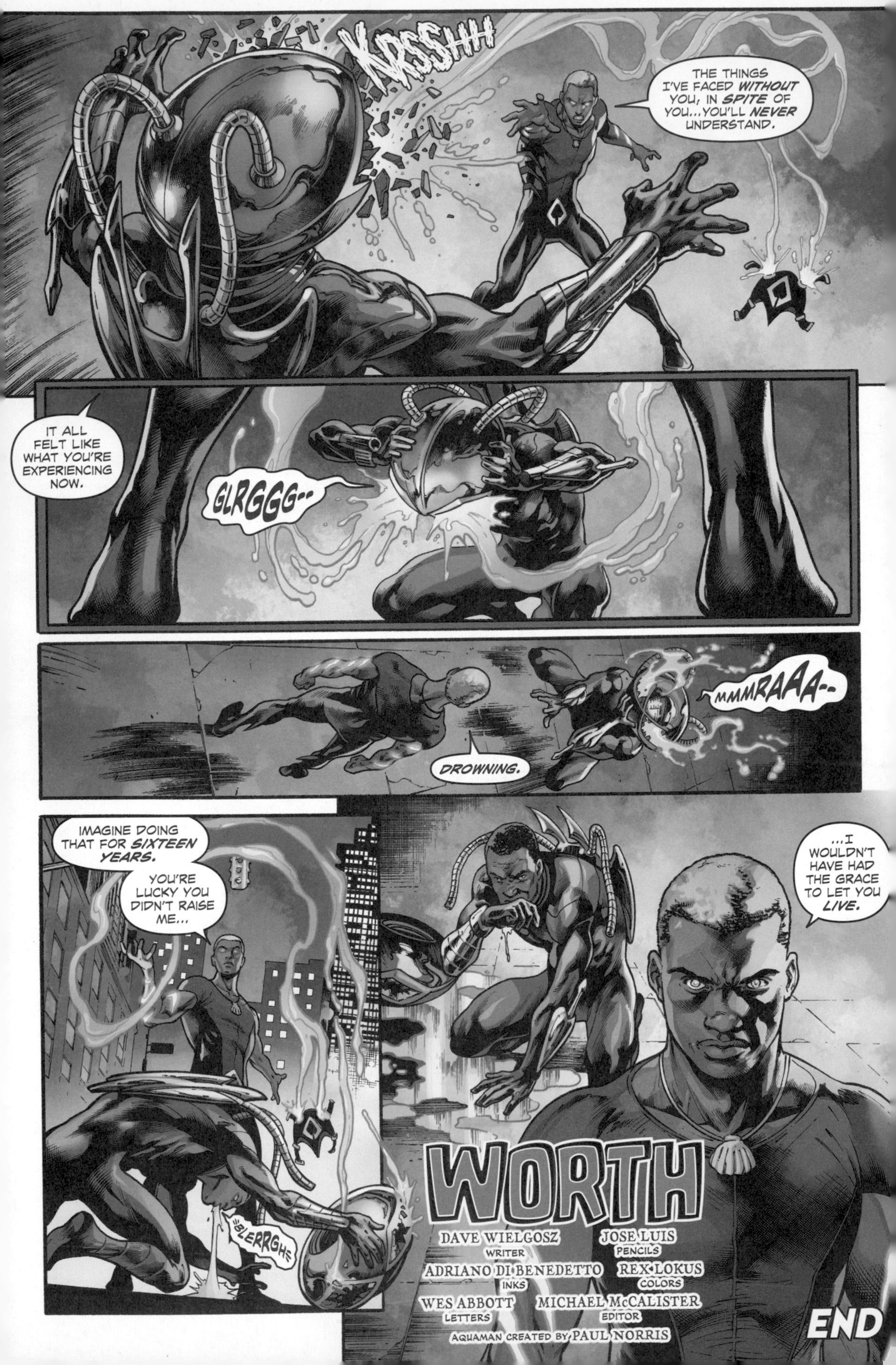
KRSSHHH
THE THINGS I'VE FACED WITHOUT YOU, IN SPITE OF YOU...YOU'LL NEVER UNDERSTAND.
IT ALL FELT LIKE WHAT YOU'RE EXPERIENCING NOW.
GLRGGG--
MMMRAAA--
DROWNING.
IMAGINE DOING THAT FOR SIXTEEN YEARS.
YOU'RE LUCKY YOU DIDN'T RAISE ME...
...I WOULDN'T HAVE HAD THE GRACE TO LET YOU LIVE.
BLERRGH
WORTH
DAVE WIELGOSZ WRITER
JOSE LUIS PENCILS
ADRIANO DI BENEDETTO INKS
REX LOKUS COLORS
WES ABBOTT LETTERS
MICHAEL McCALISTER EDITOR
AQUAMAN CREATED BY PAUL NORRIS
END

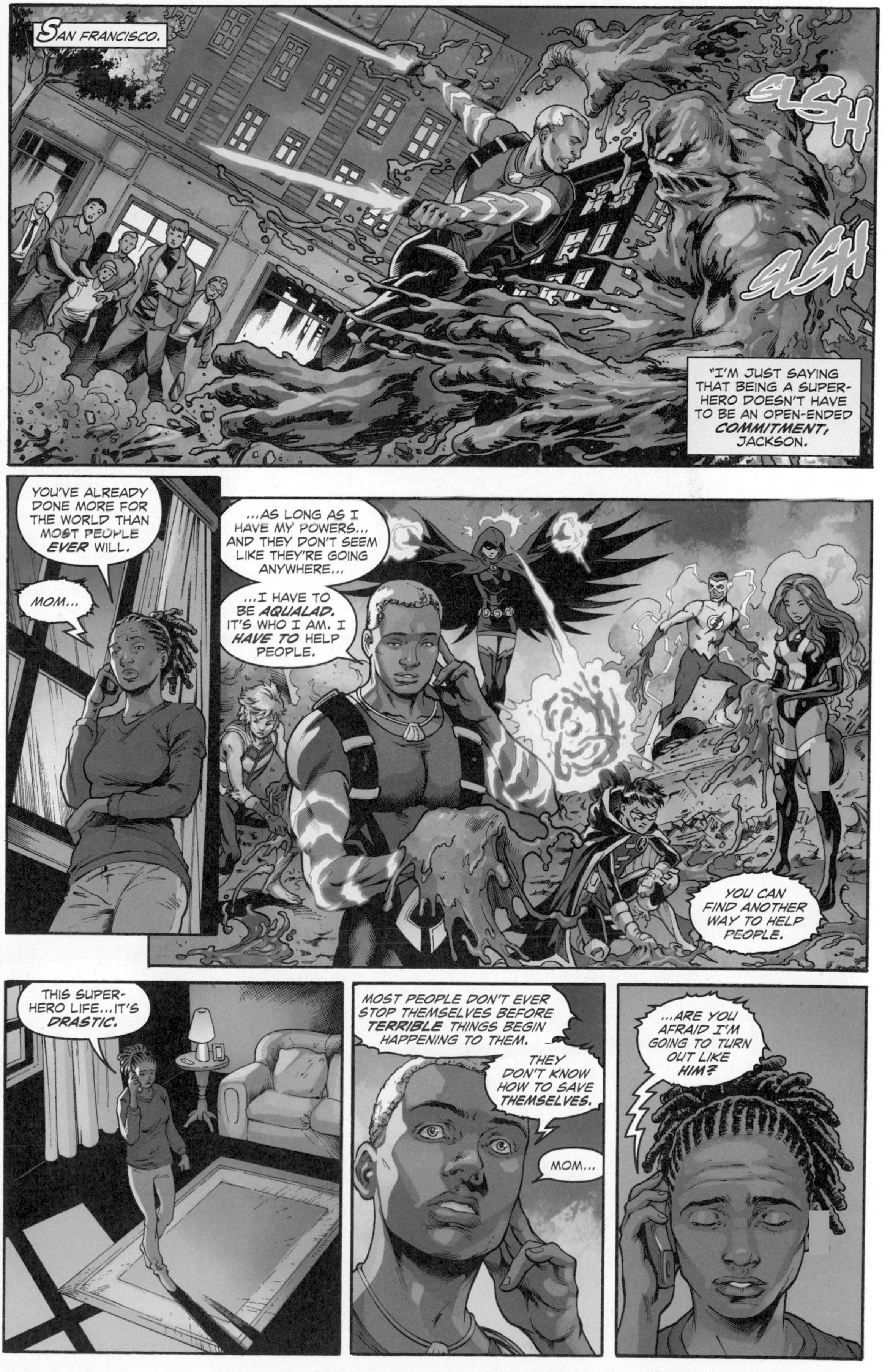

SAN FRANCISCO.
SLSH
SLSH
"I'M JUST SAYING THAT BEING A SUPER-HERO DOESN'T HAVE TO BE AN OPEN-ENDED COMMITMENT, JACKSON.
YOU'VE ALREADY DONE MORE FOR THE WORLD THAN MOST PEOPLE EVER WILL.
MOM...
...AS LONG AS I HAVE MY POWERS... AND THEY DON'T SEEM LIKE THEY'RE GOING ANYWHERE...
...I HAVE TO BE AQUALAD. IT'S WHO I AM. I HAVE TO HELP PEOPLE.
YOU CAN FIND ANOTHER WAY TO HELP PEOPLE.
THIS SUPER-HERO LIFE...IT'S DRASTIC.
MOST PEOPLE DON'T EVER STOP THEMSELVES BEFORE TERRIBLE THINGS BEGIN HAPPENING TO THEM.
THEY DON'T KNOW HOW TO SAVE THEMSELVES.
MOM...
...ARE YOU AFRAID I'M GOING TO TURN OUT LIKE HIM?

TITANS TOWER. HEADQUARTERS OF THE TEEN TITANS.

"LIKE *BLACK MANTA?*"

SPLSSH

JACKSON.

MANTA.

I NEED YOUR HELP.

IS THE REST OF THE *LEGION OF DOOM* BUSY?

WHAT I'VE COME TO ASK, I COULDN'T ASK OF ANYONE OTHER THAN *FAMILY.*

YOU ARE SON

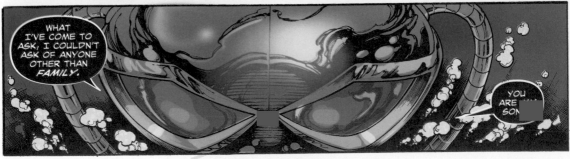

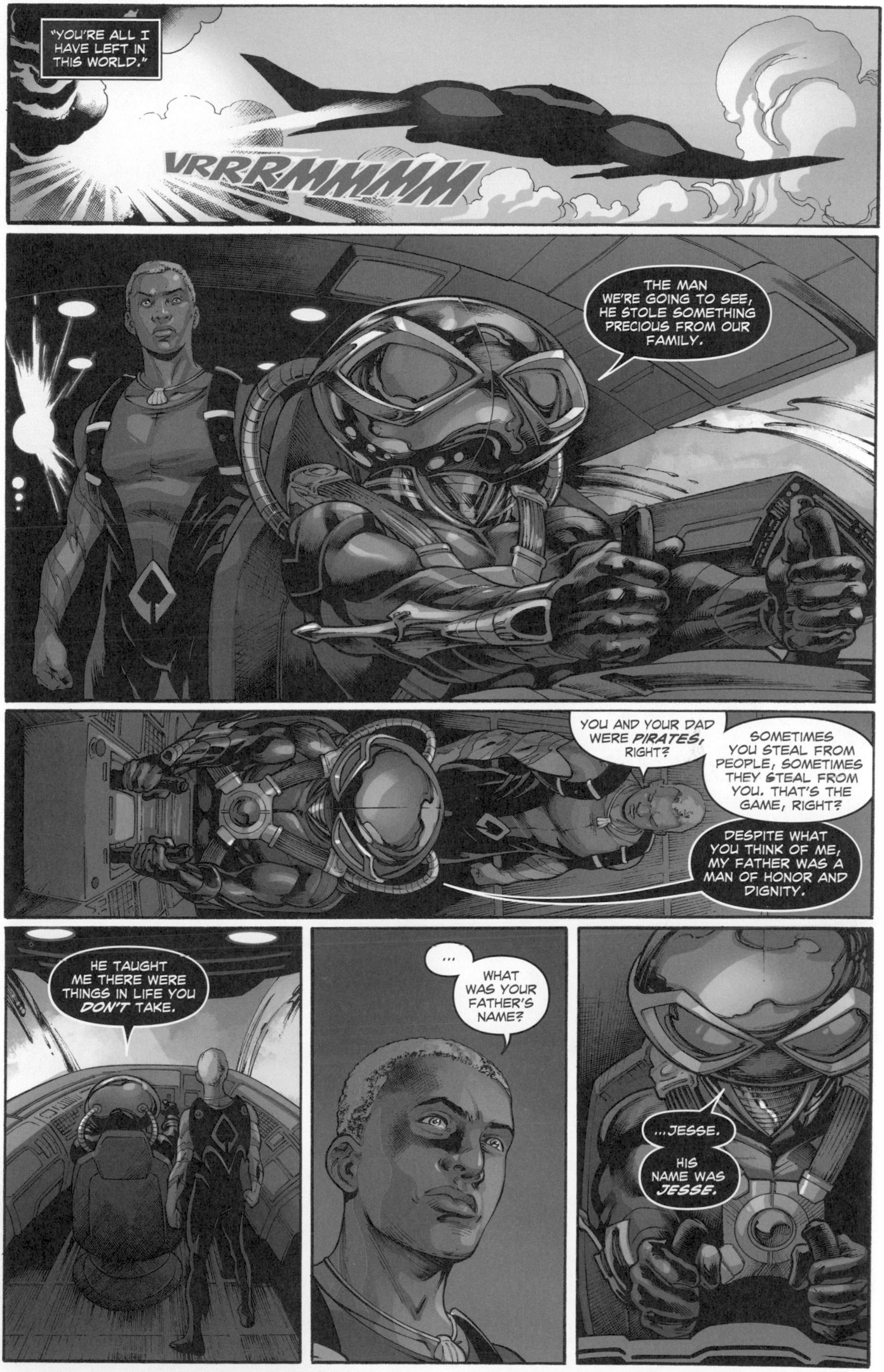
"YOU'RE ALL I HAVE LEFT IN THIS WORLD."
VRRRMMMMM
THE MAN WE'RE GOING TO SEE, HE STOLE SOMETHING PRECIOUS FROM OUR FAMILY.
YOU AND YOUR DAD WERE PIRATES, RIGHT?
SOMETIMES YOU STEAL FROM PEOPLE, SOMETIMES THEY STEAL FROM YOU. THAT'S THE GAME, RIGHT?
DESPITE WHAT YOU THINK OF ME, MY FATHER WAS A MAN OF HONOR AND DIGNITY.
HE TAUGHT ME THERE WERE THINGS IN LIFE YOU DON'T TAKE.
...
WHAT WAS YOUR FATHER'S NAME?
...JESSE.
HIS NAME WAS JESSE.

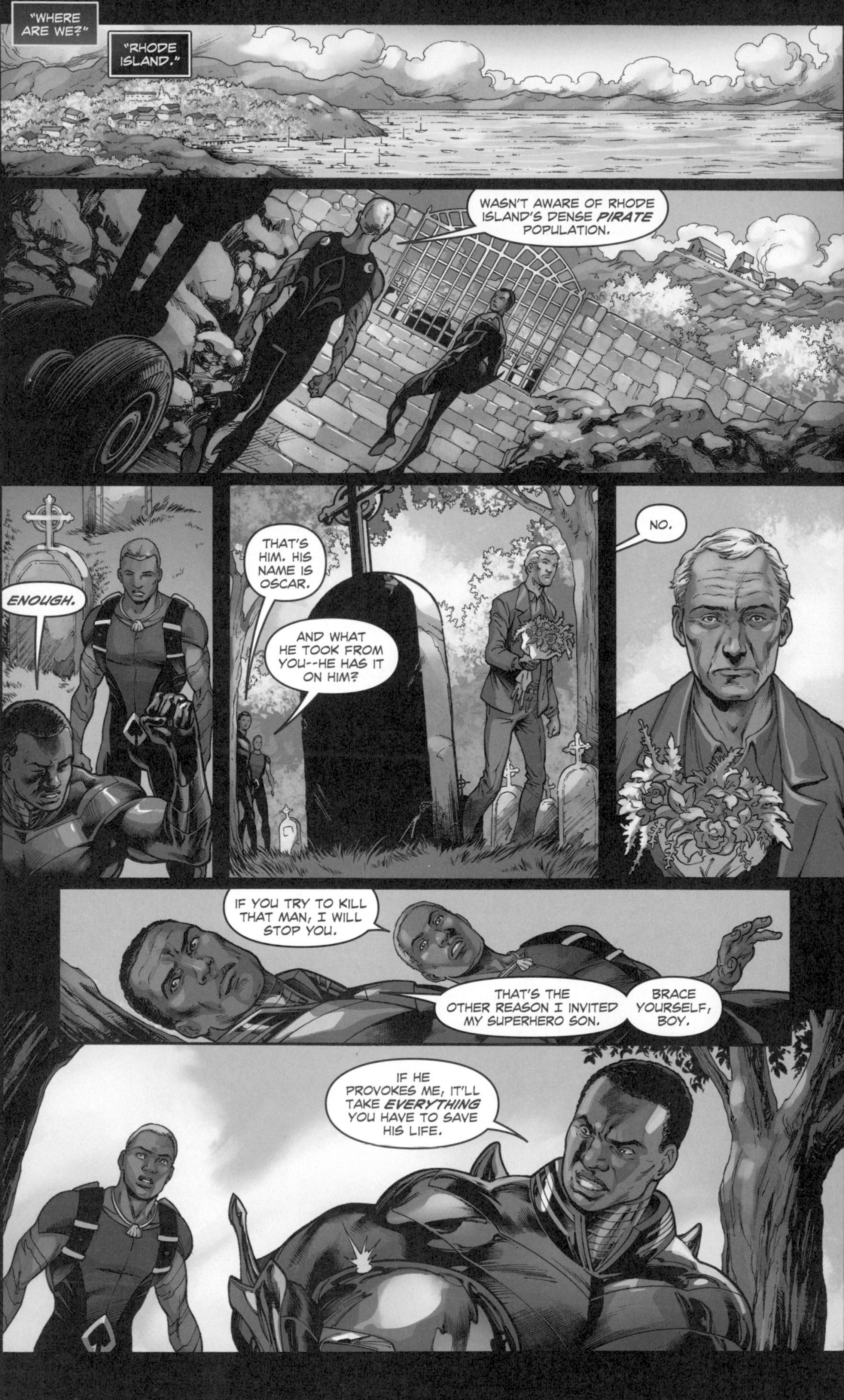
"WHERE ARE WE?"
"RHODE ISLAND."
WASN'T AWARE OF RHODE ISLAND'S DENSE *PIRATE* POPULATION.
ENOUGH.
THAT'S HIM. HIS NAME IS OSCAR.
AND WHAT HE TOOK FROM YOU--HE HAS IT ON HIM?
NO.
IF YOU TRY TO KILL THAT MAN, I WILL STOP YOU.
THAT'S THE OTHER REASON I INVITED MY SUPERHERO SON.
BRACE YOURSELF, BOY.
IF HE PROVOKES ME, IT'LL TAKE *EVERYTHING* YOU HAVE TO SAVE HIS LIFE.

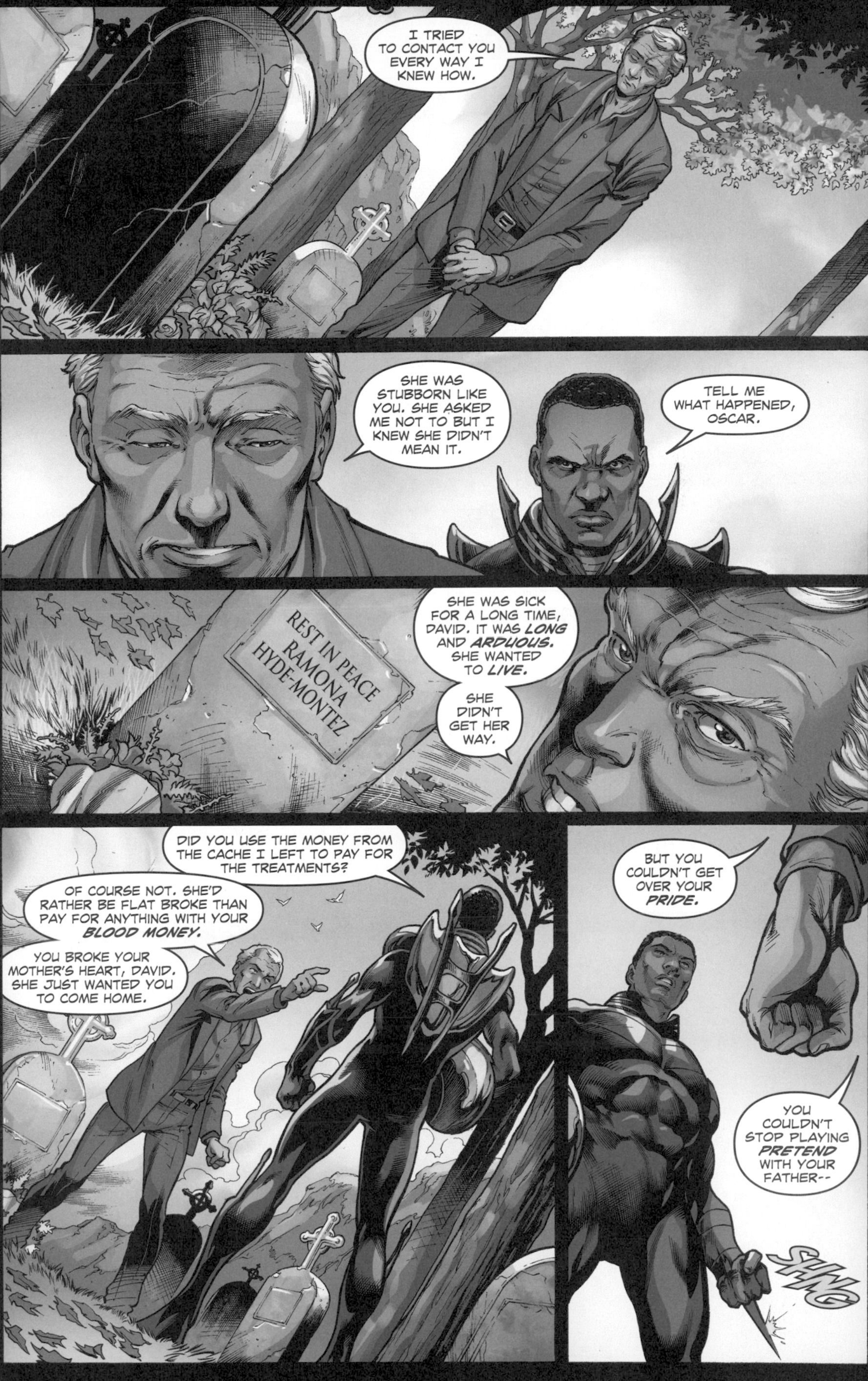
I TRIED TO CONTACT YOU EVERY WAY I KNEW HOW.
SHE WAS STUBBORN LIKE YOU. SHE ASKED ME NOT TO BUT I KNEW SHE DIDN'T MEAN IT.
TELL ME WHAT HAPPENED, OSCAR.
REST IN PEACE RAMONA HYDE-MONTEZ
SHE WAS SICK FOR A LONG TIME, DAVID. IT WAS LONG AND ARDUOUS. SHE WANTED TO LIVE.
SHE DIDN'T GET HER WAY.
DID YOU USE THE MONEY FROM THE CACHE I LEFT TO PAY FOR THE TREATMENTS?
OF COURSE NOT. SHE'D RATHER BE FLAT BROKE THAN PAY FOR ANYTHING WITH YOUR BLOOD MONEY.
YOU BROKE YOUR MOTHER'S HEART, DAVID. SHE JUST WANTED YOU TO COME HOME.
BUT YOU COULDN'T GET OVER YOUR PRIDE.
YOU COULDN'T STOP PLAYING PRETEND WITH YOUR FATHER--
SHNG

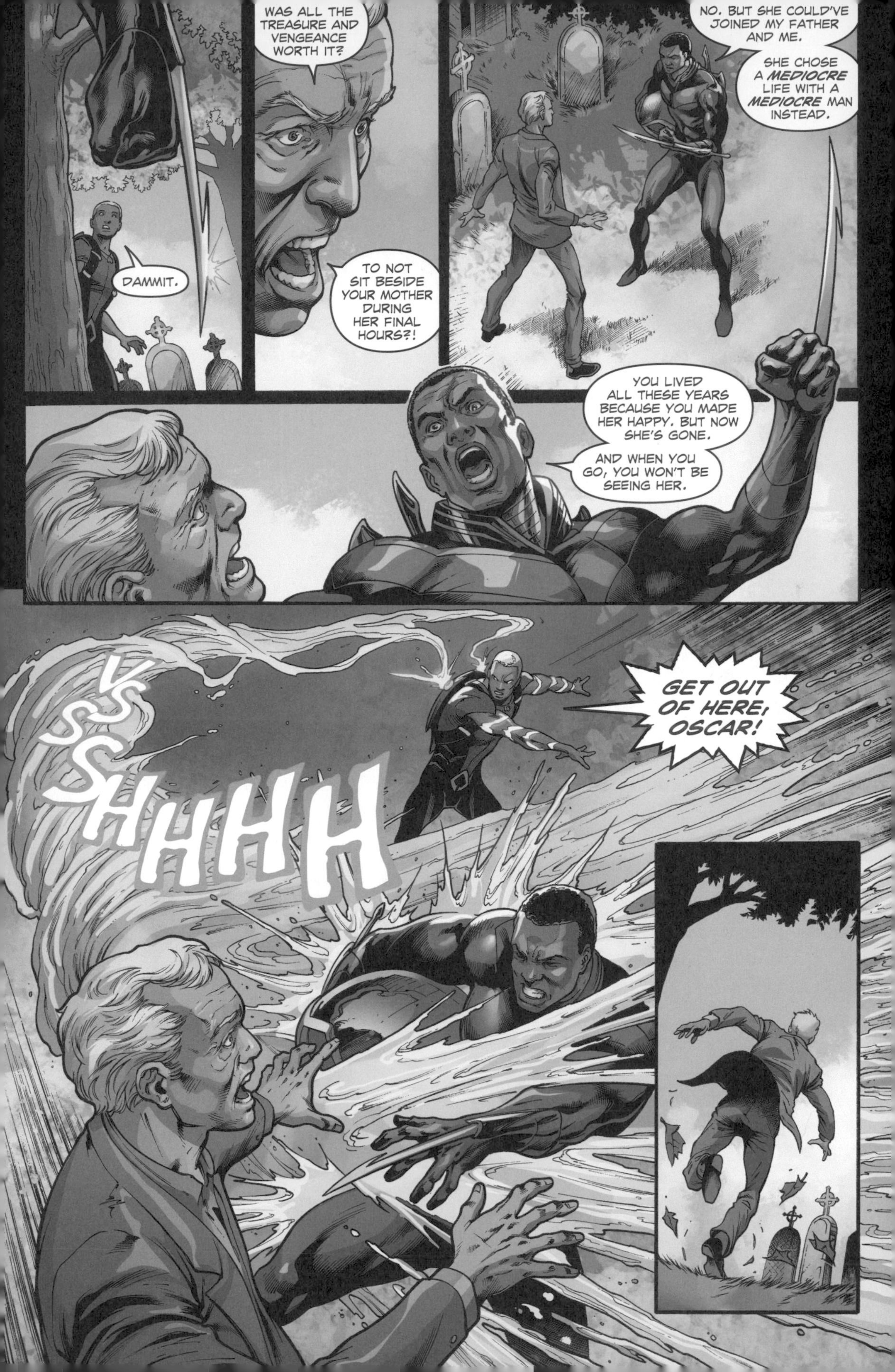
DAMMIT.
WAS ALL THE TREASURE AND VENGEANCE WORTH IT?
TO NOT SIT BESIDE YOUR MOTHER DURING HER FINAL HOURS?!
NO. BUT SHE COULD'VE JOINED MY FATHER AND ME.
SHE CHOSE A MEDIOCRE LIFE WITH A MEDIOCRE MAN INSTEAD.
YOU LIVED ALL THESE YEARS BECAUSE YOU MADE HER HAPPY. BUT NOW SHE'S GONE.
AND WHEN YOU GO, YOU WON'T BE SEEING HER.
VSSSHHHH
GET OUT OF HERE, OSCAR!

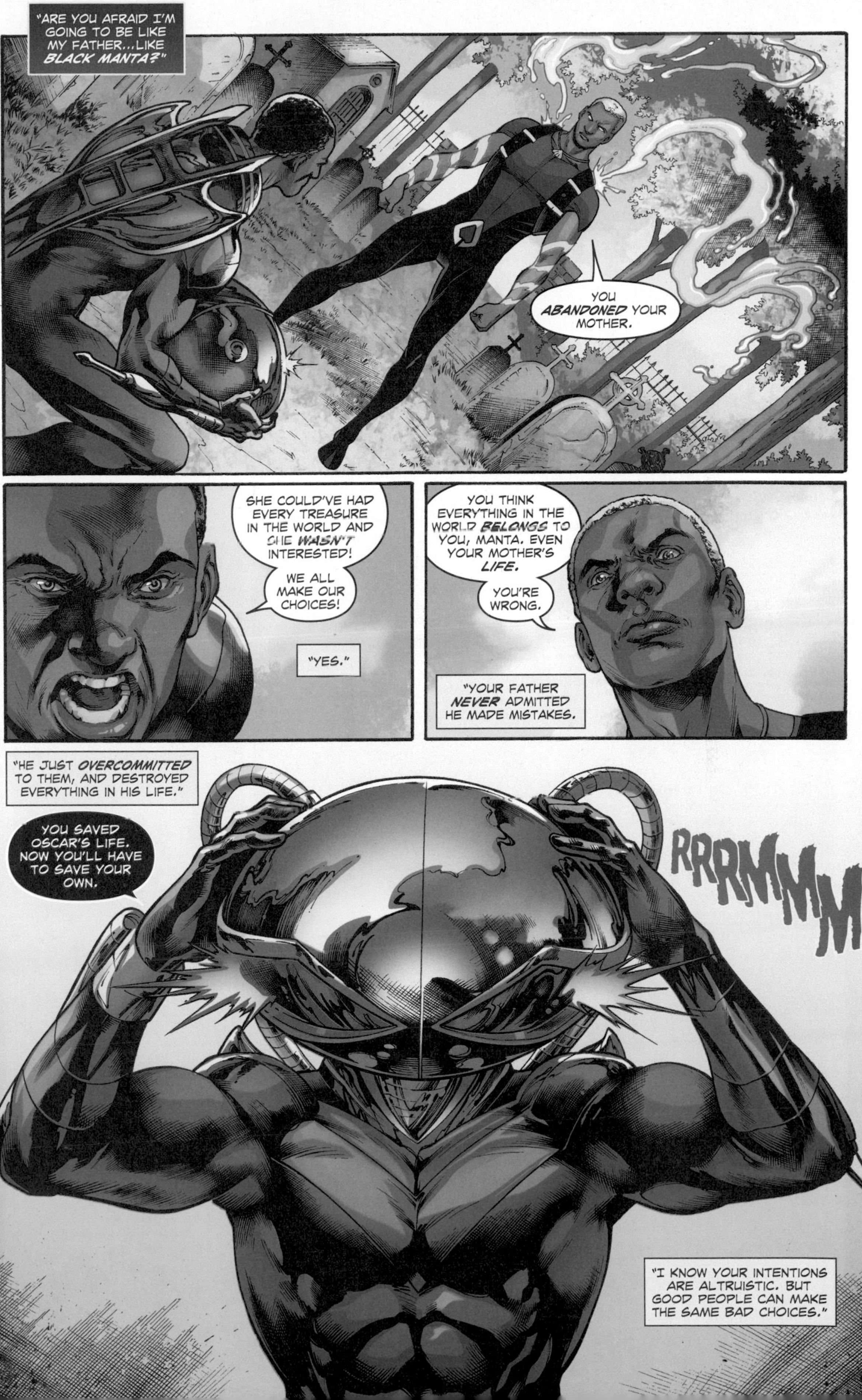
"ARE YOU AFRAID I'M GOING TO BE LIKE MY FATHER...LIKE BLACK MANTA?"
YOU ABANDONED YOUR MOTHER.
SHE COULD'VE HAD EVERY TREASURE IN THE WORLD AND SHE WASN'T INTERESTED!
WE ALL MAKE OUR CHOICES!
"YES."
YOU THINK EVERYTHING IN THE WORLD BELONGS TO YOU, MANTA. EVEN YOUR MOTHER'S LIFE.
YOU'RE WRONG.
"YOUR FATHER NEVER ADMITTED HE MADE MISTAKES.
"HE JUST OVERCOMMITTED TO THEM, AND DESTROYED EVERYTHING IN HIS LIFE."
YOU SAVED OSCAR'S LIFE. NOW YOU'LL HAVE TO SAVE YOUR OWN.
RRRMMMM
"I KNOW YOUR INTENTIONS ARE ALTRUISTIC. BUT GOOD PEOPLE CAN MAKE THE SAME BAD CHOICES."

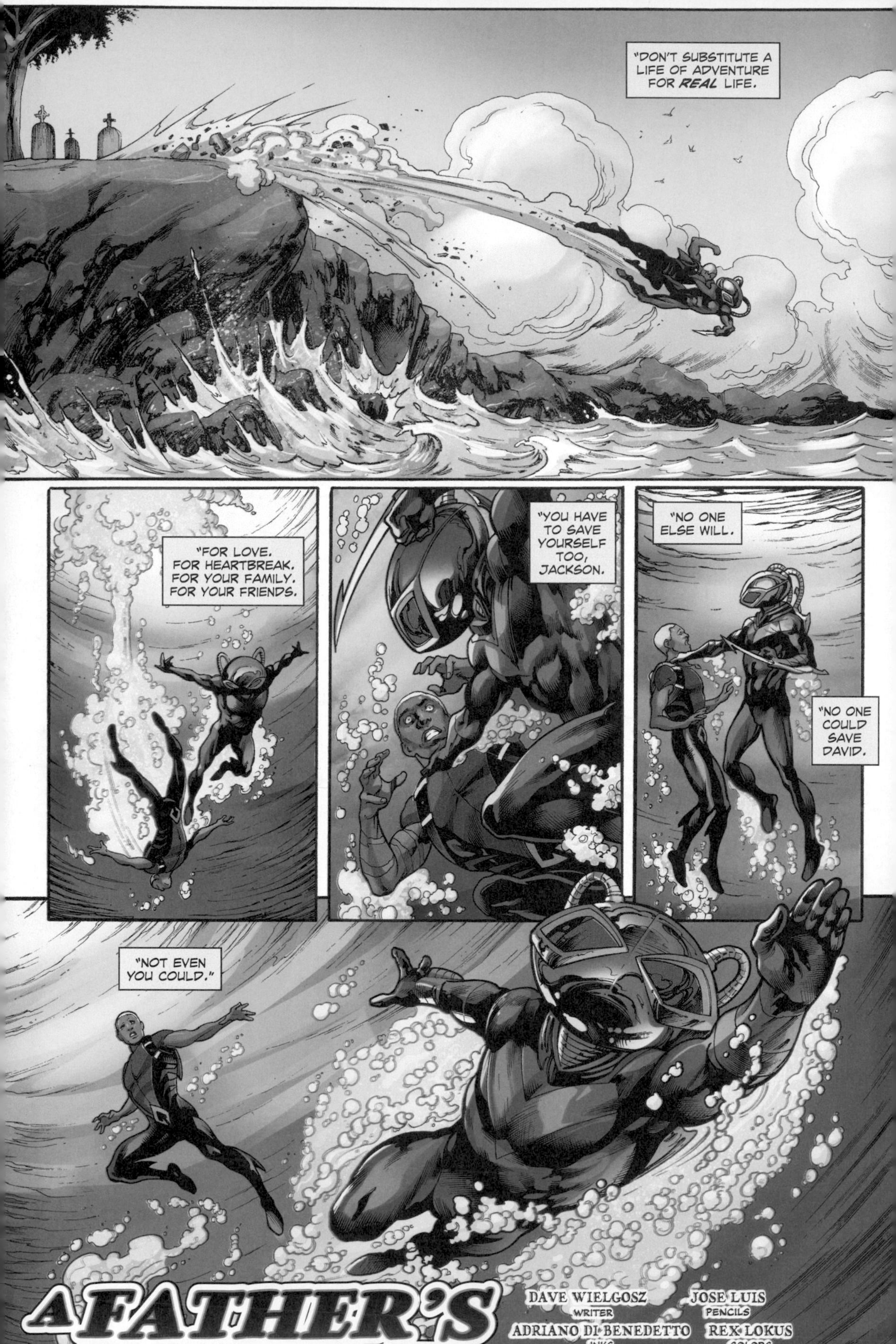
"DON'T SUBSTITUTE A LIFE OF ADVENTURE FOR REAL LIFE.
"FOR LOVE. FOR HEARTBREAK. FOR YOUR FAMILY. FOR YOUR FRIENDS.
"YOU HAVE TO SAVE YOURSELF TOO, JACKSON.
"NO ONE ELSE WILL.
"NO ONE COULD SAVE DAVID.
"NOT EVEN YOU COULD."
A FATHER'S FAVOR
DAVE WIELGOSZ WRITER
JOSE LUIS PENCILS
ADRIANO DI BENEDETTO INKS
REX LOKUS COLORS
WES ABBOTT LETTERS
MICHAEL McCALISTER EDITOR
AQUAMAN CREATED BY PAUL NORRIS
END

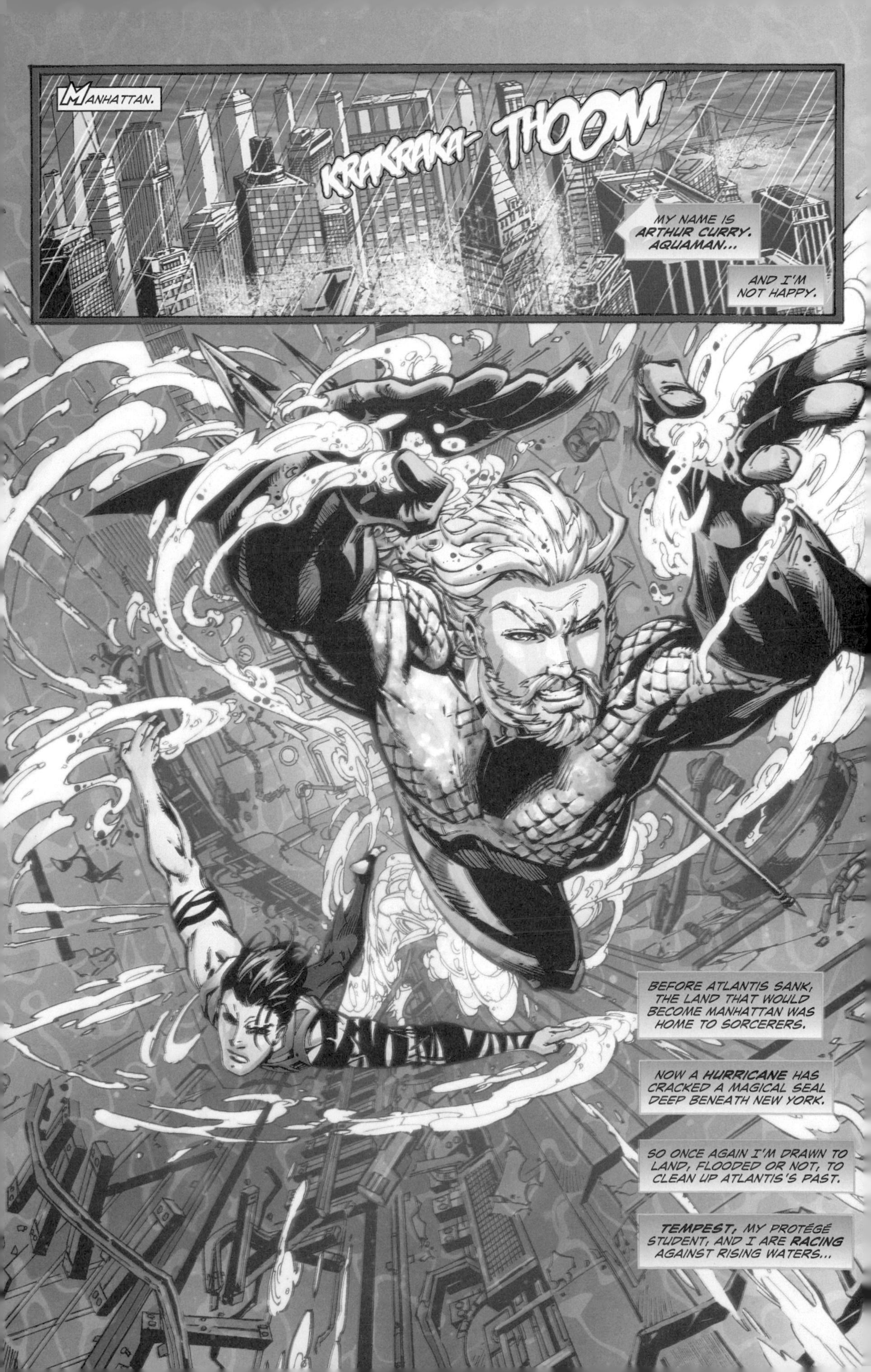

MANHATTAN.
KRAKRAKA-THOOM
MY NAME IS ARTHUR CURRY. AQUAMAN...
AND I'M NOT HAPPY.
BEFORE ATLANTIS SANK, THE LAND THAT WOULD BECOME MANHATTAN WAS HOME TO SORCERERS.
NOW A HURRICANE HAS CRACKED A MAGICAL SEAL DEEP BENEATH NEW YORK.
SO ONCE AGAIN I'M DRAWN TO LAND, FLOODED OR NOT, TO CLEAN UP ATLANTIS'S PAST.
TEMPEST, MY PROTÉGÉ STUDENT, AND I ARE RACING AGAINST RISING WATERS...

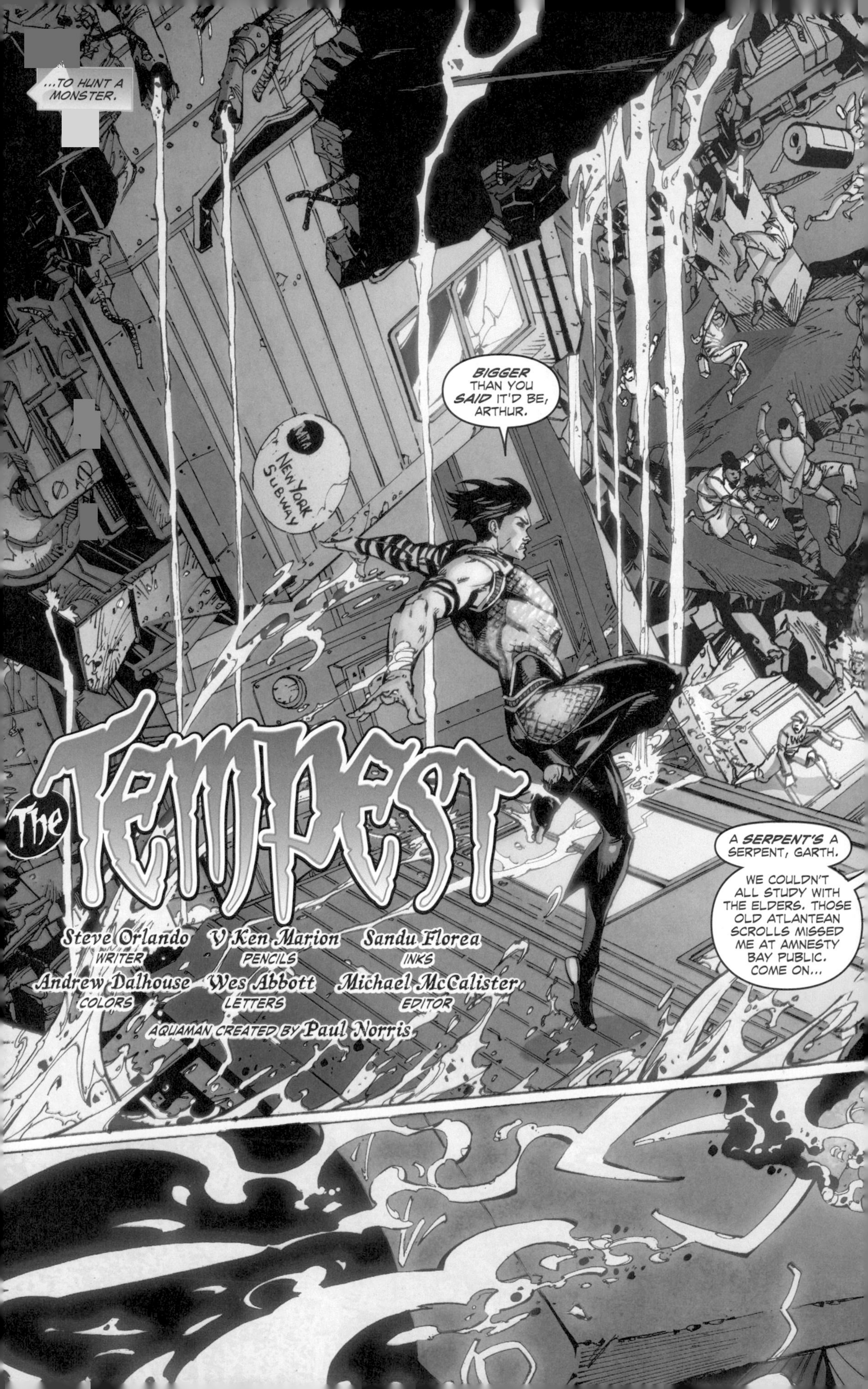

...TO HUNT A MONSTER.
BIGGER THAN YOU SAID IT'D BE, ARTHUR.
NEW YORK SUBWAY
The Tempest
Steve Orlando WRITER
V Ken Marion PENCILS
Sandu Florea INKS
Andrew Dalhouse COLORS
Wes Abbott LETTERS
Michael McCalister EDITOR
AQUAMAN CREATED BY Paul Norris
A SERPENT'S A SERPENT, GARTH.
WE COULDN'T ALL STUDY WITH THE ELDERS. THOSE OLD ATLANTEAN SCROLLS MISSED ME AT AMNESTY BAY PUBLIC. COME ON...

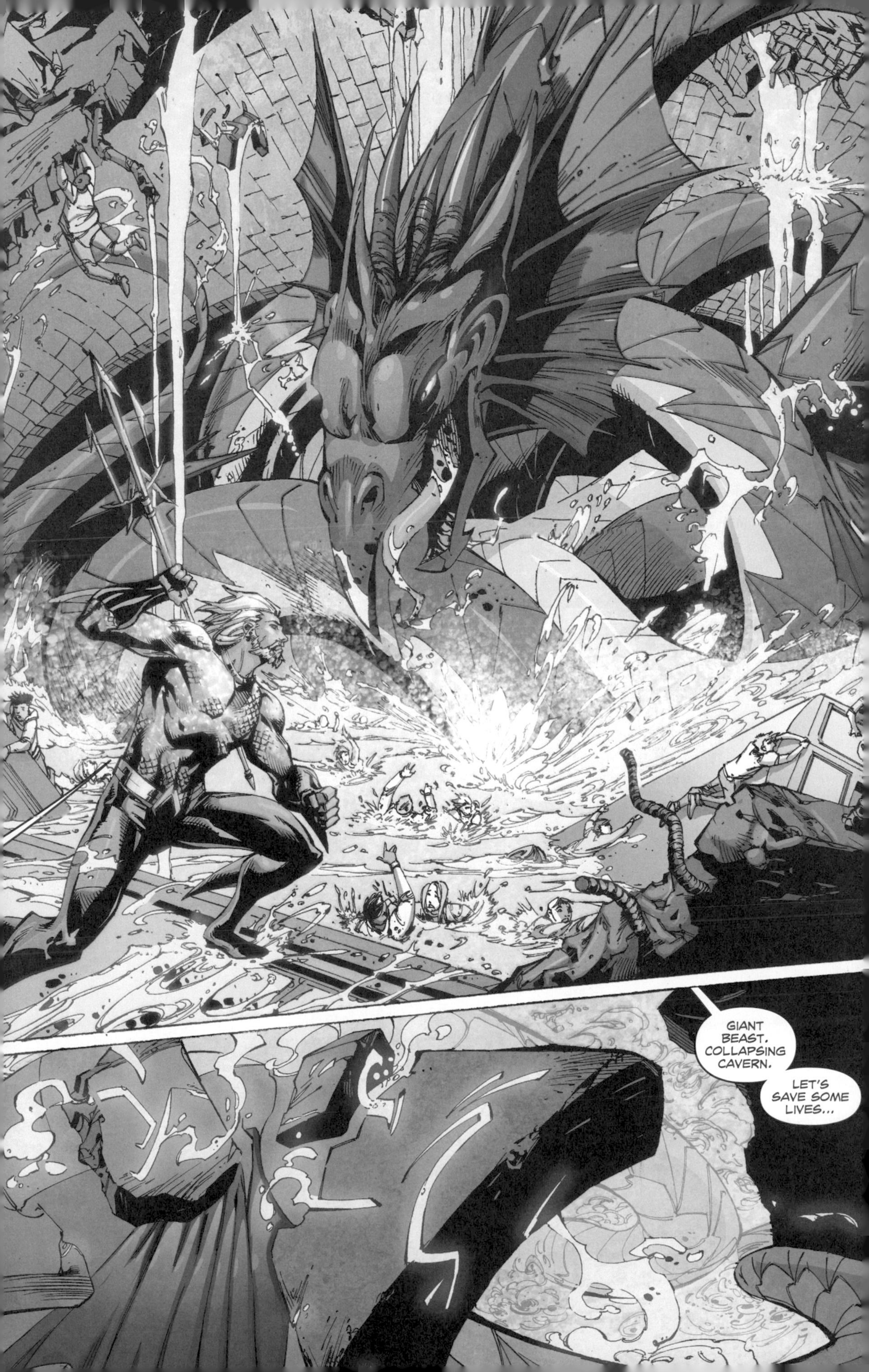
GIANT BEAST. COLLAPSING CAVERN.
LET'S SAVE SOME LIVES...

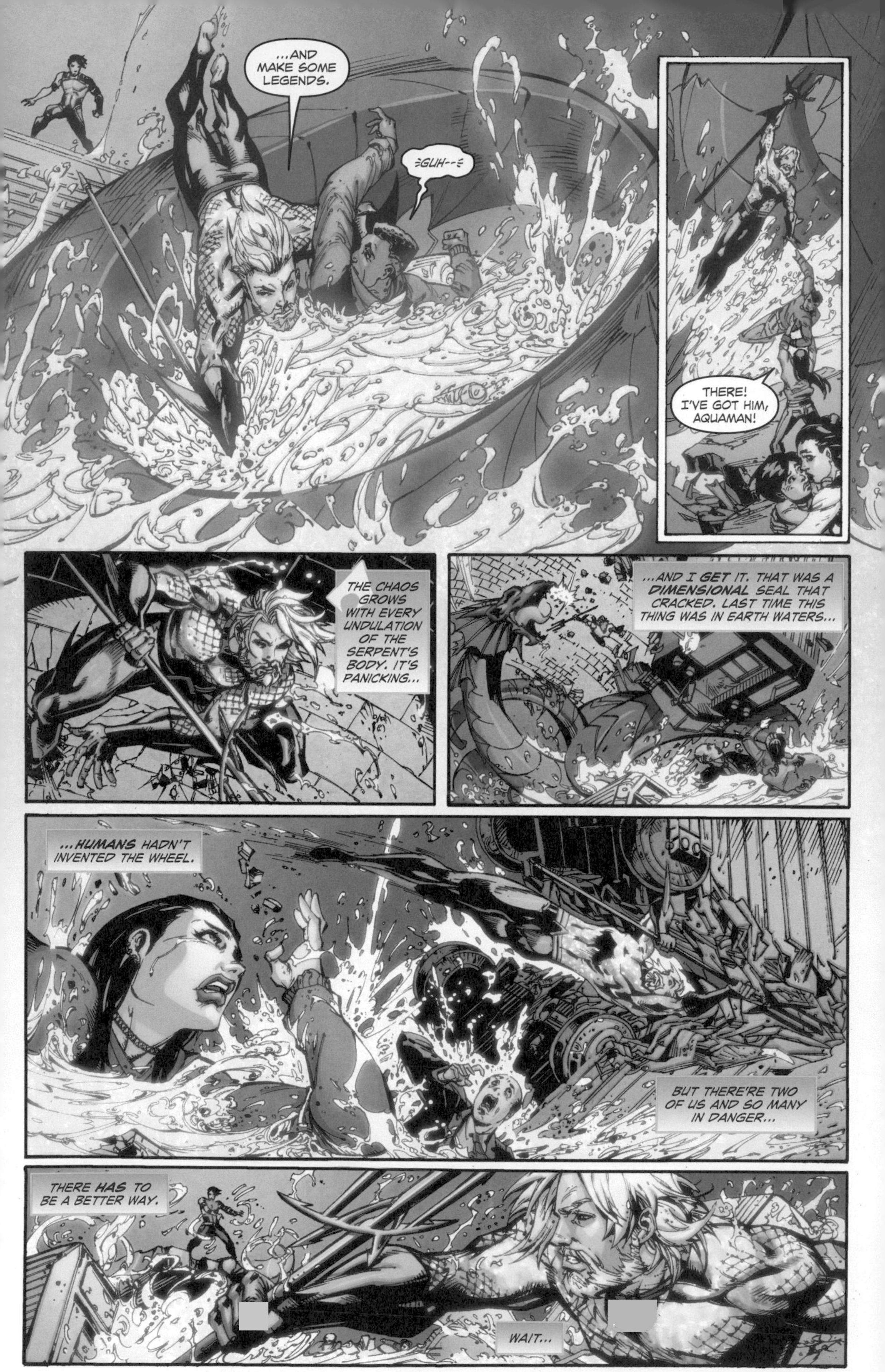
...AND MAKE SOME LEGENDS.
GUH--
THERE! I'VE GOT HIM, AQUAMAN!
THE CHAOS GROWS WITH EVERY UNDULATION OF THE SERPENT'S BODY. IT'S PANICKING...
...AND I GET IT. THAT WAS A DIMENSIONAL SEAL THAT CRACKED. LAST TIME THIS THING WAS IN EARTH WATERS...
...HUMANS HADN'T INVENTED THE WHEEL.
BUT THERE'RE TWO OF US AND SO MANY IN DANGER...
THERE HAS TO BE A BETTER WAY.
WAIT...

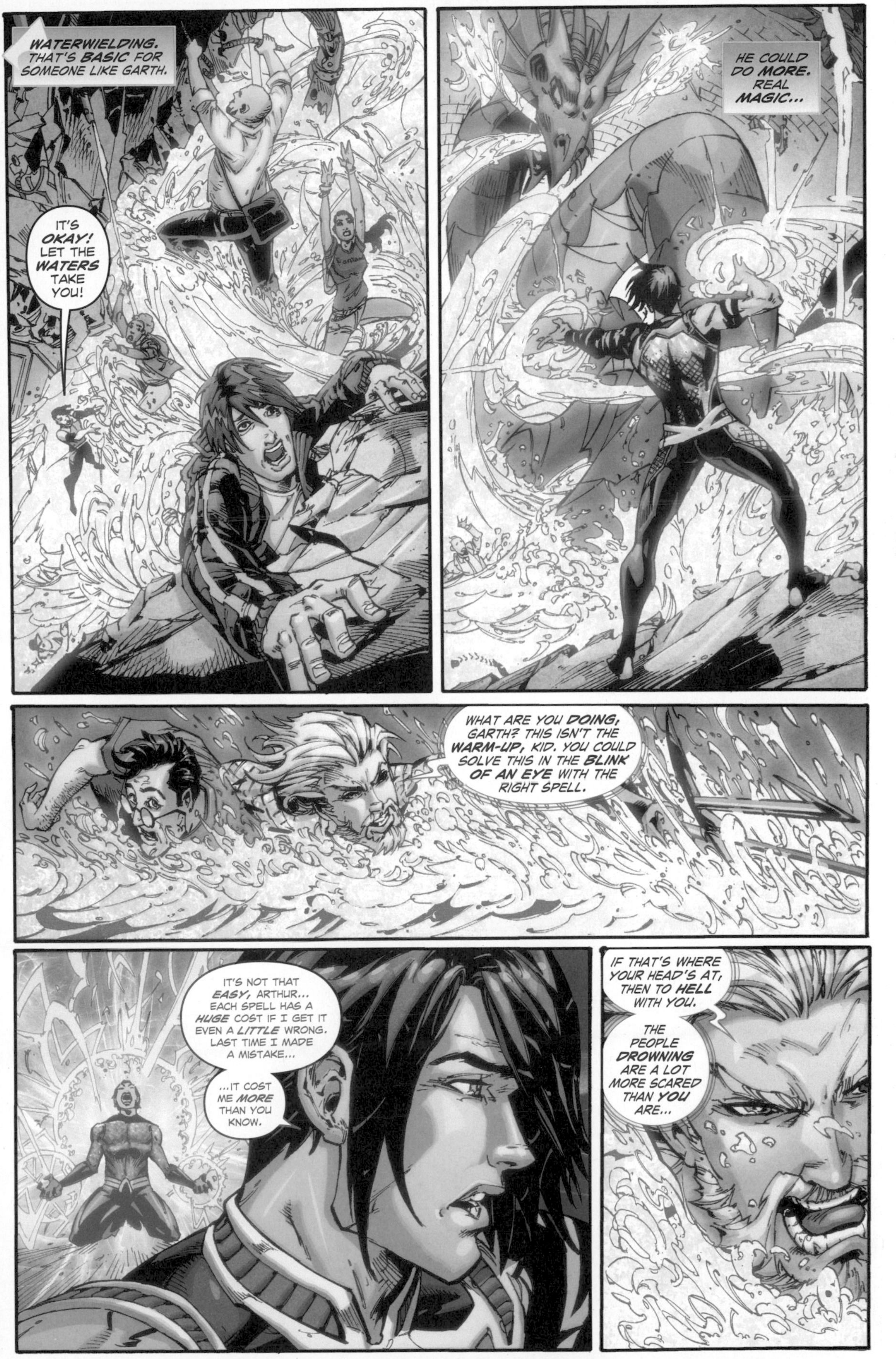
WATERWIELDING. THAT'S BASIC FOR SOMEONE LIKE GARTH.
IT'S OKAY! LET THE WATERS TAKE YOU!
HE COULD DO MORE. REAL MAGIC...
WHAT ARE YOU DOING, GARTH? THIS ISN'T THE WARM-UP, KID. YOU COULD SOLVE THIS IN THE BLINK OF AN EYE WITH THE RIGHT SPELL.
IT'S NOT THAT EASY, ARTHUR... EACH SPELL HAS A HUGE COST IF I GET IT EVEN A LITTLE WRONG. LAST TIME I MADE A MISTAKE...
...IT COST ME MORE THAN YOU KNOW.
IF THAT'S WHERE YOUR HEAD'S AT, THEN TO HELL WITH YOU.
THE PEOPLE DROWNING ARE A LOT MORE SCARED THAN YOU ARE...

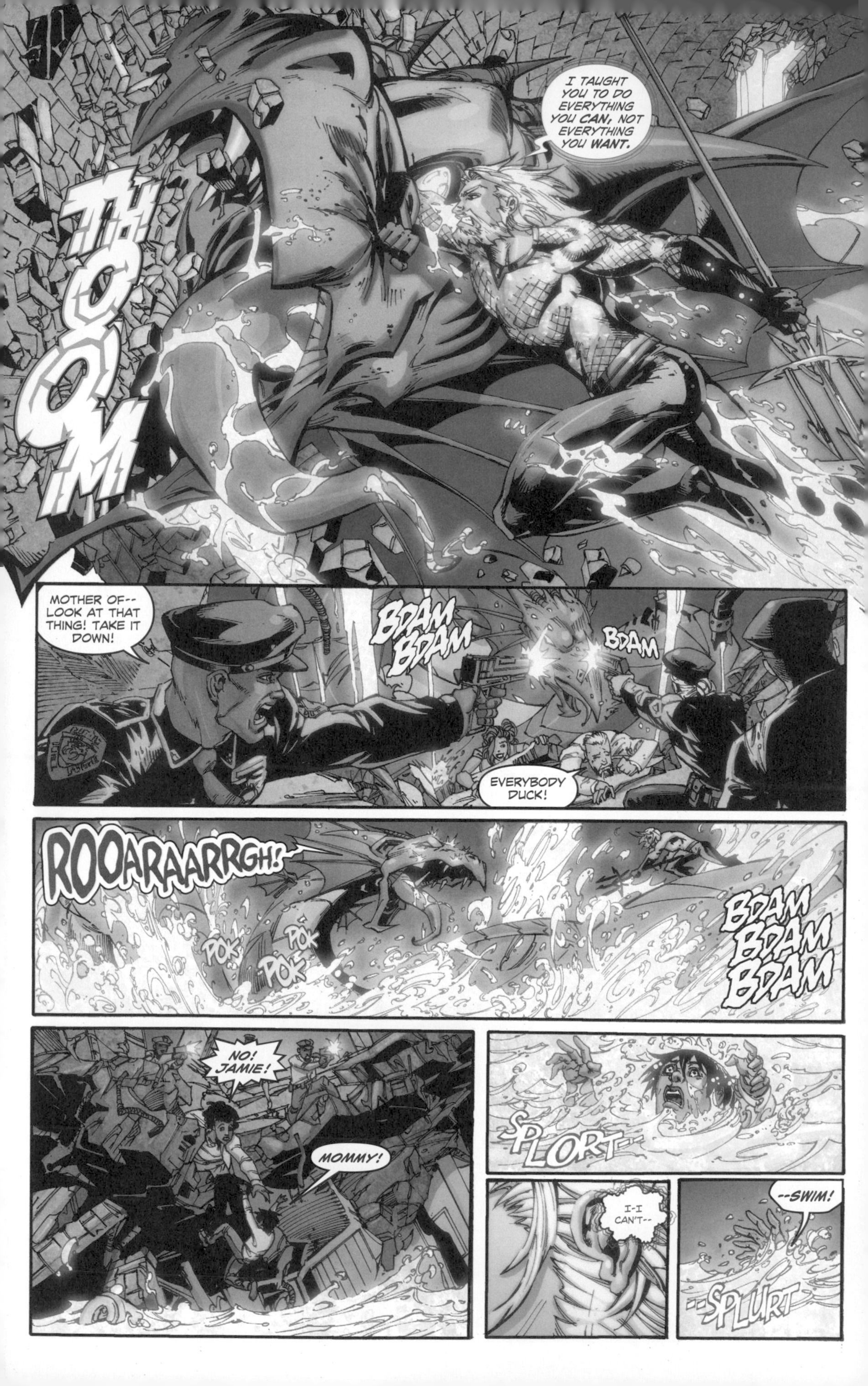
I TAUGHT YOU TO DO EVERYTHING YOU CAN, NOT EVERYTHING YOU WANT.
THOOOM
MOTHER OF-- LOOK AT THAT THING! TAKE IT DOWN!
BDAM BDAM
BDAM
EVERYBODY DUCK!
ROOARAARRGH!
POK POK POK
BDAM BDAM BDAM
NO! JAMIE!
MOMMY!
SPLORT--
I-I CAN'T--
--SWIM!
--SPLURT

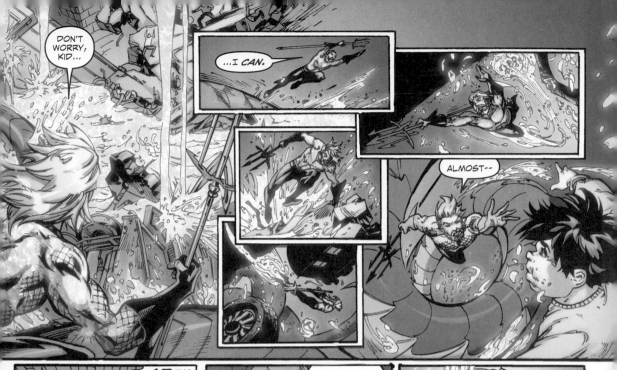

DON'T WORRY, KID...

...I CAN.

ALMOST--

ARGH!

TEMPEST! THE KID'S GOING TO *DROWN!*

I CAN PULL HIM FREE WITH A *TIDECURL...* JUST NEED TO-- *HGRRNK!*

VUUVUUVUU

DAMN. I COULD *REALLY* USE...

...A LOCAL ASSIST.

THANK YOU, MY FRIENDS.

NOW THAT THE *KID'S* SAFE, I CAN--

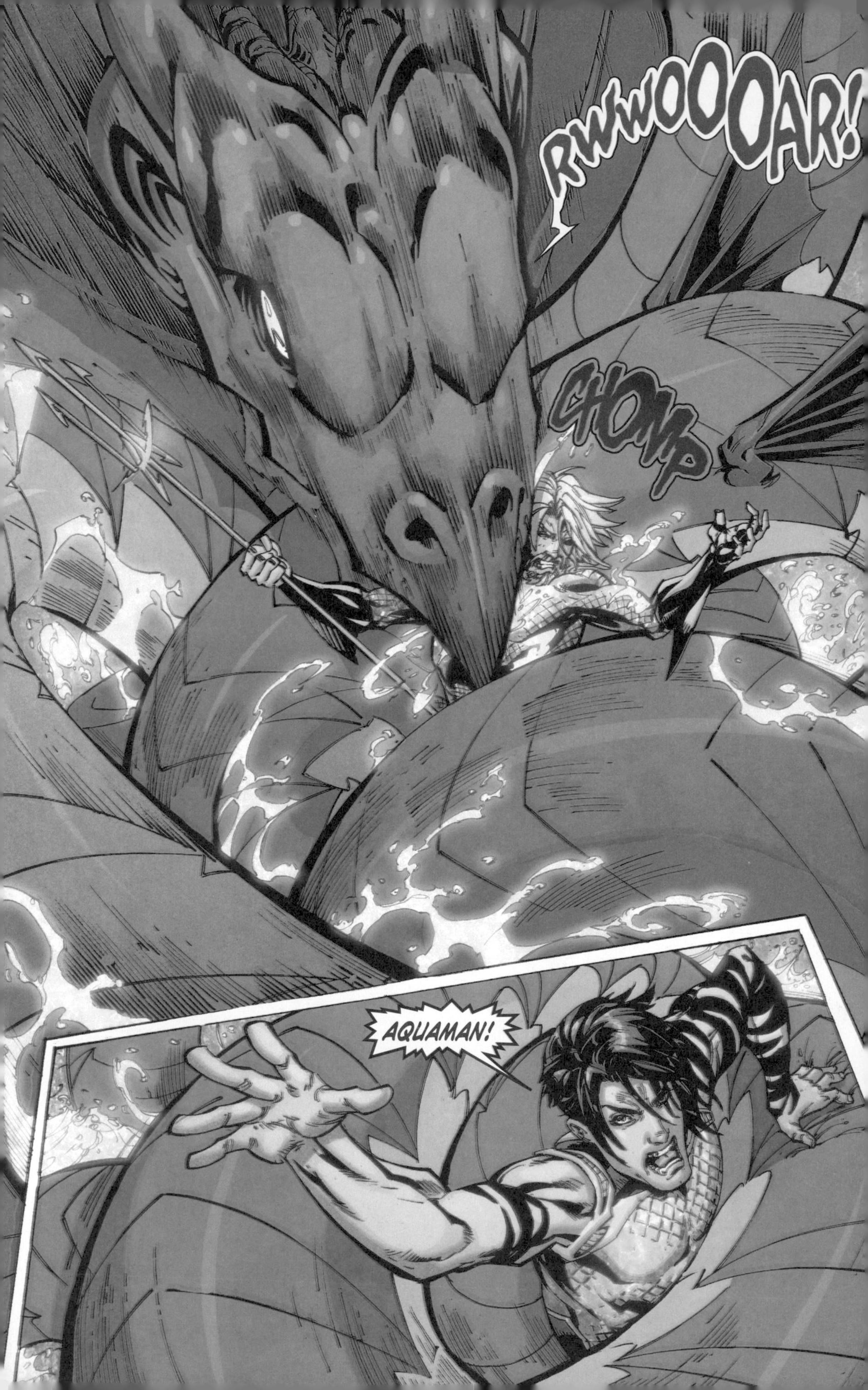
RWWOOOOAR!
CHOMP
AQUAMAN!

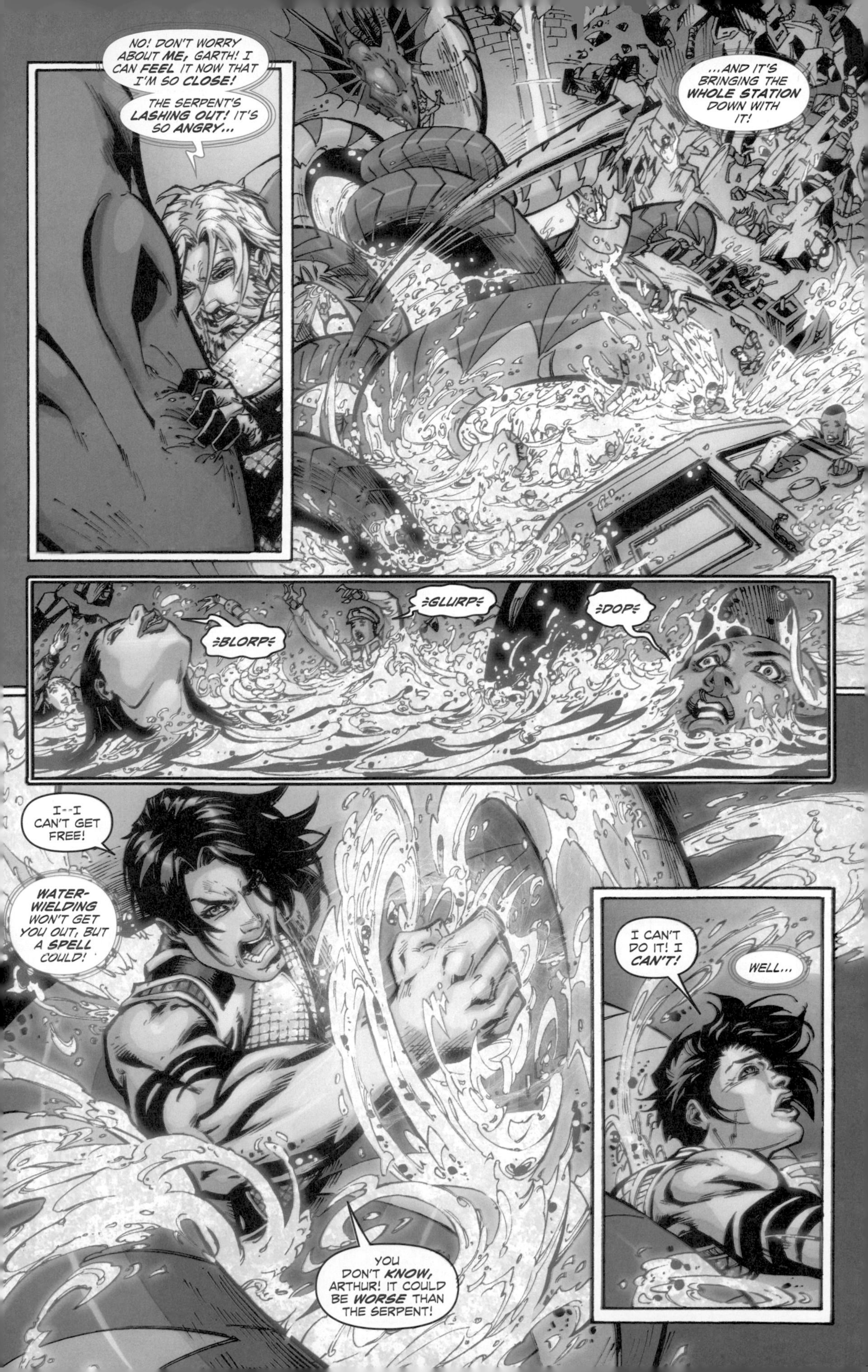
NO! DON'T WORRY ABOUT ME, GARTH! I CAN FEEL IT NOW THAT I'M SO CLOSE!
THE SERPENT'S LASHING OUT! IT'S SO ANGRY...
...AND IT'S BRINGING THE WHOLE STATION DOWN WITH IT!
BLORP
GLURP
DOP
I--I CAN'T GET FREE!
WATER-WIELDING WON'T GET YOU OUT, BUT A SPELL COULD!
YOU DON'T KNOW, ARTHUR! IT COULD BE WORSE THAN THE SERPENT!
I CAN'T DO IT! I CAN'T!
WELL...

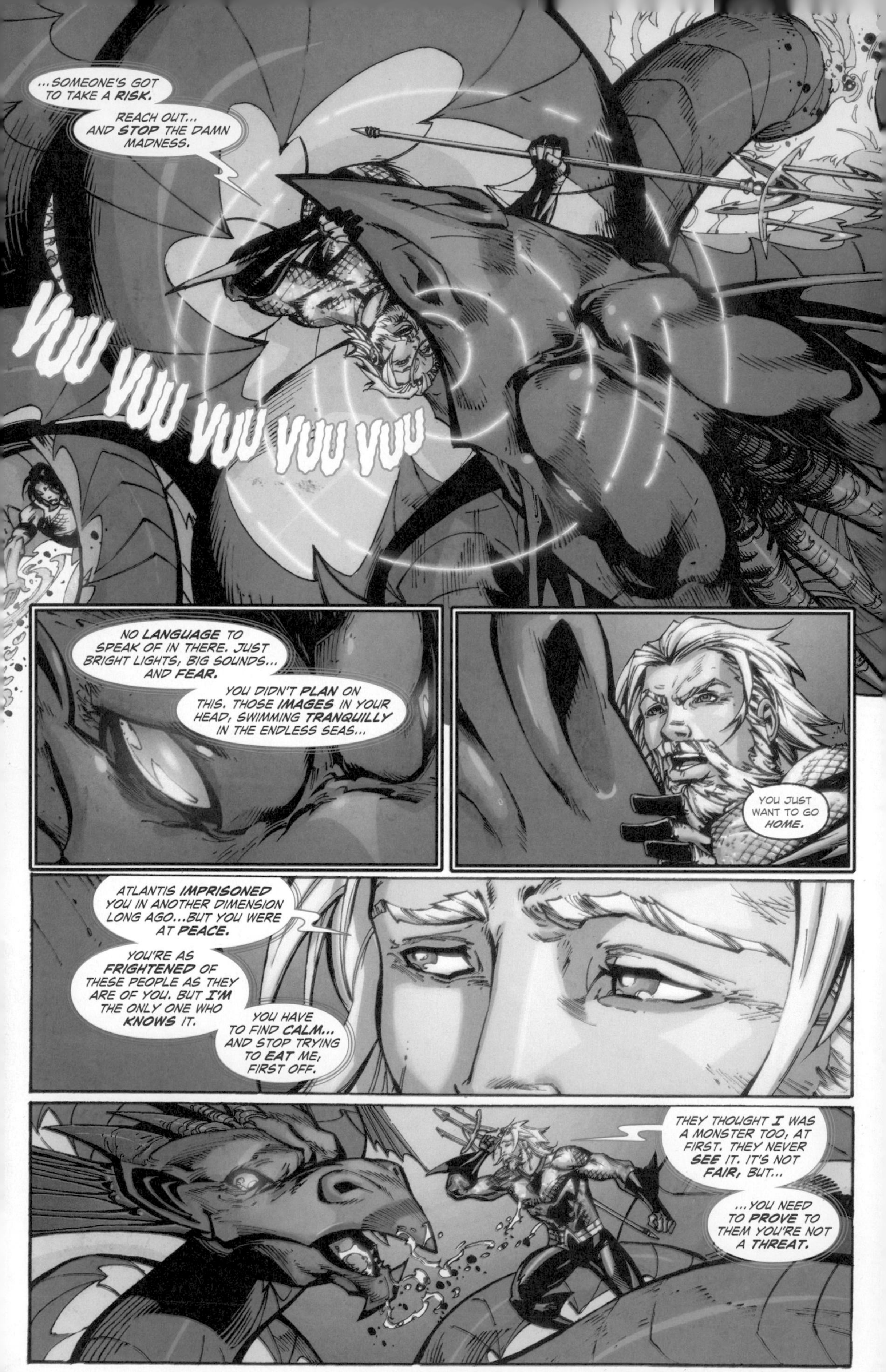
...SOMEONE'S GOT TO TAKE A RISK.
REACH OUT... AND STOP THE DAMN MADNESS.
VUU VUU VUU VUU VUU
NO LANGUAGE TO SPEAK OF IN THERE. JUST BRIGHT LIGHTS, BIG SOUNDS... AND FEAR.
YOU DIDN'T PLAN ON THIS. THOSE IMAGES IN YOUR HEAD, SWIMMING TRANQUILLY IN THE ENDLESS SEAS...
YOU JUST WANT TO GO HOME.
ATLANTIS IMPRISONED YOU IN ANOTHER DIMENSION LONG AGO...BUT YOU WERE AT PEACE.
YOU'RE AS FRIGHTENED OF THESE PEOPLE AS THEY ARE OF YOU. BUT I'M THE ONLY ONE WHO KNOWS IT.
YOU HAVE TO FIND CALM... AND STOP TRYING TO EAT ME, FIRST OFF.
THEY THOUGHT I WAS A MONSTER TOO, AT FIRST. THEY NEVER SEE IT. IT'S NOT FAIR, BUT...
...YOU NEED TO PROVE TO THEM YOU'RE NOT A THREAT.

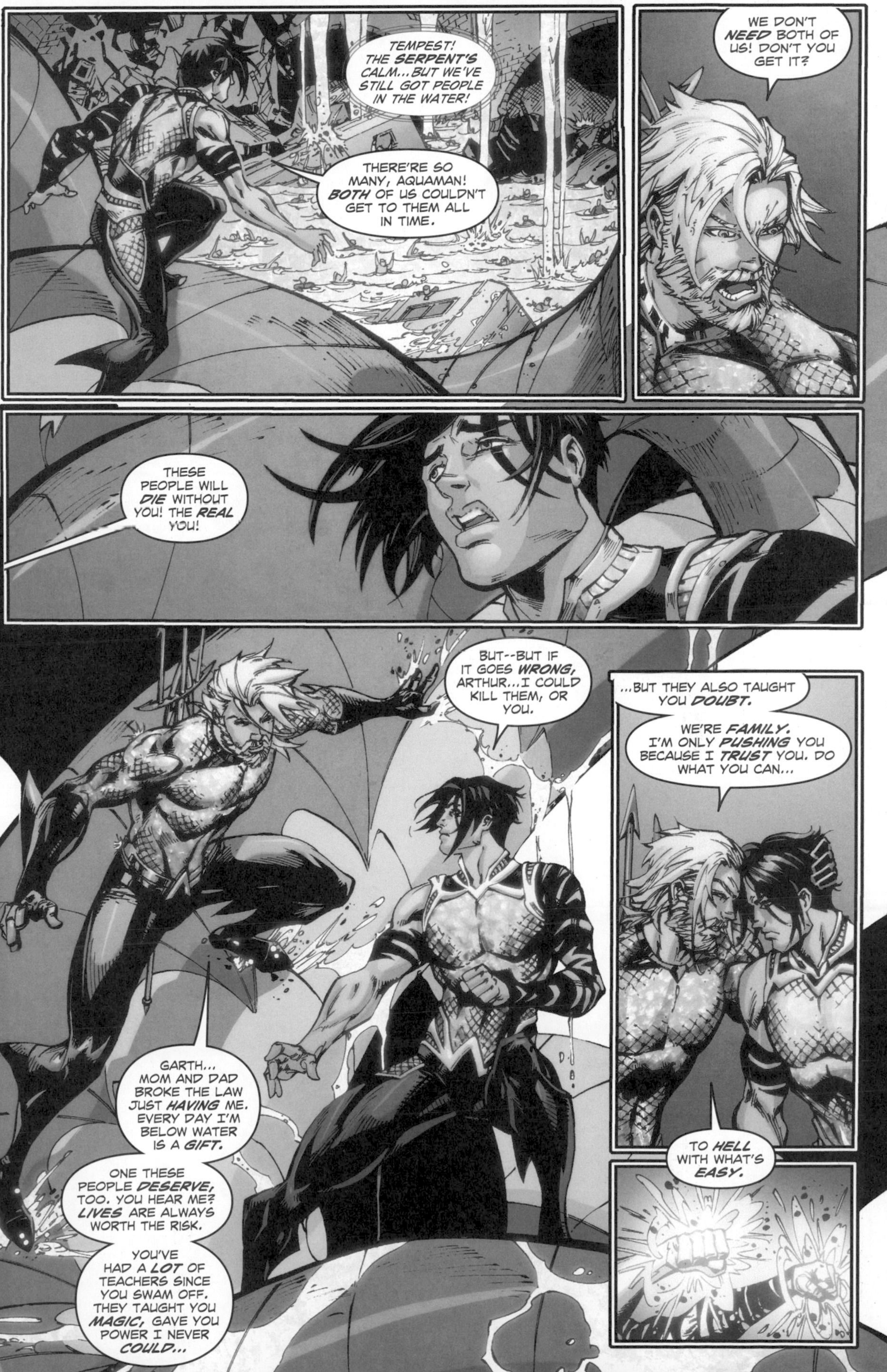
TEMPEST! THE SERPENT'S CALM...BUT WE'VE STILL GOT PEOPLE IN THE WATER!
THERE'RE SO MANY, AQUAMAN! BOTH OF US COULDN'T GET TO THEM ALL IN TIME.
WE DON'T NEED BOTH OF US! DON'T YOU GET IT?
THESE PEOPLE WILL DIE WITHOUT YOU! THE REAL YOU!
BUT--BUT IF IT GOES WRONG, ARTHUR...I COULD KILL THEM, OR YOU.
GARTH... MOM AND DAD BROKE THE LAW JUST HAVING ME. EVERY DAY I'M BELOW WATER IS A GIFT.
ONE THESE PEOPLE DESERVE, TOO. YOU HEAR ME? LIVES ARE ALWAYS WORTH THE RISK.
YOU'VE HAD A LOT OF TEACHERS SINCE YOU SWAM OFF. THEY TAUGHT YOU MAGIC, GAVE YOU POWER I NEVER COULD...
...BUT THEY ALSO TAUGHT YOU DOUBT.
WE'RE FAMILY. I'M ONLY PUSHING YOU BECAUSE I TRUST YOU. DO WHAT YOU CAN...
TO HELL WITH WHAT'S EASY.

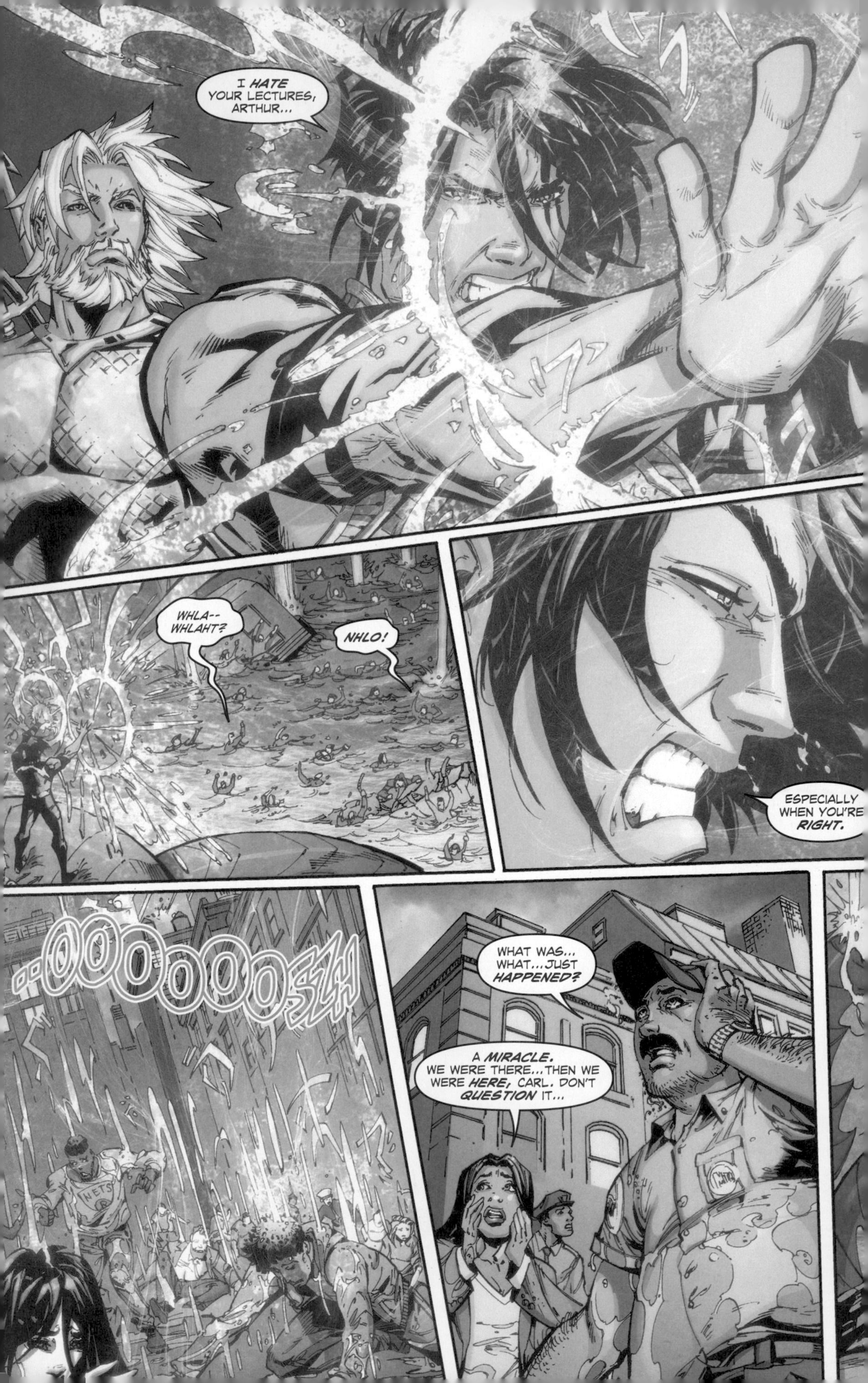
I *HATE* YOUR LECTURES, ARTHUR...
WHLA--WHLAHT?
NHLO!
ESPECIALLY WHEN YOU'RE *RIGHT.*
OOOOOOOOOSH
WHAT WAS... WHAT...JUST *HAPPENED?*
A *MIRACLE.* WE WERE THERE...THEN WE WERE *HERE,* CARL. DON'T *QUESTION* IT...

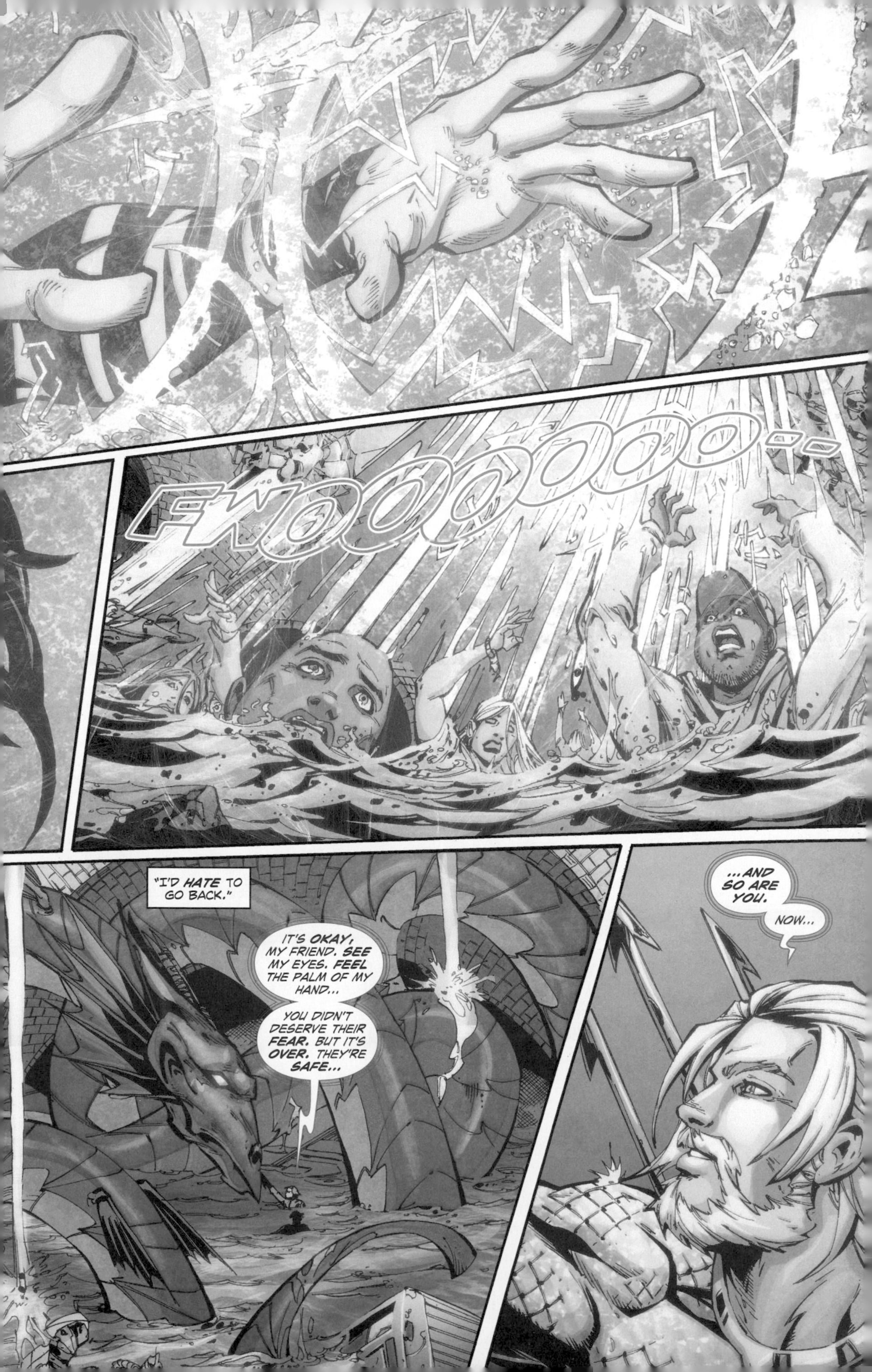
FWOOOOOOOO--
"I'D HATE TO GO BACK."
IT'S OKAY, MY FRIEND. SEE MY EYES. FEEL THE PALM OF MY HAND...
YOU DIDN'T DESERVE THEIR FEAR. BUT IT'S OVER. THEY'RE SAFE...
...AND SO ARE YOU.
NOW...

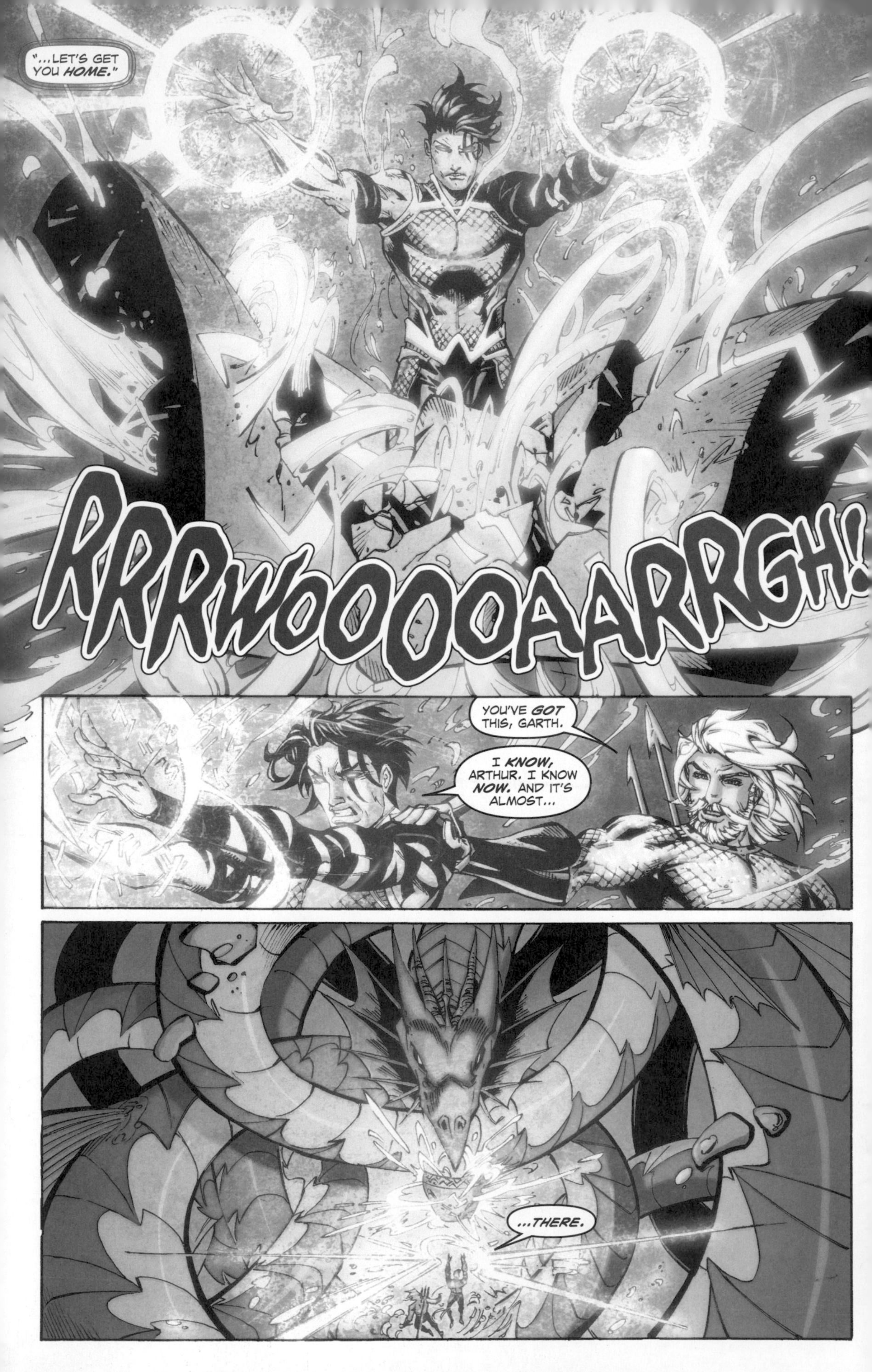
"...LET'S GET YOU HOME."
RRRWOOOOAARRGH!
YOU'VE GOT THIS, GARTH.
I KNOW, ARTHUR. I KNOW NOW. AND IT'S ALMOST...
...THERE.

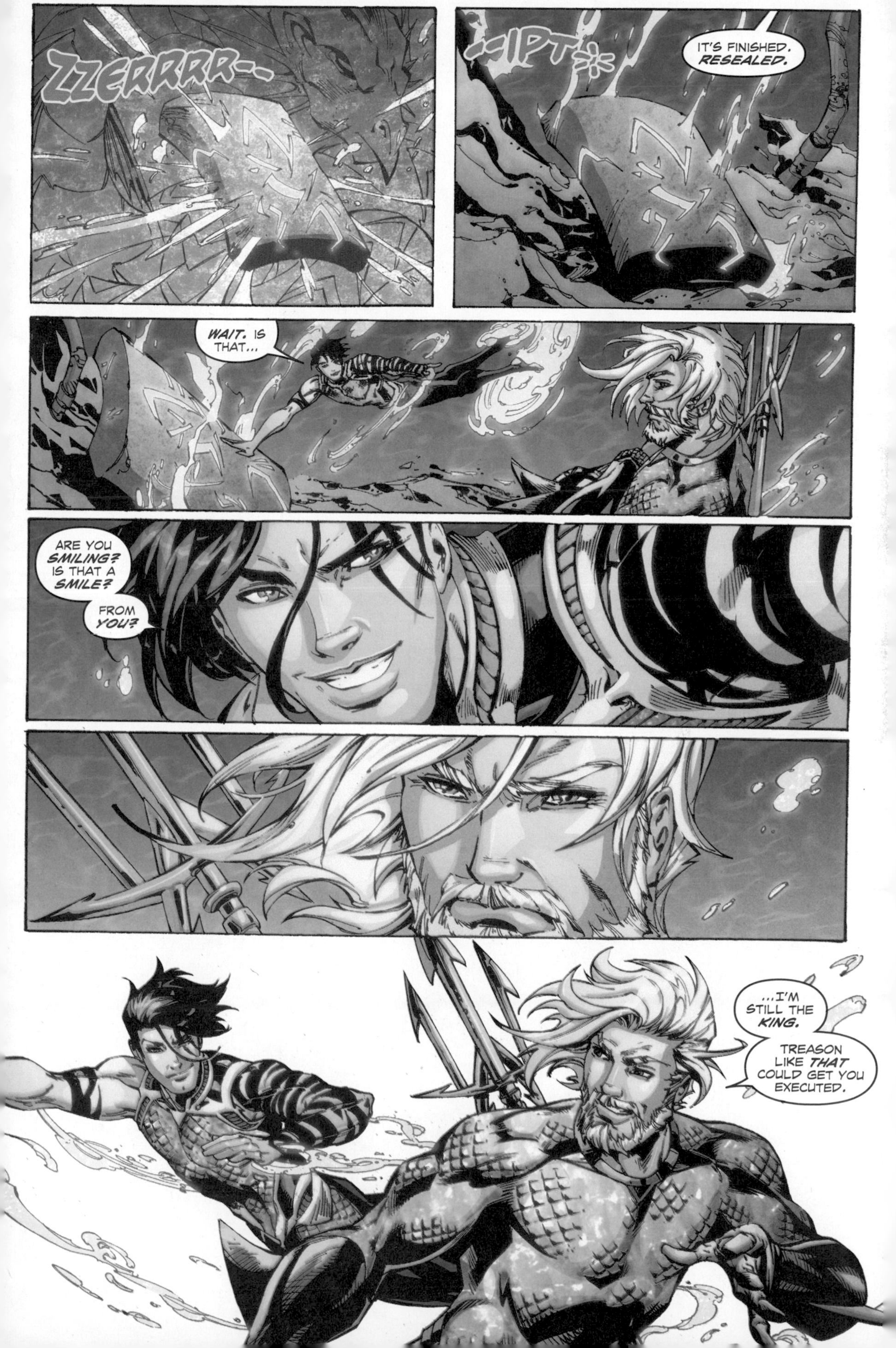
ZZERRRR--
--IPT
IT'S FINISHED. RESEALED.
WAIT. IS THAT...
ARE YOU SMILING? IS THAT A SMILE?
FROM YOU?
...I'M STILL THE KING.
TREASON LIKE THAT COULD GET YOU EXECUTED.

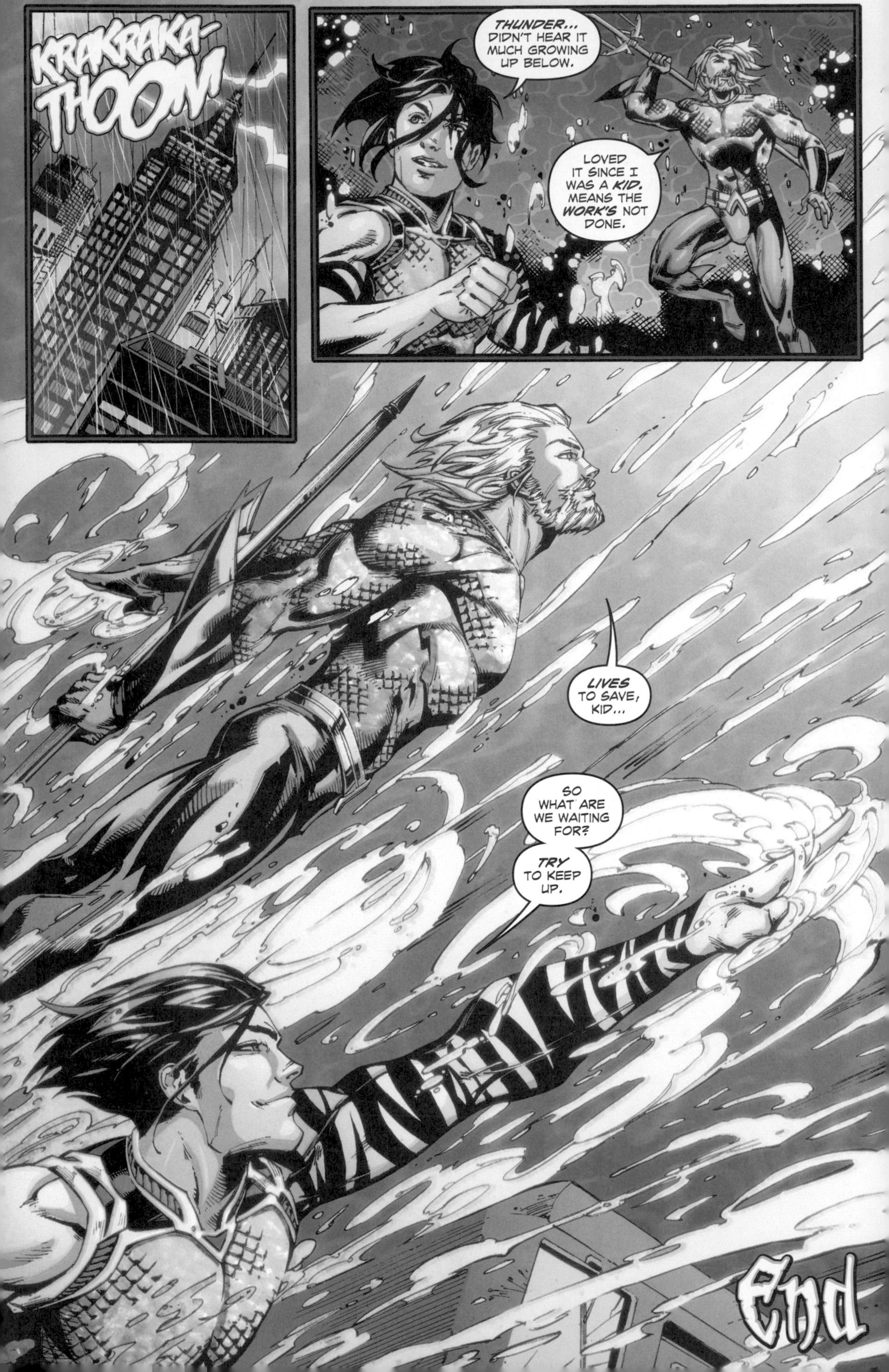
KRAKRAKA-THOOM
THUNDER... DIDN'T HEAR IT MUCH GROWING UP BELOW.
LOVED IT SINCE I WAS A KID. MEANS THE WORK'S NOT DONE.
LIVES TO SAVE, KID...
SO WHAT ARE WE WAITING FOR?
TRY TO KEEP UP.
End

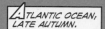

ATLANTIC OCEAN, LATE AUTUMN.

WHALE WATCH

LAST SEASON THIS POD HAD ZERO BIRTHS. THEY'RE ENDANGERED.

IT'S BECAUSE THE WATER TEMPERATURE HAS CHANGED UP NORTH AND SO HAS THE CURRENT.

THEY JUST NEED A LITTLE NUDGE TO STAY SOUTH FOR BREEDING SEASON.

YOU'LL MAKE A GREAT DAD, ARTHUR... ONE DAY. THE OCEAN IS LUCKY TO HAVE A CARING SOUL LIKE YOU.

WHY, MERA, ARE YOU WOOING ME?

I'M ALWAYS WOOING YOU. BUT EYES ON THE WHALES NOW, MY LOVE.

CECIL CASTELLUCCI
WRITER

POP MHAN
ARTIST

REX LOKUS
COLORS

WES ABBOTT
LETTERS

MICHAEL McCALISTER
EDITOR

AQUAMAN CREATED BY PAUL NORRIS

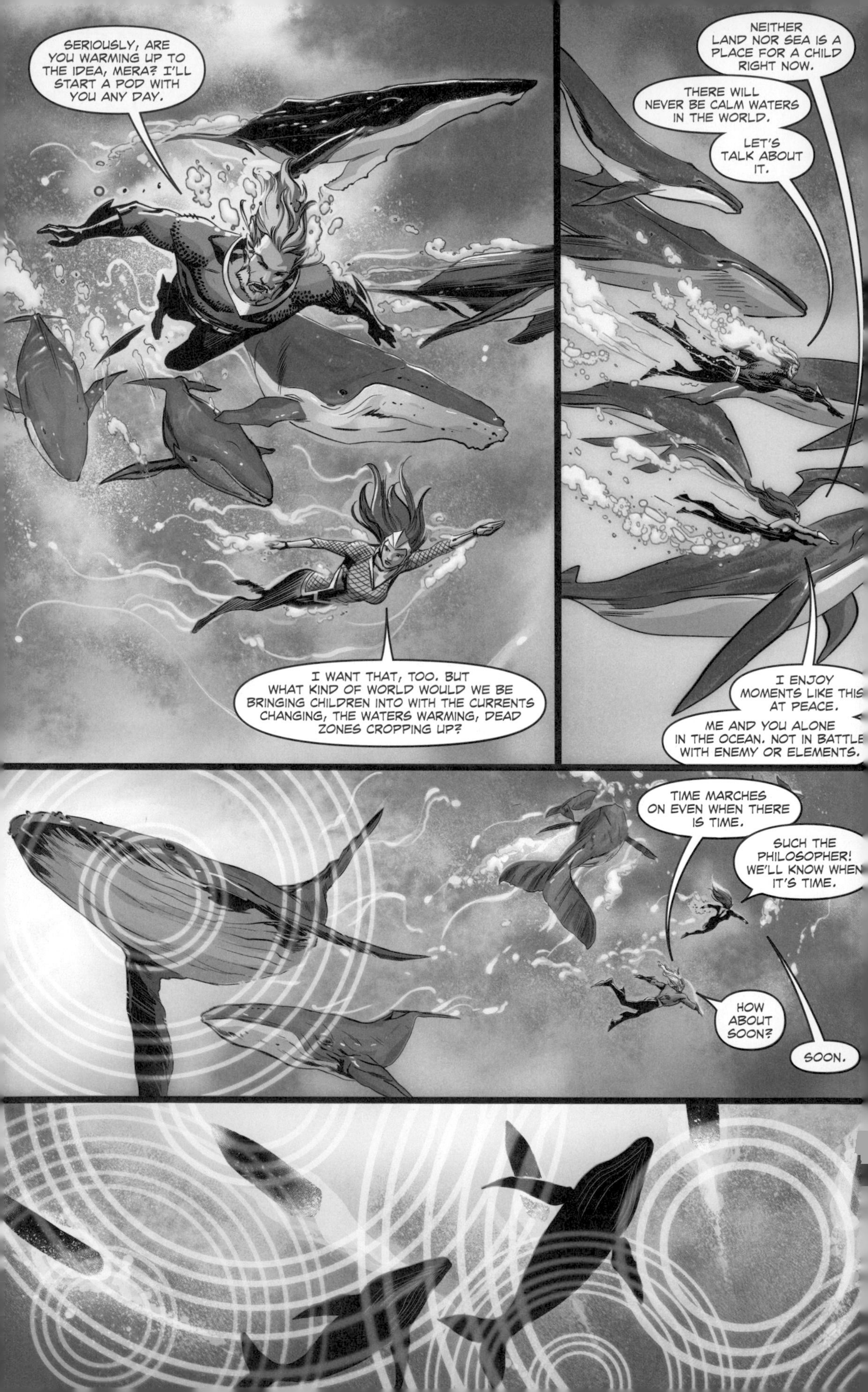
SERIOUSLY, ARE YOU WARMING UP TO THE IDEA, MERA? I'LL START A POD WITH YOU ANY DAY.
I WANT THAT, TOO. BUT WHAT KIND OF WORLD WOULD WE BE BRINGING CHILDREN INTO WITH THE CURRENTS CHANGING, THE WATERS WARMING, DEAD ZONES CROPPING UP?
NEITHER LAND NOR SEA IS A PLACE FOR A CHILD RIGHT NOW.
THERE WILL NEVER BE CALM WATERS IN THE WORLD.
LET'S TALK ABOUT IT.
I ENJOY MOMENTS LIKE THIS AT PEACE.
ME AND YOU ALONE IN THE OCEAN. NOT IN BATTLE WITH ENEMY OR ELEMENTS.
TIME MARCHES ON EVEN WHEN THERE IS TIME.
SUCH THE PHILOSOPHER! WE'LL KNOW WHEN IT'S TIME.
HOW ABOUT SOON?
SOON.

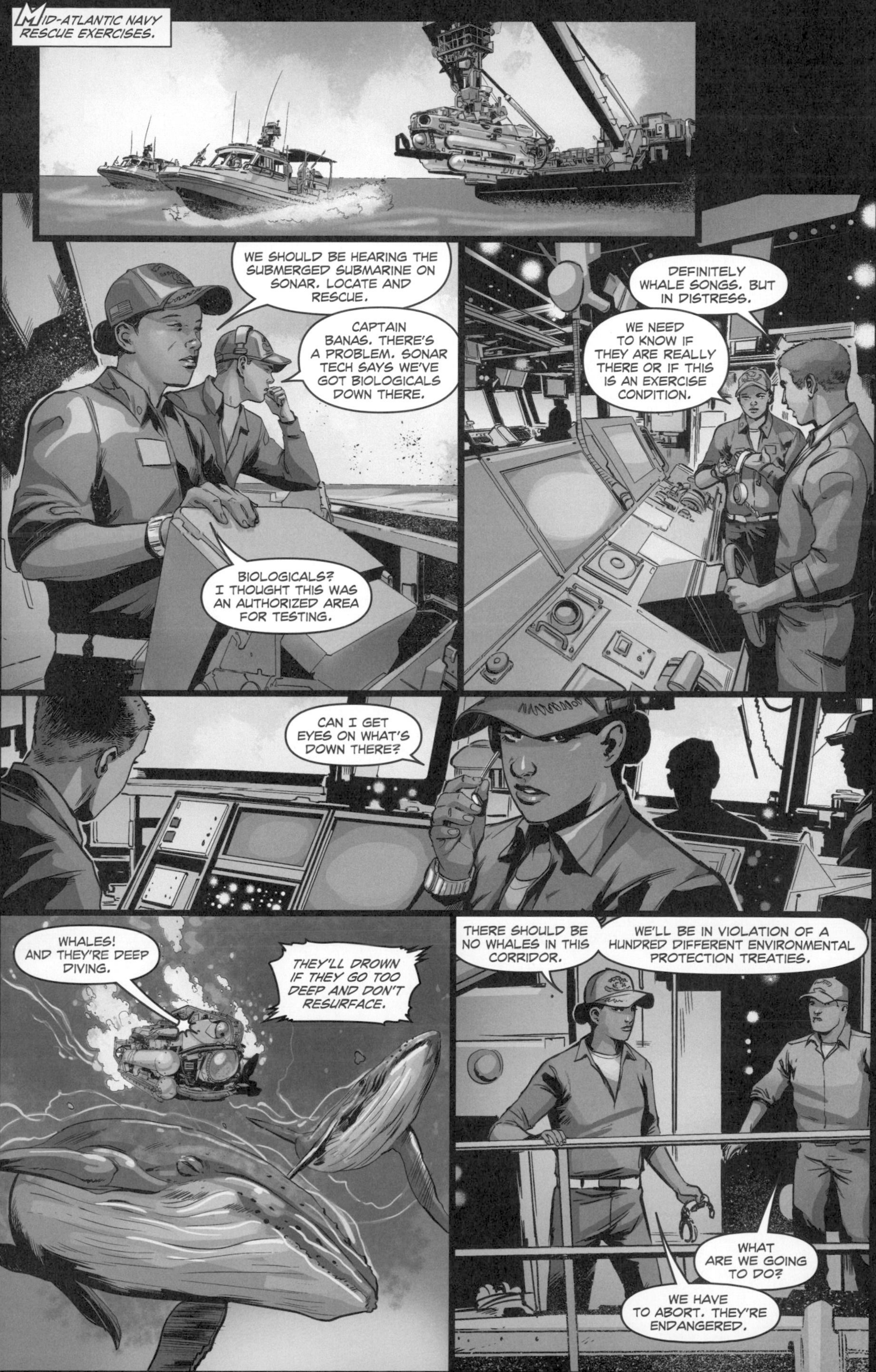
MID-ATLANTIC NAVY RESCUE EXERCISES.
WE SHOULD BE HEARING THE SUBMERGED SUBMARINE ON SONAR. LOCATE AND RESCUE.
CAPTAIN BANAS. THERE'S A PROBLEM. SONAR TECH SAYS WE'VE GOT BIOLOGICALS DOWN THERE.
BIOLOGICALS? I THOUGHT THIS WAS AN AUTHORIZED AREA FOR TESTING.
DEFINITELY WHALE SONGS. BUT IN DISTRESS.
WE NEED TO KNOW IF THEY ARE REALLY THERE OR IF THIS IS AN EXERCISE CONDITION.
CAN I GET EYES ON WHAT'S DOWN THERE?
WHALES! AND THEY'RE DEEP DIVING.
THEY'LL DROWN IF THEY GO TOO DEEP AND DON'T RESURFACE.
THERE SHOULD BE NO WHALES IN THIS CORRIDOR.
WE'LL BE IN VIOLATION OF A HUNDRED DIFFERENT ENVIRONMENTAL PROTECTION TREATIES.
WHAT ARE WE GOING TO DO?
WE HAVE TO ABORT. THEY'RE ENDANGERED.

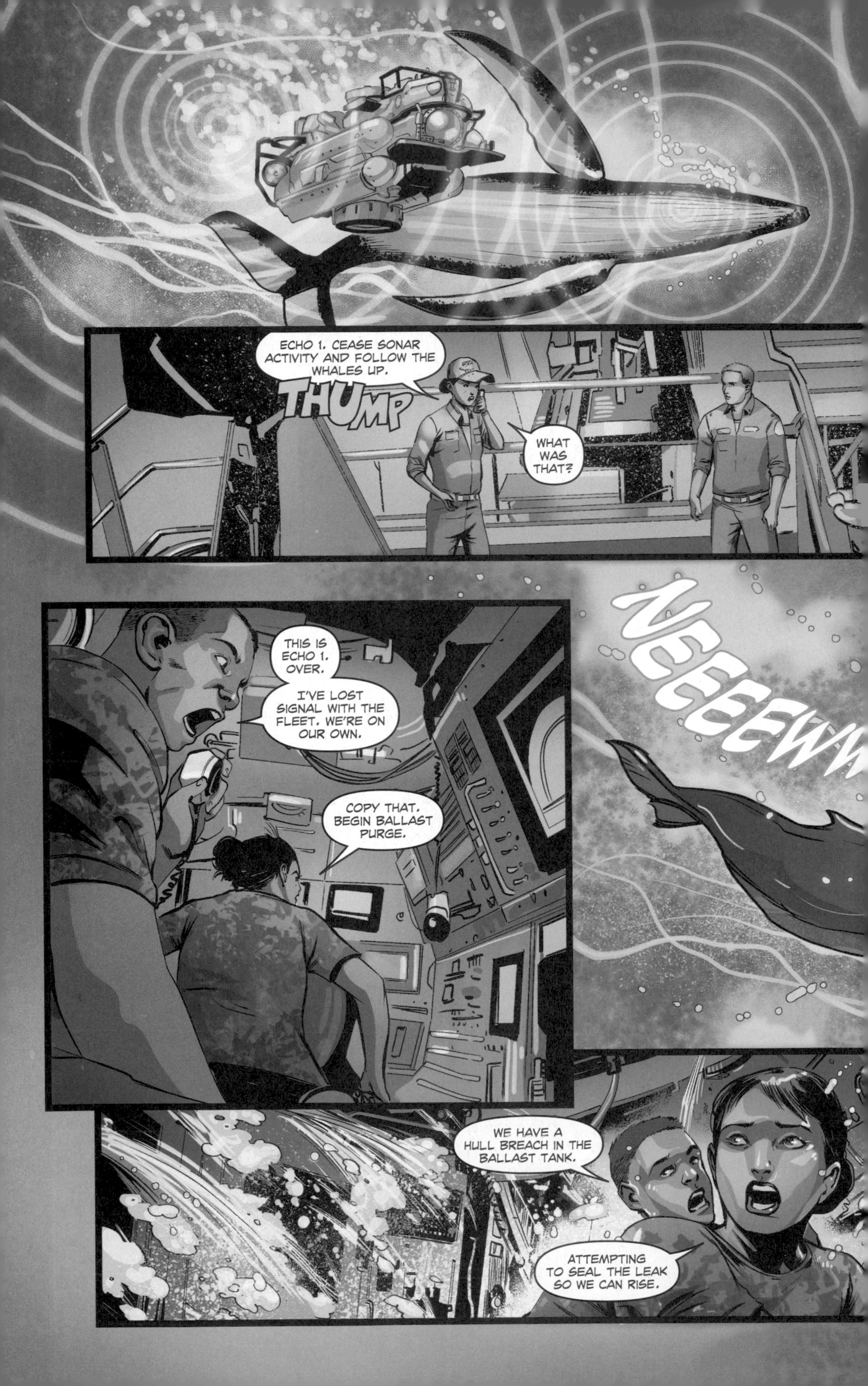

ECHO 1. CEASE SONAR ACTIVITY AND FOLLOW THE WHALES UP.
THUMP
WHAT WAS THAT?
THIS IS ECHO 1. OVER.
I'VE LOST SIGNAL WITH THE FLEET. WE'RE ON OUR OWN.
COPY THAT. BEGIN BALLAST PURGE.
NEEEEWW
WE HAVE A HULL BREACH IN THE BALLAST TANK.
ATTEMPTING TO SEAL THE LEAK SO WE CAN RISE.

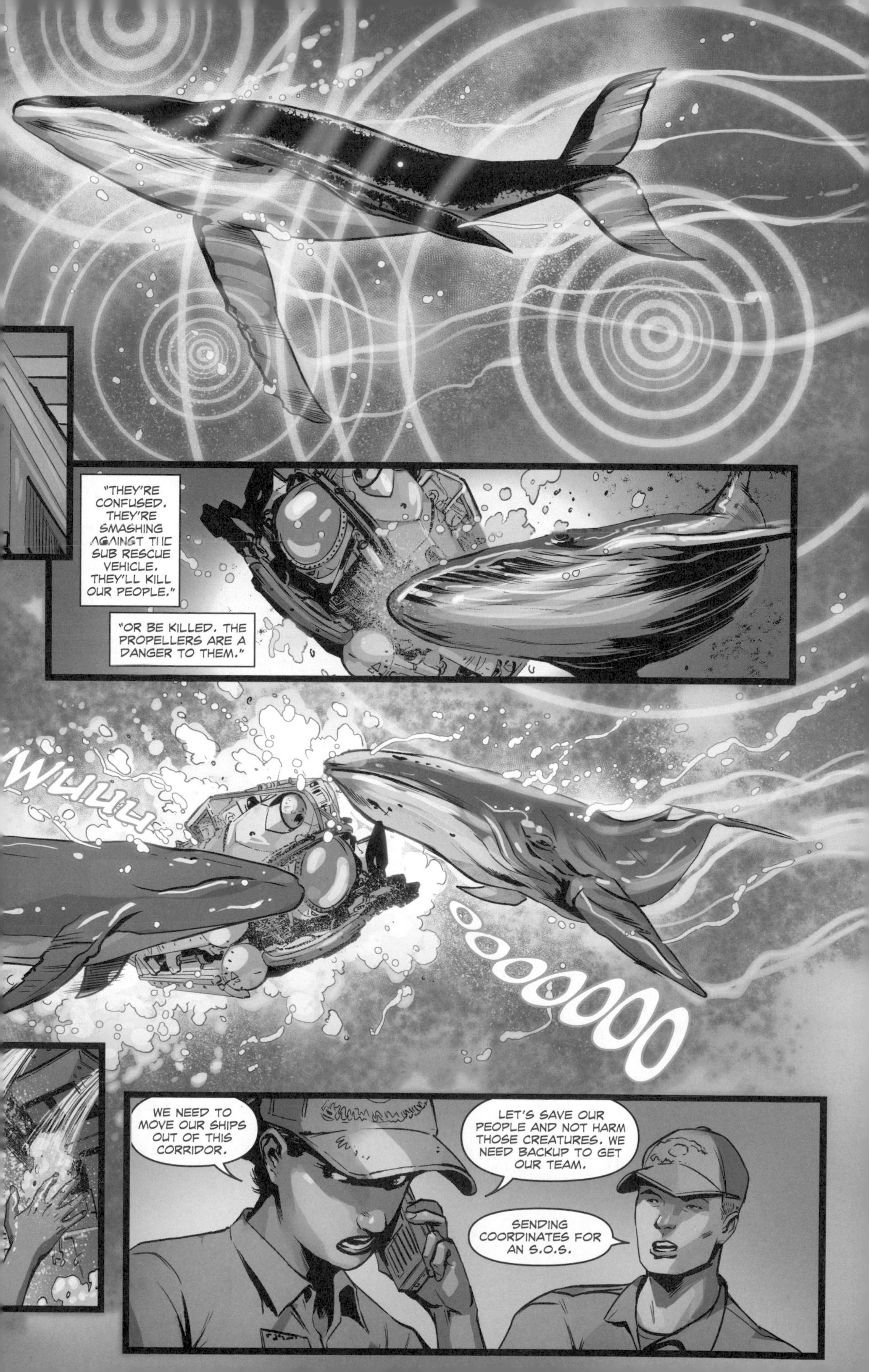
"THEY'RE CONFUSED. THEY'RE SMASHING AGAINST THE SUB RESCUE VEHICLE. THEY'LL KILL OUR PEOPLE."
"OR BE KILLED. THE PROPELLERS ARE A DANGER TO THEM."
WE NEED TO MOVE OUR SHIPS OUT OF THIS CORRIDOR.
LET'S SAVE OUR PEOPLE AND NOT HARM THOSE CREATURES. WE NEED BACKUP TO GET OUR TEAM.
SENDING COORDINATES FOR AN S.O.S.

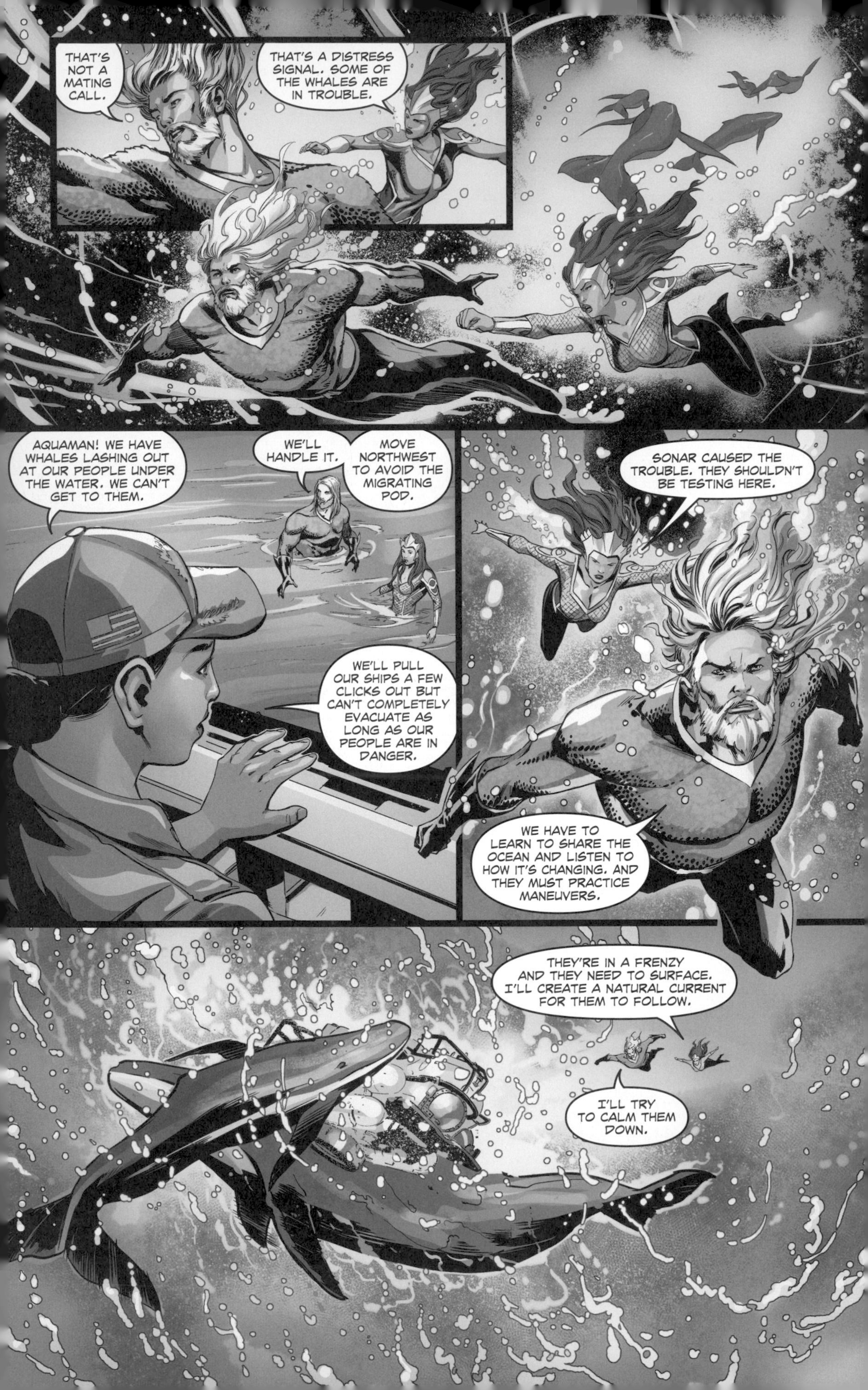

THAT'S NOT A MATING CALL.
THAT'S A DISTRESS SIGNAL. SOME OF THE WHALES ARE IN TROUBLE.
AQUAMAN! WE HAVE WHALES LASHING OUT AT OUR PEOPLE UNDER THE WATER. WE CAN'T GET TO THEM.
WE'LL HANDLE IT.
MOVE NORTHWEST TO AVOID THE MIGRATING POD.
WE'LL PULL OUR SHIPS A FEW CLICKS OUT BUT CAN'T COMPLETELY EVACUATE AS LONG AS OUR PEOPLE ARE IN DANGER.
SONAR CAUSED THE TROUBLE. THEY SHOULDN'T BE TESTING HERE.
WE HAVE TO LEARN TO SHARE THE OCEAN AND LISTEN TO HOW IT'S CHANGING. AND THEY MUST PRACTICE MANEUVERS.
THEY'RE IN A FRENZY AND THEY NEED TO SURFACE. I'LL CREATE A NATURAL CURRENT FOR THEM TO FOLLOW.
I'LL TRY TO CALM THEM DOWN.

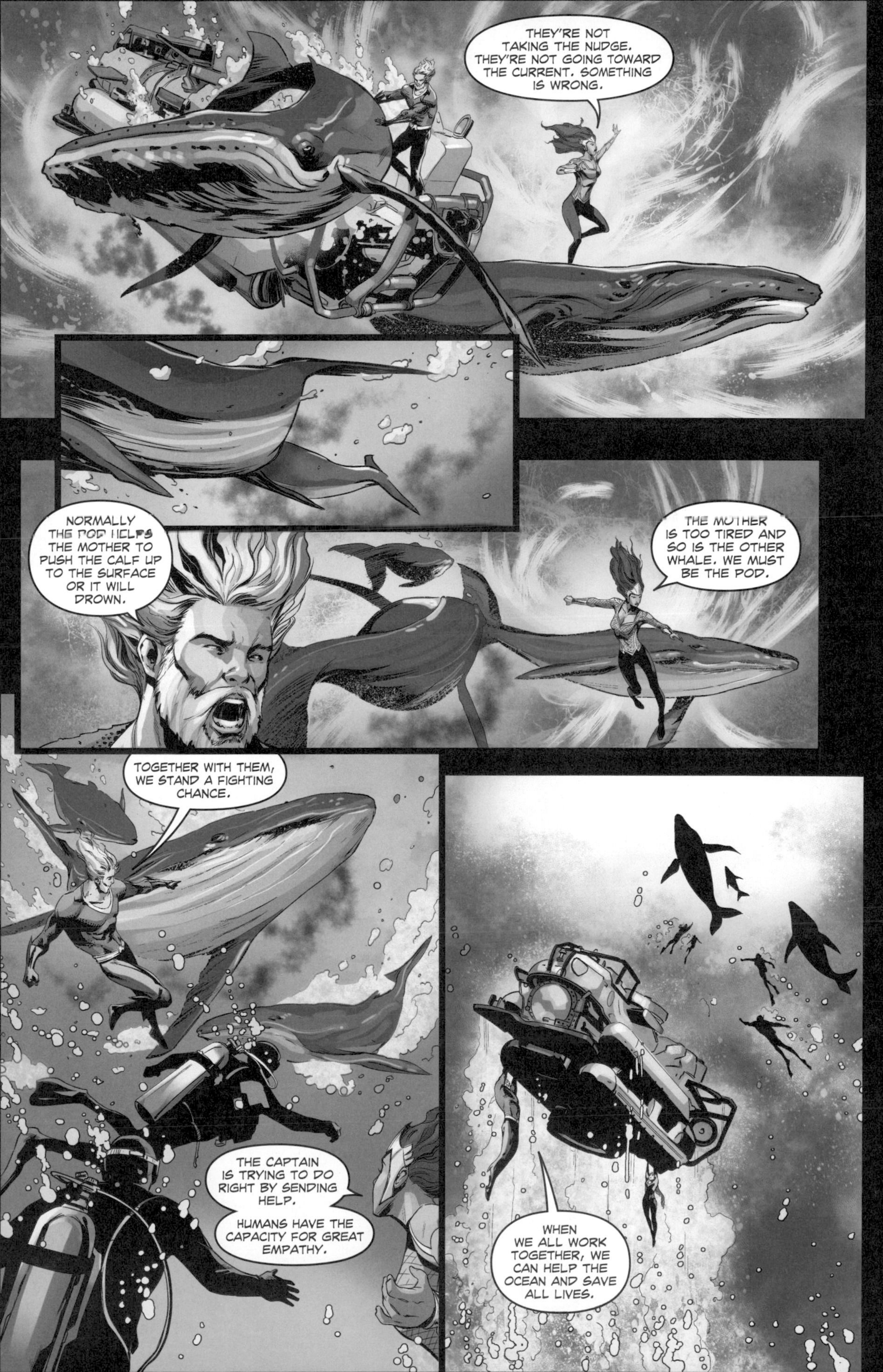
THEY'RE NOT TAKING THE NUDGE. THEY'RE NOT GOING TOWARD THE CURRENT. SOMETHING IS WRONG.
NORMALLY THE POD HELPS THE MOTHER TO PUSH THE CALF UP TO THE SURFACE OR IT WILL DROWN.
THE MOTHER IS TOO TIRED AND SO IS THE OTHER WHALE. WE MUST BE THE POD.
TOGETHER WITH THEM, WE STAND A FIGHTING CHANCE.
THE CAPTAIN IS TRYING TO DO RIGHT BY SENDING HELP.
HUMANS HAVE THE CAPACITY FOR GREAT EMPATHY.
WHEN WE ALL WORK TOGETHER, WE CAN HELP THE OCEAN AND SAVE ALL LIVES.

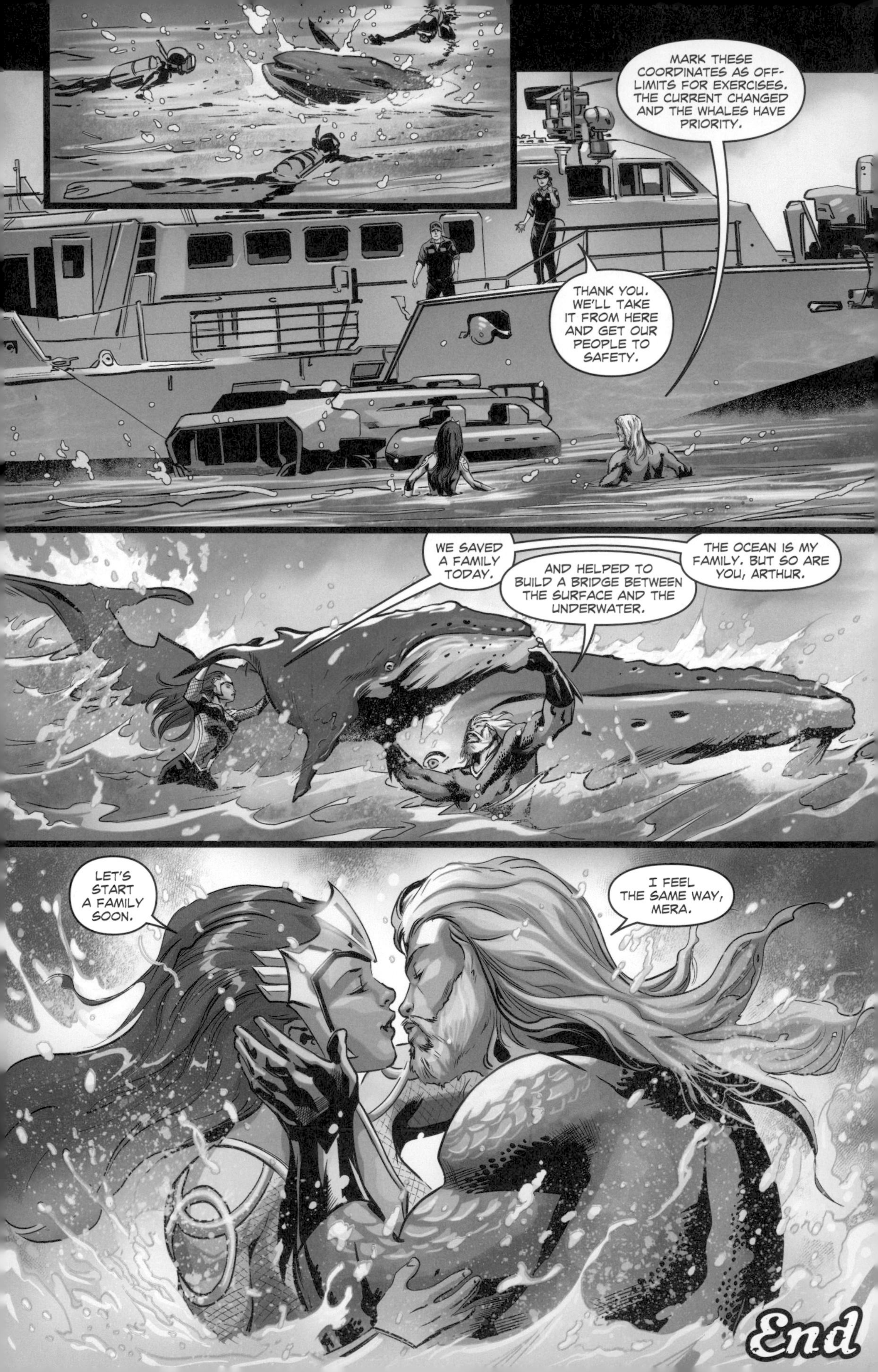
MARK THESE COORDINATES AS OFF-LIMITS FOR EXERCISES. THE CURRENT CHANGED AND THE WHALES HAVE PRIORITY.
THANK YOU. WE'LL TAKE IT FROM HERE AND GET OUR PEOPLE TO SAFETY.
WE SAVED A FAMILY TODAY.
AND HELPED TO BUILD A BRIDGE BETWEEN THE SURFACE AND THE UNDERWATER.
THE OCEAN IS MY FAMILY. BUT SO ARE YOU, ARTHUR.
LET'S START A FAMILY SOON.
I FEEL THE SAME WAY, MERA.
End

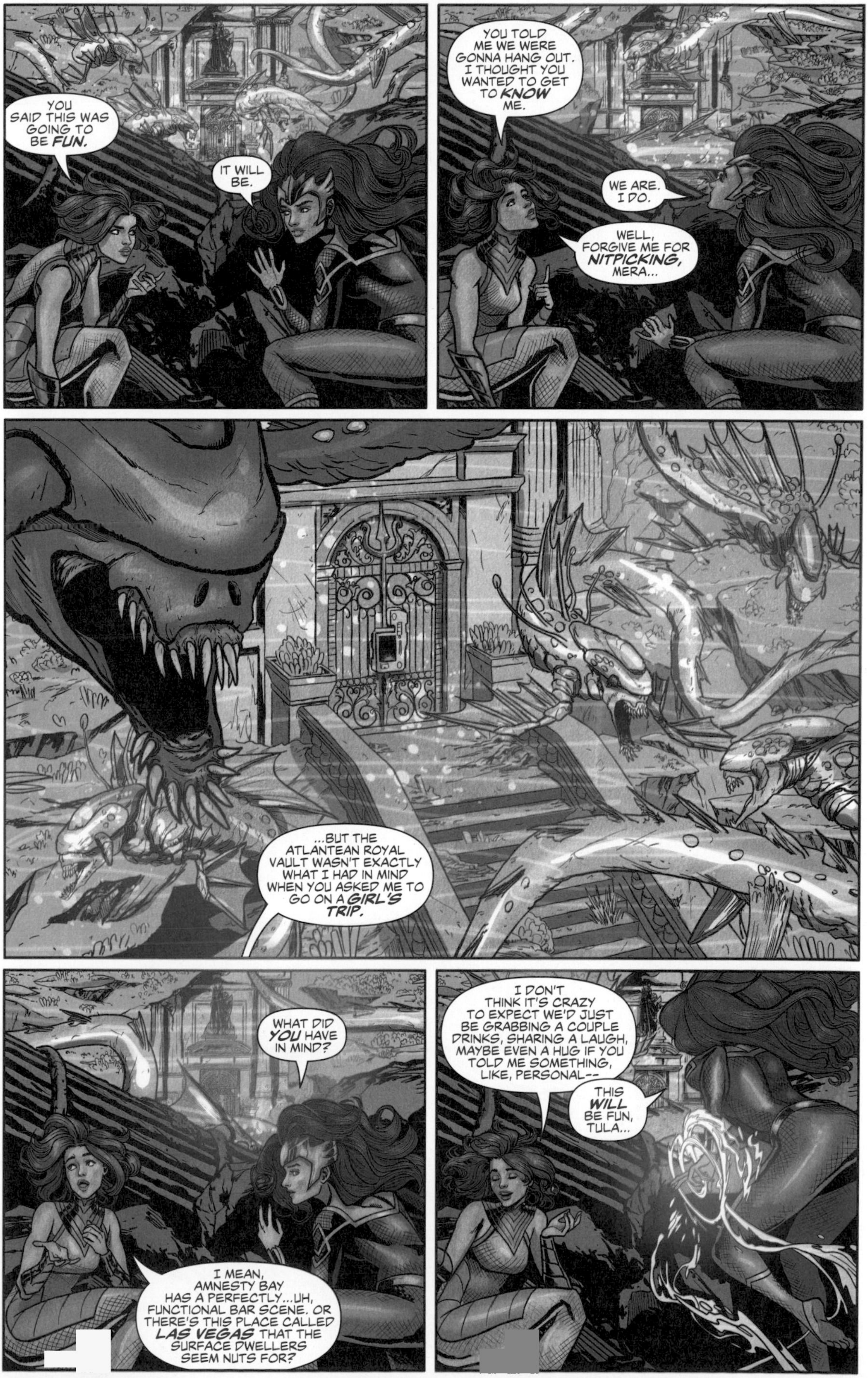
YOU SAID THIS WAS GOING TO BE FUN.
IT WILL BE.
YOU TOLD ME WE WERE GONNA HANG OUT. I THOUGHT YOU WANTED TO GET TO KNOW ME.
WE ARE. I DO.
WELL, FORGIVE ME FOR NITPICKING, MERA...
...BUT THE ATLANTEAN ROYAL VAULT WASN'T EXACTLY WHAT I HAD IN MIND WHEN YOU ASKED ME TO GO ON A GIRL'S TRIP.
WHAT DID YOU HAVE IN MIND?
I MEAN, AMNESTY BAY HAS A PERFECTLY...UH, FUNCTIONAL BAR SCENE. OR THERE'S THIS PLACE CALLED LAS VEGAS THAT THE SURFACE DWELLERS SEEM NUTS FOR?
I DON'T THINK IT'S CRAZY TO EXPECT WE'D JUST BE GRABBING A COUPLE DRINKS, SHARING A LAUGH, MAYBE EVEN A HUG IF YOU TOLD ME SOMETHING, LIKE, PERSONAL--
THIS WILL BE FUN, TULA...

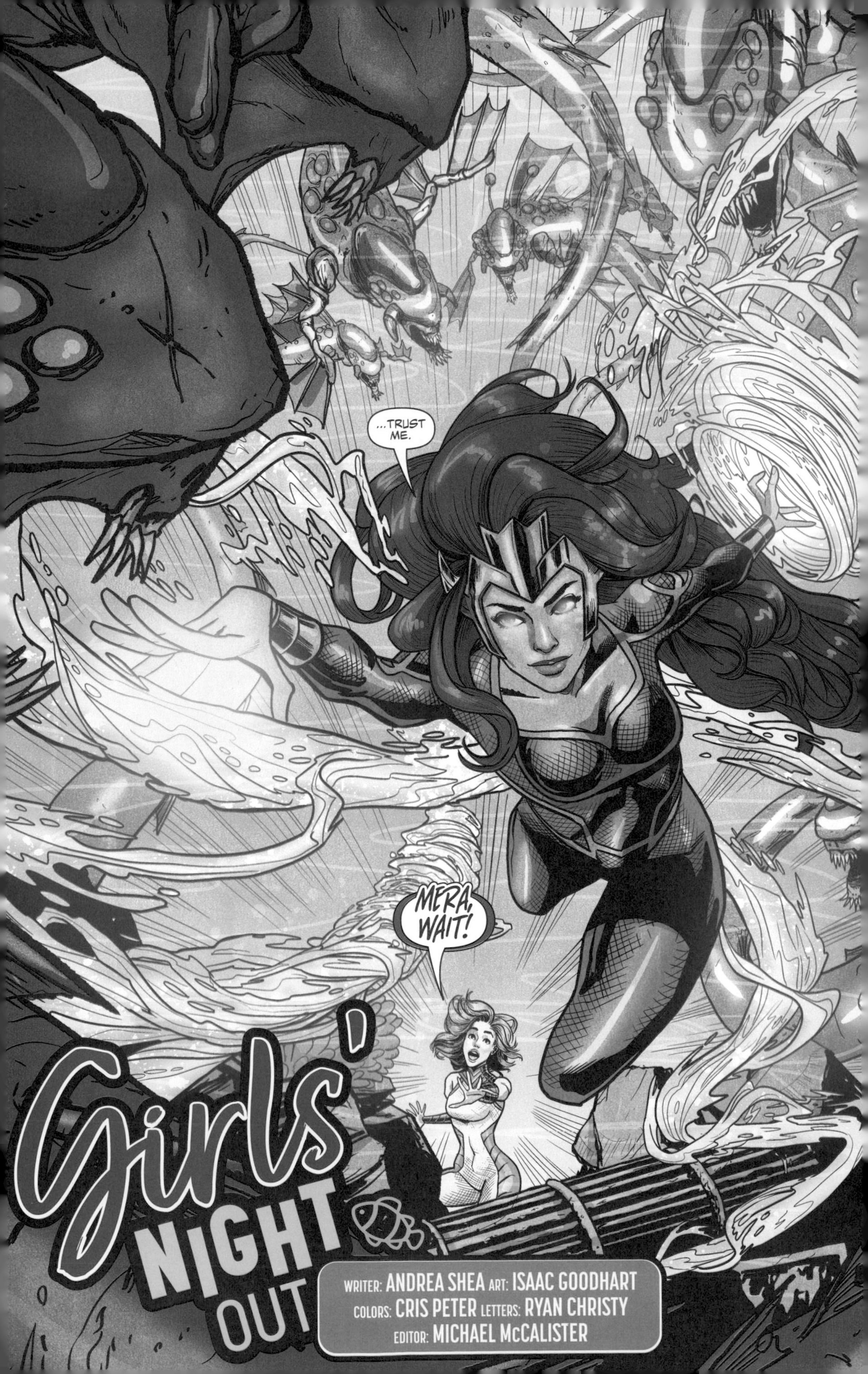
...TRUST ME.
MERA, WAIT!
Girls' NIGHT OUT
WRITER: ANDREA SHEA ART: ISAAC GOODHART
COLORS: CRIS PETER LETTERS: RYAN CHRISTY
EDITOR: MICHAEL McCALISTER

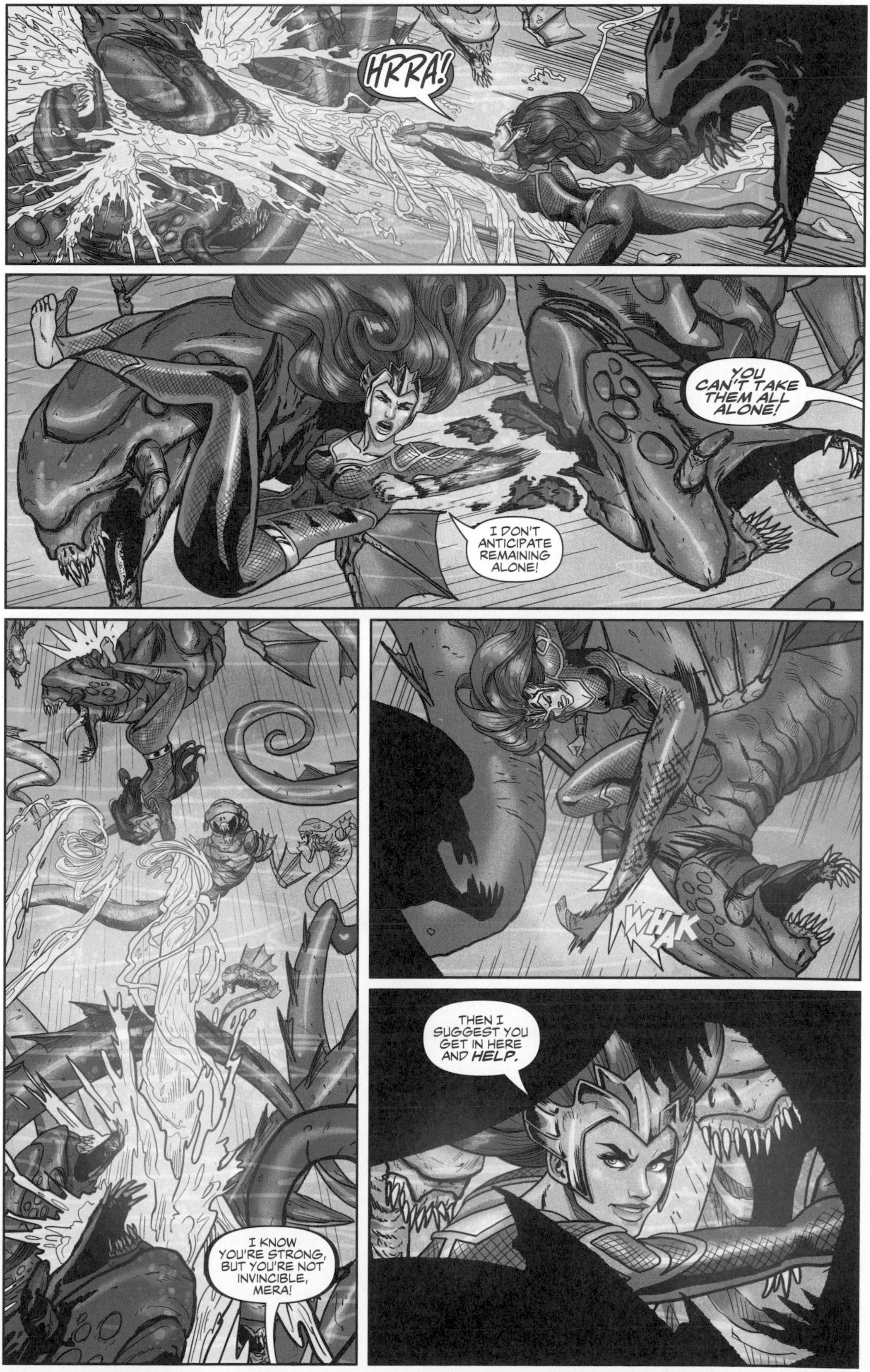
HRRA!
YOU CAN'T TAKE THEM ALL ALONE!
I DON'T ANTICIPATE REMAINING ALONE!
I KNOW YOU'RE STRONG, BUT YOU'RE NOT INVINCIBLE, MERA!
WHAK
THEN I SUGGEST YOU GET IN HERE AND HELP.

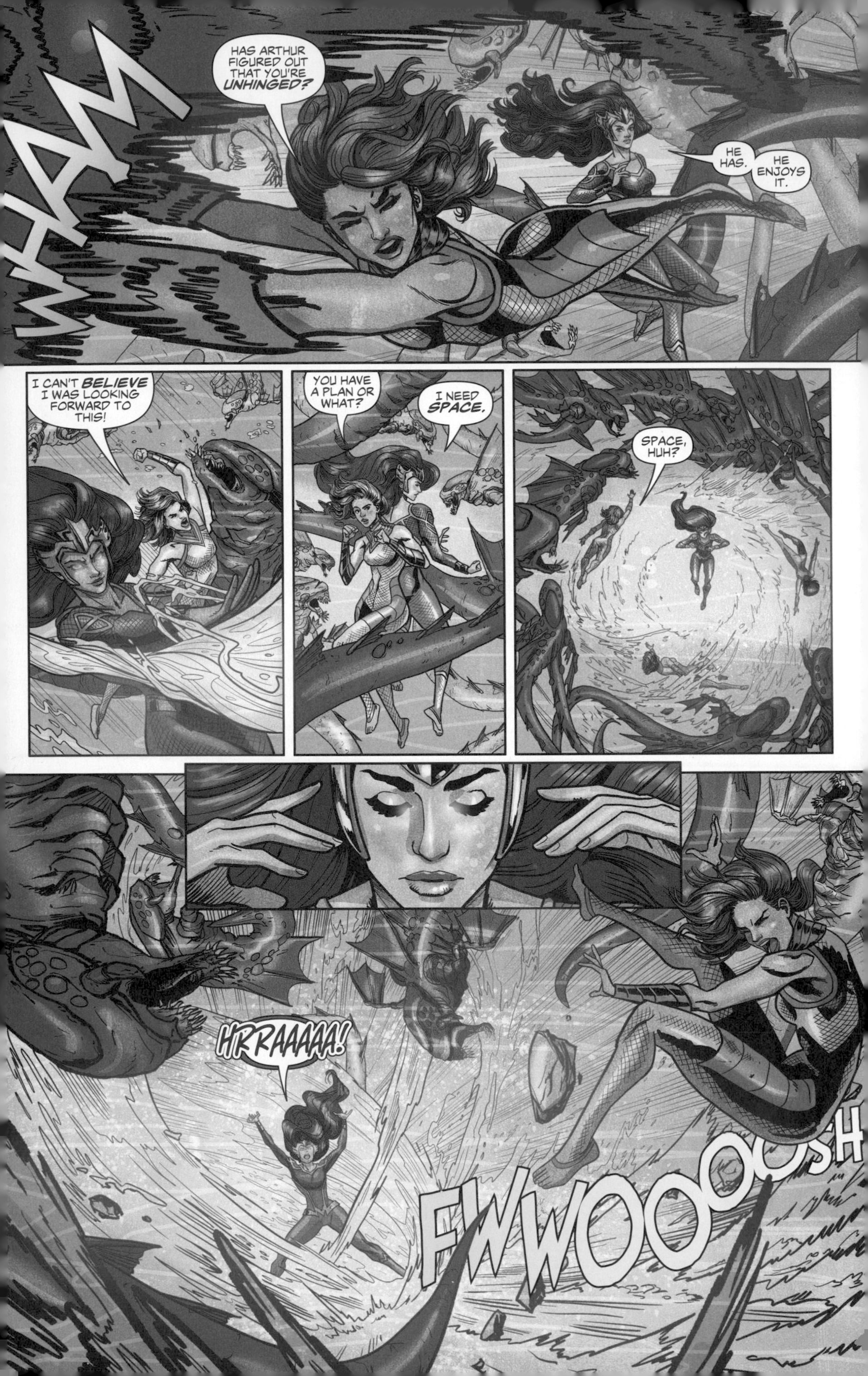
WHAM
HAS ARTHUR FIGURED OUT THAT YOU'RE UNHINGED?
HE HAS.
HE ENJOYS IT.
I CAN'T BELIEVE I WAS LOOKING FORWARD TO THIS!
YOU HAVE A PLAN OR WHAT?
I NEED SPACE.
SPACE, HUH?
HRRAAAAA!
FWOOOOSH

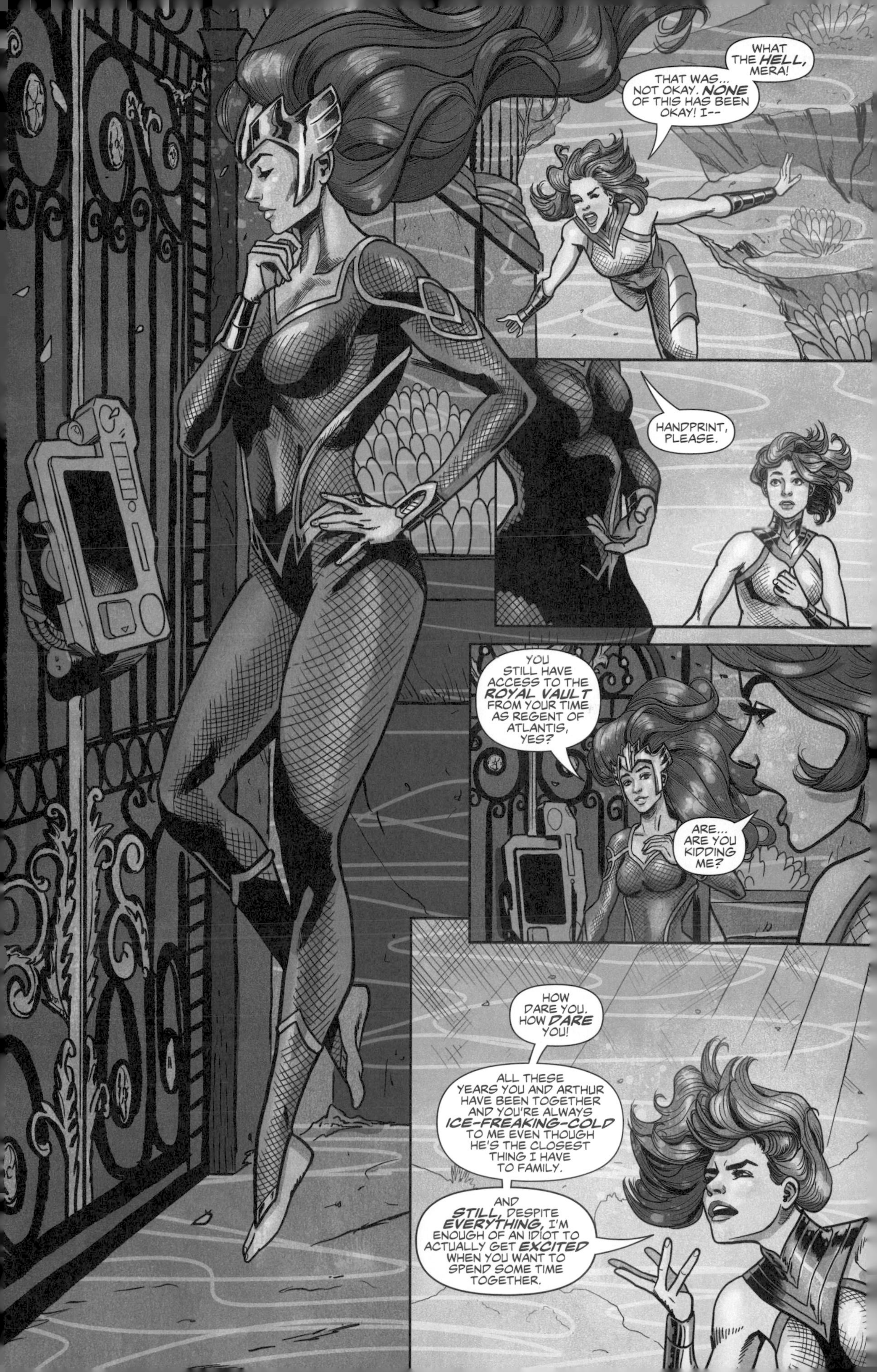

WHAT THE HELL, MERA!
THAT WAS... NOT OKAY. NONE OF THIS HAS BEEN OKAY! I--
HANDPRINT, PLEASE.
YOU STILL HAVE ACCESS TO THE ROYAL VAULT FROM YOUR TIME AS REGENT OF ATLANTIS, YES?
ARE... ARE YOU KIDDING ME?
HOW DARE YOU. HOW DARE YOU!
ALL THESE YEARS YOU AND ARTHUR HAVE BEEN TOGETHER AND YOU'RE ALWAYS ICE-FREAKING-COLD TO ME EVEN THOUGH HE'S THE CLOSEST THING I HAVE TO FAMILY.
AND STILL, DESPITE EVERYTHING, I'M ENOUGH OF AN IDIOT TO ACTUALLY GET EXCITED WHEN YOU WANT TO SPEND SOME TIME TOGETHER.

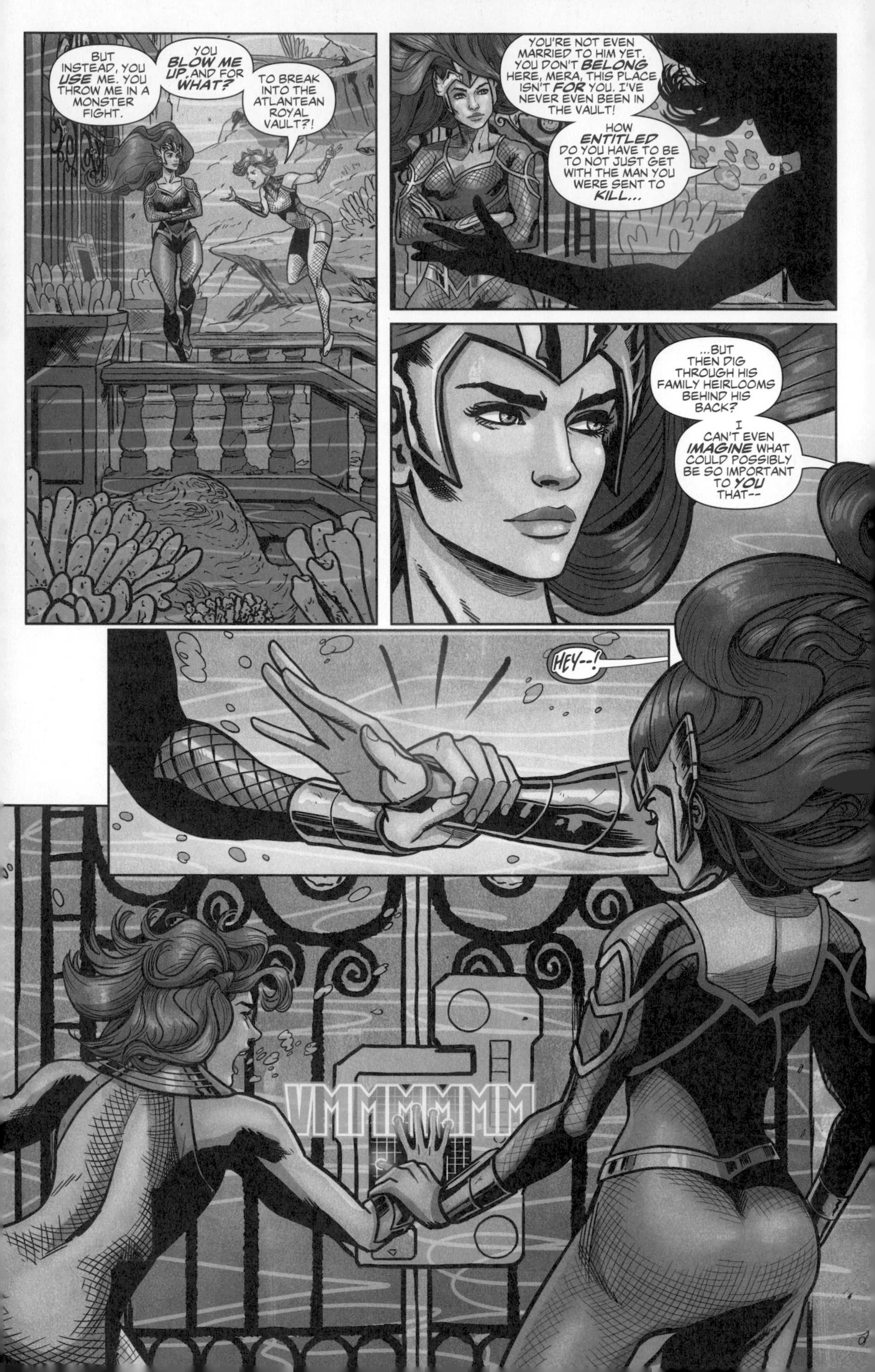

BUT INSTEAD, YOU USE ME. YOU THROW ME IN A MONSTER FIGHT.
YOU BLOW ME UP, AND FOR WHAT?
TO BREAK INTO THE ATLANTEAN ROYAL VAULT?!
YOU'RE NOT EVEN MARRIED TO HIM YET. YOU DON'T BELONG HERE, MERA, THIS PLACE ISN'T FOR YOU. I'VE NEVER EVEN BEEN IN THE VAULT!
HOW ENTITLED DO YOU HAVE TO BE TO NOT JUST GET WITH THE MAN YOU WERE SENT TO KILL...
...BUT THEN DIG THROUGH HIS FAMILY HEIRLOOMS BEHIND HIS BACK?
I CAN'T EVEN IMAGINE WHAT COULD POSSIBLY BE SO IMPORTANT TO YOU THAT--
HEY--!
VMMMMMM

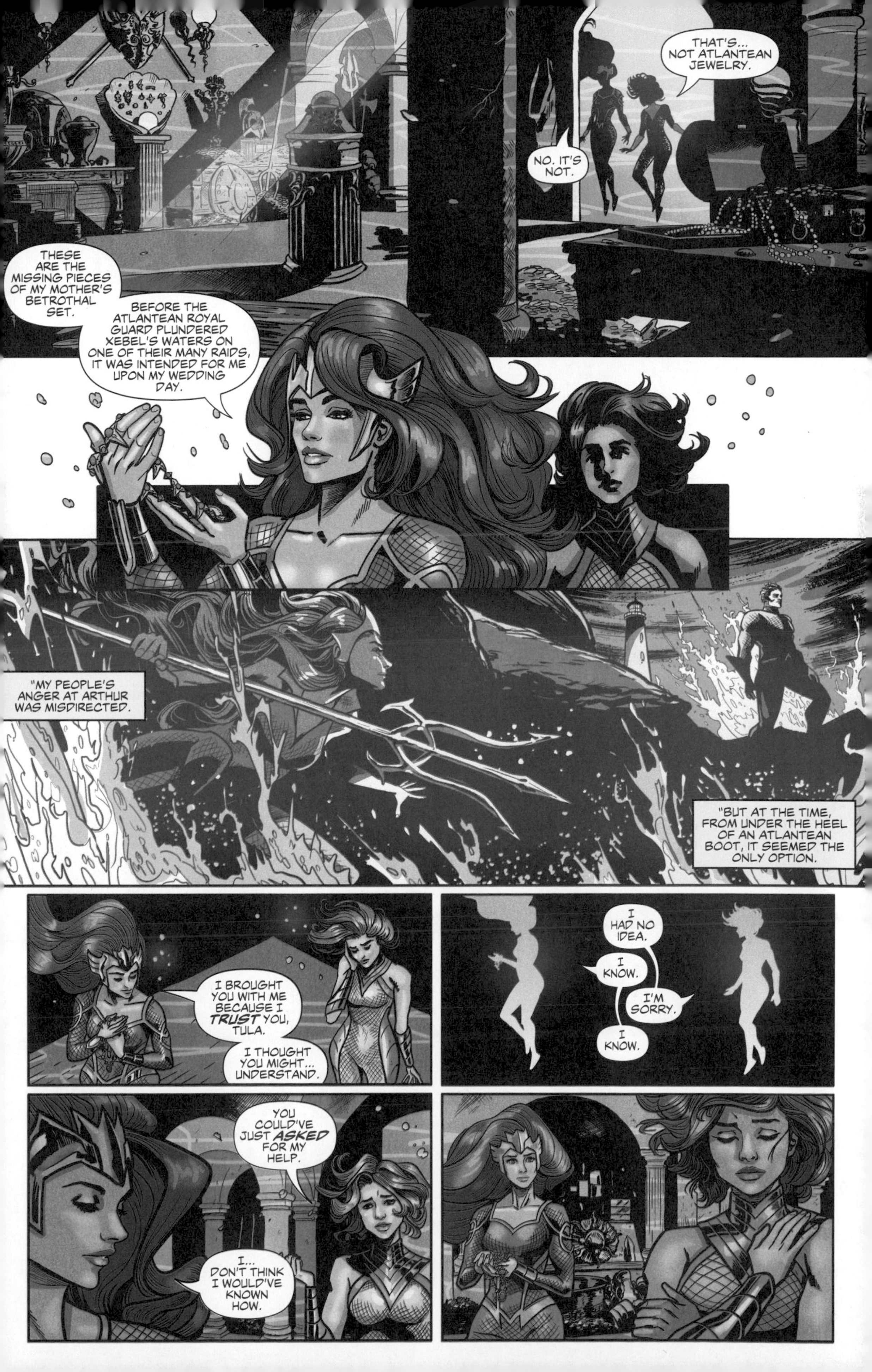
THAT'S... NOT ATLANTEAN JEWELRY.
NO. IT'S NOT.
THESE ARE THE MISSING PIECES OF MY MOTHER'S BETROTHAL SET.
BEFORE THE ATLANTEAN ROYAL GUARD PLUNDERED XEBEL'S WATERS ON ONE OF THEIR MANY RAIDS, IT WAS INTENDED FOR ME UPON MY WEDDING DAY.
"MY PEOPLE'S ANGER AT ARTHUR WAS MISDIRECTED.
"BUT AT THE TIME, FROM UNDER THE HEEL OF AN ATLANTEAN BOOT, IT SEEMED THE ONLY OPTION.
I BROUGHT YOU WITH ME BECAUSE I TRUST YOU, TULA.
I THOUGHT YOU MIGHT... UNDERSTAND.
I HAD NO IDEA.
I KNOW.
I'M SORRY.
I KNOW.
YOU COULD'VE JUST ASKED FOR MY HELP.
I... DON'T THINK I WOULD'VE KNOWN HOW.

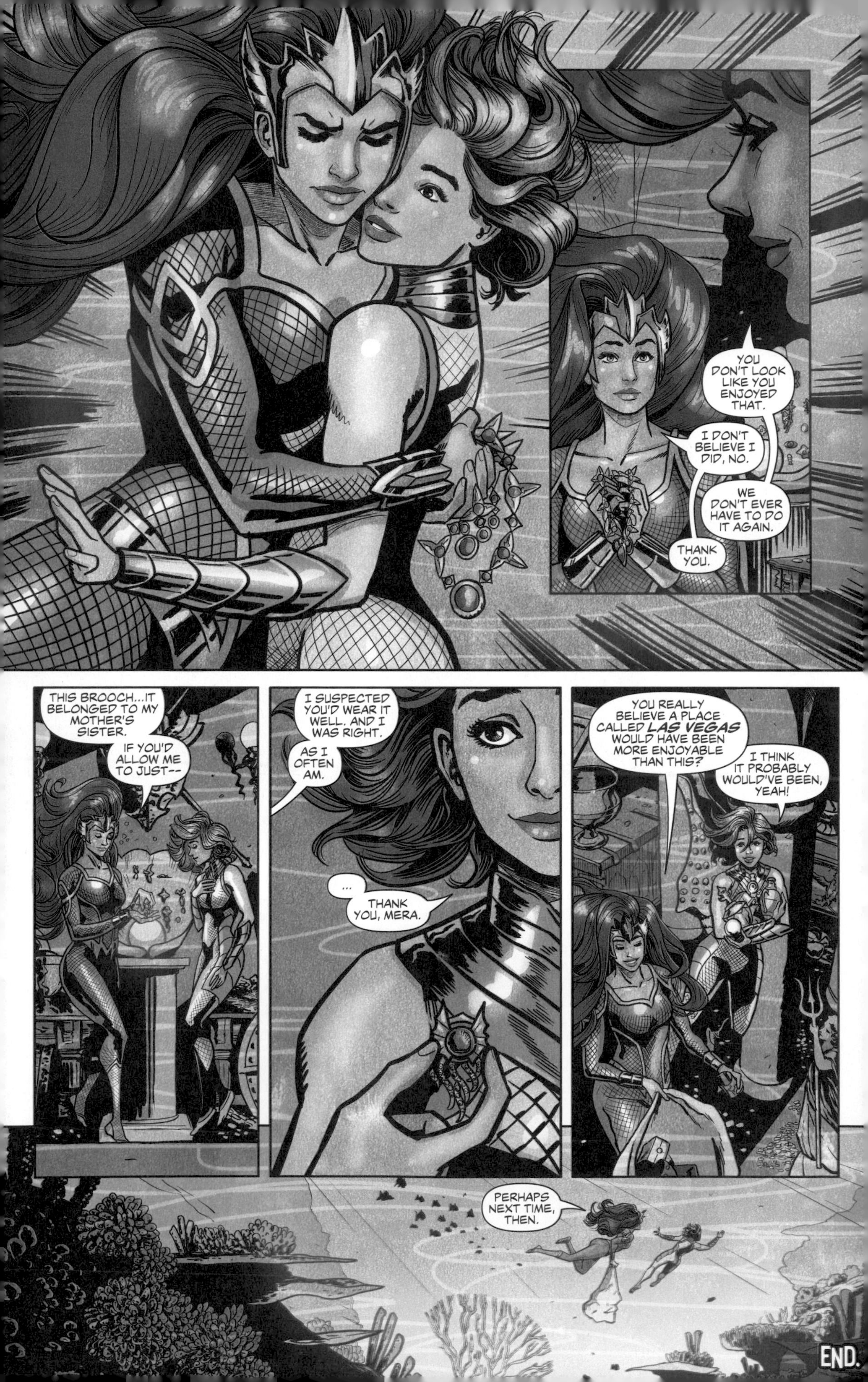
YOU DON'T LOOK LIKE YOU ENJOYED THAT.
I DON'T BELIEVE I DID, NO.
WE DON'T EVER HAVE TO DO IT AGAIN.
THANK YOU.
THIS BROOCH...IT BELONGED TO MY MOTHER'S SISTER.
IF YOU'D ALLOW ME TO JUST--
I SUSPECTED YOU'D WEAR IT WELL. AND I WAS RIGHT.
AS I OFTEN AM.
... THANK YOU, MERA.
YOU REALLY BELIEVE A PLACE CALLED *LAS VEGAS* WOULD HAVE BEEN MORE ENJOYABLE THAN THIS?
I THINK IT PROBABLY WOULD'VE BEEN, YEAH!
PERHAPS NEXT TIME, THEN.
END.

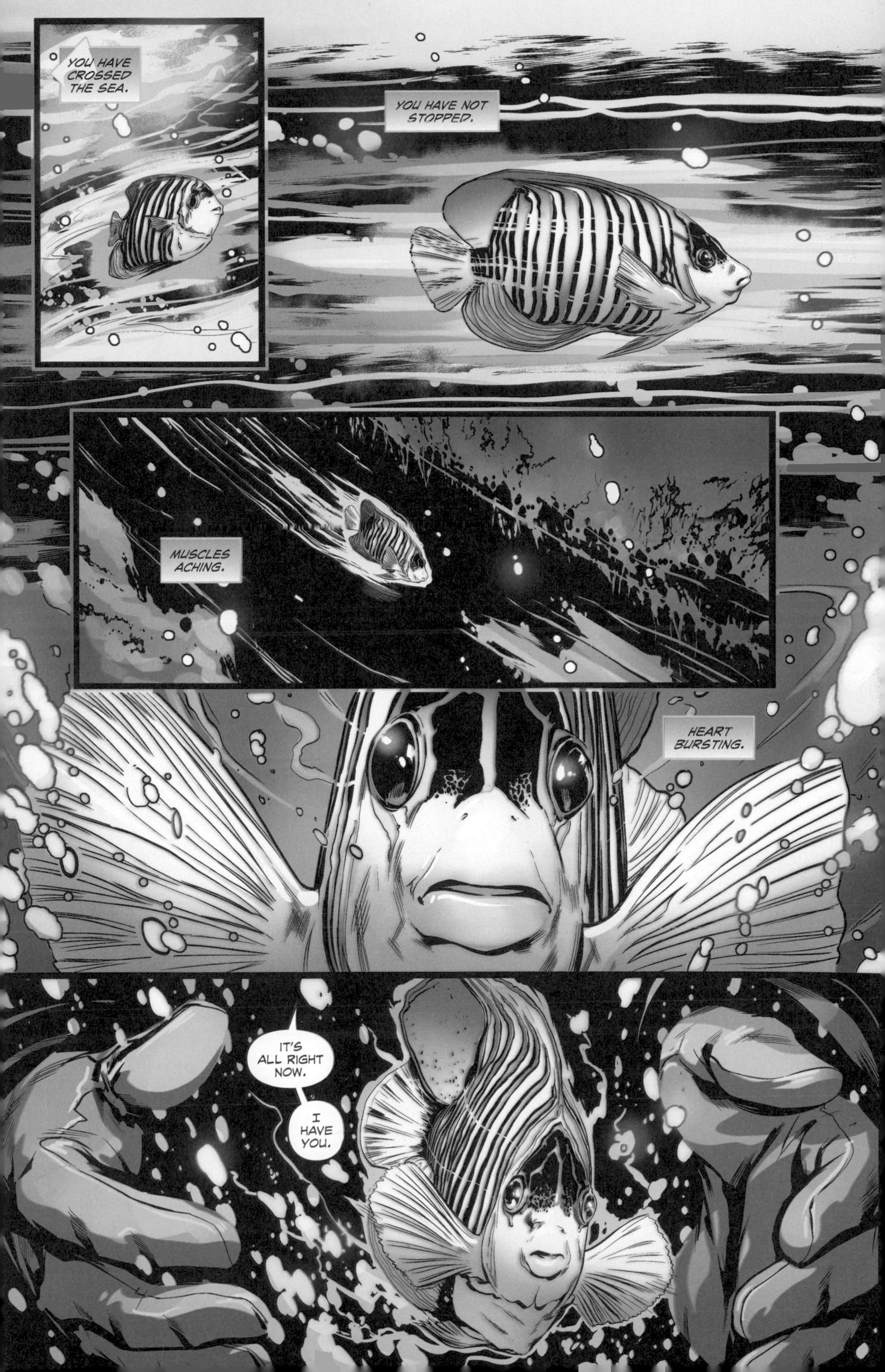
YOU HAVE CROSSED THE SEA.
YOU HAVE NOT STOPPED.
MUSCLES ACHING.
HEART BURSTING.
IT'S ALL RIGHT NOW.
I HAVE YOU.

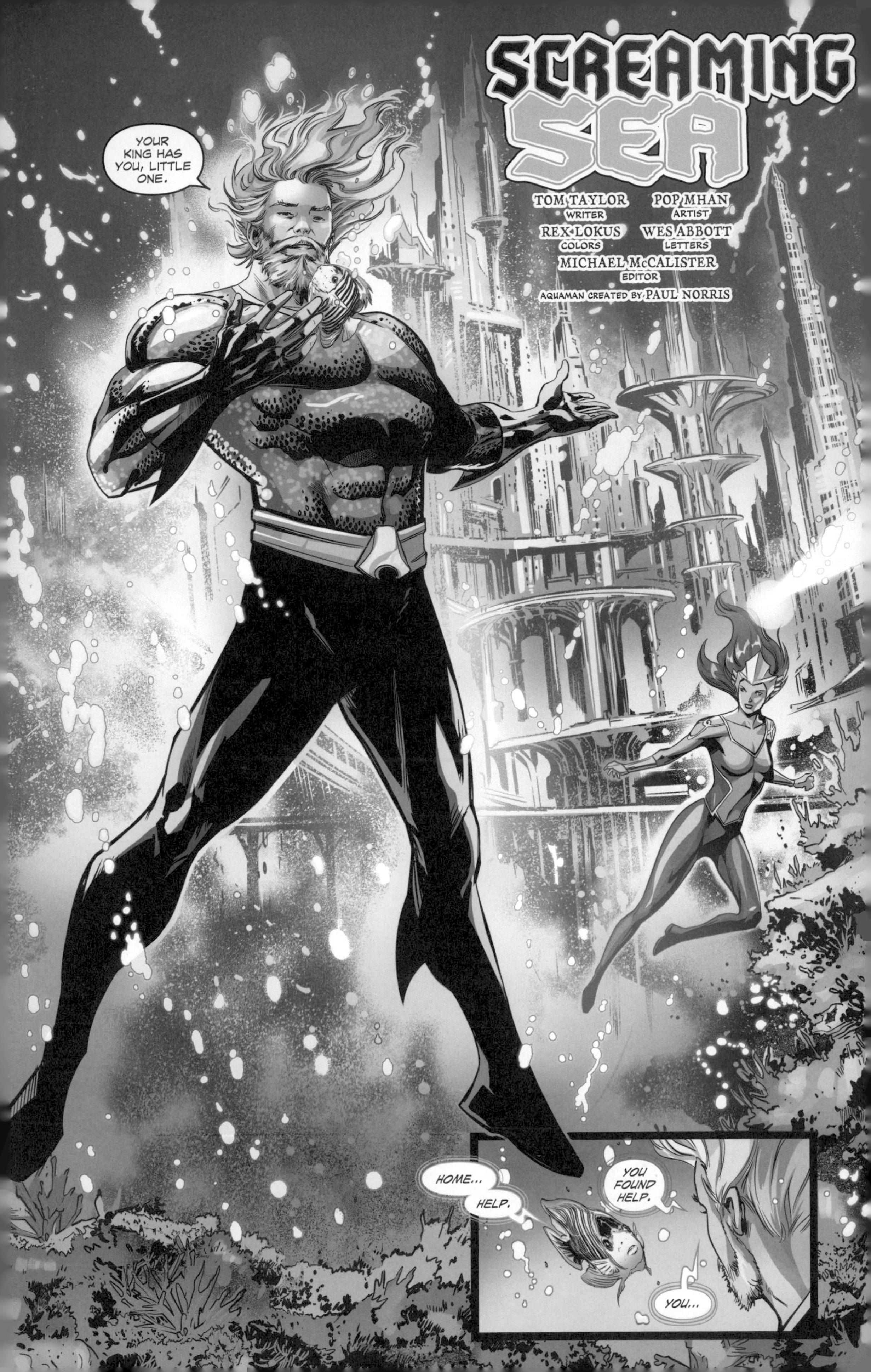
SCREAMING SEA
TOM TAYLOR WRITER
POP MHAN ARTIST
REX LOKUS COLORS
WES ABBOTT LETTERS
MICHAEL McCALISTER EDITOR
AQUAMAN CREATED BY PAUL NORRIS
YOUR KING HAS YOU, LITTLE ONE.
HOME...
HELP.
YOU FOUND HELP.
YOU...

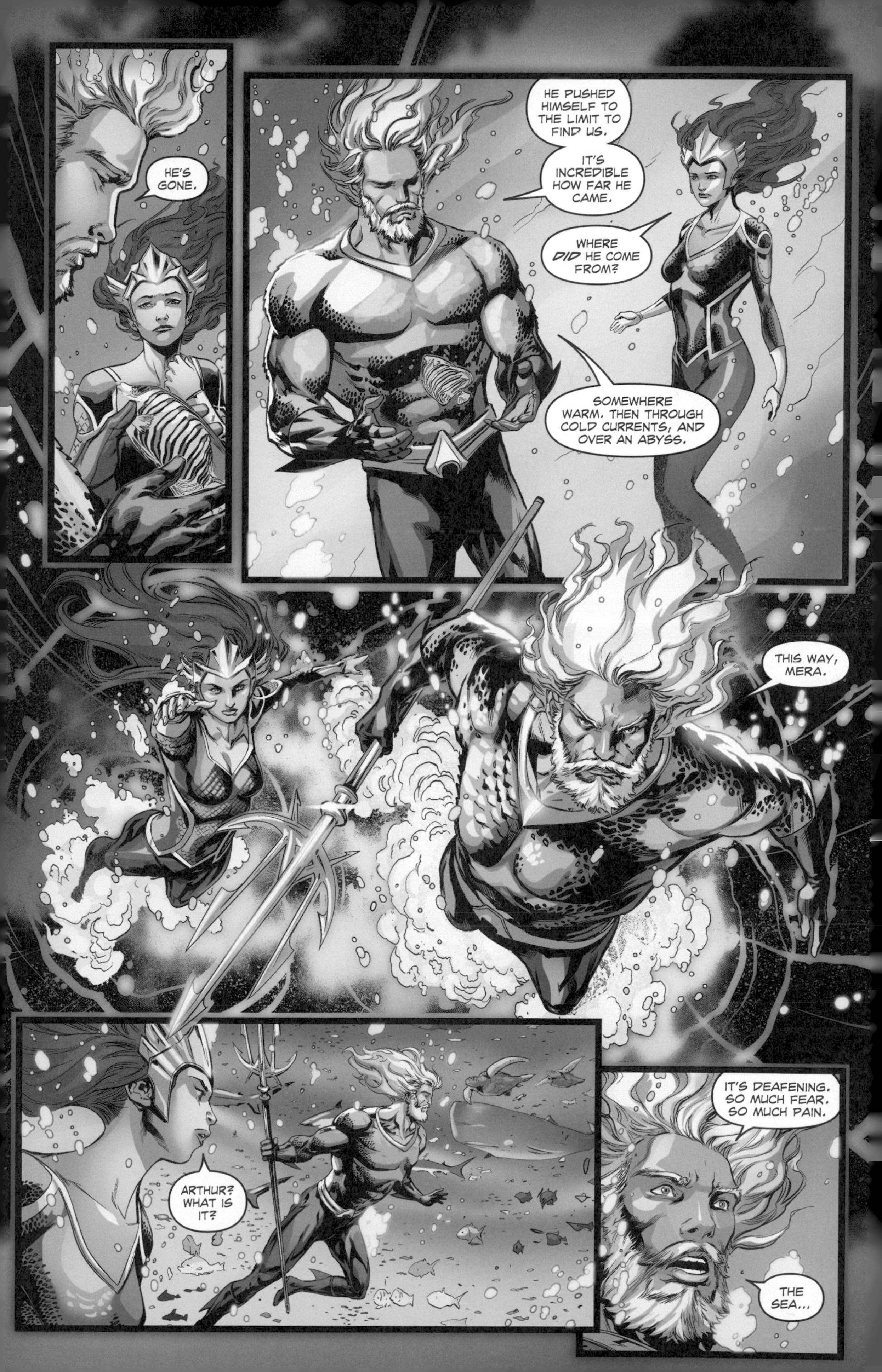

HE'S GONE.
HE PUSHED HIMSELF TO THE LIMIT TO FIND US.
IT'S INCREDIBLE HOW FAR HE CAME.
WHERE DID HE COME FROM?
SOMEWHERE WARM. THEN THROUGH COLD CURRENTS, AND OVER AN ABYSS.
THIS WAY, MERA.
ARTHUR? WHAT IS IT?
IT'S DEAFENING. SO MUCH FEAR. SO MUCH PAIN.
THE SEA...

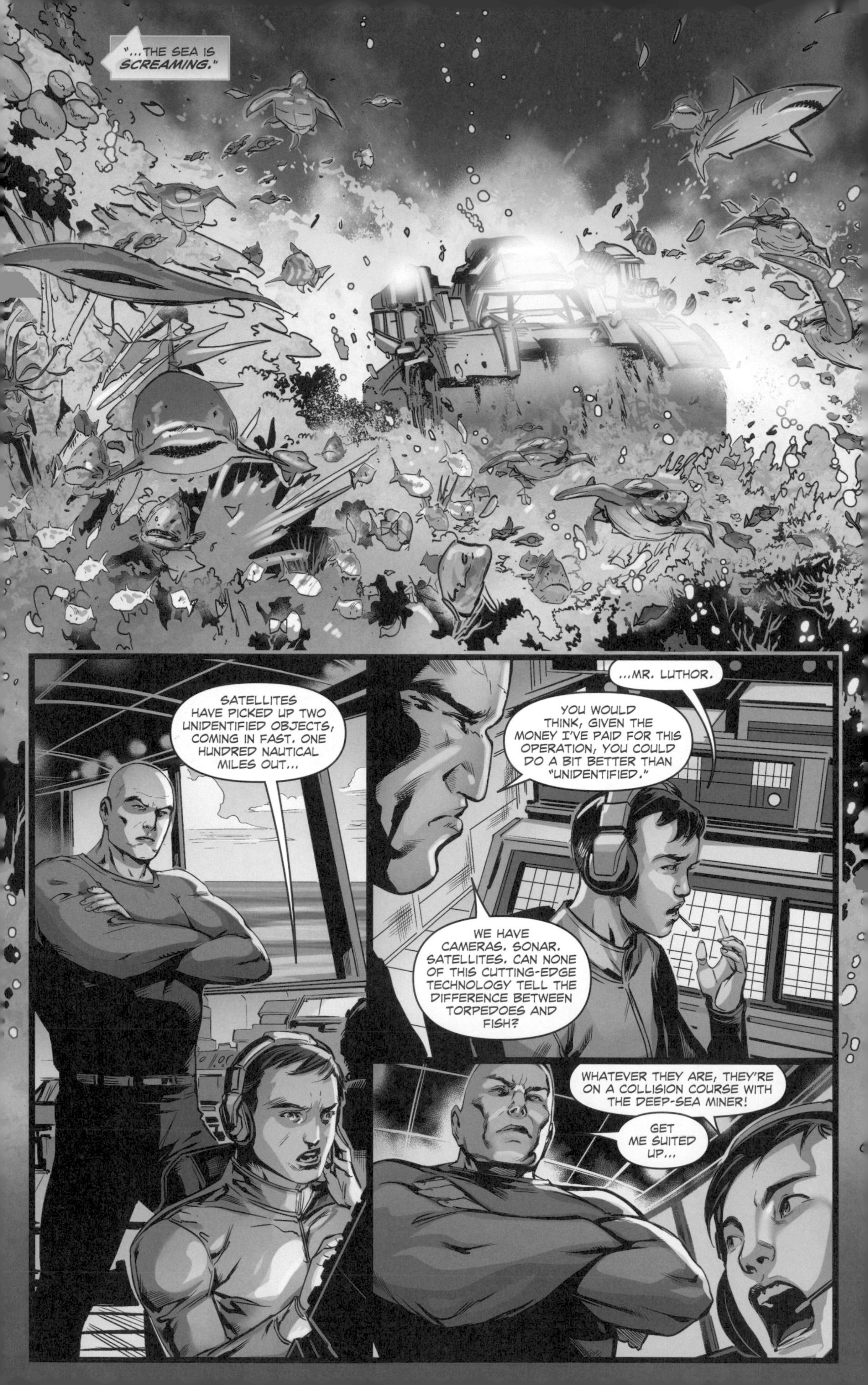
"...THE SEA IS SCREAMING."
SATELLITES HAVE PICKED UP TWO UNIDENTIFIED OBJECTS, COMING IN FAST. ONE HUNDRED NAUTICAL MILES OUT...
...MR. LUTHOR.
YOU WOULD THINK, GIVEN THE MONEY I'VE PAID FOR THIS OPERATION, YOU COULD DO A BIT BETTER THAN "UNIDENTIFIED."
WE HAVE CAMERAS. SONAR. SATELLITES. CAN NONE OF THIS CUTTING-EDGE TECHNOLOGY TELL THE DIFFERENCE BETWEEN TORPEDOES AND FISH?
WHATEVER THEY ARE, THEY'RE ON A COLLISION COURSE WITH THE DEEP-SEA MINER!
GET ME SUITED UP...

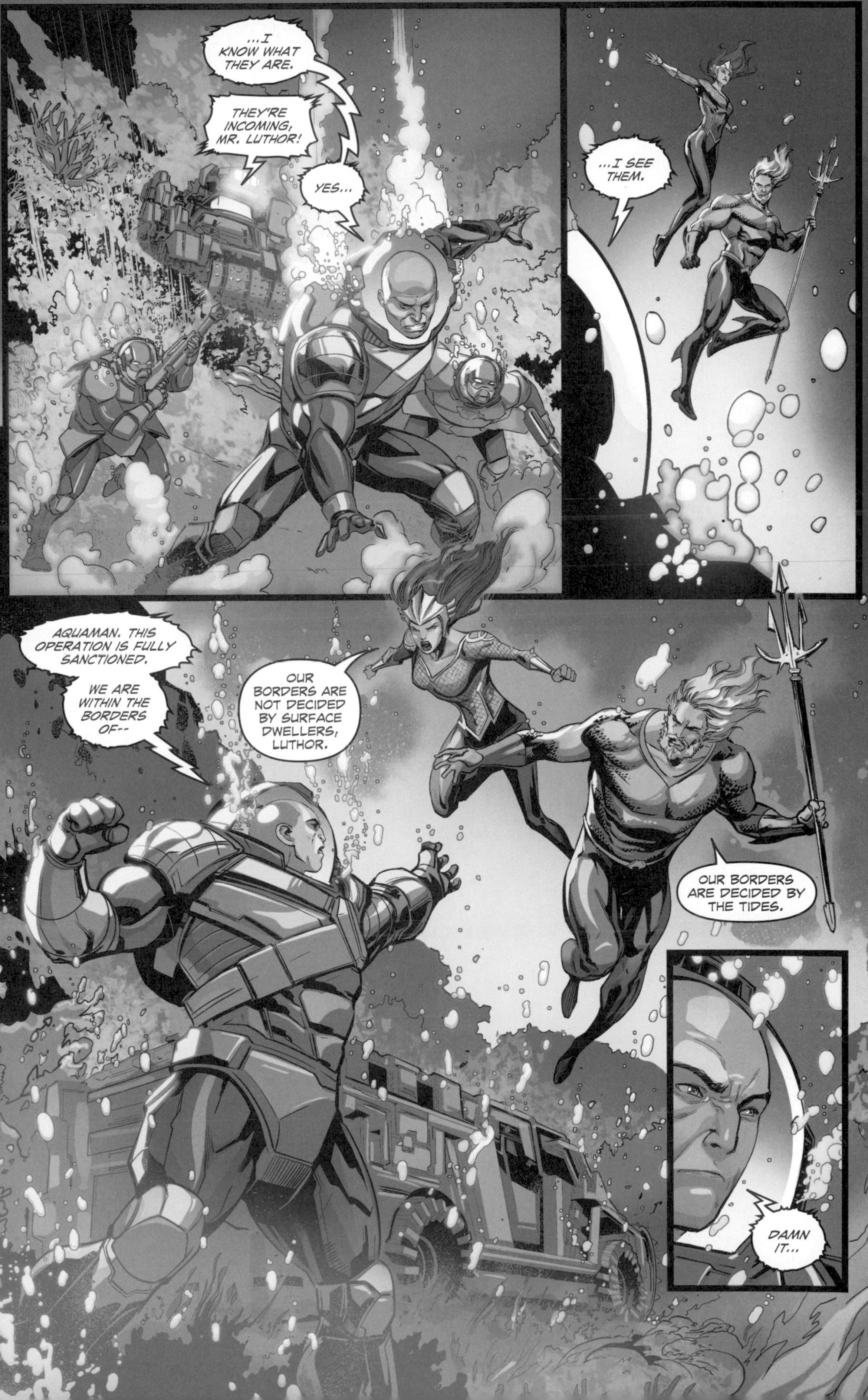
...I KNOW WHAT THEY ARE.
THEY'RE INCOMING, MR. LUTHOR!
YES...
...I SEE THEM.
AQUAMAN. THIS OPERATION IS FULLY SANCTIONED.
WE ARE WITHIN THE BORDERS OF--
OUR BORDERS ARE NOT DECIDED BY SURFACE DWELLERS, LUTHOR.
OUR BORDERS ARE DECIDED BY THE TIDES.
DAMN IT...

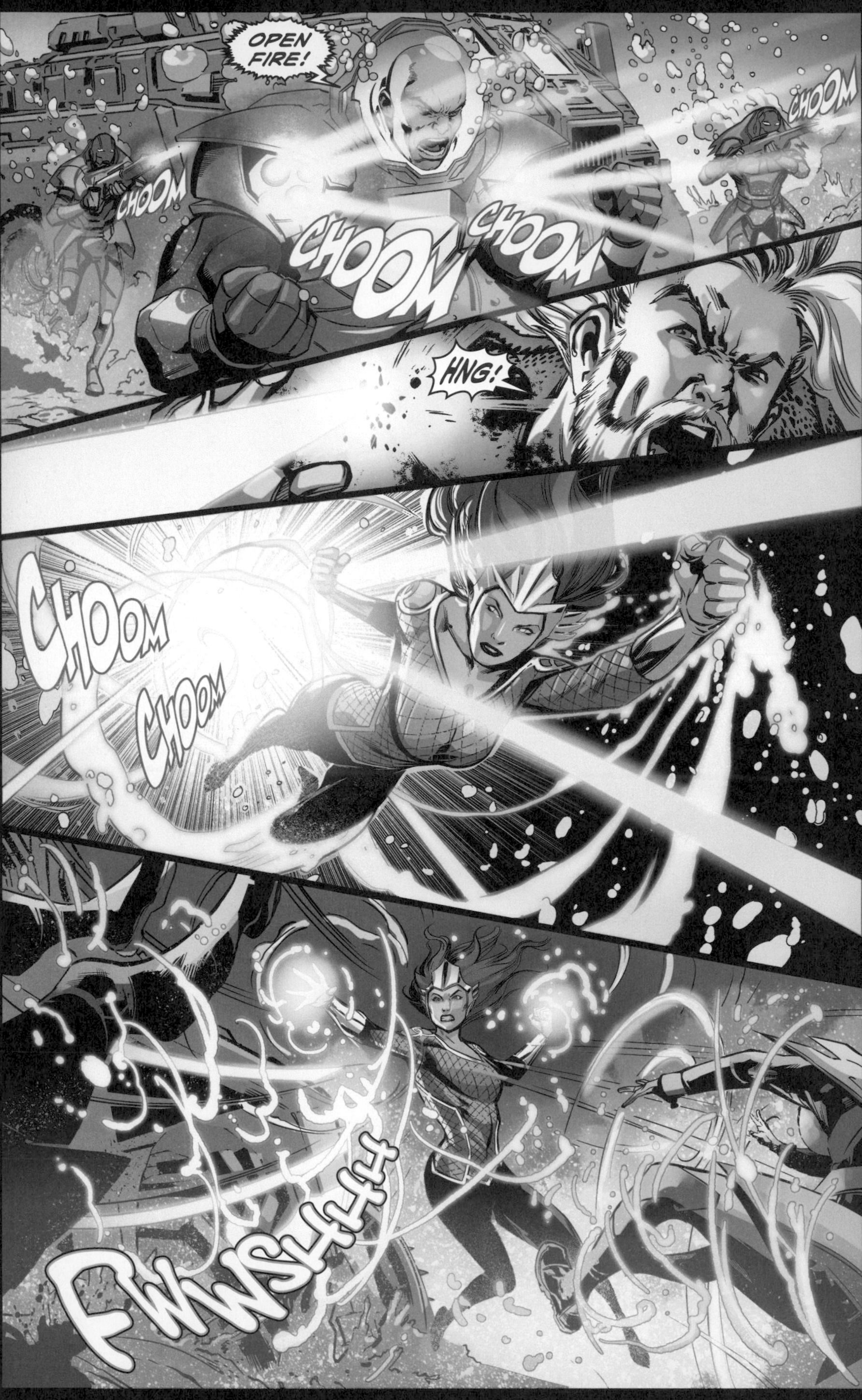

OPEN FIRE!
CHOOM
CHOOM
CHOOM
CHOOM
HNG!
CHOOM
CHOOM
FWWSHHHH

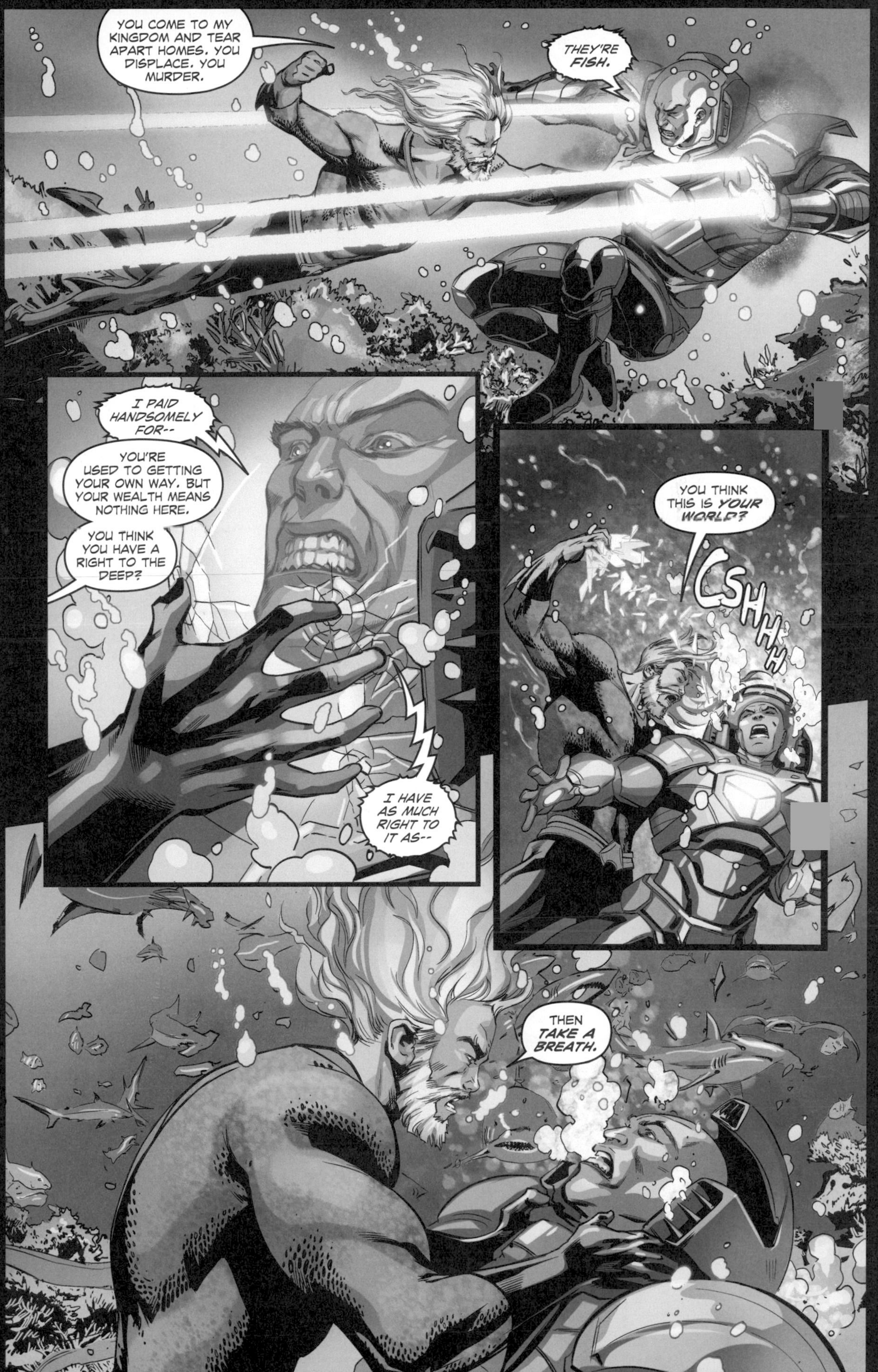

YOU COME TO MY KINGDOM AND TEAR APART HOMES. YOU DISPLACE. YOU MURDER.
THEY'RE FISH.
I PAID HANDSOMELY FOR--
YOU'RE USED TO GETTING YOUR OWN WAY. BUT YOUR WEALTH MEANS NOTHING HERE.
YOU THINK YOU HAVE A RIGHT TO THE DEEP?
I HAVE AS MUCH RIGHT TO IT AS--
YOU THINK THIS IS YOUR WORLD?
CSHHH
THEN TAKE A BREATH.

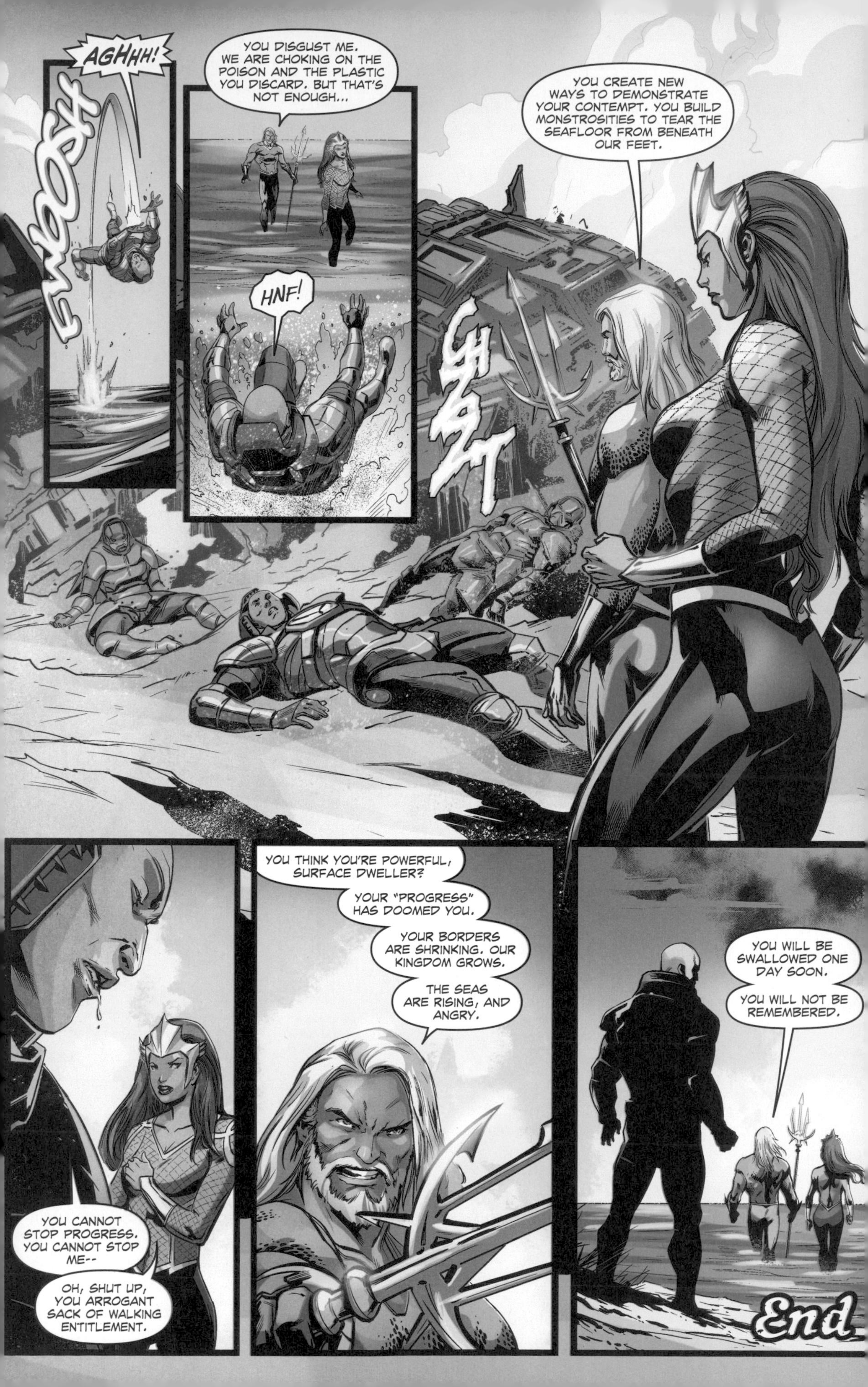
AGHHH!
FWOOSH
YOU DISGUST ME. WE ARE CHOKING ON THE POISON AND THE PLASTIC YOU DISCARD. BUT THAT'S NOT ENOUGH...
HNF!
YOU CREATE NEW WAYS TO DEMONSTRATE YOUR CONTEMPT. YOU BUILD MONSTROSITIES TO TEAR THE SEAFLOOR FROM BENEATH OUR FEET.
CHZZT
YOU CANNOT STOP PROGRESS. YOU CANNOT STOP ME--
OH, SHUT UP, YOU ARROGANT SACK OF WALKING ENTITLEMENT.
YOU THINK YOU'RE POWERFUL, SURFACE DWELLER?
YOUR "PROGRESS" HAS DOOMED YOU.
YOUR BORDERS ARE SHRINKING. OUR KINGDOM GROWS.
THE SEAS ARE RISING, AND ANGRY.
YOU WILL BE SWALLOWED ONE DAY SOON.
YOU WILL NOT BE REMEMBERED.
End

COVER GALLERY

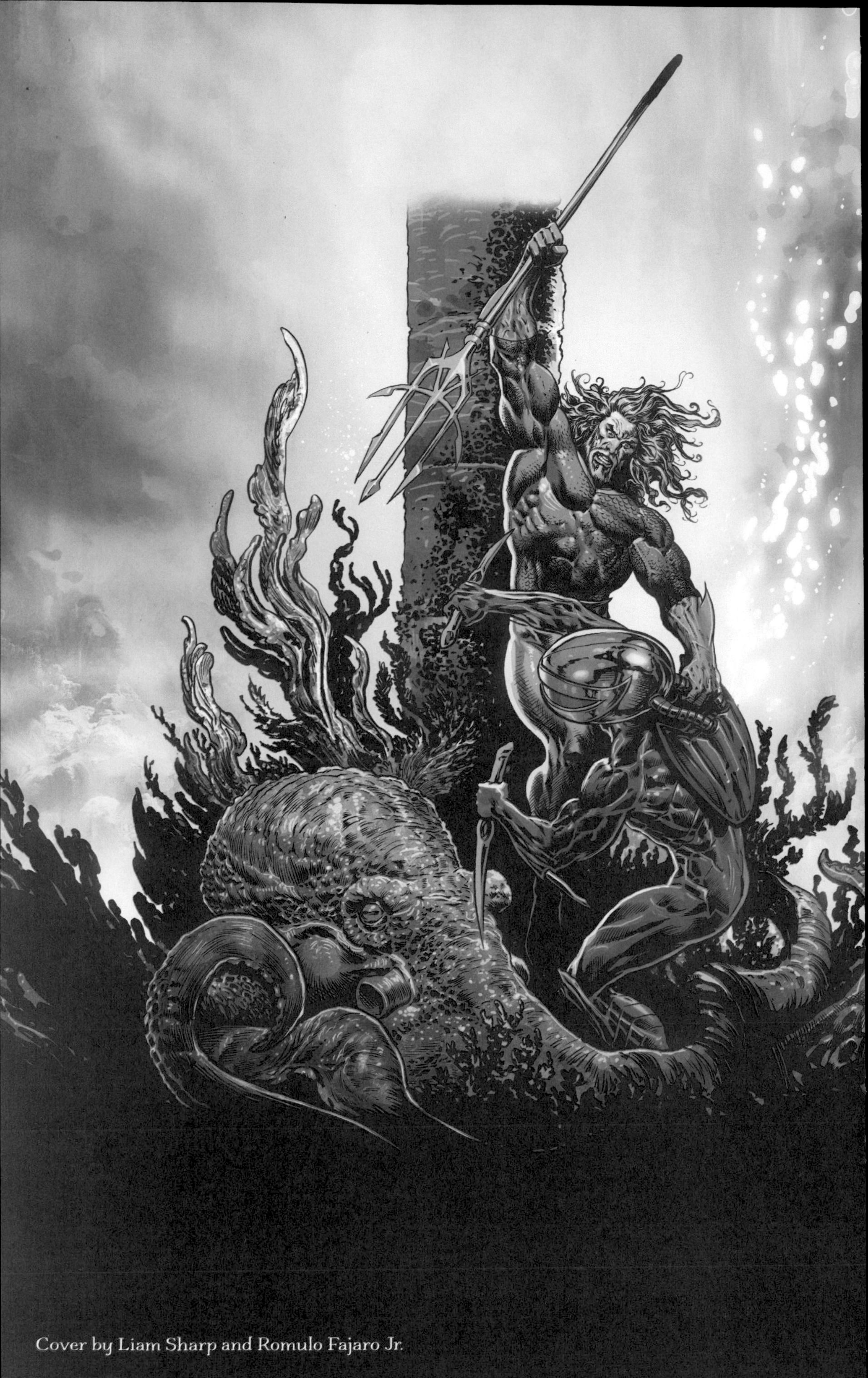

Cover by Liam Sharp and Romulo Fajaro Jr.

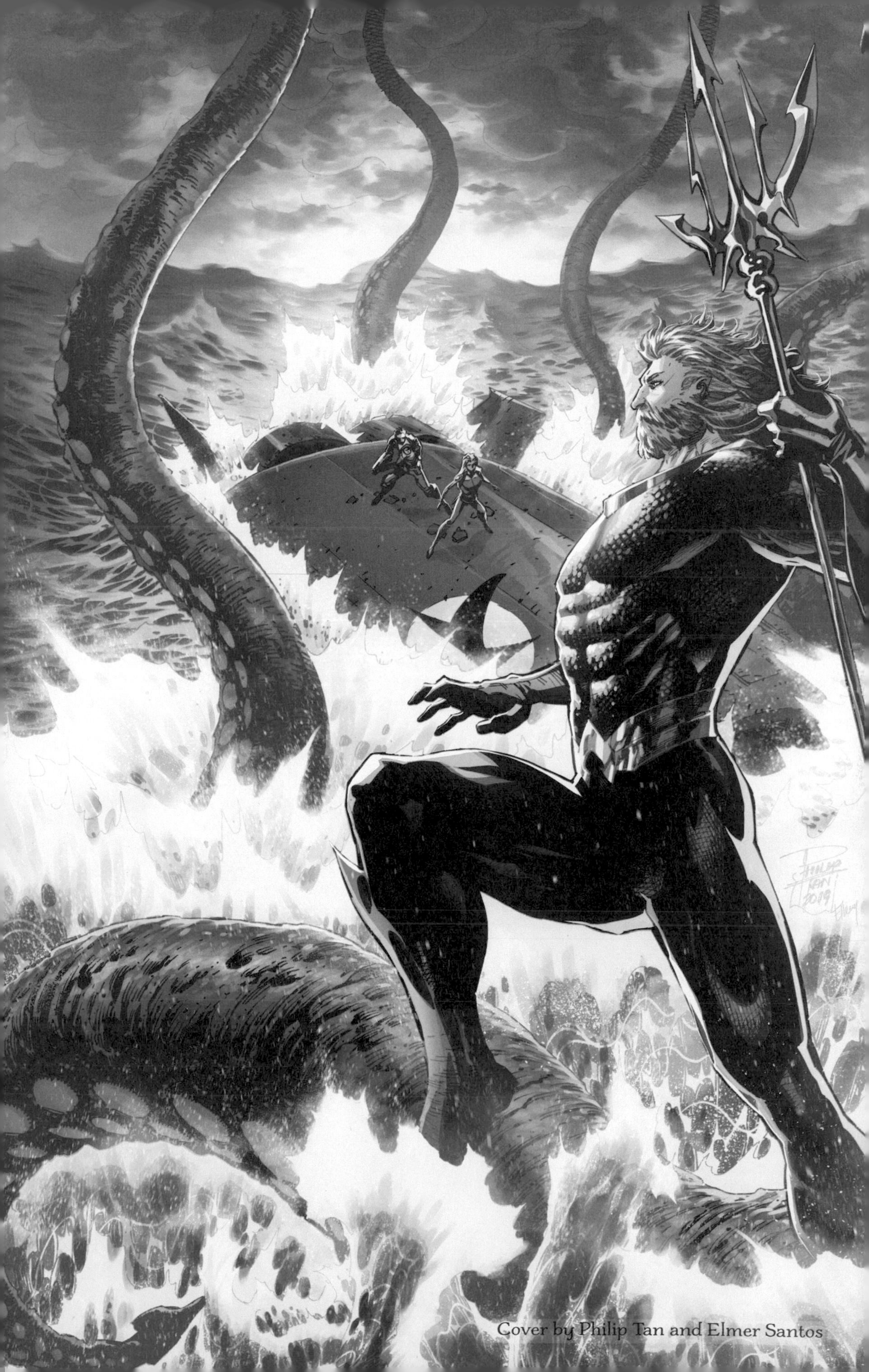

Cover by Philip Tan and Elmer Santos

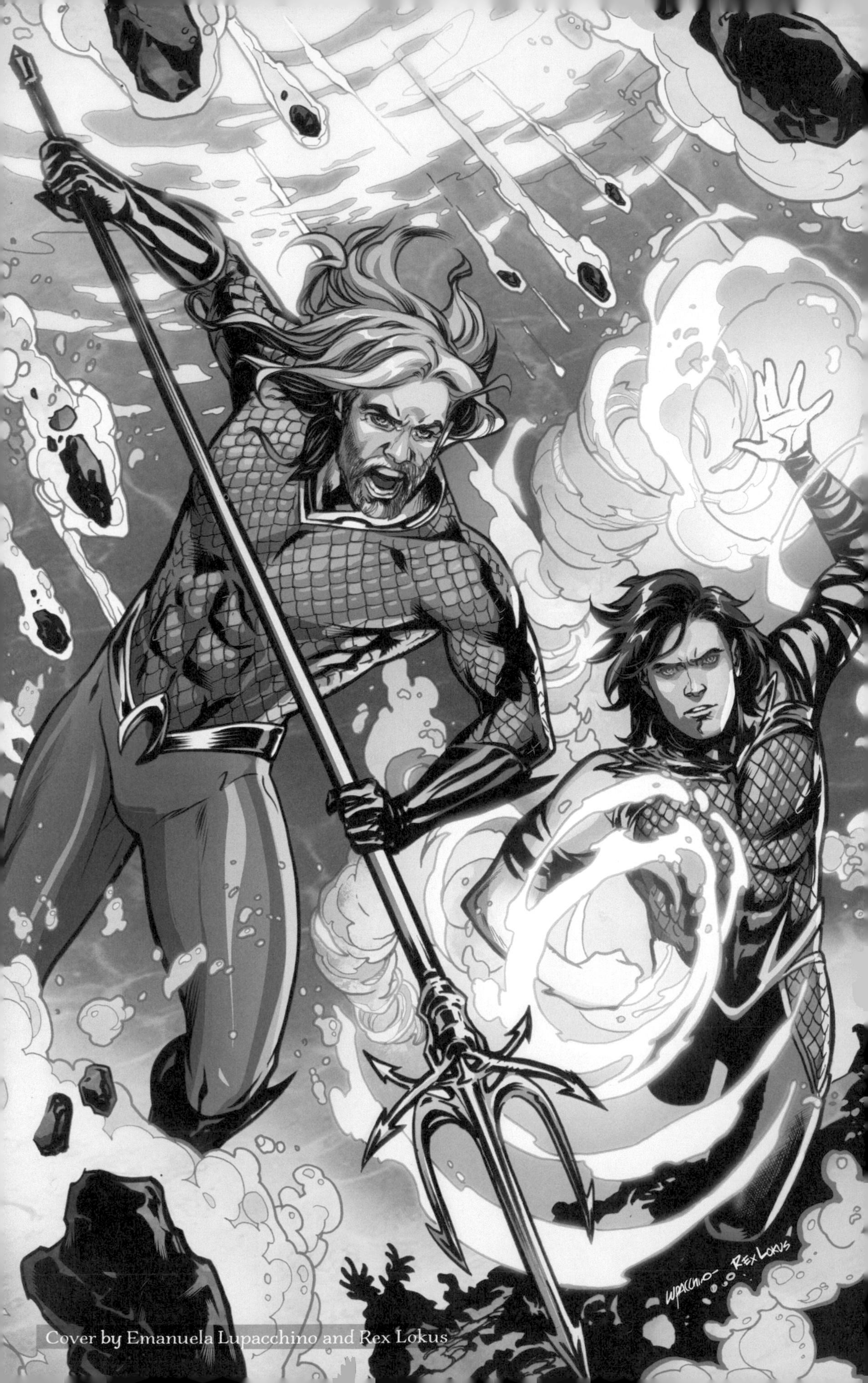

Cover by Emanuela Lupacchino and Rex Lokus

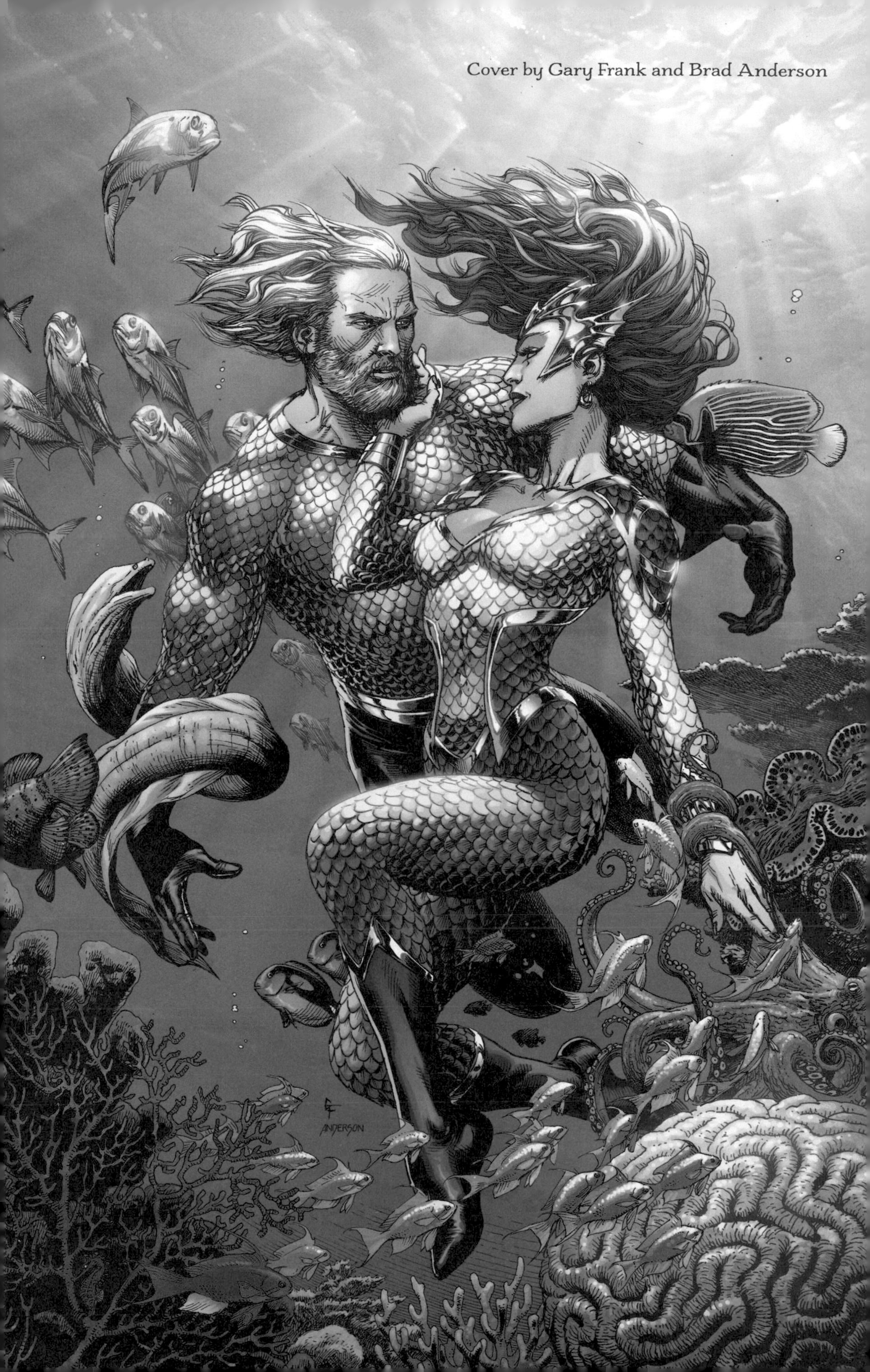
ANDERSON

Cover by Gary Frank and Brad Anderson

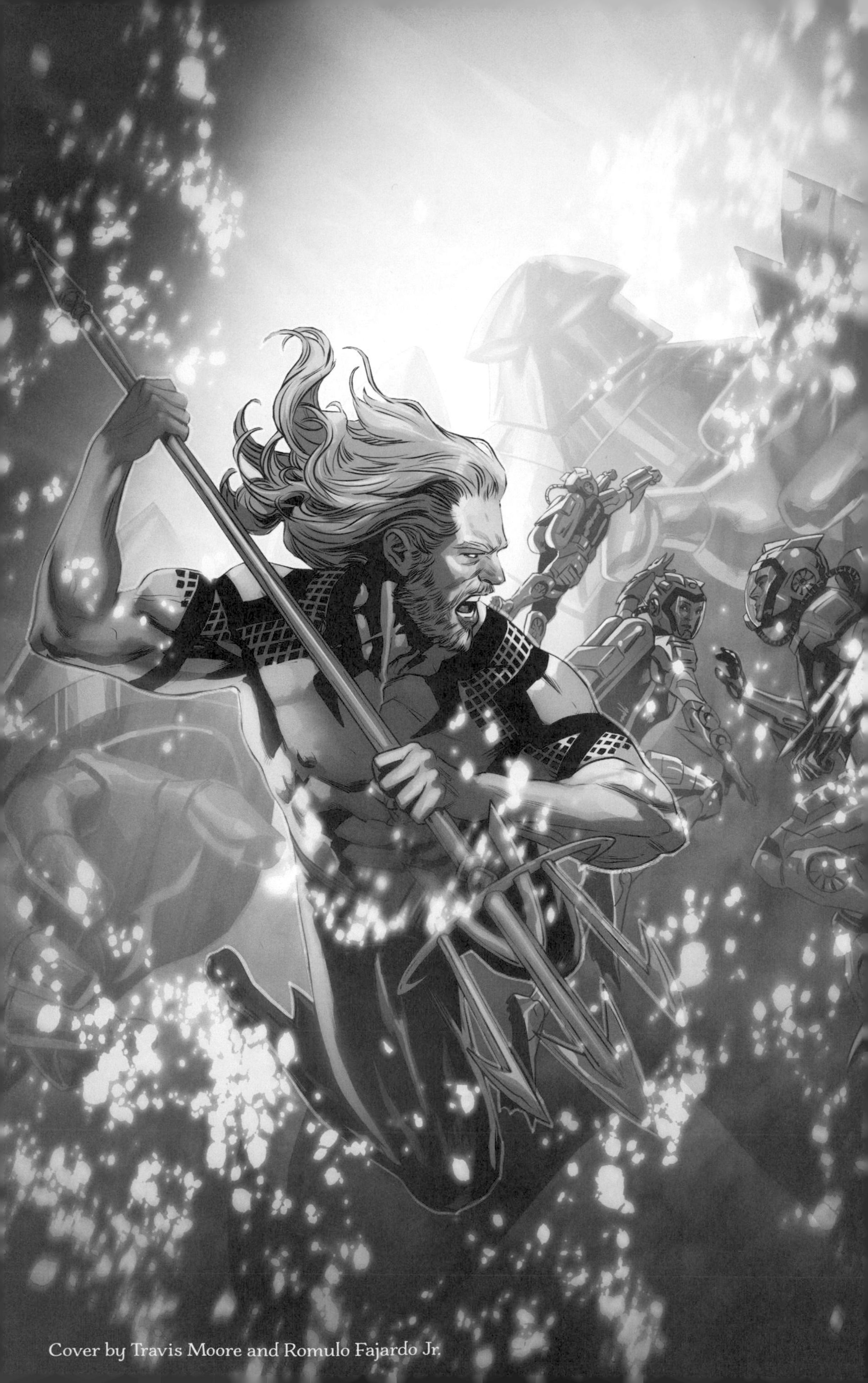
Cover by Travis Moore and Romulo Fajardo Jr.

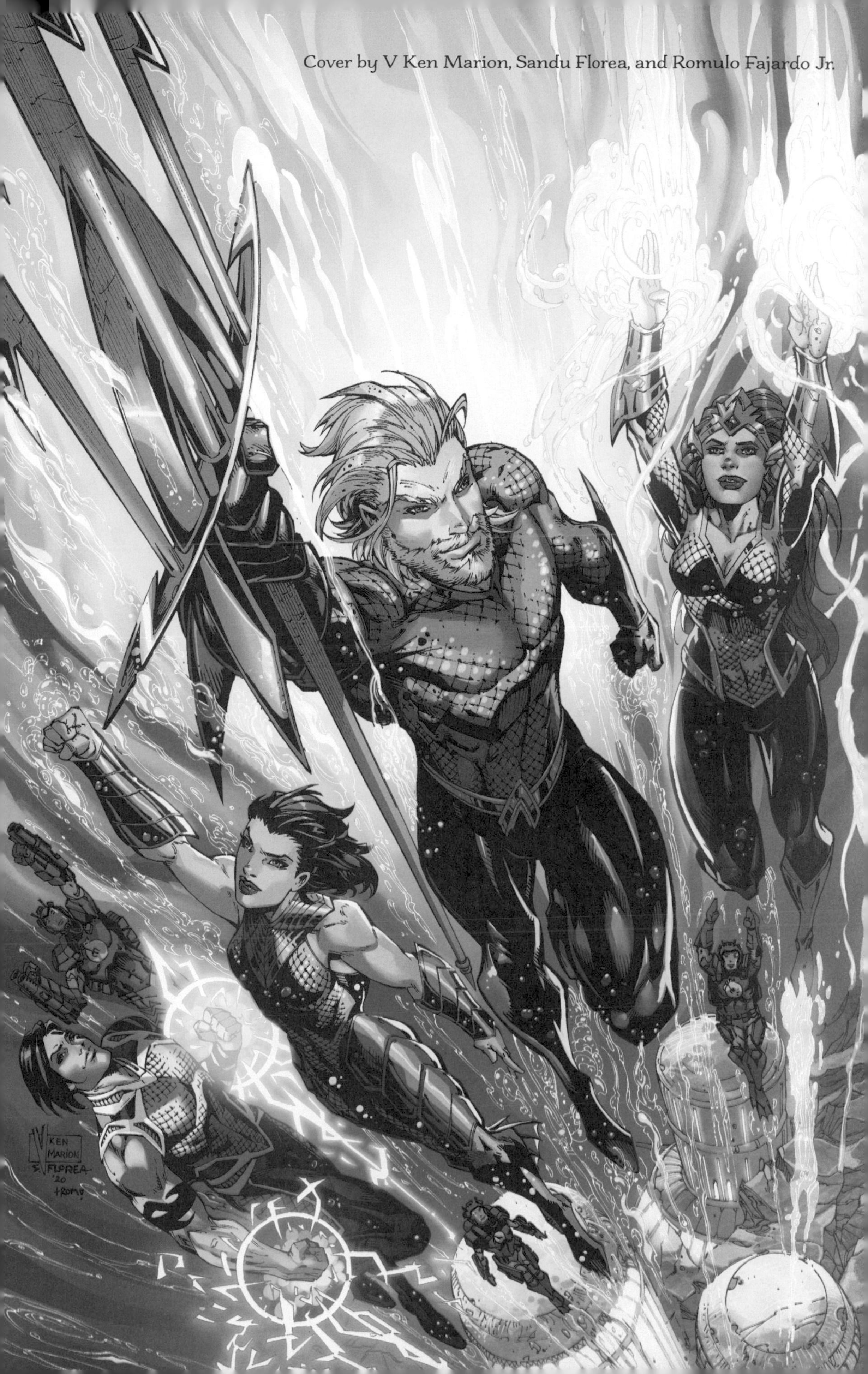
KEN MARION
S. FLOREA '20
+ROMO!
Cover by V Ken Marion, Sandu Florea, and Romulo Fajardo Jr.

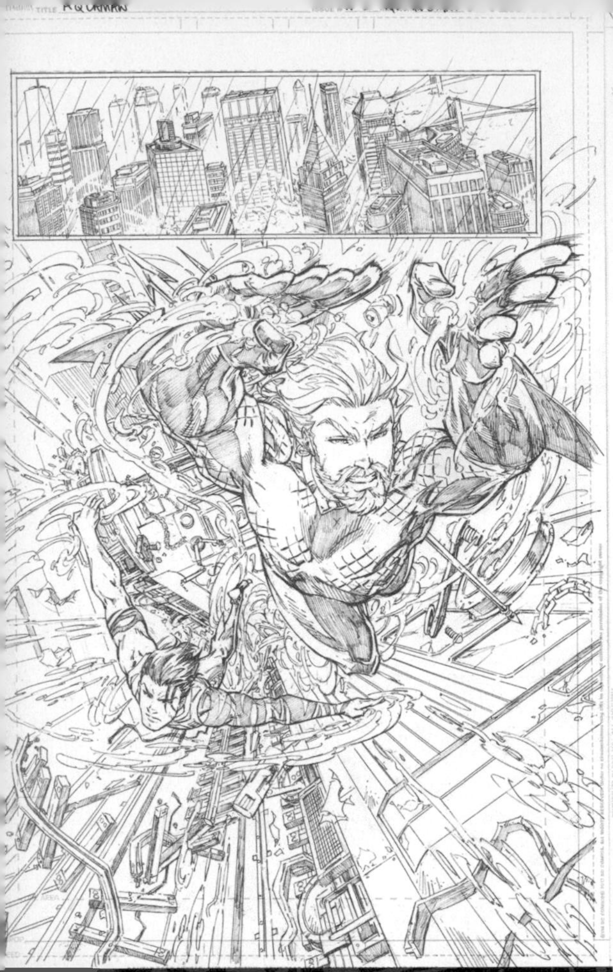

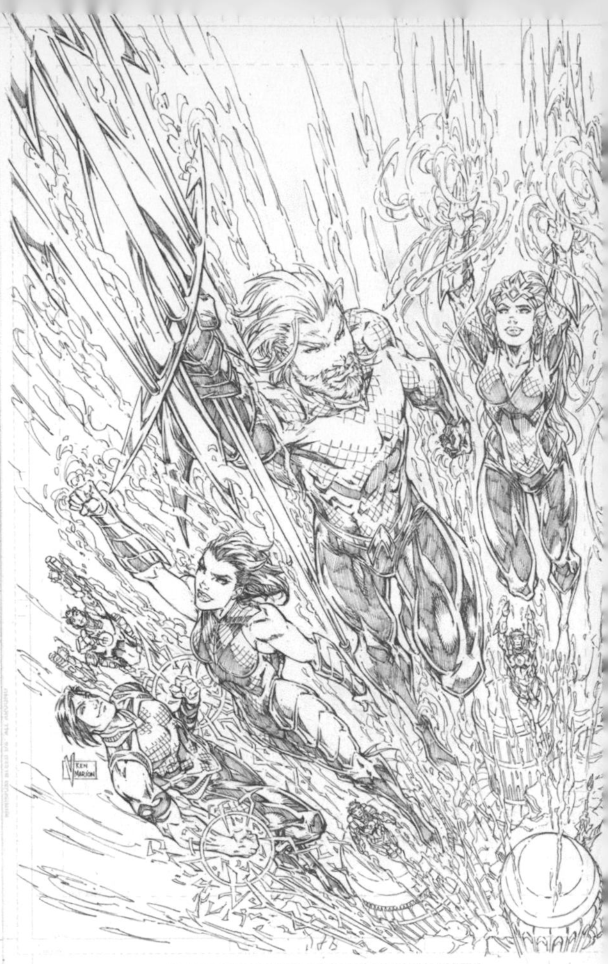
KEN MARION

Character Designs by V Ken Marion

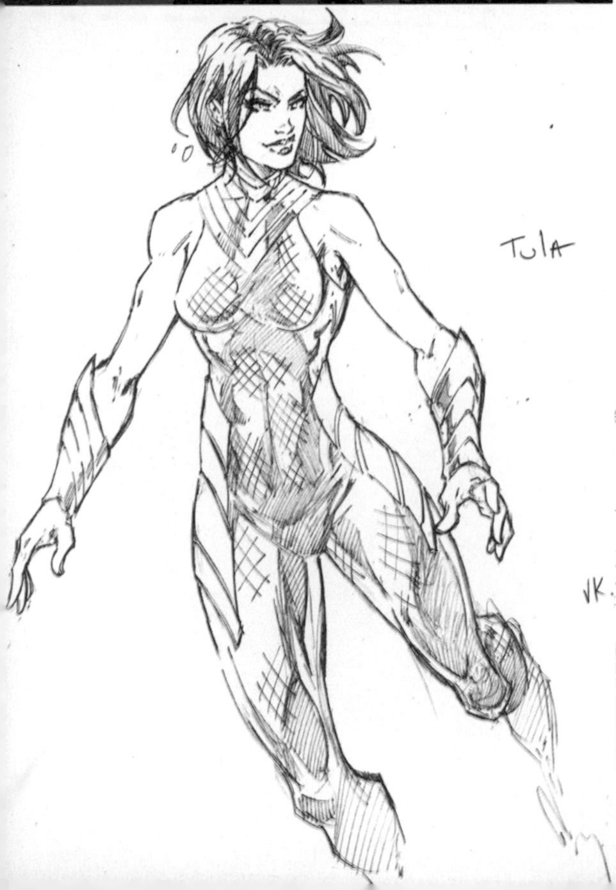
TuLA
VK.

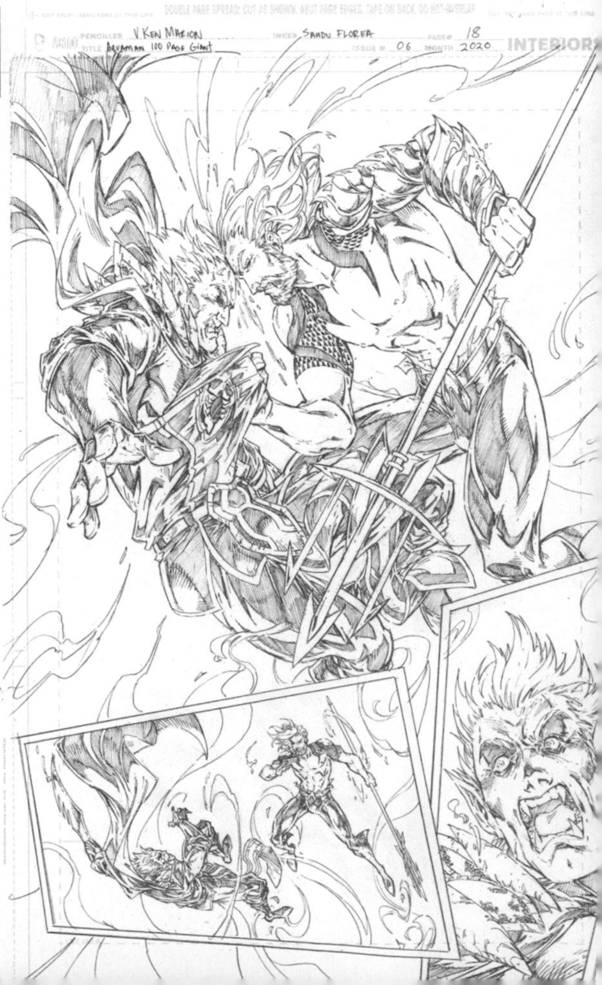
PENCILLER V KEN MARION
TITLE AQUAMAN 100 PAGE GIANT
INKER SANDU FLOREA
PAGE# 18
ISSUE # 06
MONTH 2020
INTERIOR

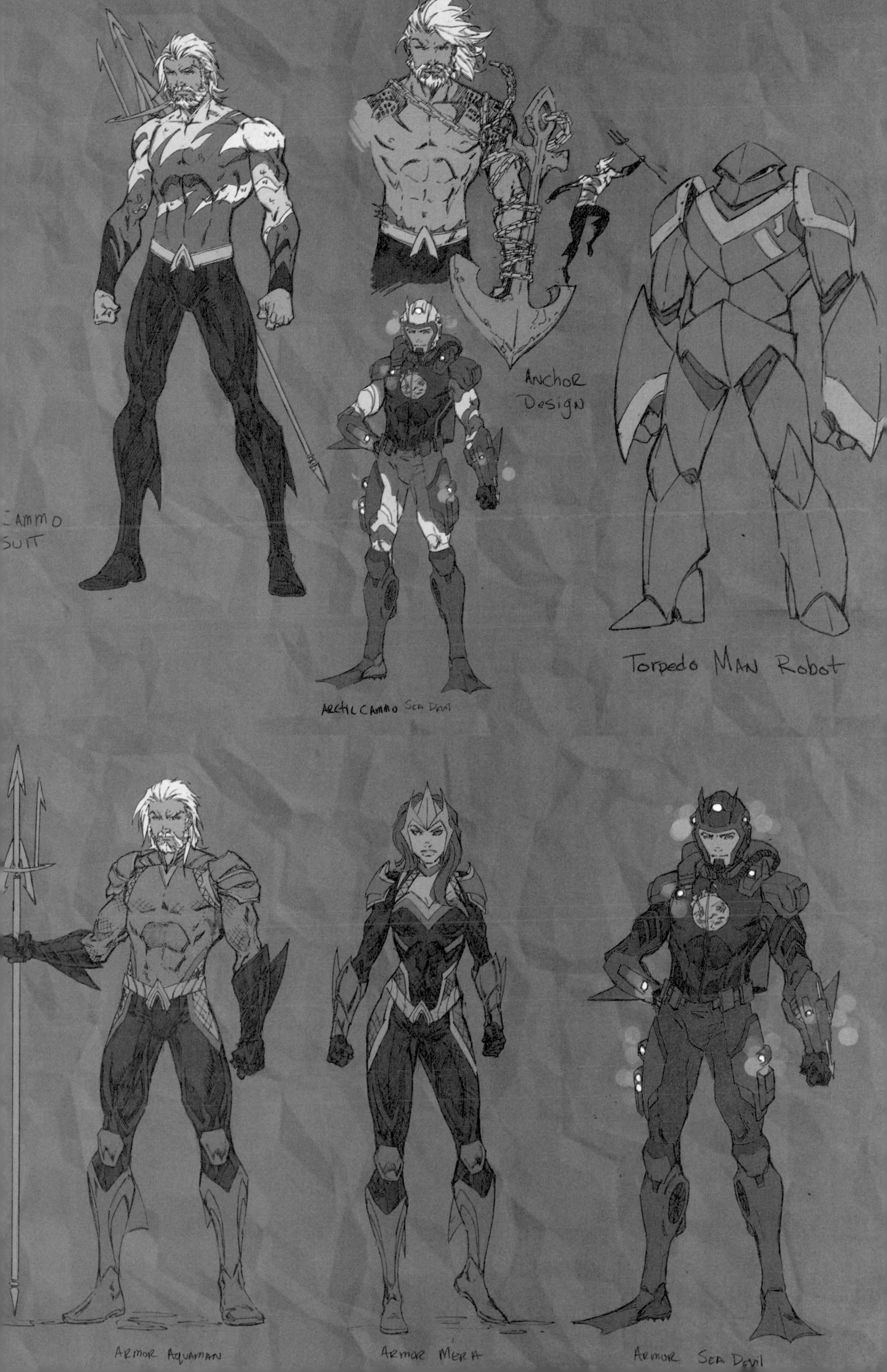
CAMMO SUIT
ANCHOR DESIGN
Torpedo MAN Robot
ARCTIC CAMMO SEA DEVIL
ARMOR AQUAMAN
ARMOR MERA
ARMOR SEA DEVIL

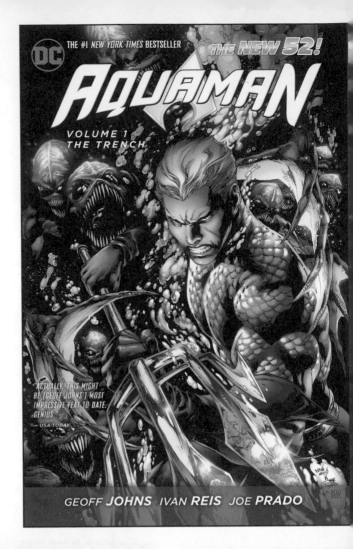

"AQUAMAN has been a rollicking good ride so far… The mythology Johns has been building up here keeps getting teased out at just the right rate, like giving a junkie their fix." – **MTV GEEK**

"With Reis on art and Johns using his full creative juices, AQUAMAN is constantly setting the bar higher and higher." – **CRAVE ONLINE**

AQUAMAN
VOL. 1: THE TRENCH
GEOFF JOHNS
with IVAN REIS

**AQUAMAN VOL. 2:
THE OTHERS**

**AQUAMAN VOL. 3:
THRONE OF ATLANTIS**

READ THE ENTIRE EPIC!

AQUAMAN VOL. 4
DEATH OF A KING

AQUAMAN VOL. 5
SEA OF STORMS

AQUAMAN VOL. 6
MAELSTROM

AQUAMAN VOL. 7
EXILED

AQUAMAN VOL. 8
OUT OF DARKNESS

"All aboard for AQUAMAN!"
–NERDIST

"A solid primer on Aquaman's new status quo."
–COMIC BOOK RESOURCES

AQUAMAN
VOL. 1: THE DROWNING

DAN ABNETT with PHILIPPE BRIONES, SCOT EATON and BRAD WALKER

DC UNIVERSE REBIRTH

AQUAMAN

VOL.1 THE DROWNING
DAN ABNETT • PHILIPPE BRIONES • SCOT EATON • BRAD WALKER

AQUAMAN VOL. 2:
BLACK MANTA RISING

AQUAMAN VOL. 3:
CROWN OF ATLANTIS

READ THE ENTIRE EPIC!

AQUAMAN VOL. 4:
UNDERWORLD

AQUAMAN VOL. 5:
THE CROWN COMES DOWN

Read more adventures of the World's Greatest Super Heroes in these graphic novels!

JLA VOL. 1

GRANT MORRISON and HOWARD PORTER

JLA VOL. 2

JLA VOL. 3

JLA VOL. 4